AMERICA'S LONGEST WAR:
The United States and Vietnam, 1950–1975

Second Edition

❦ *America in Crisis*

A series of books on American Diplomatic History

Editor: *Robert A. Divine*

America's Longest War:

The United States and Vietnam, 1950–1975

SECOND EDITION

George C. Herring
University of Kentucky

McGRAW-HILL, INC.
New York St. Louis San Francisco Auckland Bogotá Caracas
Lisbon London Madrid Mexico Milan Montreal New Delhi
Paris San Juan Singapore Sydney Tokyo Toronto

This book is printed on recycled, acid-free paper containing a minimum of 50% recycled de-inked fiber.

AMERICA'S LONGEST WAR
Cover Photo: Mark Antman/The Image Works
Cover Design: Katherine Von Urban

Second Edition

9 10 11 12 13 14 15 DOH DOH 9 9 8 7 6 5 4 3 2

Library of Congress Cataloging in Publication Data

Herring, George C., 1936-
  America's longest war.

  (America in crisis)
  Bibliography: p. 283
  Includes index.
  1. Vietnamese Conflict, 1961-1975—United States.
2. Vietnam—History—1945-1975.   3. United States—
History—1945- .   4. United States—Foreign
relations—Vietnam.   5. Vietnam—Foreign relations—
United States.   I. Title.   II. Series.
DS558.H45   1986   959.704   85-17204
ISBN 0-07-554795-3

For Nancy, John, and Lisa

FOREWORD

The initial volumes in the "America in Crisis" series appeared in 1965, the year Lyndon Johnson first sent American combat troops into Vietnam. As editor of the series, I had no thought then of including a volume on the history of the Vietnam conflict. As the war intensified during the next few years, it would have been difficult to write an account free from the deep emotions that the conflict engendered in the United States. The release of the *Pentagon Papers* in 1971 made many revealing, behind-the-scenes documents available to historians for the first time, but the continuing controversy over the wisdom of the American commitment prevented calm and objective analysis. When the end of direct American participation in 1973 and the final North Vietnamese victory two years later brought the war to a close, the nation reacted by trying to erase the tragic conflict from its memory. In the late 1970s, however, historians began a long-overdue reappraisal of the quarter century of American involvement in Vietnam.

George Herring draws upon the *Pentagon Papers,* the recently opened material in the presidential libraries, and the many articles, books, and memoirs about Vietnam to offer a comprehensive and balanced account of the American role from 1950 to 1975. He portrays American participation in the Vietnam War as the logical culmination of the containment policy that began under Harry Truman in the late 1940s. Successive administrations never questioned the assumption that the national interest required the denial of South Vietnam to Communism. The result was the gradual, yet inescapable, intervention in a local civil conflict. At first the United States sought to uphold French control, then to build and maintain South Vietnamese independence, and finally to deny victory to North Vietnam. Five Presidents struggled with the dilemma of Vietnam; none was successful, and for two, Lyndon Johnson and Richard Nixon, the effort proved politically disastrous. Throughout, as Herring makes clear, no one examined the basic premises—

the importance of South Vietnam to America's position in the world and the viability of South Vietnam as a political entity. The ultimate failure in Vietnam, Herring concludes, revealed the inherent flaws in a policy of global containment. Yet, he understands that the Vietnam story was not a simple case of diplomatic failure; the strength of his account lies in his portrayal of the complex challenge that Vietnam posed for the United States and the varied responses it evoked from the American people and their leaders.

ROBERT A. DIVINE

PREFACE TO THE SECOND EDITION

The first edition of *America's Longest War* was written immediately after the end of the Vietnam conflict. Numerous important studies have since been published, and although most of the official U.S. documentation remains unavailable to scholars, significant new material has been released. The purpose of this second edition is to update the book in terms of new information and interpretations and developments in the United States, Southeast Asia, and the world since the end of the war. As in the first edition, the emphasis remains on the American side of the conflict, but I have attempted to sharpen my discussion of the Vietnamese and especially the North Vietnamese/Vietcong role, an area where important revelations have emerged in recent years. I have also expanded the coverage of the antiwar protest movement at home and have attempted to interpret with greater precision its impact on the conduct of the war, the subject of much mythmaking since 1975 and a topic on which important scholarly work is now under way. Despite the "revisionism" of recent years, my primary thesis has not changed. I believe, as I did in 1979, that U.S. intervention in Vietnam was based on a policy fundamentally flawed in its assumptions and major premises. I do not believe that the war could have been "won" in any meaningful sense at a moral or material cost most Americans deemed acceptable.

Numerous people and institutions have assisted me in this revision, and I can single out only a few here. I am grateful to the many reviewers and colleagues who offered constructive criticism of the first edition. I am especially grateful to those colleagues who offered detailed suggestions for this second edition. They were: Richard H. Immerman, the University of Hawaii at Manoa; Gary R. Hess, Bowling Green State University; and Stephen E. Pelz, The University of Massachusetts—Amherst. A special word of thanks goes to Professor Richard W. Leopold of Northwestern University, for his support and encouragement over the years and for reading

the first edition with his customarily keen critical eye. The U.S.
Army Military History Institute and the Lyndon Baines Johnson
Foundation provided travel grants to facilitate my research involving their important holdings on Vietnam. At Carlisle Barracks,
Pennsylvania, Richard Sommers and David Keough provided invaluable assistance, and in Austin, Texas, David Humphrey exceeded
the call of archival duty in helping me to secure newly declassified
materials in the Johnson Library.

I have learned far more than I have taught in the various symposia on Vietnam in which I have had the good fortune to participate during the past few years. I thank the sponsors at the
Woodrow Wilson International Center for Scholars, the University
of Southern California, the Center for Military History, and especially Dr. Harry Wilmer and The Institute for the Humanities at
Salado, Texas, for inviting me to take part in these most enlighten-
ing gatherings. I also wish to thank my graduate students, past and
present, for their assistance and especially for their friendship.
Their influence is present in these pages far more than the foot-
notes and bibliography will indicate.

To Katie Vignery, David Follmer, and Christopher J. Rogers,
my thanks for prodding me into undertaking this effort and a belated but by no means grudging admission that revision was justified and indeed necessary.

A very special acknowledgment is due Carol Reardon, who
read the proofs and prepared the index with her customary skill
and dispatch and whose invaluable assistance in editing *Diplomatic
History* enabled me to complete this revision close to the deadline.

GEORGE C. HERRING
Lexington, Kentucky
September 1985

PREFACE TO THE FIRST EDITION

"Vietnam, Vietnam. . . . There are no sure answers," the veteran Southeast Asian correspondent Robert Shaplen wrote during an especially perplexing period of a long and confusing war.[1] Despite the passage of time, the publication of hundreds of books, and the declassification of thousands of documents, Shaplen's lament remains as real today as when it was penned ten years ago. Why did the United States make such a vast commitment in an area of so little apparent importance, one in which it had taken scant interest before? What did it attempt to do during the nearly quarter of a century of its involvement there? Why, despite the expenditure of more than $150 billion, the application of its great technical expertise, and the employment of a huge military arsenal, did the world's most powerful nation fail to achieve its objectives and suffer its first defeat in war, a humiliating and deeply frustrating experience for a people accustomed to success? What have been the consequences for American foreign policy of the nation's longest and most divisive war? Although the problems remain as complex and baffling as in Shaplen's day, this book seeks to place American involvement in Vietnam in historical perspective and to offer some answers to these vital questions.

Because of its length, its immensely confusing nature, its proximity to the present, and the emotions that still surround it, the Vietnam War presents extraordinary problems for the historian. I have chosen to give most detailed treatment to the period 1963 to 1973, the decade of heaviest American involvement in Vietnam. But I have also devoted considerable attention to the years 1950–1963. The assumptions that led to the crucial commitments took form during these years. In addition, as Edward Lansdale has observed, without an understanding of this formative period, "one

[1] Robert Shaplen, *The Road from War: Vietnam, 1965–1970* (New York, 1970), p. 283.

is like a spectator arriving in the middle of a complex drama, without true knowledge of the plot or of the identity and motivation of those in the drama."[2] I have relied on the large body of secondary literature on the war, but a vast amount of documentation has been declassified in the United States in recent years and I have attempted to use this material wherever possible. This is not primarily a military history. Rather, in keeping with the purpose of the series, it seeks to integrate military, diplomatic, and political factors in such a way as to clarify America's involvement and ultimate failure in Vietnam. My focus is on the American side of the equation, but I have sought to provide sufficient consideration of the Vietnamese side to make the events comprehensible. I have also attempted to consider American decision-making in the broader context of the nation's global outlook and policies. The United States' involvement in Vietnam was not primarily a result of errors of judgment or of the personality quirks of the policymakers, although these things existed in abundance. It was a logical, if not inevitable, outgrowth of a world view and a policy, the policy of containment, which Americans in and out of government accepted without serious question for more than two decades. The commitment in Vietnam expanded as the containment policy itself grew. In time, it oulived the conditions that had given rise to that policy. More than anything else, America's failure in Vietnam calls into question the basic premises of that policy and suggests the urgent need for a searching reappraisal of American attitudes toward the world and their place in it. Finally, I have tried to treat the events and personalities with as much detachment as possible in recognition that there was never an easy solution and that choices which at the time seemed most logical and least costly can only in retrospect be judged to have been so injurious and tragic in their consequences.

GEORGE C. HERRING
Lexington, Kentucky
May 1979

[2] Quoted in W. Scott Thompson and Donaldson D. Frizzell, *The Lessons of Vietnam* (New York, 1977), p. 43.

ACKNOWLEDGMENTS

I take this opportunity to express my gratitude to those who have done so much to assist in the completion of this project. Travel for research was greatly facilitated by grants from the National Endowment for the Humanities and the University of Kentucky Research Foundation. Archivists in the Truman, Eisenhower, Kennedy, and Johnson libraries painstakingly guided me through the labyrinthine presidential papers of the Cold War era and assisted with the declassification of a number of important documents. It was my extraordinary good fortune, while working in the John F. Kennedy Library, to renew old friendships with William Moss and Robert Stocking. I am particularly grateful to Dr. Martin Elzy of the Lyndon B. Johnson Library, who rendered archival services beyond the call of duty and extended a Texas-size hospitality which made my several visits to Austin most pleasant and productive. Professors Thomas Paterson of the University of Connecticut and Warren Kimball of Rutgers, Newark, read various chapters and generously shared with me their knowledge of recent American diplomatic history. Professor Walter LaFeber of Cornell University provided a most insightful critique of the entire manuscript. My colleague and friend Joe Thompson listened patiently to me discuss Vietnam over the course of several years and read an early draft with great care. His encouragement and sound editorial advice have been invaluable. Robert Divine of the University of Texas, the editor of this series, responded enthusiastically to my proposal to undertake this study and provided much assistance and advice along the way. Wayne Anderson of John Wiley has been a patient—but not too patient—editor, and I appreciate his tolerance in the initial stages and his friendly prodding toward the end. Dorothy Leathers somehow managed to squeeze this manuscript into her busy typing schedule during the Christmas holidays and handled the chore with customary efficiency, skill, and good humor. From beginning to end, my wife, Nancy, and my children, John and Lisa, have shared with me the frustrations and satisfactions, and this book is dedicated to them, with my love.

G.C.H.

CONTENTS

AMERICA'S LONGEST WAR:

**The United States and Vietnam,
1950–1975**

Second Edition

CHAPTER 1

A Dead-End Alley:
The United States, France,
and the First Indochina
War,
1950–1954

When Ho Chi Minh proclaimed the independence of Vietnam from French rule on September 2, 1945, he borrowed liberally from Thomas Jefferson, opening with the words "We hold these truths to be self-evident. That all men are created equal." During independence celebrations in Hanoi later in the day, American warplanes flew over the city, U.S. Army officers stood on the reviewing stand with Vo Nguyen Giap and other leaders, and a Vietnamese band played the "Star-Spangled Banner." Toward the end of the festivities, Giap spoke warmly of Vietnam's "particularly intimate relations" with the United States—something, he noted, "which it is a pleasant duty to dwell upon."[1] The prominent role played by Americans at the birth of modern Vietnam appears in retrospect one of history's most bitter ironies. Despite the glowing professions of friendship on September 2, the United States acquiesced in the return of French troops to Vietnam and from 1950 to 1954 actively supported French efforts to suppress Ho's revolution, the first phase of a quarter-century American struggle to control the destiny of Vietnam.

[1] Quoted in R. Harris Smith, *OSS: The Secret History of America's First Central Intelligence Agency* (Delta Ed.; New York, 1973), p. 354.

French Indochina

CHINA
Red R.
Cao Bang
CHINA
Black R.
TONKIN
Dien Bien Phu
Hanoi
GULF OF TONKIN
Mekong R.
Haiphong
Luang Prabang
HAINAN
V
I
E
T
N
A
M
LAOS
Vientiane
THAILAND
ANNAM
Hue
Tourane
Bangkok
CAMBODIA
SOUTH CHINA SEA
GULF OF SIAM
Phnom Penh
COCHIN CHINA
Saigon

0   100   200
Miles

The Vietnamese revolution was in many ways the personal creation of the charismatic patriot Ho Chi Minh. Born in the province of Nghe An, the cradle of Vietnamese revolutionaries, Ho inherited from his mandarin father a sturdy patriotism and an adventurous spirit. Departing Vietnam in 1912 as a cabin boy aboard a merchant steamer, he eventually settled in France with a colony of Vietnamese nationalists, and when the Paris Peace Conference rejected his petition for democratic reforms for Vietnam, he joined the French Communist party. Then known as Nguyen Ai Quoc (Nguyen the Patriot), he worked for more than two decades as a party functionary and revolutionary organizer in the Soviet Union, China, Thailand, and Vietnam. In 1930, he organized the Indochinese Communist party and helped to incite a series of revolts which were brutally suppressed by the French. When Hitler conquered France in 1940 and Japan began to move southward into Vietnam, Ho returned to his homeland. A frail and gentle man who radiated warmth and serenity, he was also a master organizer and determined revolutionary who was willing to employ the most cold-blooded methods in the cause to which he dedicated his life.

Establishing headquarters in caves near the Chinese border, by a mountain he named Karl Marx and a river he named Lenin, Ho founded the Vietminh political organization and conceived the strategy that would eventually drive the French from Vietnam. For centuries, the Vietnamese had fought bitterly against outside invaders—the Chinese, the Mongols, and most recently the French. Ho and the other Communists who comprised the Vietminh leadership skillfully tapped the vast reservoir of Vietnamese nationalism, muting their commitment to a social revolution and adopting a broad platform stressing independence and "democratic" reforms. Having learned from the abortive uprisings of 1930 the importance of the countryside, they carefully constructed among the people in the northern provinces a solid base for revolution. Displaying an organization and discipline far superior to those of competing nationalist groups, many of which spent as much time fighting each other as the French, the Vietminh established itself as the voice of Vietnamese nationalism.[2]

---

[2] See especially William J. Duiker, *The Communist Road to Power in Vietnam* (Boulder, Colo., 1981), pp. 7–89, and Douglas Pike, *History of Vietnamese Communism, 1925–1976* (Stanford, Calif., 1978), pp. 15–54.

The Vietminh capitalized on the uniquely favorable circumstances of World War II to launch its revolution. The Japanese permitted the French colonial authorities to retain nominal power throughout most of the war, but the ease with which Japan had established its position discredited the French in the eyes of the Vietnamese. The hardships imposed by the Japanese and their French puppets, along with a devastating famine, fanned popular discontent. By the spring of 1945, Ho had mobilized a base of mass support in northern Vietnam, and with the assistance of Giap, a former professor of history, had raised an army of 5,000 men. After the Japanese deposed the French puppet government in March 1945, the Vietminh, with limited assistance from a U.S. intelligence unit (hence the American presence on September 2), began the systematic harassment of their new colonial masters. When Japan surrendered in August 1945, the Vietminh opportunistically filled the vacuum, occupying government headquarters in Hanoi. Wearing the faded khaki suit and rubber sandals that would become his trademark, Ho Chi Minh stood before cheering throngs on September 2 and proclaimed the independence of his country.[3]

Independence would not come without a struggle, however, for the French were determined to regain the empire they had ruled for more than half a century. Conscious of their nation's declining position in world affairs, many French politicians felt that France could "only be a great power so long as our flag continues to fly in all the overseas territory."[4] French Indochina, comprising Cambodia, Laos, and the three Vietnamese colonies of Annam, Tonkin, and Cochin China, was among the richest and most prestigious of France's colonial possessions. The Vietminh had been unable to establish a firm power base in southern Vietnam, and with the assistance of British occupation forces, which had been given responsibility for accepting the Japanese surrender south of the seventeenth parallel, the French were able to expel the Vietminh from Saigon and reestablish control over the southern part of the country.

For more than a year, France and the Vietminh attempted to

---

[3] Ellen Hammer, *The Struggle for Indochina, 1940–1955* (Stanford, Calif., 1966), pp. 11–53, 94–105, and John T. McAlister, Jr., *Vietnam: The Origins of Revolution* (Anchor Ed.; New York, 1971), *passim.*

[4] Jean-Jacques Juglas quoted in Ronald E. Irving, *The First Indochina War: French and American Policy, 1945–1954* (London, 1975), p. 144.

negotiate an agreement, but their goals were irreconcilable. French colonial policy had always stressed assimilation, full French citizenship, rather than independence or dominion status, and France hedged on the Vietminh's demand for immediate self-government and eventual independence. For the Vietminh, unification of their country not only represented fulfillment of the centuries-old dream of Vietnamese nationalists but was also an economic necessity since the south produced the food surplus necessary to sustain the overpopulated, industrial north. The French were determined to keep Cochin China separate from Annam and Tonkin and to maintain absolute control in the southern colony, where their economic interests were largest. Negotiations dragged on inconclusively, mutual suspicions increased, and outbreaks of violence became commonplace. The shelling of Haiphong by a French cruiser in November 1946, resulting in the death of 6,000 civilians, set off a war which in its various phases would last nearly thirty years.[5]

For a time during World War II, the United States actively opposed the return of Indochina to France. Before 1941, Americans had taken little interest in the area, but the Japanese takeover impressed upon them its importance as a source of foodstuffs and raw materials and as a strategic outpost guarding the major water routes of southern Asia. Some U.S. officials perceived the growth of nationalism in Vietnam and feared that a French attempt to regain control of its colony might provoke a long and bloody war, bringing instability to an area of economic and strategic significance. Even if France should succeed, they reasoned, it would restore monopolistic controls which would deny the United States access to raw materials and naval facilities. President Franklin D. Roosevelt seems instinctively to have recognized that colonialism was doomed and that the United States must identify with the forces of nationalism in Asia. Moreover, Roosevelt profoundly disliked France and its leader Charles de Gaulle, and regarded the French as "poor colonizers" who had "badly mismanaged" Indochina and exploited its

[5] Hammer, *Struggle for Indochina*, pp. 148–202.

[6] Edward R. Stettinius, Jr., Diary, March 17, 1944, Edward R. Stettinius, Jr., Papers, University of Virginia Library, Charlottesville, Va. For Roosevelt and Indochina, see Walter LaFeber, "Roosevelt, Churchill and Indochina,

people.[6] Roosevelt therefore advocated placing Indochina under international trusteeship as preparation for independence.

In 1945, however, Roosevelt retreated sharply from his earlier forthright stand in support of Indochinese independence. Fearing for their own colonies, the British had strenuously opposed the trusteeship scheme, and many of Roosevelt's top advisers urged him not to antagonize an important ally by forcing the issue. At Yalta in February 1945, the President watered down his policy by endorsing a proposal under which colonies would be placed in trusteeship only with the approval of the mother country. In view of France's announced intention to return to its former colony, this plan implicitly precluded a trusteeship for Indochina.

After Roosevelt's death in April 1945, the United States adopted a policy even more favorable to France. Harry S. Truman did not share his predecessor's personal interest in Indochina or his concern about colonialism. American thinking about the postwar world also underwent a major reorientation in the spring of 1945. Military and civilian strategists perceived that the war had left the Soviet Union the most powerful nation in Europe and Asia, and the subjugation of Eastern Europe raised growing fears that Joseph Stalin had broader, perhaps global, designs. Assigning top priority to the promotion of stable, friendly governments in Western Europe that could stand as bulwarks against Russian expansion, the Truman administration concluded that the United States "had no interest" in "championing schemes of international trusteeship" that would weaken and alienate the "European states whose help we need to balance Soviet power in Europe."[7] France assumed a role of special importance in the new scheme of things, and the State Department insisted that the United States repair the rift which had opened under Roosevelt by cooperating "wholeheartedly" with France and allaying "her apprehensions that we are

1942–1945," *American Historical Review*, 80 (December 1975), 1277–1295; Gary R. Hess, "Franklin D. Roosevelt and Indochina," *Journal of American History*, LIX (September 1972), 353–368; and Christopher Thorne, "Indochina and Anglo-American Relations, 1942–1945," *Pacific Historical Review*, XLV (February 1976), 73–96.

[7] Office of Strategic Services, "Problems and Objectives of United States Policy," April 2, 1945, Harry S. Truman Papers, Harry S. Truman Library, Independence, Mo., Rose Conway File, Box 15.

going to propose that territory be taken away from her."[8] The Truman administration quickly scrapped what remained of Roosevelt's trusteeship plan and in the summer of 1945 gave de Gaulle firm assurances that it would not stand in the way of the restoration of French sovereignty in Indochina.

The United States viewed the outbreak of war in Indochina with concern. Along with revolutions in Burma, Malaya, and Indonesia, the Vietnamese upheaval underscored the strength and explosiveness of nationalism in Southeast Asia. France's stubborn pursuit of outmoded colonial goals seemed to preclude anything other than a military solution, but the State Department's Far Eastern Office doubted that France had the capacity to subdue the revolution by force and feared that a French defeat would eliminate Western influence from an area of economic and strategic importance. The State Department's Asian experts warned of the dangers of identifying with French colonialism and pressed the administration to use its influence to force France to come to terms with Vietnamese nationalism.

American skepticism about French policy in Asia continued to be outweighed by European concerns, however. In the spring of 1947, the United States formally committed itself to the containment of Soviet expansion in Europe, and throughout the next two years American attention was riveted on France, where economic stagnation and political instability aroused grave fears of a possible Communist takeover. Warned by moderate French politicians that outside interference in colonial matters would play into the hands of the French Communist party, the United States left France to handle the Indochina question in its own way. An "immediate and vital interest" in keeping in power a "friendly government to assist in the furtherance of our aims in Europe," the State Department concluded, must "take precedence over active steps looking toward the realization of our objectives in Indochina."[9]

By early 1947, moreover, the Truman administration had

---

[8] James Dunn memorandum, April 23, 1945, 851G.00/4-2345, Department of State Records, National Archives, Washington, D.C. See also George C. Herring, "The Truman Administration and the Restoration of French Sovereignty in Indochina," *Diplomatic History,* I (Spring 1977), 97–117.

[9] Department of State, "Policy Statement on Indochina," September 27, 1948, in Department of State, *Foreign Relations of the United States, 1948* (Washington, D.C., 1974), VI, 48. Hereafter cited as *FR* with date and volume number.

drawn conclusions about Ho's revolution that would determine American policy in Vietnam for the next two decades. On numerous occasions, Ho had openly appealed for American support, even indicating that Indochina would be a "fertile field for American capital and enterprise" and raising the possibility of an American naval base at Camranh Bay.[10] U.S. diplomats in Vietnam insisted that they could find no evidence of direct Soviet contact with the Vietminh, and they stressed that, regardless of his ideology, Ho had established himself as the "symbol of nationalism and the struggle for freedom to the overwhelming majority of the population."[11] But these arguments failed to persuade an administration increasingly obsessed with the Communist menace in Europe. Intelligence reports stressed that Ho had remained loyal to Moscow throughout his career, and the lack of close ties with the Soviet Union simply meant that he was trusted to carry out Stalin's plans without supervision. In the absence of irrefutable evidence to the contrary, the State Department concluded, the United States could not "afford to assume that Ho is anything but Moscow-directed." Unwilling, as Secretary of State George C. Marshall put it, to see "colonial empires and administrations supplanted by philosophies and political organizations emanating from the Kremlin," the administration refused to take any step which might facilitate a "Communist" triumph in Indochina.[12]

As a consequence, during the first three years of the Indochina war, the United States maintained a distinctly pro-French "neutrality." Reluctant to place itself in the awkward position of openly supporting colonialism, the Truman administration gave France covert financial and military aid.[13] In addition, substantial American funds provided under the Marshall Plan enabled France to use its own resources to prosecute the war in Indochina. Fearful of antagonizing its European ally and of assisting the Vietminh, even in-

[10] Robert Blum, "Ho Chi Minh and the United States, 1944–1946," in U.S. Senate, Committee on Foreign Relations, *The United States and Vietnam: 1944–1947* (Washington, 1972), p. 13.

[11] "Policy and Information Statement on Indochina," July 1947, Philippine and Southeast Asia Branch File, Department of State Records, Box 10.

[12] George C. Marshall to U.S. Embassy Paris, February 3, 1947, *FR, 1947*, VI, 67–68.

[13] George McT. Kahin, *Power and Reality: America's Vietnam Intervention* (New York, 1986), Chap. I.

directly, Washington also refused to acknowledge receipt of Ho's appeals for support and declined to use its leverage to end the fighting or bring about a negotiated settlement.

The possibility of a French defeat, along with the Communist victory in China, brought forth in early 1950 a decision to support France in Indochina, the first step toward direct American involvement in Vietnam. The French had launched the war in 1946 confident of victory, but Ho had predicted the nature and eventual outcome of the conflict more accurately. "If ever the tiger [Vietminh] pauses," he said, "the elephant [France] will impale him on his mighty tusks. But the tiger will not pause, and the elephant will die of exhaustion and loss of blood."[14] The Vietminh retreated into the countryside, evading major engagements, mobilizing popular support, and harassing French outposts. France held the major towns and cities, but a series of unsuccessful and costly offensives and relentless hit-and-run raids by Vietminh guerrillas placed a growing strain on French manpower and resources and produced increasing war-weariness at home. The collapse of Chiang Kai-shek's government in China in 1949 and the southward advance of Mao Tse-tung's army raised the ominous possibility of Chinese Communist collaboration with the Vietminh. From late 1949 on, French officials issued increasingly urgent warnings that without direct American military aid they might be compelled to withdraw from Indochina.

The French appeals came at a time when Washington, already gripped by near-panic, was frantically reassessing its global Cold War strategy. The fall of China and Russia's successful testing of a nuclear device persuaded many American officials that the Communist threat had assumed even more menacing proportions than that posed by the Axis a decade earlier. Any doubts about the direction of Stalin's foreign policy had long since been waved aside: the Soviet Union, "animated by a new fanatic faith," was determined to "impose its absolute authority on the rest of the world." Recent successes seemed to have spurred the Soviet leadership to a new level of confidence and militancy, and Communist expansion, in the eyes of American policymakers, had already reached a point beyond which it must not be permitted to go. Any further "exten-

[14] Quoted in Jean Lacouture, *Ho Chi Minh: A Political Biography* (New York, 1968), p. 171.

sion of the area under the domination of the Kremlin," the National Security Council warned, "would raise the possibility that no coalition adequate to confront the Kremlin with greater strength could be assembled."[15] Facing a world divided into two hostile blocs, a precarious balance of power, and the possibility, if not likelihood, of global war, the Truman administration initiated plans to increase American military capabilities, shore up the defense of Western Europe, and extend the containment policy to the Far East.

In the dramatically altered strategic context of 1950, support for France in Indochina was considered essential for the security of Western Europe. Massive expenditures for the war against the Vietminh had retarded France's economic recovery and the attainment of that level of political stability required to fend off the threat of Communism. Certain that Europe was more vulnerable than ever to the Soviet threat, American policymakers in early 1950 began to formulate plans to raise the military forces necessary to defend against the Red Army. Their preliminary proposals required France to contribute sizable numbers of troops and provided for the rearmament of West Germany, measures the French were likely to resist. The administration thus feared that if it did not respond positively to its ally's appeals for aid in Indochina, France might refuse to cooperate with its strategic design for Western Europe.

American willingness to support France in Indochina also reflected a growing concern about the future of Southeast Asia. The raging conflict in Indochina and insurgencies in Burma, Malaya, and Indonesia all sprang from indigenous roots, but in a seemingly polarized world the mere existence of these revolutions and their leftist orientation persuaded Americans that Southeast Asia was the "target of a coordinated offensive directed by the Kremlin." The European colonial powers and the fragile, newly independent governments of the region seemed incapable of subduing the revolutions, and the presence of a hostile China to the north added enormously to the danger.

In the aftermath of the fall of China, American strategists concluded that Southeast Asia was vital to the security of the United States. Should the region be swept by Communism, the National Security Council warned, "we shall have suffered a major political

[15] NSC 68, April 14, 1950, printed in *Naval War College Review* (May–June 1975), 51–108.

rout the repercussions of which will be felt throughout the world."
The loss of an area so large and populous would tip the balance of
power against the United States. Recent Communist triumphs had
already aroused nervousness in Europe, and another major victory
might tempt the Europeans to reach an accommodation with the
Soviet Union. The economic consequences could be equally profound. The United States and its European allies would be denied
access to important markets, and the Europeans would lose a major
source of the dollars they desperately needed to rebuild their shattered economies. Southeast Asia was the world's largest producer
of natural rubber and was an important source of oil, tin, tungsten,
and other strategic commodities. Should control of these vital raw
materials suddenly change hands, the Soviet bloc would be enormously strengthened at the expense of the West.

American policymakers also feared that the loss of Southeast
Asia would irreparably damage the nation's strategic position in
the Far East. Control of the offshore island chain extending from
Japan to the Philippines, America's first line of defense in the Pacific, would be endangered. Air and sea routes between Australia
and the Middle East and the United States and India could be cut,
severely hampering military operations in the event of war. Japan,
India, and Australia, those nations where the West retained predominant influence, would be cut off from each other and left vulnerable.

The impact on Japan, America's major Far Eastern ally and the
richest economic prize in the area, would be especially disastrous.
Even before China fell, the United States was pushing for the rein-
tegration of Japan with Southeast Asia, its rice bowl and breadbas-
ket and an essential source of raw materials and markets. With
China having already fallen to Communism, the loss of Southeast
Asia would leave Japan no choice but to accommodate with the
adversary. The United States thus moved rapidly to defend a region
perceived to be a "vital segment" of the "great crescent" of containment extending from Japan to India.[16]

American officials agreed that Indochina, and especially Viet-

---

[16] NSC 48/1, "The Position of the United States with Respect to Asia," December 23, 1949, U.S. Congress, House, Committee on Armed Services, *United
States-Vietnam Relations, 1945–1967: A Study Prepared by the Department of
Defense* (Washington, 1971), Book 8, 226–272. Hereafter cited as *USVN* with
book number. Michael Schaller "Securing the Great Crescent: Occupied Japan
and the Origins of Containment in Southeast Asia," *Journal of American History*,
69 (September 1982), 392–413.

nam, was the key to the defense of Southeast Asia. Soviet recognition of the Vietminh on January 30, 1950, confirmed long-standing beliefs about Ho's allegiance, revealing him, in Secretary of State Dean Acheson's words, in his "true colors as the mortal enemy of native independence in Indochina." It was also interpreted as a "significant and ominous" portent of Stalin's intention to "accelerate the revolutionary process" in Southeast Asia.[17] Ho's well-organized guerrillas had already scored major gains against France, and with increased Soviet and Chinese backing might be able to force a French withdrawal, removing the last military bulwark between China and the rest of Southeast Asia. Indochina was in the "most immediate danger," the State Department concluded, and was therefore "the most strategically important area of Southeast Asia."[18]

Indochina was considered intrinsically important for its raw materials, rice, and naval bases, but it was deemed far more significant for the presumed effect its loss would have on other areas. By early 1950, American policymakers had firmly embraced what would become known as the "domino theory," the belief that the fall of Indochina would bring in rapid succession the collapse of the other nations of Southeast Asia. Acceptance of this concept reflects the perceived fragility of the region in 1950, as well as the experience of World War II, when Hitler had overrun Western Europe in three months and the Japanese had seized much of Southeast Asia in even less time. First employed to justify aid to Greece in 1947, the idea, once applied to Southeast Asia, quickly became an article of faith. Americans were certain that if Indochina fell the rest of Southeast Asia would be imperiled. The strategic reassessment of 1950 thus ended American "neutrality" and produced a commitment in early March to furnish France military and economic assistance for the war against the Vietminh. It also established principles that would provide the basis for U.S. policy in Vietnam for years to come and would eventually lead to massive involvement.

The creation of nominally independent governments in Indo-

---

[17] *Department of State Bulletin* (February 13, 1950), 244; Charles Yost memorandum, January 31, 1950, *FR 1950*, VI, 710–711.

[18] Dean Rusk to James H. Burns, March 7, 1950, U.S. Congress, Senate, Subcommittee on Public Buildings and Grounds, *The Pentagon Papers* (*The Senator Gravel Edition*) (4 vols.; Boston, 1971), I, 363. Hereafter cited as *Pentagon Papers* (*Gravel*).

china made it easier for the United States to rationalize support of France. Unable to defeat the Vietminh militarily, the French had attempted to undercut it politically by forming native governments in Laos, Cambodia, and Vietnam, the latter headed by the former Emperor of Annam, Bao Dai, and according them the status of "free states" within the French Union. Many U.S. officials were skeptical of the so-called Bao Dai solution, warning that it was only a smokescreen for continued French domination and had little chance of success. The State Department acknowledged the strength of these arguments, but Bao Dai seemed the only alternative to "Commie domination of Indochina," as Acheson put it, and while American support did not guarantee his success, the lack of it seemed likely to ensure his failure.[19] By backing Bao Dai, moreover, the United States would at least avoid the appearance of being an accomplice of French imperialism. In February 1950, the Truman administration formally recognized the Bao Dai government and the free states of Laos and Cambodia and initiated plans to support them with economic and technical assistance.

In retrospect, the assumptions upon which American policy-makers acted in 1950 appear misguided. The Southeast Asian revolutions were not inspired by Moscow and, although the Soviet Union and China at times sought to control them, their capacity to do so was limited by their lack of military and especially naval power and by the strength of local nationalism. The American assessment of the situation in Vietnam seems to have been well off the mark. Although a dedicated Communist, Ho was no mere tool of the Soviet Union, and while he was willing to accept help from the major Communist powers—indeed, he had no choice but to do so—he was not prepared to subordinate Vietnamese independence to them. Vietnam's historic fears of its larger northern neighbor made submission to China especially unlikely. "It is better to sniff French dung for a while than eat China's all our life," Ho once said, graphically expressing a traditional principle of Vietnamese foreign policy.[20] Perhaps most important, regardless of his ideology, Ho by 1950 had captured the standard of Vietnamese nationalism, and by supporting France, even under the guise of the Bao Dai solution, the United States was attaching itself to a losing cause.

[19] Dean Acheson to U.S. Embassy Manila, January 7, 1950, *FR, 1950*, VI, 692; Gary R. Hess, "The First American Commitment in Indochina: The Acceptance of the Bao Dai Solution," *Diplomatic History*, 2 (Fall 1978), 331–350.

[20] Quoted in Lacouture, *Ho Chi Minh*, p. 119.

American policymakers were not unaware of the pitfalls of intervention in Indochina. Should the United States commit itself to Bao Dai and should he turn out to be a French puppet, a State Department Asian specialist warned, "we must then follow blindly down a dead-end alley, expending our limited resources . . . in a fight that would be hopeless."[21] Some American officials even dimly perceived that the United States might get sucked into direct involvement in Vietnam. But the initial commitment seemed limited and the risks seemed smaller than those of inaction. Caught up in a global struggle reminiscent of World War II, with Russia taking Germany's place in Europe and China Japan's place in Asia, U.S. officials were certain that if they did not back France and Bao Dai, Southeast Asia might be lost, leaving the more awesome choice of making a "staggering investment" to recover the losses or falling back to a "much contracted" line of defense in the western Pacific.[22]

By the time the United States committed itself to assist France, the Vietminh had gained the military initiative in Indochina. Ho Chi Minh controlled an estimated two-thirds of the countryside, and Vietminh regulars and guerrillas numbered in the hundreds of thousands. The Chinese were furnishing sanctuaries across the border and large stocks of weapons. By early 1950, Giap felt sufficiently confident of his strength to take the offensive for the first time. The French maintained tenuous control in the cities and the major production centers, but at a very high cost, suffering 1,000 casualties per month and in 1949 alone spending 167 million francs on the war. Even in the areas under nominal French control, the Vietminh spread terror after dark, sabotaging power plants and factories, tossing grenades into cafés and theaters, and brutally assassinating French officials. "Anyone with white skin caught outside protected areas after dark is courting horrible death," an American correspondent reported.[23]

---

[21] Charles Reed to C. Walton Butterworth, April 14, 1949, 851G.00/4–1449, Department of State Records.

[22] Acheson to Truman, May 14, 1950, Truman Papers, Confidential File. For an excellent discussion of the initial commitment in Indochina, see Robert M. Blum, *Drawing the Line: The Origin of the American Containment Policy in Asia* (New York, 1982), especially pp. 198–213.

[23] Tilman Durdin, "War 'Not for Land But for People,' " *New York Times Magazine* (May 28, 1950), 48.

The Bao Dai solution, Bao Dai himself ruefully conceded, was "just a French solution."[24] The much-maligned "playboy Emperor" was in fact a tragic figure. An intelligent man, genuinely concerned about the future of his nation, he had spent most of his life as a puppet of France and then Japan, whiling away the years by indulging an apparently insatiable taste for sports cars, women, and gambling. The agreement of February 1950 gave him little to work with. Under this impossibly complex document of 258 pages, the French retained control of Vietnam's treasury, commerce, and foreign and military policies. They refused even to turn over Saigon's Norodom Palace as the seat of the new government. The government itself was composed largely of wealthy southern landowners, many of them more European than Vietnamese and in no sense representative of the people. Nationalists of stature refused to support Bao Dai, and the masses either backed the resistance or remained aloof. The emperor may have wished to become a leader, but he lacked the experience and temperament to do so. Introverted and given to periodic moods of depression and indolence, he lived in isolation in one of his palaces or aboard his 600-ton air-conditioned yacht or escaped to the French Riviera, all the while salting away large sums of money in Swiss bank accounts— not "the stuff of which Churchills are made," U.S. Ambassador Donald Heath lamented with marvelous understatement.[25]

The onset of the Korean War in the summer of 1950 complicated an already difficult problem. The Truman administration perceived North Korea's invasion of South Korea as confirmation of its suspicion that the Soviet Union sought to conquer all of Asia, even at the risk of war, and the defense of Indochina assumed even greater importance in American eyes. By the end of the year, however, the United States and France had suffered major reversals. Chinese intervention in Korea forced General Douglas MacArthur into a headlong retreat from the Yalu. In the meantime, Giap had inflicted upon France its "greatest colonial defeat since Montcalm had died at Quebec," trapping an entire army at Cao Bang in northeastern Vietnam and costing the French more than 6,000 troops and enough equipment to stock an entire Vietminh divi-

---

[24] Robert Shaplen, *The Lost Revolution: The U.S. in Vietnam, 1946–1966* (New York, 1966), p. 64.

[25] Heath to John Foster Dulles, April 28, 1953, *FR, 1952–1954*, XIII, 523; Ellen Hammer, "The Bao Dai Experiment," *Pacific Affairs*, 23 (March 1950), 58.

sion.[26] Chinese intervention in Korea raised fears of a similar plunge across the border into Vietnam, and American policymakers were increasingly concerned that a growing defeatism in France would raise demands for withdrawal from Indochina.

Against this background of stunning defeat in the Far East, the Truman administration struggled to devise a workable policy for Indochina. With large numbers of American troops committed to Korea and with Europe vulnerable to a possible Soviet invasion, the Joint Chiefs of Staff agreed that even should the Chinese invade Indochina, the United States could not commit military forces to its defense. France must remain and bear primary responsibility for the war. More certain than ever that Indochina was essential to American security, the administration was forced to rely on military assistance to bolster French defenses. In late 1950, the United States committed more than $133 million for aid to Indochina and ordered immediate delivery of large quantities of arms and ammunition, naval vessels, aircraft, and military vehicles.

Most Americans agreed, however, that military equipment by itself would not be enough. As early as May, Acheson complained that the French seemed "paralyzed, in a state of moving neither forward or backward," and a fact-finding mission dispatched to Indochina *before* the Cao Bang disaster confirmed his fears.[27] American observers reported that the French state of mind was "fatuous, even dangerous," and warned that unless France prosecuted the war with greater determination, made more effective use of native manpower, and moved boldly and generously to win over the Vietnamese, the United States and its ally might be "moving into a debacle which neither of us can afford."[28] The Joint Chiefs of Staff proposed that the United States condition its military aid on French pledges to take drastic measures, including the promise of eventual independence.

The administration approached this question with great caution. Acheson conceded that if the United States supported France's "old-fashioned colonial attitudes," it might "lose out." But the French presence was essential to defend Indochina against Communism, he quickly added, and the United States could not

[26] Bernard Fall, *Street Without Joy* (New York, 1972), p. 33.

[27] Minutes of meeting, National Security Council, May 4, 1950, Truman Papers, President's Secretary's File.

[28] Melby Mission Report, August 6, 1950, *FR, 1950*, VI, 843–844; Policy Planning Staff Memorandum, August 16, 1950, *ibid.*, 857–858.

press France to the point where it would say, "All right, take over the damned country. We don't want it." Admitting the inconsistency of American policy, he concluded that the only choice was to encourage the French to remain until the crisis had eased but at the same time persuade them to "play with the nationalist movement and give Bao Dai a chance really to get the nationalists on his side."[29] Rejecting any form of pressure, the administration would go no further than to gently urge France to make symbolic concessions and build a Vietnamese army. The State Department, in the meantime, would hold Bao Dai's "feet to the fire" to get him to assert effective leadership under French tutelage.[30]

To strengthen the governments of Indochina and increase their popular appeal, the United States established a program of economic and technical assistance in 1950 and over the next two years spent more than $50 million on various projects. American experts provided fertilizer and seeds to increase agricultural production, constructed dispensaries, developed malaria-control programs, and distributed food and clothing to refugees. To ensure that the program would achieve its objectives the United States insisted that the aid go directly to the native governments rather than through France. To secure maximum propaganda advantage, zealous U.S. aid officials tacked posters on pagoda walls and air-dropped pamphlets into villages indicating that the programs were gifts of the United States and contrasting the "real gains" made possible by them with "Communism's empty promises."[31]

The Truman policy brought only limited results. Their hopes of victory revived by the prospect of large-scale American assistance, the French in late 1950 appointed the flamboyant Jean de Lattre de Tassigny to command the armed forces in Indochina and instructed him to prosecute the war vigorously. A born crusader and

[29] U.S. Congress, Senate, *Reviews of the World Situation: 1949–1950 Hearings Held in Executive Session Before the Committee on Foreign Relations* (Washington, D.C., 1974), pp. 266–268, 292–293.

[30] Livingston Merchant to Dean Rusk, October 19, 1950, *FR, 1950*, VI, 901–902.

[31] Mutual Security Agency, *Dateline Saigon—Our Quiet War in Indochina* (Washington, D.C., 1952). The United States Information Service even prepared a Vietnamese-language edition of the *Outline History of the United States* with an introduction by President Truman expressing hope that an "account of the progress of the American people toward a just and happy society can be an inspiration to those Vietnamese who today know something of the same difficulties as they build a new nation." Roger Tubby to Joseph Short, March 8, 1951, Truman Papers, Official File 203–F.

practitioner of what he called *dynamisme*, de Lattre announced upon arriving in Vietnam that he would win the war within fifteen months, and under his inspired leadership French forces repulsed a major Vietminh offensive in the Red River Delta in early 1951. But when de Lattre attempted to follow up his success by attacking Vietminh strongholds just south of Hanoi, France suffered its worst defeat of the war. De Lattre himself would die of cancer in early 1952, and the French military position was more precarious at the time of his death than when he had come to Vietnam.

In other areas as well there was little progress. Desperately short of manpower, the French finally put aside their reluctance to arm the Vietnamese, and de Lattre made determined efforts to create a Vietnamese National Army (VNA). The Vietnamese were understandably reluctant to fight for what they regarded as a French cause, however, and by the end of 1951 the VNA numbered only 38,000 men, far short of its projected strength of 115,000. Responding to American entreaties, the French vaguely promised to "perfect" the independence of the Associated States, but the massive infusion of American supplies and de Lattre's early victories seemed to eliminate any compelling need for real concessions. The French were unwilling to fight for *Vietnamese* independence and never seriously considered the only sort of concession that would have satisfied the aspirations of Vietnamese nationalism. France transferred to the native governments some additional responsibilities, but they remained shadow governments lacking in real authority and in popular support.

By 1952, the United States was bearing roughly one-third of the cost of the war, but it was dissatisfied with the results and it found itself with no influence over French military policy. A small Military Assistance and Advisory Group (MAAG) had been sent to Vietnam in 1950 to screen French requests for aid, assist in the training of Vietnamese soldiers, and advise on strategy. By going directly to Washington to get what he wanted, however, de Lattre reduced the MAAG to virtual impotence. Proud, sensitive, and highly nationalistic, he ignored the American "advisers" in formulating strategy, denied them any role in training the Vietnamese, and refused even to keep them informed of his current operations and future plans.[32]

[32] Ronald H. Spector, *Advice and Support: The Early Years, 1941–1960* (Washington, D.C., 1983), pp. 115–121.

Deeply suspicious of American intrusion into their domain, the French expressed open resentment against the aid program and placed numerous obstacles in its way. De Lattre bitterly complained that there were too many Americans in Vietnam spending too much money, that the American aid program was making France "look like a poor cousin in Vietnamese eyes," and that the Americans were "fanning the flames of extreme nationalism." French officials attempted to block projects which did not contribute directly to the war and encouraged Vietnamese suspicions by warning that American aid contained "hidden traps" to subvert their "independence." Largely as a result of French obstructionism, the aid program touched only a small number of people. American officials conceded that its "beneficial psychological results were largely negated because the United States at the same time was pursuing a program of [military] support to the French." America was looked upon "more as a supporter of colonialism than as a friend of the new nation."[33]

While firmly resisting American influence in Indochina, France demanded larger military assistance and an expanded American commitment. Already facing the threat of a military and political collapse in Indochina, the French grew more concerned when American efforts to negotiate an end to the war in Korea raised the possibility that Chinese troops would be freed for a drive southward. In early 1952, France pressed Washington relentlessly for additional military aid, a collective security arrangement for the defense of Southeast Asia, and a firm commitment to provide American combat forces should Chinese troops cross the border into Vietnam.

Washington was extremely wary of expanding its commitments. The proposal for a collective security arrangement appeared to be a snare to draw the United States more deeply into the conflict, and the Truman administration promptly rejected it. The "line we took," Acheson later recalled, was that "in some places such as Europe and NATO, we had a common responsibility. In other places, one or the other of these nations had to take a leading part."[34] The United States also refused to commit ground forces to

[33] Shaplen, *Lost Revolution,* pp. 86–89; Embassy Saigon to Secretary of State, May 15, 1951, *FR, 1951,* VI, 419.

[34] Dean Acheson, "Princeton Seminar," March 14, 1954, Dean Acheson Papers, Harry S. Truman Library, Independence, Mo., Box 66. See also "Defense of

Indochina under any circumstances. The administration had initiated a massive rearmament program, but progress had been
slowed by the war in Korea, and the National Security Council
concluded that the nation faced the "continuing danger of global
war, as well as local aggression in a situation of inadequate military
strength."[35] The drawn-out, costly stalemate in Korea had produced considerable frustration among the American people and
had made abundantly clear the difficulties of fighting a land war in
Asia. It would be "futile and a mistake to defend Indochina in Indochina," Acheson observed. We "could not have another Korea,
we could not put ground forces into Indochina."[36]

The administration was not prepared to abandon France, however. By early 1952, the domino theory was firmly rooted as a principle of American foreign policy. Policymakers agreed that
Southeast Asia must not be permitted to "fall into the hands of the
Communists like a ripe plum" and that a continued French presence in Indochina was essential to the defense of that critical region.[37] Aware that the threat to Indochina had increased since
1950, and fearful that the French might pull out if their requests
were not met, the administration in June 1952 approved an additional $150 million in military assistance. Moving one step beyond
its commitment of 1950, the National Security Council agreed that
if China intervened directly in the war, the United States would
have to send naval and air units to defend Indochina and would
have to consider the possibility of naval and air operations against
China itself.[38]

Although thoroughly dissatisfied with France's performance in
the war and deeply annoyed by its secretiveness and obstructionism, the administration refused to attach any strings to its new
commitments. The Defense Department urged that the United
States use its leverage to force France to adopt a "dynamic pro-

---

Southeast Asia," January 2, 1952, Truman Papers, President's Secretary's File,
Churchill-Truman Meetings, Box 116.

[35] NSC Staff Study, December 20, 1951, Truman Papers, President's Secretary's
File, Box 216.

[36] Acheson memorandum, June 17, 1952, *Pentagon Papers* (*Gravel*), I, 381.

[37] NSC 124/2, June 24, 1952, *ibid.*, 385–386; "Pacific Security Pact," January 2,
1952, Truman Papers, President's Secretary's File, Churchill-Truman Meetings,
Box 116.

[38] NSC 124/2, June 25, 1952, *Pentagon Papers* (*Gravel*), I, 385–386.

gram geared to produce positive improvement in the military and political situation." The State Department feared, however, that if the administration "pressed the French too hard they would withdraw and leave us holding the baby."[39]

America's Indochina policy continued to be a hostage of its policy in Europe, the area to which Truman and Acheson assigned the highest priority. Since 1951, the United States had been pressing for allied approval of the European Defense Community, a plan for the integration of French and German forces into a multinational army originally put forward by France to delay German rearmament. The French repeatedly warned that they could not furnish troops for European defense without generous American support in Indochina, a ploy Acheson accurately described as "blackmail." The European Defense Community had also become a volatile political issue in France, where there was strong nationalistic resistance to surrendering the identity of the French army and to collaborating with a recent, and still despised, enemy. With the question awaiting ratification by the French parliament, Acheson later recalled, no one "seriously advised" that it would be "wise to end, or threaten to end, aid to Indochina unless an American plan of military and political reform was carried out."[40] NSC 124/2, a major policy statement on Indochina of June 1952, would go no further than state that the United States should use its "influence" to "promote positive political, military, economic, and social policies. . . ."[41]

During the last half of 1952, Acheson did make a concerted effort to break through French secretiveness. The Secretary of State bluntly informed French officials in July that since the United States was paying about one-third of the cost of the war, it did not seem "unreasonable" to expect some detailed information about its progress. The French did not dissent, Acheson later recalled, but "not much happened as a result." Following a long and heated session of the Council of Foreign Ministers in Paris in December, the French again requested additional military assistance. "At this point tired, hungry and exasperated," Acheson later wrote, "I ran

---

[39] Quoted in John M. Allison, *Ambassador from the Prairie, or Allison Wonderland* (New York, 1976), pp. 191, 194.

[40] Dean G. Acheson, *Present at the Creation* (New York, 1969), p. 676.

[41] NSC 124/2, June 25, 1952, *Pentagon Papers (Gravel)*, I, 387.

out of patience." He complained forcefully that the United States was "thoroughly dissatisfied" with the information it was getting and warned that this situation "had to be remedied. We must know exactly what the situation was and what we were doing if, as and when we were to take any further step."[42] Acheson's protest revealed the depth of American frustration with more than two years of partnership with France, but it came too late to have any effect. Within less than a month, the Truman administration would leave office, freeing it from further responsibility.

Despite a considerable investment in Indochina, Truman and Acheson left to their successors a problem infinitely more complex and dangerous than the one they had taken on in 1950. What had begun as a localized rebellion against French colonialism had expanded into an international conflict of major proportions. The United States was now bearing more than 40 percent of the cost of the war and had established a stake in its outcome. Chinese aid to the Vietminh had increased from 400 tons per month to more than 3,000, and as many as 4,000 Chinese "volunteers" assisted the Vietminh in various ways. The war had spilled over into neighboring Laos and Thailand, where China and the Vietminh backed insurgencies against governments supported by the United States and France. In Vietnam itself, French control had been reduced to enclaves around Hanoi, Haiphong, and Saigon, and a narrow strip along the Cambodian border, and France faced a new and much more ominous type of military threat. "The enemy, once painted as a bomb-throwing terrorist or hill sniper lurking in night ambush," the veteran correspondent Theodore White observed, "has become a modern army, increasingly skillful, armed with artillery, organized into divisional groups."[43] The French had naively hoped that American aid might be a substitute for increased sacrifice on their own part, but they had come to realize that it only required more of them. Fearful of their nation's growing dependence on the United States and aware that victory would require nothing short of an all-out effort, in late 1952 some French political leaders outside the Communist party began for the first time to recommend withdrawal from Indochina. The "real" problem, Acheson warned

[42] Acheson, *Present at the Creation*, pp. 676–677.
[43] Theodore H. White, "France Holds on to the Indo-China Tiger," *New York Times Magazine* (June 8, 1952), 9.

the incoming administration, was the "French will to carry on the . . . war."[44]

The Republican administration of Dwight D. Eisenhower accepted without modification the principles of Indochina policy bequeathed by the Democrats. Eisenhower and his Secretary of State, John Foster Dulles, agreed that Ho Chi Minh was an instrument of international Communism and that the fall of Indochina would cause the loss of all of Southeast Asia with disastrous political, economic, and strategic consequences for the United States. In the campaign of 1952, the Republicans had attacked the Democrats for failing to halt the advance of Communism, and they were even more determined than their predecessors to prevent the fall of Indochina. While vowing to wage the Cold War with vigor, Eisenhower and Dulles had also promised cuts in defense spending, and their "New Look" defense policy called for sharp reductions in American ground forces. They were even more reluctant than Truman and Acheson to commit American combat forces to Southeast Asia and agreed that France must remain in Indochina and bear the burden of the conflict.

The changes introduced by Eisenhower and Dulles were changes of mood and tactics rather than of substance. As would happen so often during the long history of American involvement in Vietnam, a new administration came into office confident that new methods or the more persistent application of old ones could turn a deteriorating situation around. The Republicans quickly concluded that the United States and France had made critical errors. Eisenhower insisted that the French generals in Indochina were a "poor lot" and that new leadership was needed. The U.S. military deplored France's cautious, defensive strategy and its reluctance to use Vietnamese troops. The United States Army had achieved great success in the Korean War by training South Korean troops and employing aggressive, offensive tactics against the Chinese and the North Koreans. The Joint Chiefs of Staff therefore concluded that France could win the war within a year if it made greater use of Vietnamese forces and adopted an aggressive strategy designed to destroy the enemy's regular units. Most U.S. officials also agreed that France had not done enough to win nationalist support by making timely and substantive political con-

---

[44] Henry Cabot Lodge, Jr., *As It Was* (New York, 1976), p. 36.

cessions. Eisenhower and Dulles felt that the Truman administration had carelessly squandered the leverage available to it, and they concurred with General J. Lawton Collins that it was necessary to "put the squeeze on the French to get them off their fannies."[45]

The new administration set out zealously to correct the mistakes of its predecessor. Alarmed by growing signs of war-weariness in France, Eisenhower and Dulles gave firm assurances of continued assistance and promised that the nation's "tiredness" would "evaporate in the face of a positive and constructive program."[46] The administration also made clear, however, that continued aid would be conditioned on detailed and specific information about French military operations and plans and on firm French pledges to expand the Vietnamese National Army and to develop a new, aggressive strategy with an explicit timetable for the defeat of the enemy's main forces. Eisenhower himself advised Ambassador Douglas Dillon in Paris to impress upon the French the importance of appointing a *"forceful and inspirational leader,* empowered with the means and authority to win victory," and of making "clear and unequivocal public announcements, repeated as often as may be desirable," that complete independence would be granted "as soon as victory against the Communists had been won."[47]

Under mounting pressure to do something or withdraw from Indochina, the French government responded quickly. In early May 1953, it appointed General Henri Navarre to command French forces in Indochina. Two months later, a new cabinet, headed by Joseph Laniel, promised to "perfect" the independence of the Associated States by turning over responsibilities exercised by France. Shortly after, the French presented for American approval a new strategic concept, the so-called Navarre Plan. Tailored to meet many of the specifications set down earlier by the American Joint Chiefs, the plan called for a vast augmentation of the Vietnamese National Army and for the establishment of a new training program, along with the commitment to Indochina of an additional nine battalions of French regulars. Navarre proposed to withdraw his scattered forces from their isolated garrisons, com-

---

[45] J.C.S. meeting, April 24, 1953, *FR, 1952–1954,* XIII, 500.

[46] Dulles to American Embassy Paris, March 27, 1953, *USVN,* Book 9, 20.

[47] Eisenhower to Dillon, May 6, 1953, Dwight D. Eisenhower Papers, Dwight D. Eisenhower Library, Abilene, Kans., International File: France, 1953 (3), Box 10.

bine them with the new forces available to him, and initiate a major offensive to drive the Vietminh from its stronghold in the Red River Delta. In a secret report to Paris, Navarre warned that the war could not be won in a strictly military sense and that the best that could be hoped for was a draw. The Laniel government apparently adopted the plan as a last-ditch measure to salvage some return on the huge investment that had been made and to ensure continued American support. It also attached a high price tag, advising Washington that without an additional $400 million in aid it could not implement the plan and would have to consider withdrawal from Indochina.

Although dubious of French intentions and capabilities, Washington saw no alternative but to accept the proposal. Eisenhower privately complained that Laniel's promise of independence had been made "in an obscure and roundabout fashion—instead of boldly, forthrightly and repeatedly."[48] The Joint Chiefs were skeptical of France's willingness and ability to pursue the Navarre Plan vigorously. By this time, however, the two nations were caught up in a tangle of mutual dependence and spiraling commitments, and the United States felt compelled to go along with France. The Joint Chiefs concluded that the Navarre Plan at least offered a hope of success. The State Department warned that the Laniel government was the first French government which seemed "prepared to do what needs to be done to wind up the war in Indo-China," and if it fell it would probably be succeeded by a government committed to a negotiated settlement, which would mean "the eventual loss to Communism not only of Indochina but of the whole of Southeast Asia."[49] After extracting a formal French promise to pursue the Navarre Plan with determination, the administration in September 1953 agreed to provide France with an additional $385 million in military assistance. With characteristic bravado, Dulles publicly proclaimed that the new French strategy would "break the organized body of Communist aggression by the end of the 1955 fighting season."[50]

Within six months after the United States and France had

[48] Eisenhower to Ralph Flanders, July 7, 1953, Eisenhower Papers, Diary Series, Box 2.

[49] State Department report to NSC, August 5, 1953, *USVN*, Book 9, 128.

[50] Quoted in Bernard Fall, *The Two Vietnams: A Political and Military Analysis* (New York, 1967), p. 122.

agreed upon the "end-the-war offensive," the military and political situation in Indochina drastically deteriorated. Navarre was forced to scrap his ill-fated plan in its initial stages. In the fall of 1953, he began to mobilize his forces for the anticipated offensive in the delta. Recognizing that he must strike a decisive blow before the impact of expanded American aid could be felt, Giap invaded central and southern Laos, intensified guerrilla activity in the delta, and prepared for a major strike into northern Laos. The only response Navarre could devise was to scatter the very forces he had just combined to counter the Vietminh thrusts.

By early 1954, both sides had committed major forces to the remote village of Dienbienphu in the northwest corner of Vietnam. Navarre established a position at the intersection of several major roads near the Laotian border in hopes of cutting off the anticipated invasion and luring Vietminh main units into open battle. In a broad valley surrounded by hills as high as 1,000 feet, he constructed a garrison ringed with barbed wire and bunkers, and hastily dispatched twelve battalions of regulars supported by aircraft and heavy artillery. Giap took the "bait." After a quick strike into Laos, he retraced his steps and encircled the French garrison. Navarre now found 12,000 of his elite forces isolated in a far corner of Vietnam. Although increasingly uncertain that they could hold out against superior Vietminh numbers, in January he decided to remain.

In the meantime, an outburst of Vietnamese nationalism further undercut France's already tenuous political position. When the French opened negotiations to "perfect" Vietnamese independence, non-Communist nationalists, including some of Bao Dai's associates, demanded not only complete independence but also severance of all ties with France. The United States found itself in an awkward predicament. Although it had taken a forthright stand in favor of eventual independence, it feared that the Vietnamese demands would provoke a French withdrawal, and it was certain that the Bao Dai government could not survive by itself. Ambassador Heath charged the Vietnamese with "childlike" and "irresponsible" behavior. Dulles angrily denounced the "ill-considered" actions of the nationalists and dangled in front of them promises of large-scale American aid if they cooperated.[51] The American Em-

[51] Heath to State Department, October 18, 1953, *FR, 1952–1954,* XIII, 836; Dulles to American Embassy Saigon, October 21, 1953, *USVN,* Book 9, 169–170.

bassy in Saigon pressed the Vietnamese to tone down their demands—"We are the last French colonialists in Indochina," an American diplomat remarked with wry humor.[52] Despite American attempts to mediate, the French and Vietnamese could not reach an agreement on the status of an independent Vietnam.

The political crisis of late 1953, along with an apparent shift in Soviet foreign policy, heightened French tendencies toward a negotiated settlement. Many French politicians concluded that Vietnamese association with the French Union, if only symbolic, was all that could be salvaged from the war and without this there was no reason to prolong the agony. The leaders who had assumed power in the Kremlin after Stalin's death in February had taken a conciliatory line on a number of major Cold War issues, Indochina included, and the French government hoped that Soviet influence would enable it to secure a favorable settlement. Over Dulles's vigorous opposition, France in early 1954 agreed to place Indochina on the agenda of an East-West conference scheduled to meet in Geneva to consider Far Eastern problems.

Eisenhower and Dulles could only acquiesce. Distrustful of the Soviet overtures and skeptical of the wisdom of the French decision, they were nevertheless unwilling to put the United States in the position of being the only great power to oppose peaceful settlement of a major international crisis. Moreover, despite Dulles's threats of an "agonizing reappraisal" of American commitments, the French still refused to ratify the European Defense Community, and the new Soviet line had complicated the prospect by easing European fears of a Russian attack. Like Acheson before him, Dulles hesitated to press France too hard on Indochina lest it reject the European Defense Community altogether, splitting the Western alliance and playing into the hands of the Russians.

In January 1954, the United States for the first time faced the prospect of direct military intervention in Indochina. Speaking with "great force," Eisenhower told the National Security Council how "bitterly opposed" he was to putting American troops into the jungles of Indochina. He went on to insist, however, that the United States must not forget its vital interests there. Comparing the region to a "leaky dike," he warned that with such situations it was "sometimes better to put a finger in than to let the whole

[52] Quoted in Hammer, *Struggle for Indochina*, p. 319.

structure wash away."[53] American officials especially feared that French war-weariness would result in a surrender at Geneva. A special committee appointed by the President to review Indochina policy recommended in mid-March that prior to the conference the United States should attempt to discourage defeatist tendencies in France and should use its influence at Geneva to ensure that no agreements were reached. If, despite American efforts, the French accepted an unsatisfactory settlement, the United States might have to arrange with the Associated States and other interested nations to continue the war without France.[54]

While Eisenhower and his advisers pondered the long-range possibility of American intervention in Indochina, Giap tightened the noose around Dienbienphu. On March 13, the Vietminh launched an all-out attack and within twenty-four hours had seized hills Gabrielle and Beatrice, the outposts established by France to protect the fortress in the valley below. American and French experts had predicted that it would be impossible to get artillery up to the high ground surrounding the garrison. But the Vietminh formed "human anthills," carrying disassembled weapons up piece by piece, then reassembling them and camouflaging them so effectively that they were impervious to artillery and strafing. The heavy Vietminh guns quickly knocked out the airfield, making resupply impossible except by parachute drop and leaving the garrison of 12,000 men isolated and vulnerable.

The spectacular Vietminh success at Dienbienphu raised the prospect of immediate American intervention. During a visit to Washington in late March, French Chief of Staff General Paul Ely still estimated a "50-50 chance of success" at Dienbienphu and merely requested the transfer of additional American aircraft to be used by France for attacks on Vietminh lines around the fortress. Ely was deeply concerned about the possibility of Chinese intervention, however, openly inquiring of Dulles how the United States would respond in such a contingency.[55] Much less optimistic about Dienbienphu was Admiral Arthur Radford, Chairman of the Joint

---

[53] Record of NSC meeting, January 8, 1954, *FR, 1952–1954*, XIII, 949, 952.

[54] *Pentagon Papers (Gravel)*, I, 90–92.

[55] Memorandum of conversation, Ely and Dulles, March 23, 1954, 751G.00/3-2354, Department of State Records. For a more detailed discussion of these events, see George C. Herring and Richard H. Immerman, "Eisenhower, Dulles, and Dienbienphu: 'The Day We Didn't Go to War' Revisited," *Journal of American History*, 71 (September 1984), 343–363.

Chiefs of Staff, who during the Ely visit began to give serious consideration to a scheme originally devised by French and American officers in Saigon. The plan called for a massive strike by American B-29s and carrier-based aircraft, possibly using tactical atomic weapons, to relieve the siege of Dienbienphu. Although Radford made no commitments, he apparently led Ely to believe that he would push for approval of the plan should the French formally request it.

The proposed air attack won little support in Washington. Eisenhower briefly toyed with the idea of a "single strike [flown by U.S. pilots in unmarked planes], if it were almost certain this would produce decisive results." "Of course, if we did, we'd have to deny it forever," he quickly added.[56] Dulles was prepared to consider air and naval operations in Indochina, but only as a last resort. Less worried about the immediate threat to Dienbienphu than about the long-range threat to Southeast Asia, the Secretary preferred what he called "United Action," the formation of a coalition composed of the United States, Great Britain, France, Australia, New Zealand, the Philippines, Thailand, and the Associated States, to guarantee the security of Southeast Asia. Such a coalition, by its very existence, might deter Chinese intervention in the Indochina War and Chinese aggression elsewhere in Asia. If military intervention became necessary, United Action would remove the stigma of a war for French colonialism and would ensure that the entire burden did not fall upon the United States. In keeping with the doctrine of the New Look defense policy, local and regional forces could bear the brunt of the ground fighting while the United States provided air and naval support, furnished money and supplies, and trained indigenous troops.

Dulles and Eisenhower were also unwilling to intervene unless they could extract major concessions from the French. Dulles warned that if the United States intervened, its prestige would be "engaged to a point where we would want to have a success. We could not afford a defeat that would have world-wide repercussions."[57] The administration attributed France's failure to its mishandling of the Vietnamese and its refusal to wage the war aggres-

[56] Memorandum of conversation, Eisenhower and Dulles, March 24, 1954, Lot 64D199, Box 222, Department of State Records; James Hagerty Diary, April 1, 1954, James Hagerty Papers, Dwight D. Eisenhower Library, Abilene, Kans.

[57] Dwight D. Eisenhower, *Mandate for Change, 1953–1956* (New York, 1963), p. 345.

sively; persistent efforts to change French attitudes had been fruitless. Indeed, Ely had only recently rebuffed a proposal to expand
the role of the American military advisory group, bitterly complaining about the "invading nature" of the Americans and their
"determination to control and operate everything of importance."[58] Dulles and Eisenhower agreed that the United States
must not risk its prestige in Indochina until France had made
firm commitments to keep its troops there, accelerate the move
toward eventual independence, and permit the United States a
larger role in training indigenous forces and in formulating military strategy.

Most of Eisenhower's top military advisers raised serious objections to air intervention at Dienbienphu. Some questioned whether
an air strike could relieve the siege without destroying the fortress
itself; others wondered whether intervention, once undertaken,
could be kept limited—"One cannot go over Niagara Falls in a
barrel only slightly," a Defense Department analyst warned.[59]
Among the Joint Chiefs of Staff, only Air Force General Nathan F.
Twining approved an air attack on Dienbienphu and he insisted on
attaching conditions that the French were unlikely to accept. The
other chiefs warned that air intervention posed major risks and
would not decisively affect the outcome of the war. Army Chief of
Staff Matthew Ridgway was particularly outspoken, responding to
Radford's query about the proposed air strike with an "emphatic
and immediate 'No.'" Alarmed by what he viewed as "the old delusive idea . . . that we could do things the cheap and easy way,"
Ridgway later warned Eisenhower that air power alone could not
ensure victory in Indochina and that any ground forces sent there
would have to fight under difficult logistic circumstances and in a
uniquely inhospitable terrain.[60]

Although profoundly skeptical concerning the proposed air
strike at Dienbienphu, the administration was sufficiently alarmed
by the emerging crisis in Indochina to seek Congressional support
for possible American military intervention. The fall of Dienbien-

---

[58] Radford to Eisenhower, March 29, 1954, *USVN*, Book 9, 283–284.

[59] *Pentagon Papers (Gravel)*, I, 89.

[60] Ridgway memorandum for the Joint Chiefs, April 2, 1954, Matthew B. Ridgway Papers, U.S. Army Military History Institute, Carlisle Barracks, Pa.;
Matthew B. Ridgway, *Soldier* (New York, 1956), pp. 276–277.

phu seemed certain by early April. Eisenhower and Dulles preferred to act in concert with other nations, but they feared that a
defeat at Dienbienphu might produce a French collapse before
plans for United Action could be put into effect, leaving American
naval and air power as the only means to save Indochina. Sensitive
to Truman's fate in Korea, they were unwilling to act without
backing from Congress, and Eisenhower instructed Dulles to explore with Congressional leaders the conditions under which the
use of American military power might be approved. The purpose
of the dramatic meeting at the State Department on April 3 was
not, as has often been assumed, to secure approval for an immediate air attack, but rather to gain discretionary authority to employ
American naval and air forces—with allies if possible, without
them if necessary—should the fall of Dienbienphu threaten the loss
of all Indochina.

The administration encountered stubborn resistance. Dulles
and Radford grimly warned that failure to act decisively might cost
the United States all of Southeast Asia and advised that the President should have the power to use naval and air forces "if he felt it
necessary in the interest of national security." No one questioned
this assessment of the gravity of the situation, but the Congressmen
insisted that there must be "no more Koreas, with the United States
furnishing 90% of the manpower," and made clear that they would
approve nothing until the administration had obtained firm commitments of support from other nations. Dulles persisted, assuring
the legislators that the administration had no intention of sending
ground troops to Indochina and indicating that he could more easily gain commitments from allies if he could specify what the
United States would do. The Congressmen were not swayed by the
Secretary's arguments. "Once the flag is committed," they warned,
"the use of land forces would surely follow." Sharing the administration's distrust of France, they also insisted that the United States
must not go to war in support of colonialism. They would only
agree that if "satisfactory commitments" could be secured from
Great Britain and other allies to support military intervention, and
from France to "internationalize" the war and speed up the move
toward independence, a resolution could be obtained authorizing
the President to commit American forces to the defense of Indochina. Congressional insistence on prior allied commitments, particularly from Great Britain, eliminated the option of unilateral

American intervention and placed major obstacles in the way of United Action.[61]

The April 3 session doomed any possibility of an air strike at Dienbienphu. Although unenthusiastic about the prospect of American intervention in any form, the French government eventually concluded that an air strike offered the only hope of saving the beleaguered fortress and on April 5 requested implementation of the plan. Eisenhower promptly rejected the French request, expressing great annoyance with Radford for misleading the French about American intentions and emphatically stating that the proposal was "politically impossible."[62] At a meeting on April 6, the National Security Council agreed that planning and mobilization for possible later intervention should "promptly be initiated," while the administration made a determined effort to meet the essential preconditions for United Action.[63]

While the fate of Dienbienphu hung in the balance, the United States frantically promoted United Action. Dulles immediately departed for London and Paris to consult with British and French leaders. Eisenhower penned a long personal letter to Prime Minister Winston Churchill urging British support for a coalition that would be "willing to fight" to check Communist expansion in Southeast Asia. At a much publicized news conference on April 7, the President laid the foundation for possible American intervention. Outlining in simple language the principles that had formed the basis for American policy for four years, he emphasized that Indochina was an important source of tin, tungsten, and rubber, and that having lost China to "Communist dictatorship," the United States "simply can't afford greater losses." More important, he warned, should Indochina fall, the rest of Southeast Asia would "go over very quickly," like a "row of dominoes" when the first one is knocked down, causing much greater losses of raw materials and people, jeopardizing America's strategic position in the Far East, and driving Japan into the Communist camp. "So the possible con-

[61] Dulles memorandum, April 5, 1954, "Conference with Congressional Leaders, April 3, 1954," John Foster Dulles Papers, Dwight D. Eisenhower Library, Abilene, Kans.

[62] Record of telephone conversation, Eisenhower and Dulles, April 5, 1954, Eisenhower Papers, Diary Series, Box 3.

[63] Record of NSC meeting, April 6, 1954, *FR, 1952–1954*, XIII, 1253.

sequences of the loss," he concluded, "are just incalculable to the free world."[64]

The flurry of American diplomatic activity in April 1954 revealed deep differences between the United States and its allies. The Churchill government was prepared to join a collective security arrangement *after* Geneva, but it was adamantly opposed to immediate intervention in Indochina. Churchill and his Foreign Secretary, Anthony Eden, did not share the American fear that the loss of all or part of Indochina would bring the fall of Southeast Asia. They were convinced that France retained sufficient influence to salvage a reasonable settlement at Geneva, and they feared that outside military intervention would destroy any hope of a negotiated settlement and perhaps even provoke a war with China. Most important, they had no desire to entangle Britain in a war they felt could not be won.

Dulles's discussions with France were equally unproductive and made clear the widely divergent approaches of the two nations toward the war and the Geneva negotiations. The United States was willing to intervene in Indochina, but only on condition that France resist a negotiated settlement at Geneva, agree to remain in Indochina and fight indefinitely, concede to its ally a greater role in planning strategy and training indigenous forces, and accept Vietnamese demands for complete independence. The French insisted that Vietnam must retain ties with the French Union. They wanted nothing more than an air strike to relieve the siege of Dienbienphu. They opposed internationalization of the war, which would not only threaten their prestige in Indochina but would also remove control from their hands. Dulles may have hoped that by offering help to France he could yet save the European Defense Community, but the French government made clear that EDC would have no chance of approval if France had to commit itself to keep troops in Indochina indefinitely.

The administration was deeply annoyed by the response of its allies. U.S. officials complained that the British were "weak-kneed," and Eisenhower privately lamented that Churchill and Eden showed a "woeful unawareness" of the risks of inaction in

---

[64] Eisenhower, *Mandate for Change*, pp. 346–347; *Dwight D. Eisenhower, Public Papers, 1954* (Washington, D.C., 1955), pp. 382–384.

Southeast Asia.[65] Dulles misinterpreted Eden's willingness to discuss long-range security arrangements as a tentative commitment to United Action, and when informed of the actual British position he was incensed. The White House and State Department were outraged by the French intransigence. Eisenhower placed full blame on the French for their present plight—they had used "weasel words in promising independence," he wrote a friend, "and through this reason as much as anything else have suffered reverses that have been inexcusable." He refused to consider intervention on France's terms. The French "want us to come in as junior partners and provide materials, etc., while they themselves retain authority in that region" and he would "not go along with them . . . on any such notion."[66]

Congressional opposition reinforced the administration's determination to avoid unilateral intervention in support of France. In a speech that won praise from both sides of the aisles, Democratic Senator John F. Kennedy of Massachusetts warned that no amount of military aid could conquer "an enemy of the people which has the support and covert appeal of the people," and that victory could not be attained in Indochina as long as France remained. When a "high administration source," subsequently identified as Vice President Richard M. Nixon, remarked "off the record" that if United Action failed the United States might have to act alone, the reaction was immediate and strong.[67]

Thus, even when France relented a bit, continued British opposition to military intervention settled the fate of United Action. In late April, Foreign Minister Georges Bidault, whom Dulles described as "close to the breaking point," made a last desperate appeal for American support, warning that only a "massive" air attack would save Dienbienphu and hinting that France was prepared to accept internationalization of the war. With his hopes of implementing United Action suddenly revived, Dulles informed

[65] Hagerty Diary, April 25, 1954, Hagerty Papers; Eisenhower Diary, April 27, 1954, Eisenhower Papers, Diary Series, Box 3.

[66] Eisenhower to E. E. Hazlett, April 27, 1954, Eisenhower Papers, Diary Series, Box 4; record of telephone conversation, Eisenhower and Walter Bedell Smith, April 24, 1954, *ibid.*, Box 3.

[67] The Nixon statement has sometimes been regarded as a trial balloon, but it was unauthorized and did not reflect the administration's thinking at this time. See Hagerty Diary, April 17, 1954, Hagerty Papers, and Richard M. Nixon, *RN: The Memoirs of Richard Nixon* (New York, 1978), pp. 152–153.

Bidault that if the British could be persuaded to go along, the administration would seek a Congressional resolution authorizing intervention. Over the next three days, the Secretary made frantic efforts to convert Eden, urgently warning that without support from its allies France might give up the fight. The British would have none of it, however, and the administration was forced to back off. Eisenhower informed Congressional leaders on April 26 that it would be a "tragic error to go in alone as a partner of France" and made clear that the United States would intervene only as part of a "grouping of interested nations." Three days later, the National Security Council formally decided to "hold up for the time any military action in Indo China until we see how Geneva is coming along."[68]

The American decision sealed Dienbienphu's doom. Without American air power, France had no means of saving the fortress. Subjected to merciless pounding from Vietminh artillery and to a series of human-wave assaults, the hopelessly outmanned defenders finally surrendered on May 7 after fifty-five days of stubborn but futile resistance. The attention of belligerents and interested outside parties immediately shifted to Geneva, where the following day the Indochina phase of the conference was set to begin. Buoyed by its victory, the Vietminh confidently savored the prize for which it had been fighting for more than seven years. Its influence in northern Vietnam now reduced to a small pocket around Hanoi, France began preparations to abandon the north and to salvage as much as possible in the area below the sixteenth parallel. The French delegation came to Geneva, Bidault lamented, holding a "two of clubs and a three of diamonds."[69]

The United States was a reluctant participant at Geneva. Negotiation with any Communist nation was anathema, but the presence of Communist China made the conference especially unpalatable. Dulles remained in Geneva only briefly and, in the words of his biographer, conducted himself like a "puritan in a house of ill repute."[70] On one occasion, he remarked that the only

[68] Dulles to State Department, April 22, 23, 1954, Eisenhower Papers, Ann Whitman File; Summary of meeting, April 26, 1954, Eisenhower Papers, "Cleanup" File, Box 16; Hagerty Diary, April 29, 1954, Hagerty Papers.

[69] Quoted in Chester Cooper, *The Lost Crusade: America in Vietnam* (New York, 1970), p. 79.

[70] Townsend Hoopes, *The Devil and John Foster Dulles* (Boston, 1973), p. 222.

way he and Chou En-lai, the top Chinese delegate, would meet was if their cars collided, and when they actually met face-to-face and Chou extended his hand, the Secretary reportedly turned his back. The administration had long feared that the conference would merely provide a fig leaf of respectability for the French surrender of Indochina, and the fall of Dienbienphu increased its concern. After departing Geneva, Dulles instructed the American delegation that it should participate in the conference only as an "interested nation," not as a "belligerent or a principal in the negotiations," and should not endorse an agreement which in any way impaired the territorial integrity of the Associated States.[71] Given the military position of the Vietminh when the conference opened, Dulles was saying that the United States would approve no settlement at all.

Indeed, the administration probably hoped there would be no agreement, and during the first five weeks of the conference it kept alive the prospect of military intervention. When Laniel requested American military support in the event the Chinese should stall the talks while the Vietminh pressed on for military victory, Dulles and Eisenhower seriously considered a new plan for intervention. The Joint Chiefs of Staff drew up detailed contingency plans for deploying U.S. forces, one provision of which was that nuclear weapons would be used if it were militarily advantageous. Administration officials drafted a Congressional resolution authorizing the President to employ military forces in Indochina. As before, however, the United States and France could not agree on the terms. This time, the administration did not make intervention conditional on British backing, but it stiffened the concessions demanded of France, insisting upon an unequivocal advance commitment to internationalize the war and a guarantee that the Associated States could withdraw from the French Union at any time. The French indicated a willingness only to discuss the American conditions and added demands of their own which were unacceptable to Washington, including at least a token commitment of American ground forces and a prior commitment to employ air power should the Chinese intervene. As the discussions dragged on inconclusively, each side grew wary. The French government eventually concluded that it must exhaust every possibility of a negotiated settlement before considering prolongation of the war. Eisen-

---

[71] Dulles to Smith, May 12, 1954, *USVN*, Book 9, 457–459.

hower and Dulles surmised that France was interested primarily in keeping alive the possibility of American intervention "as a card to play at Geneva," and they were unwilling to "grant France an indefinite option on us." The talks had all but ended by mid-June.[72]

In the meantime, the conferees at Geneva struggled toward an agreement. As a result of pressure applied by the Chinese and Russians, the Vietminh reluctantly agreed to the principle of a temporary partition of Vietnam to permit the regrouping of military forces following a cease-fire. Laniel had made firm commitments to Bao Dai not to accept any form of partition, but his government fell on June 12 and was replaced by a government headed by Pierre Mendès-France. The new Prime Minister was flexible on the issue of partition, and upon taking power he had also promised to resign if a settlement were not reached by July 21. Although many details remained to be worked out, the outlines of a political agreement had begun to take form when the heads of the delegation agreed to a short recess on June 19.

At this point, the Eisenhower administration adopted a change of policy with momentous long-range implications. Recognizing that the war could not be prolonged without unacceptable risks and that part of Vietnam would probably be lost at Geneva, the administration began to lay plans for the defense of the rest of Indochina and Southeast Asia. Dulles informed Congressional leaders on June 24 that any agreement that emerged from Geneva would be "something we would have to gag about," but he nevertheless expressed optimism that the United States might still be able to "salvage something" in Southeast Asia "free of the taint of French colonialism." The United States would have to take over from France responsibility for defending Laos, Cambodia, and that part of Vietnam beneath the partition line. The first essential was to draw a line which the Communists would not cross and then to "hold this area and fight subversion within it with all the strength we have" by providing economic assistance and building a strong military force. The United States would also have to take the lead in forming a strong regional defense grouping "to keep alive freedom" in Southeast Asia.[73]

---

[72] Dulles to American Consulate Geneva, June 8, 1954, *ibid.*, 541.
[73] Hagerty Diary, June 23, 24, 28, 1954, Hagerty Papers.

Over the next few weeks, Dulles worked relentlessly to get the kind of settlement that would enable the United States to defend Indochina and Southeast Asia after Geneva. He secured British agreement to a set of principles that would constitute an "acceptable" settlement, including the freedom of Laos, Cambodia, and southern Vietnam to maintain "stable, non-communist regimes" and to accept foreign arms and advisers. He applied extreme pressure, even threatening to disassociate the United States entirely from Geneva, until Mèndes-France accepted the so-called seven points as the basis for the French bargaining position. Although armed with firm British and French promises, Dulles still approached the last stages of the conference with great caution and with a determination to retain complete freedom of action. The United States should play no more than a passive role in the negotiations, he instructed the head of the American delegation, Walter Bedell Smith. If the agreement lived up to its standards, the administration would issue a unilateral statement of endorsement, but if it fell short the United States would reserve the freedom to "publicly disassociate itself." Under no circumstances would it be a "cosignatory with the Communists," and it would not be placed in a position of guaranteeing the results.[74]

When the conference reconvened, pressures for a settlement had increased significantly. The July 21 deadline was rapidly approaching for Mèndes-France, and Anglo-American support strengthened his bargaining position. Perhaps more important, although the Vietminh's military position gave it strong claim for influence throughout Vietnam, both the Russians and the Chinese exerted heavy pressure for a compromise peace. The Soviet Union had only limited interests in Southeast Asia and appears to have pursued a conciliatory line toward France in order to encourage French rejection of the European Defense Community. China sought to enhance its international prestige and to cultivate influence among the neutral nations of South and Southeast Asia by playing the role of peacemaker. Moreover, the Chinese apparently feared that a prolonged war ran serious risks of American intervention, and they may have felt that a partition arrangement would make the Vietminh more susceptible to their influence. For reasons of their own, the Russians and the Chinese moderated the Vietminh demands and played a crucial role in arranging the settlement.

[74] *Pentagon Papers (Gravel)*, I, 152.

The Geneva Accords of 1954 reflected these influences. Vietnam was to be partitioned along the seventeenth parallel to permit the regrouping of military forces from both sides. The agreements stressed that the division was to be only temporary and that it should not be "interpreted as constituting a political or territorial boundary." The country was to be reunified by elections scheduled for the summer of 1956 and to be supervised by an international commission composed of Canada, Poland, and India. To insulate Vietnam against a renewal of conflict during the transitional period, the agreements provided that forces should be withdrawn from the respective partition zones within 300 days, and they prohibited the introduction of new forces and equipment and the establishment of foreign military bases. Neither portion of Vietnam was to join a military alliance. The agreements also established cease-fire arrangements for Laos and Cambodia. The two nations' right to self-defense was explicitly recognized, but to assuage Chinese fears of American intervention, they were not to enter military alliances or permit foreign bases on their soil except in cases where their security was clearly threatened.

The Eisenhower administration viewed the Geneva Agreements with mixed feelings. As had been feared, the settlement produced some domestic political backlash; Republican Senate Leader William Knowland denounced it as the "greatest victory the Communists have won in twenty years." The administration itself regarded the loss of northern Vietnam—"the keystone to the arch of Southeast Asia"—with concern. Eisenhower and Dulles realized, as Smith put it, that "diplomacy has rarely been able to gain at the conference table what cannot be held on the battlefield." The administration protected itself against domestic criticism and retained its freedom of action by refusing to associate itself directly with the agreements. In a unilateral statement, Smith simply "took note" of the Geneva Accords and said that the United States would not "disturb them" by the "threat or the use of force."[75]

The administration was not altogether displeased with the results, however. The agreements were better than had been anticipated when the conference opened, and they allowed sufficient latitude to proceed along the lines Dulles had already outlined. Partition was unpalatable, but it gave the United States the opportunity to build up non-Communist forces in southern Vietnam, a

[75] *Ibid.*, 571–572.

challenge Eisenhower and Dulles took up eagerly. The accords placed some limits on outside intervention, to be sure, but the administration did not view them as prohibitive. And some of the provisions seemed advantageous. Eisenhower and Dulles agreed, for example, that if elections were held immediately, Ho Chi Minh would be an easy victor. But the two-year delay gave the United States "fairly good time" to get ready, and Canada's presence on the commission would enable it to "block things."[76]

Eisenhower and Dulles viewed the apparent demise of French colonialism in Southeast Asia with equanimity, if not outright enthusiasm. From the start, the Franco-American partnership in Indochina had been marked by profound mutual suspicion and deep-seated tensions. From 1950 to 1954, the United States had provided France more than $2.6 billion in military aid, but its efforts to influence French policies by friendly persuasion and by attaching strings had failed, and the commitment to France had indeed turned out to be a "dead-end-alley." Eisenhower and Dulles attributed France's failure primarily to its attempts to perpetuate colonialism in Indochina, and they were confident that without the problems posed by France, the United States could build a viable non-Communist alternative to the Vietminh. "We must work with these people, and then they themselves will soon find out that we are their friends and that they can't live without us," Eisenhower observed.[77] Conceding that the Geneva Accords contained "many features which we did not like," Dulles nevertheless insisted that they included many "good aspects," most important, the "truly independent status" of Laos, Cambodia, and southern Vietnam. The "important thing," he concluded, was "not to mourn the past but to seize the future opportunity to prevent the loss in Northern Vietnam from leading to the extension of communism throughout Southeast Asia and the Southwest Pacific."[78]

[76] Record of telephone conversation, Eisenhower and Dulles, July 20, 1954, Eisenhower Papers, Diary Series, Box 4.

[77] Hagerty Diary, July 23, 1954, Hagerty Papers.

[78] Dulles news conference, July 23, 1954, John Foster Dulles Papers, Seeley G. Mudd Manuscript Library, Princeton, N.J.

CHAPTER 2

Our Offspring: Nation-Building in South Vietnam, 1954–1961

"The fundamental tenets of this nation's foreign policy . . . depend in considerable measure upon a strong and free Vietnamese nation," Senator John F. Kennedy stated in 1956. "Vietnam represents the cornerstone of the Free World in Southeast Asia, the keystone in the arch, the finger in the dike," and should the "red tide of Communism" pour into it, Kennedy warned, much of Asia would be threatened. Vietnam's economy was essential to the economy of Southeast Asia, the Senator went on to say, its "political liberty" an "inspiration to those seeking to obtain or maintain their liberty in all parts of Asia—and indeed of the world." The United States had special obligations to Vietnam which extended beyond mere considerations of the national interest, Kennedy stressed in conclusion: "It is our offspring, we cannot abandon it, we cannot ignore its needs."[1]

Kennedy was addressing the American Friends of Vietnam, and he may have been indulging in hyperbole, but his speech summed up the rationale of American policy in Vietnam in the 1950s, touched on the pivotal role played by the United States at its birth, and highlighted the importance it came to assume. Certain that the fall of Vietnam to Communism would lead to the loss of all of Southeast Asia, the Eisenhower administration after Geneva firmly committed itself to creating in the southern part of the country a nation that would stand as a bulwark against Communist expansion

[1] John F. Kennedy, "America's Stake in Vietnam," *Vital Speeches*, 22 (August 1, 1956), 617–619.

and serve as a proving ground for democracy in Asia. Originating out of the exigencies of the Cold War, the experiment in nation-building tapped the wellsprings of American idealism and took on many of the trappings of a crusade. Begun as a high-risk gamble, it appeared for a time one of the great success stories of postwar American foreign policy. Only at the end of the decade, when South Vietnam was swept by revolution, did Americans fully perceive the magnitude and complexity of the problem they had taken on.

Warning that Geneva had been a "disaster" which had made possible a "major forward stride of Communism," the National Security Council (NSC) in the summer of 1954 called for a "new initiative" to shore up the United States's position in Southeast Asia. The NSC recommended, among other things, the use of "all available means" to weaken the infant Vietminh regime in northern Vietnam.[2] Throughout the rest of the year, a CIA team stationed in Saigon and headed by Colonel Edward Lansdale devised numerous clandestine methods to harass the Hanoi government. Paramilitary groups infiltrated across the demilitarized zone on sabotage missions, attempting to destroy the government's printing presses and pouring contaminants into the engines of busses to demobilize the transportation system. The teams also carried out "psywar" operations to embarrass the Vietminh regime and encourage emigration to the south. They distributed fake leaflets announcing the harsh methods the government was prepared to take and even hired astrologers to predict hard times in the north and good times in the south.[3]

In the meantime, Dulles hastened off to Manila and negotiated the Southeast Asian security pact he had promoted so vigorously during the Dienbienphu crisis. The Southeast Asian Treaty Organization (SEATO) had obvious weaknesses. The major neutralist nations of the region, Burma, India, and Indonesia, declined to join, and because of restrictions imposed by the Geneva Accords, Laos, Cambodia, and southern Vietnam could not formally participate.

[2] NSC, "Review of U.S. Policy in the Far East," August 1954, U.S. Congress, House, Committee on Armed Services, *United States–Vietnam Relations, 1945–1967: A Study Prepared by the Department of Defense* (Washington, D.C., 1971), Book 10, 731–741.

[3] Neil Sheehan et al., *The Pentagon Papers as Published by the New York Times* (New York, 1971), pp. 16–18. Hereafter cited as *Pentagon Papers (NYT)*.

The member nations bound themselves only to "meet common danger" in accordance with their own "constitutional processes" and to "consult" with each other. From Dulles's standpoint, however, SEATO was more than satisfactory. He hoped that the mere existence of the alliance would deter Communist aggression in the region. More important, a separate protocol specifically designated Laos, Cambodia, and southern Vietnam as areas which, if threatened, would "endanger" the "peace and security" of the signatories. During the Dienbienphu crisis, Dulles had felt hampered by the lack of any legal basis for intervention in Indochina. The SEATO protocol not only remedied this defect, but also established the foundation should United Action become necessary in the future and gave South Vietnam a semblance of international status as a "free" nation.[4]

The key to the new American "initiative" was South Vietnam. The National Security Council recommended in August that the United States "must make every possible effort, not openly inconsistent with the U.S. position as to the armistice agreements . . . to maintain a friendly non-Communist South Vietnam and to prevent a Communist victory through all-Vietnam elections."[5] Violating the spirit and sometimes the letter of the Geneva Accords, the Eisenhower administration in 1954 and after firmly committed itself to the fragile government of Ngo Dinh Diem, eased the French out of Vietnam, and used its resources unsparingly to construct in southern Vietnam a viable, non-Communist nation that would stand as the "cornerstone of the Free World in Southeast Asia."

Had it looked all over the world, the United States could not have chosen a less promising place for an experiment in nation-building. The partition settlement left an estimated 14 of 25 million Vietnamese above the seventeenth parallel. The North Vietnamese regime was not without internal opposition, and it faced an enormous challenge of postwar reconstruction. At the same time, it had a large, reasonably well-equipped army and a tightly organized government. Ho Chi Minh was the best-known nationalist leader in

[4] The members of SEATO were the United States, the United Kingdom, France, Australia, New Zealand, Thailand, the Philippines, and Pakistan. For an insightful view of Dulles's attitudes toward the alliance, see Richard Bissell oral history interview, Dulles Papers, Princeton, N.J.

[5] NSC, "Review of U.S. Policy in the Far East," August 1954, *USVN*, Book 10, 731–741.

all of Vietnam, and the Vietminh had won broad popular respect for having led the struggle against France. Ho and his colleagues remained deeply committed to the unification of Vietnam, and they left between 10,000 and 15,000 operatives in the south to promote that goal by legal and extralegal means.

In southern Vietnam, chaos reigned. The colonial economy depended entirely on exports of rice and rubber to finance essential imports. It had been devastated by nearly fourteen years of war and was held together by enormous French military expenditures that would soon cease. The French had finally granted unqualified independence to the State of Vietnam in June 1954, but the government, still nominally presided over by Bao Dai, was a fiction. Assuming the premiership in the summer of 1954, the staunchly anti-French Ngo Dinh Diem inherited antiquated institutions patterned on French practices and ill-suited to the needs of an independent nation—an "oriental despotism with a French accent," one American scornfully labelled it. Diem's government lacked experienced civil servants. Tainted by its long association with France, it had no base of support in the countryside or among the non-Communist nationalists in Saigon. Its army had been created by the French out of desperation in the last stages of the war, and was accurately dismissed by General Navarre as a "rabble."[6]

The French had employed the classical imperialist device of divide and conquer to rule their Indochinese colonies, and political fragmentation was the fundamental fact of life in post-Geneva South Vietnam. The French army remained, and the French government clung stubbornly to hopes of exerting some influence in its former colony. The Vietminh retained pockets of control, even on the doorstep of Saigon. The so-called sects, politico-religious organizations with their own governments and armies, ruled the Mekong Delta and the suburbs of Saigon as their private fiefdoms. Viewing a mass emigration from North Vietnam as a possible means of tipping the political balance toward the south and perhaps even winning the 1956 elections, the French and the Americans actively encouraged northerners to cross the seventeenth parallel. Within weeks after Geneva, northern Catholics began pouring into predominantly Buddhist South Vietnam at the rate of 7,000 a day, adding new religious and ethnic tensions to an already volatile mix.

[6] Robert McClintock to State Department, May 20, 1953, and May 8, 1954, *FR, 1952–1954*, XIII, 575, 1519.

Some American officials issued stern warnings about the pitfalls of nation-building in South Vietnam. A National Intelligence Estimate of August 1954 admonished that even with solid support from the United States, the chances of establishing a strong, stable government were "poor."[7] When asked to formulate a program for training a South Vietnamese army, the Joint Chiefs of Staff demurred, advising that it would be "hopeless" to build an army without a "reasonably strong, stable civil government in control."[8] Agreeing that the situation in South Vietnam was "utterly hopeless," Secretary of Defense Charles E. Wilson urged that the United States get out as "completely and as soon as possible." In words that would take on the ring of prophecy in little more than a decade, Wilson warned that he could "see nothing but grief in store for us if we remained in that area."[9]

Eisenhower and Dulles were not deterred by these gloomy forecasts. Dulles admitted that the chances of success might not be better than one in ten. On the other hand, he and the President agreed that to do nothing risked the probable loss of a vital area to Communism. They seem also to have felt that because of the purity of its motives and the superiority of its methods, the United States might succeed where the French had failed in creating a strong South Vietnamese army and a viable government. In its first two years in office, moreover, the administration with limited effort had toppled unfriendly governments in Iran and Guatemala, and Eisenhower and Dulles may have concluded that they could beat the odds in Vietnam as well. Admitting that he was indulging in the "familiar hen-and-egg argument as to which comes first," Dulles flatly informed the Joint Chiefs that a strong army would do more than anything else to stabilize the government of South Vietnam.[10] His arguments eventually prevailed with the President. At an NSC meeting on October 22, 1954, Eisenhower resorted to aphorism, affirming with "great conviction" that "in the lands of the blind, one-eyed men are kings," by which he presumably meant that despite the obstacles the United States had the resources and ingenu-

---

[7] National Intelligence Estimate 63-5-54, "Post-Geneva Outlook in Indochina," August 3, 1954, *USVN*, Book 10, 692.

[8] Joint Chiefs of Staff to Secretary of Defense, August 4, 12, 1954, *ibid.*, 701–702, 759–760.

[9] Record of National Security Council meeting, October 26, 1954, *FR, 1952–1954*, XIII, 2184–2186.

[10] Dulles to Charles E. Wilson, August 18, 1954, *USVN*, Book 10, 728–729.

ity to succeed.[11] Shortly after, the administration committed itself
to a major aid program for South Vietnam. The commitment was
carefully limited and was made conditional on Diem's instituting
major reforms, but the significance of the step was unmistakable:
the experiment in nation-building was under way.

The man to whom Eisenhower made the fateful commitment
had impeccable credentials as a nationalist and, from the American
standpoint, more important, as an anti-Communist. One of nine
children of Ngo Dinh Kha, an official at the imperial court of Hue,
Ngo Dinh Diem attended French Catholic schools in Hue and the
school of public administration in Hanoi, where, after finishing at
the top of his class, he was given an appointment in the bureaucracy of the protectorate of Annam. A devout Catholic, he became
a staunch opponent of Communism before he became a nationalist.
As a village supervisor in central Vietnam, he unearthed a Commu-
nist-inspired uprising in 1929 and severely punished its leaders. The
French rewarded him with an appointment as Minister of the Interior, the highest position in the government, but when they refused
to enact reforms which he had proposed, he resigned and would not
return to his post even when threatened with deportation. For most
of the next two decades, Diem was a virtual exile in his own land,
living as a scholar-recluse and refusing offers from the Japanese, the
Vietminh, and Bao Dai to participate in the various governments
formed after World War II. He eventually left the country, trav-
eling to Rome and then settling at a Maryknoll seminary in Lake-
wood, New Jersey. While in the United States he lectured widely,
and his fervent appeals for an independent, non-Communist Vietnam attracted him to such luminaries as Francis Cardinal Spellman
and Democratic Senators John F. Kennedy and Mike Mansfield.[12]

Diem's nationalism and his administrative experience made
him appear a logical choice for the premiership of an independent
Vietnam, but he lacked many of the qualities required for the im-
posing challenges he faced. His most noteworthy characteristics
seemed to have been a stubborn determination to persist in the face
of great danger and a remarkable penchant for survival. A man of
principle, he inclined toward an all-or-nothing integrity which de-

[11] Record of National Security Council meeting, October 22, 1954, *FR,
1952–1954*, XIII, 2154.

[12] Frances FitzGerald, *Fire in the Lake: The Vietnamese and the Americans in
Vietnam* (Boston, 1972), pp. 80–84, 98–99.

prived him of the flexibility necessary to deal with the intractable problems and deep-seated conflicts he confronted. His love for his country in the abstract was profound, but he was an elitist who had little sensitivity to the needs and problems of the Vietnamese people. Not perceiving the extent to which the French and the Vietminh had destroyed traditional political processes and values, he looked backward to an imperial Vietnam that no longer existed. He had no blueprint for building a modern nation or mobilizing his people. Introverted and absorbed in himself, he lacked the charisma of Ho Chi Minh. "He was a short, broadly built man with a round face and a shock of black hair, who walked and moved jerkily, as if on strings," Robert Shaplen has recalled. "He always dressed in white and looked as if he were made out of ivory." A compulsive talker—"a single question was likely to provoke a dissertation for an hour or more"—he was a poor listener who seemed almost indifferent to the reaction he evoked in others.[13]

Diem's route to the premiership of South Vietnam remains obscure. The Catholic leader approached the U.S. government as early as 1951, attacking Bao Dai's leadership and expressing "somewhat wistfully" his hope that American troops might be used in Vietnam. Diem's virulent Francophobia seems to have been too much for Dean Acheson's State Department, and American diplomats regarded the self-exiled nationalist as too rigid, too Catholic, and too "monkish" to be an effective leader. Diem also came to the attention of General William Donovan, chief of U.S. intelligence in World War II, who at this time was orchestrating from his Wall Street office a global network of anti-Communist operations. Donovan and prominent Catholic-Americans such as Spellman and Mansfield, with or without the support of the CIA, may have forced Diem on a reluctant Bao Dai. Or the emperor may have turned to Diem as a means of getting the American support he needed to break free from French dominance.[14]

Although the United States may have influenced the appoint-

---

[13] Robert Shaplen, *The Lost Revolution: The U.S. in Vietnam, 1946–1966* (New York, 1966), p. 104.

[14] Acheson to Legation Saigon, January 16, 1951, document #3051, William J. Donovan Papers, U.S. Army Military History Institute, Carlisle Barracks, Pa. Donovan's anti-Communist activities are discussed in Anthony Cave Brown, *The Last Hero: Wild Bill Donovan* (New York, 1984), pp. 820–822, 828. For possible Catholic lobby and CIA involvement in Diem's rise to power, see Congressional Research Service, *The U.S. Government and the Vietnam War*, Part I (Washington, D.C., 1983), pp. 261–262.

ment, many top U.S. officials found little encouragement in Diem's assumption of power. Indeed, what is striking in retrospect is the extent to which early on-the-scene estimates of the prime minister's leadership potential pointed directly toward the major problems that would develop later. From Geneva, Walter Bedell Smith did express hope that Diem might be a "modern political Joan of Arc" who could "rally the country behind him." In Paris, however, Ambassador Douglas Dillon was reassured by the emergence of this "Yogi-like mystic" only because the standard set by his predecessors had been so low. Within weeks after Diem took office, Chargé Robert McClintock in Saigon characterized him as a "messiah without a message," complained of his "narrowness of view," and commented scornfully that his only "formulated policy is to ask immediate American assistance in every form."[15]

Throughout the fall and winter of 1954–1955, Diem was the focal point of a bitter and protracted conflict between the United States and France. Controversy was probably inevitable given the accumulated tensions of four years of uneasy partnership, and it was sharpened by profound mutual suspicions which extended from top policy levels in Paris and Washington down to the operational level in Saigon. French support for Diem was at best lukewarm, and the Americans feared, probably with some justification, that Paris was playing a double game, seeking to maintain its position in the south while attempting to build bridges to Hanoi. U.S. officials also feared that the French government's apparent inclination to let the best man win the upcoming election might facilitate a Ho Chi Minh victory. The French had always resented American intrusion in Vietnam, and they suspected that the United States was using Diem to try to supplant them. Diem has that "one rare quality, so precious in Asia," a French journalist snarled, "he is pro-American."[16] Differences over Vietnam were exacerbated by French rejection of the European Defense Community, which strained Franco-American relations to the breaking point and, at least momentarily, left the Western alliance in disarray.

In Vietnam, the United States held most of the cards and it was

[15] T. B. Millar, ed., *Australian Foreign Minister: The Diaries of R. G. Casey, 1951–1960* (London, 1972), p. 159; Dillon to State Department, May 24, 1954, *FR, 1952–1954*, XIII, 1608–1609; McClintock to State Department, July 4, 1954, *ibid.*, 1783–1784.

[16] Quoted in *FR, 1952–1954*, XIII, 2333.

eventually able to impose its policy on a recalcitrant France. The French still depended upon American aid to support their army in Vietnam, and Washington used this leverage in the fall of 1954 to extract from Paris a commitment to support Diem. The Eisenhower administration also insisted on giving its economic and military aid directly to the Diem government rather than funneling it through the French mission in Saigon, as Paris had proposed. Throughout the winter of 1954–1955, French officials insisted that Diem was incapable of running the government and proposed that he be replaced by Bao Dai or some other reputable nationalist figure. But Dulles would have none of it. If, as the French argued, Bao Dai was the only person who could save Vietnam, the Secretary concluded, "then indeed we must be desperate." He conceded Diem's shortcomings, but he accepted Ambassador Donald Heath's argument "that there is no one to take his place who would serve US interests better."[17] More than any other single factor, the unstinting support provided by Dulles and the United States enabled Diem to remain in power against strong French opposition.

Timely American support enabled Diem to thwart a series of military plots against his government. The U.S. Embassy foiled a coup attempt in the fall of 1954 by letting it be known that a change of government would result in termination of American aid. Edward Lansdale singlehandedly stopped another coup in November. A former advertising executive, Lansdale had served in the Office of Strategic Services during World War II and afterwards had assisted Philippine President Ramon Magsaysay in suppressing the Huk rebellion. A flamboyant and imaginative operator whose schemes ranged from the macabre to the bizarre, he had quickly ingratiated himself with Diem and became one of the Prime Minister's most trusted advisers and vocal supporters. Learning that a group of army officers was plotting to overthrow the government, Lansdale lured several of the ringleaders out of the country by giving them an expense-paid trip to Manila and the scheme quickly collapsed.[18]

The United States also enabled Diem to cope with some of the enormous problems he confronted in his first year, most notably the

[17] Embassy Paris to State Department, December 19, 1954, *USVN*, Book 10, 826–834; Heath to Walter Robertson, December 17, 1954, *ibid.*, 824–825.

[18] Sheehan, *Pentagon Papers (NYT)*, p. 20.

massive influx of refugees from the north. Responding to the fervent appeals of the northern Catholic hierarchy that "Christ has gone to the south" and to warnings that their lives would be in danger if they remained under Communism, an estimated 900,000 refugees, most of them Catholics, fled from the north after Geneva. The United States organized a task force of some fifty ships in what was dubbed "Passage to Freedom" and, along with private charities, established reception centers offering emergency food, clothing, and medical care to the newcomers. Himself a northerner, Diem was sympathetic to the refugees, and his government provided a subsidy to help them build new dwellings and to purchase clothing and food. Foreign Operations Administrator Harold Stassen called Passage to Freedom "one of the epochs" of modern Far Eastern history, and Diem's effective handling of the short-term problems created by the refugees was cited as early evidence of his ability to govern South Vietnam under American tutelage. The long-range problem of resettlement and integration proved much more difficult, however, and Diem's favoritism for the northerners was one of the major articles in the later indictment against him.[19]

Even with American help, Diem barely survived the sect crisis of 1955. The Cao Dai and Hoa Hao represented the most potent political forces in the fragmented society of post-Geneva Vietnam. Organized along the lines of the Catholic Church with a "pope" as head, the Cao Dai claimed two million adherents, maintained an army of 20,000, and exercised political control over much of the Mekong Delta. The Hoa Hao, with as many as one million followers and an army of 15,000, dominated the region northwest of Saigon. In addition, the Binh Xuyen, a mafia-like organization headed by a colorful brigand named Bay Vien, had an army of 25,000 men, earned huge revenues from gambling and prostitution in Saigon, and actually ran the city's police force. Unable to subdue the sects while fighting the Vietminh, the French had given them virtual autonomy. Accustomed to running their own affairs, the sects were not willing to surrender their power or fortunes to the new national government.[20]

Diem's divide-and-conquer tactics only united the sects against

[19] Stassen to Eisenhower, June 7, 1955, Eisenhower Papers, Office File 181-B, Box 862; Gertrude Samuels, "Passage to Freedom," *National Geographic,* 107 (June 1955), 858–874.

[20] FitzGerald, *Fire in the Lake,* pp. 56–57.

him. He offered the Cao Dai and Hoa Hao cabinet posts, and Lansdale journeyed deep into the jungles near the Cambodian border and bribed the most important Cao Dai leaders to work with the government. The U.S. Embassy backed Diem by warning that if the sects overthrew the President, American aid would be withdrawn, leaving South Vietnam at the mercy of the Vietminh. Diem stubbornly refused to negotiate with the Binh Xuyen, however, and his rapprochement with the Cao Dai and Hoa Hao broke down when he refused their demands for autonomy within their own territories. In the spring of 1955, the sects joined the Binh Xuyen in an all-out assault against the government. By March, government forces and sect armies waged open warfare in the streets of Saigon.

Diem's mishandling of the sects persuaded top French and American officials in Saigon that he must be removed. General Paul Ely, the French High Commissioner for Vietnam, advised the U.S. Embassy that Diem verged on megalomania, that he probably could not be saved, and that if he were saved "we shall have spared for Vietnam the worst Prime Minister it ever had." General J. Lawton Collins, whom Eisenhower had appointed Ambassador to Vietnam in December, concurred. Collins had expressed misgivings about Diem from the time he arrived in Vietnam, and the sect crisis convinced him that he had been correct. On April 7, he advised the State Department that Diem did not have the "capacity to achieve the necessary unity of purpose and action . . . to prevent the country from falling under Communist control."[21]

Several weeks later, Collins returned to Washington to plead the case for Diem's removal. Dulles stood his ground, arguing that Diem's problems were caused by French intrigue and Vietnamese "warlords" and that if the French viewpoint won out, "we will be paying the bill and the French calling the tune."[22] Collins was able to persuade the President, however, and Dulles and the State Department could do nothing more than arrange a face-saving compromise by which Diem would be retained as President, a largely titular position, while the actual authority of government was given to someone else.

While Collins was en route to Vietnam to implement the

[21] Collins to State Department, April 7, 1955, Eisenhower Papers, International File, Vietnam (2), Box 50.

[22] Hagerty Diary, March 30, April 12, 20, 1955, Hagerty Papers; *USVN*, Book 10, 909.

change, a sudden turn of events gave American backers of Diem another chance. When the Binh Xuyen launched a mortar attack against the presidential palace, Diem ordered his army into battle, and to the surprise of everyone, it quickly drove the opposition back into Cholon, the Chinese district of Saigon. Although instructed to remain neutral, many Americans openly sided with Diem. According to Lansdale, General John W. O'Daniel, the chief of the U.S military mission, "rode past the Vietnamese troops in his sedan, flying the American flag . . . and gave them the thumbs-up sign, shouting 'Give 'em hell, boys.' "[23] Lansdale himself convinced a skeptical Embassy that the successful counterattack demonstrated the loyalty of the army and Diem's strength as a leader. At a critical moment in the struggle, moreover, the ubiquitous CIA agent persuaded Diem to ignore a cable from Bao Dai demanding his resignation.

Diem's success against the Binh Xuyen produced an American policy reversal of enormous long-range significance. Senate leaders, including Mansfield and California Republican William Knowland, lobbied furiously for Diem's retention. Having lost the first round to Collins, Dulles, with the support of his brother, CIA director Allen Dulles, ably exploited the developments in Saigon. Arguing that Diem was the only means to "save South Vietnam and counteract revolution," that he must be supported "wholeheartedly," and that he could not be permitted to become "another Karensky [*sic*]," the Secretary persuaded the President to stick by a man whose political career had faced certain doom just days before.[24]

The American commitment to Diem provoked a final—and from the American standpoint not unwelcome—crisis with France. In a dramatic confrontation in Paris in mid-May, Prime Minister Edgar Faure argued heatedly that Diem was "not only incapable but mad" and that France could "no longer take risks with him": if the United States persisted in its support, France would have to withdraw from Vietnam.[25] Advised by the Joint Chiefs that a French withdrawal, although desirable from the long-term standpoint, would leave the new nation highly vulnerable, Dulles subsequently persuaded the French to remain and to support

[23] Edward G. Lansdale, *In the Midst of Wars* (New York, 1972), p. 288.

[24] Dulles to State Department, May 8, 1955, *USVN*, Book 10, 962–963.

[25] *Ibid.*

Diem until the Vietnamese themselves could settle the future of their country through elections. He also let it be known that the United States would frame its policies independently and would not feel bound to consult France before acting. In all, it was a bravura Dulles performance. The agreement ensured French support for the short run but left the United States complete freedom of action. Frustrated by Dulles and Diem and faced with rebellion in their North African colonies, the French abandoned whatever remained of their dreams of influence and began a phased withdrawal from what had been the most glittering jewel in the French Union.

Buoyed by his successes and by American support, Diem quickly consolidated his power. The army drove the Binh Xuyen deep into the swamps east of Saigon, where it eventually surrendered, and routed Hoa Hao forces in the Mekong Delta. Now isolated, the Cao Dai saw no choice but to come over to Diem's side. With American assistance, a "national" referendum was hastily arranged between Diem and Bao Dai. U.S. advisers informed the Prime Minister that 60 percent would be a more than adequate majority, but Diem and his brother Ngo Dinh Nhu left nothing to chance, securing 98.2 percent of the vote and winning more than 605,000 votes from the 405,000 registered voters in Saigon. Facing near certain downfall in May 1955, Diem, largely as a result of American support, had established uncontested control over the government of South Vietnam by the end of the year.

With firm American backing, Diem also blocked the elections called for by the Geneva Accords. Such a position was awkward for the United States given its traditional advocacy of free elections and its policies in Germany and Korea. Even Diem's most uncritical supporters realized, however, that Ho Chi Minh's reputation as a nationalist leader made elections risky and that, in any event, the more populous north—operating under iron Communist discipline—was "mathematically certain" of winning. Washington and Saigon used alleged North Vietnamese truce violations to justify their stand. They also resorted to legalism, insisting that the Geneva articles calling for elections had no "juridical value" and merely expressed a "pious wish" that committed no one. For the sake of appearances, the United States and South Vietnam affirmed that they would participate in genuinely free elections. Such a position was "unassailable in intent," Dulles argued, and it held out little danger since Communist nations never permitted a free and open political process.[26]

Diem's refusal to participate in elections ended, at least temporarily, any chance of the reunification of Vietnam, and the division of the country increasingly took on features of permanency. Diem refused to permit any traffic with the north, including even a postal arrangement, and the seventeenth parallel became one of the most restricted boundaries in the world.

Having ensured the survival of the Diem regime through its tumultuous first years, the United States supported it lavishly for the rest of the decade. The preservation of an independent South Vietnam as a bulwark against further Communist penetration of Southeast Asia remained the fundamental goal of U.S. policy. During the mid-1950s, the major battleground of the Cold War shifted from Europe to the newly emerging nations of Asia and Africa, where the United States and the Soviet Union vied for influence and sought to demonstrate the superior merits of their respective systems. In this context, South Vietnam assumed an even greater importance as a testing ground for the viability of American ideology and institutions in underdeveloped nations.

The experiment in nation-building launched by Dulles on a crash basis quickly assumed the form of a crusade. Private charitable agencies distributed to refugees food, soap, toothbrushes, and emergency medical supplies, and worked zealously to improve amenities in refugee camps. The International Rescue Committee went further. Originally established to assist refugees from Nazi Germany, the IRC had since shifted its efforts to the Cold War. In Vietnam, it professed to stand as a "lighthouse of inspiration" for those eager to preserve and broaden "concepts of democratic culture." The IRC staged anti-Communist plays in the villages and sponsored in the cities recitals and art exhibitions built around democratic themes. It also established Freedom Centers in Saigon, Hue, and Dalat to win over disaffected Vietnamese intellectuals and students through such diverse and apparently contradictory efforts as research into "pure Vietnamese culture" and English lan-

---

[26] Tran Van Chuong, "Comment on the Viet Minh's Request for General Elections in Viet Nam," document #4051, Donovan Papers; American Friends of Vietnam, "The Election Issue," n.d., copy in Hans Morgenthau Papers, Library of Congress, Washington, D.C.; Dulles news conference, August 30, 1955, Dulles Papers, Princeton, N.J., Box 95.

guage courses.[27] Meanwhile, in the United States, liberals and conservatives joined hands to form the American Friends of Vietnam, a group headed by Donovan and created to enlighten American opinion to the "realities" in Vietnam and lobby the U.S. government to support the Diem government. "A free Vietnam means a greater guarantee of freedom in the world," the AFV affirmed in its statement of purpose. "There is a little bit of all of us in that faraway country," General O'Daniel, a charter member, would write in 1960.[28]

Already deeply committed to South Vietnam, the Eisenhower administration needed no urging from private lobby groups. From 1955 to 1961, the United States poured more than $1 billion in economic and military assistance into South Vietnam, and by 1961, Diem's government ranked fifth among all recipients of American foreign aid. By the late 1950s, there were more than 1,500 Americans in South Vietnam, assisting the government in various ways, and the U.S. mission in Saigon was the largest in the world.

The American aid program accorded top priority to building a South Vietnamese army. Dulles had insisted from the outset that the development of a strong, modern army was an essential first step in promoting a stable government. The withdrawal of the French Expeditionary Force, the presence of large, experienced armies in the north, and continued instability in the south all underscored the necessity of providing South Vietnam with a strong military force. Between 1955 and 1961, military assistance constituted more than 78 percent of the total American foreign aid program.

In early 1956, the United States assumed from France full responsibility for training the Vietnamese Army, and the Military Assistance and Advisory Group (MAAG) in Saigon undertook a crash program to build it into an effective force. Limited by the Geneva Accords to a strength of 342 men, the MAAG was augmented by various subterfuges to a strength of 692. From 1955 to 1960, it was headed by Lieutenant General Samuel Williams, a spit-and-polish veteran of the two world wars and Korea whose in-

[27] Robert MacAlister reports to International Rescue Committee, May–October 1955, document #4084, Donovan Papers.

[28] American Friends of Vietnam, "Statement of Purpose," n.d., copy in Morgenthau Papers; John W. O'Daniel, *The Nation That Refused to Starve* (New York, 1960), p. 11.

sistence on rigid discipline and vicious tongue-lashings were legendary throughout the army.

The MAAG faced truly formidable obstacles. The United States inherited from France an army of more than 250,000 men, poorly organized, trained, and equipped, lacking in national spirit, suffering from low morale, and deficient in officers and trained specialists such as engineers and artillerymen. The army's supply problems were compounded by the French, who took most of the best equipment with them and dumped upon the Vietnamese tons of useless and antiquated material. The American advisers had to bridge profound language and cultural gaps. Despite good intentions, they often patronized the Vietnamese, sometimes even referring to them as "natives." "Probably the greatest single problem encountered by the MAAG," one of its officers wrote at the time, "is the continual task of assuring the Vietnamese that the United States is not a colonial power—an assurance that must be renewed on an individual basis by each new adviser."[29] From this weak foundation and in the face of serious practical difficulties, the MAAG was assigned the challenging mission of building an army capable of maintaining internal security and of holding the line against an invasion from the north until outside forces could be brought in.

Under the MAAG's direction, the United States reorganized, equipped, and trained the South Vietnamese Army. The United States provided roughly $85 million per year in military equipment, including uniforms, small arms, vehicles, tanks, and helicopters. It paid the salaries of officers and men, financed the construction of military installations, and underwrote the cost of training programs. The MAAG scaled down the army to a strength of 150,000 men and organized it into mobile divisions capable of a dual mission. It launched an ambitious training program, based on American models, including a Command and General Staff College for senior officers, officer candidate schools, and specialized schools for noncoms. In 1960 alone, more than 1,600 Vietnamese soldiers participated in the Off-Shore Program, studying in the United States and other "free world" countries. Official spokesmen proclaimed by 1960 that the United States had achieved a "minor

---

[29] Judson J. Conner, "Teeth for the Free World Dragon," *Army Information Digest* (November 1960), 41; Ronald H. Spector, *Advice and Support: The Early Years, 1941–1960* (Washington, D.C., 1983), pp. 278–282.

miracle," transforming what had been "little more than a marginal collection of armed men" into an efficient, modern army.[30]

As would so often be the case in Vietnam, however, reality was far removed from official rhetoric. The army still lacked sufficient officers in 1960, and General Williams later conceded that many of the officers holding key positions were of "marginal quality." As one of Williams' top assistants put it, "No one can make good . . . commanders by sending uneducated, poorly trained, and poorly equipped and motivated boys to Benning or Knox or Leavenworth or Quantico."[31] Diem's determination to maintain tight control over the army frustrated the MAAG's efforts to establish a smoothly functioning command system. The President personally ordered units into action, bypassing the Ministry of Defense and the General Staff. He chose safe rather than competent officers for critical posts. He promoted officers on the basis of loyalty rather than merit and constantly shuffled the high command—"generals and colonels, it was said jokingly in Saigon, were the only first-class travelers in Vietnam."[32]

The basic problem, however, was that the army was trained for the wrong mission. The MAAG would be sharply criticized for failing to prepare the South Vietnamese Army for dealing with guerrilla operations, but from the perspective of the mid-1950s its emphasis appears quite logical. Confronting the near-impossible task of building from scratch an army capable of performing two quite diverse missions, the MAAG naturally leaned toward the conventional warfare with which it was most familiar. At least until 1958, moreover, the countryside was quiescent and Diem appeared firmly entrenched. Williams and most of his staff had served in Korea, and the remarkable resemblance between the Korean and Vietnamese situations inclined them to focus on the threat of an invasion from the north. Also learning from experiences in Greece and the Philippines, they doubted that North Vietnam could mount an insurgency capable of threatening the south. The army was therefore trained, organized, and equipped primarily to fight a conventional war, and its inadequacies were obvious only after South Vietnam was enveloped by a rural insurgency.

[30] Conner, "Teeth for the Free World Dragon," 33.

[31] Robert H. Whitlow, "The United States Military in South Vietnam, 1954–1960" (M.A. thesis, University of Kentucky, 1972), 87.

[32] Jean Lacouture, *Vietnam Between Two Truces* (New York, 1966), p. 117.

A paramilitary force, the Civil Guard, was to assist the army in maintaining internal security, but it was hampered from the beginning by conflicts over organization and training. Advisers from Michigan State University assigned to help with the Civil Guard sought a small group trained and equipped for police duties at the province and village level, while Diem, supported by Lansdale and the MAAG, preferred an auxiliary military force equipped with helicopters, armored cars, and bazookas, and capable of small-scale military operations. Washington supported the Michigan State group and refused to furnish assistance for the Civil Guard until Diem acquiesced, but the guard never developed into an effective force. Diem used it as a dumping ground for inferior army officers and in general gave it little support. The training provided by the Michigan State police experts, in Lansdale's words, left the guard "pathetically unready for the realities of the Vietnamese countryside. A squad of Civil Guard policemen, armed with whistles, nightsticks and 38 caliber revolvers, could hardly be expected to arrest a squad of guerrillas armed with submachine guns, rifles, grenades and mortars."[33]

The United States also pumped millions of dollars in foreign aid into the South Vietnamese economy between 1955 and 1960, the great bulk of it through the commercial-import program. Described by one zealous U.S. official as "the greatest invention since the wheel," the commercial-import program was designed to make up South Vietnam's huge foreign exchange deficit while avoiding the runaway inflation that might have been set loose by a massive infusion of dollars into a vulnerable economy.[34] Vietnamese importers ordered from foreign export firms goods ranging from foodstuffs to automobiles, with Washington footing the bill. The importers paid for the goods in piasters, which then went into a "counterpart fund" held by the National Bank of Vietnam and were used by the Diem government to cover operating expenses and finance development projects. From 1955 to 1959, the commercial-import program generated almost $1 billion in counterpart funds. In addition, the United States furnished South Vietnam more than $127 million in direct economic assistance and more than $16 million in technical aid.

The American aid program brought significant results. The

[33] Lansdale, *Midst of Wars*, p. 353.

[34] U.S. Senate, Committee on Foreign Relations, *Situation in Vietnam, Hearings, 1959* (Washington, D.C., 1959), p. 203.

commercial-import program covered South Vietnam's foreign exchange deficit and, by making available large quantities of consumer goods, held inflation in check. American money and technology helped to repair the vast damages resulting from more than a decade of war, rebuilding highways, railroads, and canals, and spurring a modest increase in agricultural productivity. Specialists from American land-grant colleges promoted the development of new crops and established credit facilities for small farmers. Educators supervised the founding of schools and furnished textbooks. Public health experts provided drugs and medical supplies, and assisted in the training of nurses and paramedics. A group of public administration specialists from Michigan State University trained Vietnamese civil servants in skills ranging from typing to personnel management and even established a school of police administration to train what one brochure described as "Vietnam's finest."[35]

More than any other single factor, American aid enabled South Vietnam to survive the first few critical years after independence, and by the late 1950s the new nation appeared to be flourishing. In Saigon, one visitor reported, "the stores and market places are filled with consumer goods; the streets are filled with new motor scooters and expensive automobiles; and in the upper-income residential areas new and pretentious housing is being built."[36] After conducting an investigation of the uses of American economic assistance, Democratic Senator Gale McGee of Wyoming proposed that South Vietnam be made a "showcase" for the foreign aid program, a place to which people from other countries could be brought to observe firsthand the "wholesome effects of our efforts to help other peoples help themselves."[37]

Appearances were again deceptive, however, for the American aid program had at best mixed results. The recipients were undoubtedly grateful for U.S. generosity, but they could not help but be suspicious as well. "After eighty years of ruthless exploitation by the French," one American observed, "many Vietnamese wonder why America is suddenly spending so much money in Vietnam."[38]

[35] U.S. Operations Mission, *Building Economic Strength* (Washington, D.C., 1958), p. 75.

[36] Milton C. Taylor, "South Vietnam: Lavish Aid, Limited Progress," *Pacific Affairs*, 34 (1961), 242.

[37] Senate, *Hearings, 1959*, p. 369.

[38] MacAlister report to International Rescue Committee, n.d., document #4084, Donovan Papers.

More important, although U.S. aid prevented an economic collapse and served to maintain a high standard of living in Saigon, it did little to promote economic development or to improve living conditions in the villages where more than 90 percent of South Vietnam's population resided. From 1955 to 1959, military aid was four times greater than economic and technical assistance, and of the nearly $1 billion in counterpart funds, more than 78 percent went for military purposes. Such was the preoccupation with "security" among Vietnamese and American officials alike that those interested in other projects found it expedient to justify them in terms of defense. Saigon and Washington insisted that the continuing presence of serious external and internal threats allowed them no choice, but the heavy emphasis on military aid left little money for long-range economic development. As a Senate committee pointed out in 1960, the military program was the "tail that wags the dog."[39]

The commercial-import program also contained built-in weaknesses. It was enormously wasteful, with importers frequently ordering far more than could be consumed, and it created abundant opportunities for fast profits. The most serious weakness of the program, however, was that it financed an artificially high standard of living while contributing little to development. As late as 1957, about two-thirds of the imports consisted of consumer goods, and much of the wealth was drained off in conspicuous consumption rather than going into industry or agriculture. Diem stubbornly resisted American attempts to reduce the proportion of consumer goods, arguing that a lowering of living standards would create domestic unrest. The United States made some changes on its own, dropping from the list such obvious luxury items as hi-fis and water skis and reducing consumer goods to about one-third of the total, but with little effect. Robert Scigliano concluded in 1963 that the commercial-import program had been a "large-scale relief project" which had not "served to induce significant economic development in Vietnam."[40]

In spending the small percentage of funds allotted to development, Americans and Vietnamese frequently found themselves at

[39] U.S. Senate, Committee on Foreign Relations, *United States Aid Program in Vietnam, Report, February 26, 1960* (Washington, D.C., 1960), p. 8.

[40] Robert Scigliano, *South Vietnam: Nation Under Stress* (Boston, 1964), p. 125.

odds. The United States insisted that industrial development must be based on private enterprise and until the early 1960s refused to provide funds for state-owned industries. Diem and his entourage shared the mandarin's contempt for businessmen and the nationalist's distrust of foreign capital. They denounced American attitudes as "medieval and retrograde," and insisted that they must have government ownership of major industries, at least at the start. The result was a bitter stalemate which inhibited any constructive program of industrial development.

The massive infusion of American aid thus kept South Vietnam alive, but it fostered dependency rather than laying the foundation for a genuinely independent nation. Rice production doubled between 1955 and 1960, but much of the increase was taken up in increased domestic consumption, while gains in industrial productivity were insignificant. South Vietnam relied on a high level of imports to maintain its standard of living and on American money to pay for them. Vietnamese and Americans alike agreed that a cutback or termination of American assistance would bring economic and political collapse. Vietnam was the "prototype of the dependent economy," Milton Taylor wrote in 1961, "its level of national income as dependent on outside forces as was the case when the country was a French colony. . . . American aid has built a castle on sand."[41]

The basic problem of nation-building was political, however. There was much talk about assisting the Vietnamese to construct an American-style democracy, and U.S. advisers helped to draft a constitution which contained many of the trappings of Western democracies, including a President and legislature elected by popular vote and guarantees of basic political rights. In fact, the United States devoted very little attention to political matters and, despite its massive foreign aid program, exerted very little influence. Some Americans naively assumed that Diem shared their political values; others were preoccupied with the security problems which seemed most urgent. Most probably shared Dulles's view that it was enough for Diem to be "competent, anti-Communist and vigorous," and that while representative government was a desirable long-range objective, it could not be accomplished overnight.[42] For

[41] Taylor, "South Vietnam," 256.

[42] Dulles news conference, May 7, 1955, Dulles Papers, Princeton, N.J., Box 99; Frederick Reinhardt oral history interview, *ibid.*

whatever reason, the U.S. government and the American mission in Saigon did little to promote democracy, or even political reform, until South Vietnam was swept by revolution.

In any event, it would have been lost on Diem, for whom democracy was alien in terms of experience and temperament. Inasmuch as he had a political philosophy, it was the vague concept of "personalism," a fusion of Western and Eastern ideas which Diem and his brother Ngo Dinh Nhu used as a rationalization for absolute state power, distrust of popular rule, and the belief that a small elite was responsible for defining the general welfare. Diem's model was the Emperor Ming Mang, the nineteenth-century reformer who created an assembly of mandarins to approve his royal decrees. Diem's philosophy of government was succinctly expressed in a line he personally added to the constitution: "The President is vested with the leadership of the nation." He identified his principles with the general good and firmly believed that the people must be guided by the paternalistic hand of those who knew what was best for them. A deeply suspicious individual, Diem was convinced, as Bernard Fall has written, that "compromise has no place and opposition of any kind must of necessity be subversive and must be suppressed with all the vigor the system is capable of."[43]

To please his American advisers, Diem occasionally paid lip service to democracy, but in actual practice he assumed absolute powers. He personally dominated the executive branch of government, reserving to himself and his brothers, three of whom were appointed to a cabinet of six, all power of decision-making. Unable or unwilling to delegate authority, he oversaw the operations of the entire government down to the most minute detail. Cabinet members or upper-level civil servants who expressed opposition were quickly appointed to ambassadorships abroad—or worse. The executive branch completely dominated the legislature, which, in any case, was virtually handpicked through careful manipulation of the electoral process. In the first years of its existence, the National Assembly initiated nothing important on its own and pliantly approved everything which the President submitted to it.

The Diem government might have survived its authoritarianism had it pursued enlightened policies, but its inattention to the needs

[43] Bernard Fall, *The Two Vietnams: A Political and Military Analysis* (New York, 1967), p. 237.

of the people and its ruthless suppression of dissent stirred a rising discontent which eventually brought its downfall. Diem's policies toward the villages—traditionally the backbone of Vietnamese society—demonstrated a singular lack of concern and near-callous irresponsibility. Lansdale persuaded the President to initiate a Civic Action Program to extend government services to the villages, but Diem took little interest in it, and, as Lansdale later lamented, "it flopped."[44] At American insistence, the government instituted a land reform program, but it too was implemented halfheartedly and did little to meet the rising appetite for land among South Vietnam's rural population.

The only significant "reform" enacted by the government during the 1950s touched off massive resentment in the villages. In a misguided effort to centralize federal authority and curb Vietminh influence in the countryside, Diem abolished traditional local elections and began to appoint village and provincial officials. The villagers had enjoyed virtual autonomy for centuries and received the outsiders, Frances FitzGerald observes, "much as they might have received proconsuls from a conquering power."[45] The fears aroused by their mere presence were often heightened by their actions. Many of Diem's appointees were chosen on the basis of personal loyalty, and most of them were poorly trained for their tasks. Some used their positions for personal enrichment; province chiefs were known to have arrested wealthy villagers on trumped-up charges and then forced them to pay bribes for their release.

Diem's vigorous assault against political opponents spawned rising discontent in the cities as well as the countryside. Newspapers which criticized the government were promptly shut down, and Nhu's Vietnam Bureau of Investigation rooted out suspected subversives in a manner that would have made J. Edgar Hoover blanch. Using authority handed down in various presidential ordinances, the government herded into "reeducation centers" thousands of Vietnamese—Communists and non-Communists alike—who were alleged to be threats to public order. The reeducation program was originally aimed at the Vietminh "stay-behinds," but in time it was extended to anyone who dared speak out against the government. The regime admitted to the incarceration

[44] Lansdale, *Midst of Wars*, p. 212.
[45] FitzGerald, *Fire in the Lake*, p. 154.

of 20,000 people by 1956, and the campaign was subsequently intensified. The government "has tended to treat the population with suspicion or coerce it," an American intelligence report concluded in 1960, "and has been rewarded with an attitude of apathy or resentment."[46]

Diem retained a highly favorable image in the United States until South Vietnam was engulfed by revolution in the early 1960s. It is possible that even those Americans close to the government were unaware until the end of the decade of the extent to which he had alienated his people. In the eyes of most Americans, moreover, the President's vigorous anti-Communism more than compensated for his shortcomings. Apologists such as Professor Wesley Fishel of Michigan State University conceded that Diem had employed authoritarian methods, but argued that Vietnam's lack of experience with democracy and the internal threat posed by Communism left him no choice. The American media focused on the stability brought to South Vietnam by the "tough little miracle man," and when Diem visited the United States in 1957 he was widely feted and praised. The image persisted even after insurgency had spread throughout much of the country. "On his record," *Newsweek's* Ernest Lindley exclaimed in 1959, "he must be rated as one of the ablest free Asian leaders. We can take pride in our support."[47]

At the very time Americans were extolling the "miracles" wrought by Diem, the revolution that would eventually sweep him from power and provoke massive U.S. intervention was taking root. The U.S. government later went to great lengths to prove that the Second Indochina War was the result of "aggression from the north," the determination of North Vietnam to impose Communism on its southern neighbor. Critics of American policy insisted, on the other hand, that the revolution had sprung from indigenous roots largely in response to Diem's oppressiveness and that it had grown in strength without significant support from the north. Although much remains unclear about the origins of the war, the most persuasive assessment, that of William Duiker, concludes that the insurgency was a "genuine revolt based in the South" but that it was "organized and directed from the North."[48]

[46] "Special Report on Internal Security Situation in Saigon," March 7, 1960, *USVN*, Book 10, 1267–1280.

[47] Ernest K. Lindley, "An Ally Worth Having," *Newsweek* (June 29, 1959), 31.

[48] William J. Duiker, *The Communist Road to Power in Vietnam* (Boulder, Colo., 1981), p. 198.

In the years after Geneva, North Vietnam approached the issue of unification with great caution. Neither the Soviet Union nor China appears to have offered support for an aggressive policy. In any event, like Diem, Ho Chi Minh and his lieutenants faced massive problems of postwar reconstruction and nation-building. Reports of a "bloodbath" in which as many as 500,000 people were executed following implementation of a land reform program have been greatly exaggerated.[49] Hanoi's heavy-handed measures did provoke widespread opposition, however. Between 3,000 and 15,000 dissidents may in fact have been executed, and resistance in Ho Chi Minh's own Nghe An province had to be suppressed by units of the regular army. Although it did not abandon its goal of unification, a preoccupied Hanoi ordered stay-behind units in the south to protect the party apparatus but to avoid violence and confine their activities to the political sphere.

The result, according to Communist party historians, was "the darkest period" for the revolution in the south. The elections were not held, and the amnesty promised by Geneva was not granted. More important, Diem turned out to be a greater menace than his adversaries had anticipated. His anti-Communist campaigns were devastatingly successful, and by 1957, party membership had fallen to precarious levels. Facing extinction, local leaders began to defend themselves, sometimes in violation of the party line.

Between 1957 and 1959, Hanoi gradually committed itself to the growing insurgency in the south. Its leaders appear to have been bitterly divided between those who wanted to focus on consolidation of the revolution in the north and those who wanted to liberate the south. In December 1956, the factions compromised, agreeing that the north should continue to take priority, but authorizing southern insurgents to use violence to defend themselves. In March 1957, Hanoi approved plans to modernize its own armed forces. More important decisions came in 1959. Recognizing that the revolutionaries in the south were in desperate straits and also that Diem's oppressiveness had created a favorable atmosphere for revolution, the party in the spring of 1959 authorized the resumption of armed struggle and took active measures to support it. With the watchword "absolute secrecy, absolute security," it established a special force, Group 559, to construct an infiltration route to

---

[49] The most detailed and convincing account is in Edwin E. Moise, *Land Reform in China and North Vietnam* (Chapel Hill, N.C., 1983), pp. 178–268.

move men and supplies into South Vietnam through Laos and began to send back to the south to assume leadership roles Vietminh who had come north after Geneva. The Third Party Congress of September 1960 formally approved the shift to armed struggle, assigning liberation of the south equal priority with consolidation of the north. In December 1960, at Hanoi's direction, southern revolutionaries founded the National Liberation Front (NLF), a broad-based organization led by Communists but designed to rally all those disaffected with Diem by promising sweeping reforms and the establishment of genuine independence. In all of these steps, North Vietnam carefully concealed its own hand, hoping that Diem could be overthrown by what would appear an indigenous revolution without provoking U.S. intervention.

The result was a drastic intensification of revolutionary activity in the south. The level of violence increased dramatically: in 1958, an estimated 700 government officials were assassinated; in 1960, 2,500. In 1959, the insurgents shifted from hit-and-run operations to full-scale military operations against government-controlled villages and exposed units of the South Vietnamese Army. The intelligence and propaganda networks that had fallen into disuse after Geneva were reactivated, and vigorous campaigns of political agitation were launched in the villages. Largely as a result of Diem's misguided policies, the insurgents found a receptive audience—the peasants were like a "mound of straw ready to be ignited," a captured guerrilla later told an interrogator.[50] By the time the NLF was formally organized, the Vietcong (a term applied to the NLF by the Diem regime meaning Vietnam Communist, with derogatory implications) had attracted thousands of adherents from among the rural population and had established a presence in countless villages.

Diem's response to the insurgency heightened popular antagonism toward his government. The President intensified the anti-Communist campaign in the villages and tightened controls in the cities, arresting scores of alleged dissidents. Once again demonstrating the degree to which he was out of touch with rural Vietnam, in the summer of 1959 he launched an ill-fated "agroville" program to combat the rising violence in the countryside. The purpose of the

[50] U.S. Congress, Senate, Subcommitee on Public Buildings and Grounds, *The Pentagon Papers* (*The Senator Gravel Edition*) (4 vols.; Boston, 1971), I, 329. Hereafter cited as *Pentagon Papers* (*Gravel*).

program was to relocate the peasantry in areas where the army could protect them from Vietcong terror and propaganda, and the government sought to make it attractive by providing the new communities with schools, medical facilities, and electricity. But the peasants deeply resented being forcibly removed from their homes and from the lands which contained the sacred tombs of their ancestors, and the government's provisions for their relocation added to their discontent. They were given only about $5.50, which did not cover the cost of the land they were required to purchase, and they were forced to work on community projects without any compensation. The agroville program was eventually abandoned, but only after it had spawned enormous rural discontent with the government.

Throughout 1960, evidence of the government's fragility mounted. The insurgency grew unchecked in the countryside, and the level of violence increased sharply. In January 1960, at Trang Sup, a village northeast of Saigon, four Vietcong companies destroyed a South Vietnamese Army headquarters and seized large stocks of weapons, leaving the army and its U.S. advisers in a state of shock. The regime's unpopularity in Saigon was made especially clear in April when a group of non-Communist politicians, many of whom had served in Diem's cabinet, met at the Caravelle Hotel and issued a manifesto bitterly protesting the government's oppressiveness and calling for sweeping reforms. In November, Diem narrowly thwarted an attempted coup by three paratroop battalions presumed to be among those units of the army most loyal to him. American intelligence reports ominously warned that if present trends continued, the collapse of the regime was a near certainty.

Belatedly perceiving the strength of the insurgency and the inability of the South Vietnamese government and armed forces to cope with it, the United States in 1960 shifted the emphasis of its military programs from conventional warfare to counterinsurgency. U.S. military officials in Washington and Saigon began work on a comprehensive plan to expand and reorganize the army and Civil Guard and to equip and train them for anti-guerrilla operations. While this plan was being formulated, the mission in Saigon took piecemeal steps to assist the South Vietnamese. Training programs already in operation were reoriented. Special American teams were sent to train South Vietnamese Ranger Battalions, and U.S. advisers were placed at the regimental level to give on-the-spot advice and assess the capabilities and needs of individual units. Although the shift to counterinsurgency represented a tacit admission that the original advisory program had failed, it did not produce the sort of drastic changes that would have been required to defeat the guerrillas. It merely resulted in additional military aid and proposals for bureaucratic reorganization.[51]

In the meantime, civilian officials made gentle and largely unsuccessful attempts to persuade Diem to change his ways. Many U.S. officials, including Ambassador Elbridge Durbrow, feared that unless the President reformed his government and mobilized popular support, the insurgency would overwhelm South Vietnam. In October, Durbrow secured Washington's permission to broach the question directly with Diem. He tactfully urged the President to broaden his government by appointing a new cabinet, to relax his controls on the press and civil liberties, and to try to win over the rural population by restoring village elections and making credit easily available to small farmers. Diem was noncommittal, responding that the proposals conformed with his own ideas but that it would be "most difficult" to implement them while the government faced internal rebellion.[52] Over the next few weeks, he tightened the controls, clamping down on the army and arresting the politicians who had issued the Caravelle Manifesto.

By the end of the year, Americans in Saigon were thoroughly alarmed by the crisis and deeply divided over how to combat it. Durbrow warned Washington that the Saigon government was in "serious danger" and that "prompt and even drastic action" was required to save it. In return for additional military aid, he advised, the United States should require Diem to institute sweeping reforms.[53] The U.S. military mission in Saigon firmly resisted Durbrow's proposals. The MAAG's major concern was to develop an effective military response to the insurgency, and it felt that insistence upon "democratic" reform would distract attention from the war and undercut Diem during a critical period. The debate became increasingly bitter during 1960, and meetings at the Embassy, in the words of a participant, were "barely civil."[54]

---

[51] Spector, *Advice and Support*, p. 372.

[52] Durbrow memorandum, October 15, 1960, *USVN*, Book 10, 1318.

[53] Durbrow to State Department, December 5, 1960, *ibid.*, 1334–1336.

[54] William Colby, *Honorable Men* (New York, 1978), p. 160.

Although the experiment in nation-building was in obvious jeopardy by the end of the year, the Eisenhower administration did not resolve the debate in Saigon or take any major steps to salvage its huge investment. Throughout much of 1960, attention was focused elsewhere. A new flareup over Berlin sharpened Cold War tensions in Europe, and the U-2 incident and an abortive summit meeting in Paris produced enormous strains in Soviet-American relations. The emergence in Cuba of a revolutionary government headed by Fidel Castro and the establishment of close ties between Cuba and the Soviet Union aroused fears of Communist intrusion into the hemisphere. The deterioration in South Vietnam was gradual, and a sense of impending crisis did not develop until late in the year, by which time Eisenhower was already planning the transfer of power to the newly elected Democratic administration of John F. Kennedy.

Even then, Laos, rather than South Vietnam, was viewed as the most dangerous problem in Indochina. A mildly pro-Western government had assumed power in Laos after Geneva and had been given lavish American support, but when it attempted to reach an accommodation with the Pathet Lao insurgents who had fought with the Vietminh, the United States had instigated a right-wing coup. The American-sponsored government launched an ambitious military campaign against the Pathet Lao, but it achieved little success and in 1960 was overthrown by a group of so-called neutralists. Rejecting a compromise political settlement, the Eisenhower administration firmly supported its client government and forced the neutralists into an uneasy alliance with the Pathet Lao. By the end of the year, North Vietnam and the Soviet Union had begun to furnish substantial support to the anti-American forces, and intensification of the civil war seemed certain.

By the beginning of 1961, Eisenhower was seriously considering American military intervention in Laos. As early as September 1959, he had grimly warned that Laos might "develop into another Korea."[55] In a briefing for President-elect Kennedy on January 19, 1961, he advised that the fall of Laos would threaten Thailand, Cambodia, and South Vietnam, and that if the United States did not draw the line in Laos, it might have to "write off" the rest of Southeast Asia. Intervention should be multilateral, Eisenhower

[55] Gordon Gray memorandum, September 14, 1959, Eisenhower Papers, "Cleanup" File, Box 5.

observed, but the defense of Laos was sufficiently important that if the United States could not persuade its SEATO allies to participate, it might have to go in alone. Compared to Laos, South Vietnam seemed a "back-burner" problem and was not even mentioned during the January briefing on Southeast Asia.[56]

Between 1954 and 1961, the United States came full circle in Vietnam. Facing the likelihood of a French collapse, the Eisenhower administration had briefly considered military intervention to save Indochina from Communism. Confident that the United States, free of the taint of colonialism, could succeed where France had failed, Eisenhower and Dulles had eventually acquiesced in a French military defeat and assumed the burden of nation-building. Vietnam must have seemed comparable to Greece and Korea, where the United States had shored up embattled allies. Lacking knowledge of Vietnamese history and culture, Americans seriously underestimated the difficulties of nation-building in an area with only the most fragile basis for nationhood. The ambitious programs developed in the 1950s merely papered over rather than corrected South Vietnam's problems. To have constructed a viable nation in southern Vietnam, moreover, would have required the most enlightened, imaginative, and determined *Vietnamese* leadership, an ingredient the United States could not provide. Ngo Dinh Diem may well have been the "best available man," as Dulles described him, and the United States pinned its hopes exclusively on him and helped him to survive the tumultuous years 1954–1955.[57] But Diem lacked the qualities necessary for the formidable challenge of nation-building and by 1960 he faced a potent internal opposition supported by North Vietnam which he, like the French before him, seemed increasingly incapable of handling. The quirks of the electoral calendar spared Eisenhower from facing the ultimate failure of his policies in Vietnam. Within a short time after taking office, however, John F. Kennedy would have to choose between abandoning what he had earlier called "our offspring" or significantly increasing the American commitment.

---

[56] Clark Clifford memorandum of conversation, January 19, 1961, *Pentagon Papers (Gravel)*, II, 635–637.

[57] Dulles news conference, March 1, 1955, Dulles Papers, Princeton, N.J., Box 99.

CHAPTER 3

Limited Partnership: Kennedy and Diem, 1961–1963

"Our problems are critical," John F. Kennedy warned the nation in January 1961. "The tide is unfavorable. The news will be worse before it is better."[1] It was a theme Kennedy had sounded throughout the 1960 campaign, and it set the tone for his administration. In 1961, the world *did* appear to be entering the most perilous stage in its history. The struggle of hundreds of new nations to break from their colonial past and establish modern institutions unleashed chaos across much of the globe. The rhetoric and actions of the erratic Soviet Premier Nikita Khrushchev suggested a new Communist boldness, even recklessness, and a determination to exploit the prevailing instability. Soviet-American confrontation broadened and intensified in the late 1950s, and the development of awesome new weapons systems added an especially frightful dimension. Over the long haul, nationalism proved a more powerful force than Communism or democratic-capitalism, and within two years the eruption of the Sino-Soviet split would starkly expose the myth of a monolithic Communist "bloc." In 1961, however, the fate of the world appeared to hang in the balance, and Kennedy took office certain that the survival of the United States depended upon its capacity to defend "free" institutions. Should America falter, he warned, "the whole world, in my opinion, would inevitably begin to move toward the Communist bloc."[2]

[1] John F. Kennedy, State of the Union Address, January 30, 1961, *John F. Kennedy, Public Papers, 1961* (Washington, D.C., 1962), p. 27.

[2] Quoted in Seyom Brown, *The Faces of Power* (New York, 1969), p. 217.

Calling upon his countrymen to become the "watchmen on the walls of freedom" and promising to assert firm, vigorous leadership, Kennedy committed his administration to meet the perils of the new era. He gathered about him a youthful, energetic, and intelligent corps of advisers from the top positions in academia and industry, self-confident, activist men who shared his determination to "get the country moving again." The New Frontiersmen accepted without question the basic assumptions of the containment policy, but they also believed, as Kennedy put it, that they must "move forward to meet Communism, rather than waiting for it to come to us and then reacting to it."[3] Coming to political maturity during World War II, they were alarmed by the danger of another global holocaust. However, they were also exhilarated by the prospect of leading the nation through perilous times and winning the ultimate victory, and they shared a Wilsonian view that destiny had singled out their nation to defend and spread the democratic ideal.[4]

Kennedy and his advisers also recognized that domestic politics demanded a firm and successful foreign policy. In ringing tones during the campaign of 1960, the Senator from Massachusetts had accused Eisenhower of indecisiveness and had promised to regain the initiative in the Cold War. Having won only the most narrow of electoral victories, the new President was keenly aware of his own vulnerability. Especially in his first two years, he always kept a wary eye on his domestic flank while making foreign policy decisions, and he was ever sensitive to Republican charges of weakness or appeasement.

The Kennedy administration set out at once to meet the challenges of the Cold War. The President ordered a massive buildup of nuclear weapons and long-range missiles to establish a credible deterrent to Soviet nuclear power. Persuaded that Eisenhower's heavy reliance on nuclear weapons had left the United States muscle-bound in many diplomatic situations, Kennedy also expanded and modernized the nation's conventional military forces to permit a "flexible response" to various types and levels of aggression. Certain that the emerging nations would be the "principal battleground in which the forces of freedom and Communism [would]

---

[3] Quoted in Henry Fairlie, *The Kennedy Promise* (New York, 1973), p. 72.

[4] Thomas G. Paterson, "Bearing the Burden: A Critical Look at JFK's Foreign Policy," *Virginia Quarterly Review*, 54 (Spring 1978), p. 197.

compete," the administration devoted much attention to developing an effective response to guerrilla warfare—"an international disease" which the United States had to learn to "destroy."[5] Kennedy also felt that the United States must strike at the source of disease, however, and placed great emphasis on devising programs of economic and technical assistance which would eliminate the conditions in which Communism flourished and would channel revolutionary forces into democratic paths.

Vietnam stands as the most tragic legacy of the global activism of the Kennedy era. Kennedy had long taken a close personal interest in Vietnam, which he had once described as the "cornerstone of the free world in Southeast Asia." In his eyes and those of many of his advisers, moreover, South Vietnam would become a test case of America's determination to uphold its commitments in a menacing world and of its capacity to meet the new challenges posed by guerrilla warfare in the emerging nations. Kennedy had joined in the attacks on Truman for "losing" China, and he was extremely sensitive to the political damage that could be done by the loss of additional Asian real estate. Thus he was even less willing than Truman and Eisenhower to permit the fall of Vietnam to Communism.

Inheriting from Eisenhower an increasingly dangerous if still limited commitment, he plunged deeper into the morass. Kennedy did not, as some critics have alleged, eagerly take up the burden in Vietnam, and his actions there contrast sharply with the administration's rhetoric.[6] In settling the major policy issues, he was cautious rather than bold, hesitant rather than decisive, and improvisational rather than carefully calculating. He delayed making a firm commitment for nearly a year, and then acted only because the shaky Diem government appeared on the verge of collapse. Wary of the domestic and international consequences of a negotiated settlement but unwilling to risk a full-scale involvement, he chose a cautious middle course, expanding the American role while trying to keep it limited. In the short run, such a course offered numerous advantages, but over the long run it was delusive

---

[5] John McCloy and Walt W. Rostow quoted in Fairlie, *Kennedy Promise*, pp. 132, 264.

[6] See, for example, Bruce Miroff, *Pragmatic Illusions* (New York, 1976), especially pp. 142–166.

and dangerous. It encouraged Diem to continue on his self-destructive path, while leading Americans to believe they could secure a favorable outcome without paying a heavy price. It significantly narrowed the choices, making extrication more difficult and creating a self-supporting argument for a larger and more dangerous commitment.

Throughout the presidential campaign, Kennedy had stressed the perils the nation confronted, but the new President himself appears to have been unprepared for the problems he inherited. Khrushchev's threat to resolve the status of divided Berlin on his own terms held out the possibility of a direct confrontation of the superpowers. In January 1961, the Soviet Premier delivered a militant speech avowing Soviet support for wars of national liberation. The statement may have been designed as much for Chinese as for American ears, but the Kennedy administration interpreted it as a virtual declaration of war. Stepped-up Soviet aid to Castro's Cuba and to insurgents in the Congo and in Laos appeared to confirm the magnitude of the threat. Such was the siege mentality that gripped the White House in early 1961 that Kennedy on one occasion greeted his advisers by grimly asking, "What's gone against us today?"[7]

Vietnam was not regarded as a major trouble spot in the administration's first hundred days. Eisenhower had not even mentioned it in his briefings, and it was only in January, after reading a gloomy report by Lansdale, that Kennedy learned of the steady growth of the insurgency and the increasing problems with Diem. Lansdale predicted a large-scale Vietcong offensive before the end of the year, but he concluded optimistically that a "major American effort" could frustrate the Communist drive for power. Persuaded as Truman and Eisenhower before him that Vietnam was vital to America's global interests, Kennedy routinely approved an additional $42 million in aid to support an expansion of the South Vietnamese Army.[8]

By the end of April, Kennedy's staff was again closely watching

[7] Quoted in Walt Whitman Rostow, *The Diffusion of Power: An Essay in Recent History* (New York, 1972), p. 170.

[8] McGeorge Bundy to Rostow, January 30, 1961, Kennedy Papers, National Security File, Box 192. For a detailed analysis of Kennedy's policies in the first year, see Stephen Pelz, "John F. Kennedy's 1961 Vietnam War Decisions," *Journal of Strategic Studies*, 4 (December 1981), 356–385.

Vietnam. Acting upon Ambassador Durbrow's advice, the President had conditioned the assistance granted in January on the institution of military and political reforms. But Diem had balked, and after three months the aid program remained stalled and the war against the Vietcong languished.

At the same time, major foreign policy setbacks in Cuba and Laos appeared to increase the importance of Vietnam. Clandestine operations against Castro ended in disaster at the Bay of Pigs, leaving Kennedy in a state of acute shock and his administration profoundly embarrassed. After the Bay of Pigs, Kennedy was suspicious of the Joint Chiefs of Staff and the intelligence community, and therefore rejected various proposals to put troops into Laos to stave off the impending defeat of the American-sponsored government. The military warned that protecting U.S. troops sent to Laos against possible Chinese or North Vietnamese countermoves might require extreme measures, even the use of nuclear weapons. The country was landlocked, a poor choice for intervention from the logistic standpoint, and many of Kennedy's advisers shared the view of Ambassador John Kenneth Galbraith that as a "military ally the entire Laos nation is clearly inferior to a battalion of conscientious objectors from World War I."[9] Moreover, as Kennedy himself repeatedly pointed out, it would be difficult to explain to the American public why he sent troops to remote Laos when he had refused to send them to nearby Cuba. In late April, the President concluded that a negotiated settlement was the best he could get in Laos, and the United States agreed to participate in a peace conference at Geneva.

More than anything else, the decision to negotiate in Laos led the administration to take a careful look at its policy in Vietnam. Along with the refusal to send troops to the Bay of Pigs, the unwillingness to intervene militarily in Laos appeared to increase the symbolic importance of taking firm stands elsewhere. The administration had captured the attention of the nation with its self-conscious activism, but in its first months it had little success. "At this point we are like the Harlem Globetrotters," McGeorge Bundy conceded, "passing forward, behind, sidewise, and underneath. But nobody has made a basket yet."[10] Kennedy informed *New York*

[9] Galbraith to Kennedy, May 10, 1961, Kennedy Papers, Office File, Box 29.
[10] Fairlie, *Kennedy Promise*, p. 180.

Times columnist Arthur Krock that he had to make certain that "Khrushchev doesn't misunderstand Cuba, Laos, etc. to indicate that the United States is in a yielding mood on such matters as Berlin."[11] Moreover, with the outcome of the Laos negotiations uncertain, it seemed urgent to prepare a fallback position in Southeast Asia, and most administration officials agreed that Vietnam, in contrast to Laos, would be a suitable place to make a stand.

Despite its growing concern with Vietnam, the administration did not institute major policy changes or drastically expand American commitments in the spring of 1961. The President authorized a modest increase in the MAAG of 100 advisers and dispatched to Vietnam 400 Special Forces troops to train the Vietnamese in counterinsurgency techniques. Convinced in the light of the Laos negotiations that Diem had to be handled with special care, Kennedy recalled Ambassador Durbrow, the foremost advocate of hard bargaining tactics, and sent Vice President Lyndon B. Johnson to Saigon to give personal assurances of American support. To support its diplomacy without provoking domestic or international concern, the administration waged covert warfare in Indochina. The United States sent clandestine teams of South Vietnamese across the seventeenth parallel to attack enemy supply lines, sabotage military and civilian targets, and agitate against the Hanoi regime. At the same time, the CIA initiated its "secret war" in Laos, arming some 9,000 Meo tribesmen for operations against the Ho Chi Minh trail in what would become one of the largest paramilitary operations ever undertaken.

The reappraisal of the spring of 1961 was more important for the questions it raised than for the solutions it provided, however. The administration's decisions reflected, in the words of White House adviser Walt W. Rostow, a calculated policy of "buying time with limited commitments of additional American resources."[12] But many officials feared that this might not be enough, and a task force appointed by Kennedy to review American options in Vietnam began to consider the more drastic measures that might be required if the Laos negotiations broke down or if the Communists launched a major offensive in Vietnam. Among other things, for the

---

[11] Krock memorandum of conversation with Kennedy, May 5, 1961, Arthur Krock Papers, Seeley G. Mudd Manuscript Library, Princeton, N.J., Box 59.

[12] Rostow, *Diffusion of Power,* p. 270.

first time since 1954 the task force openly raised the possibility of sending American combat forces to Vietnam, and also discussed air and naval operations against North Vietnam.

While the administration studied various choices, pressures mounted for expanded American involvement in Vietnam. After a whirlwind trip through the Far East with a major stopover in Saigon, Johnson reported that the decision to negotiate in Laos had shaken Diem's confidence in the United States and warned that if a further decline in morale was to be arrested, "deeds must follow words—soon."[13] In the aftermath of the Johnson visit, Diem himself requested additional aid. He displayed no interest in U.S. combat troops when the Vice President discreetly raised the issue. Fiercely independent and keenly aware of the rising opposition to his regime, Diem apparently feared that the introduction of large numbers of American troops would not only give the Vietcong a powerful rallying cry but would also give the non-Communist opposition critical leverage. Shortly after Johnson departed Saigon, however, Diem warned Kennedy that the situation in Vietnam had become "very much more perilous" and requested sufficient additional American aid and advisers to expand his army by 100,000 troops.[14]

The Cold War intensified in the summer of 1961, and some of Kennedy's advisers began to urge an all-out effort in Vietnam. During a stormy summit meeting in Vienna in June, Khrushchev again affirmed the Soviet commitment to wars of liberation, reinforcing the administration's fears. Rostow had long advocated the employment in Vietnam of such "unexploited counterguerrilla assets" as helicopters and the newly created Green Berets. "It is somehow wrong to be developing these capabilities but not applying them in a crucial theater," he advised Kennedy. "In Knute Rockne's old phrase, we are not saving them for the junior prom." The economist and former MIT professor compared the summer of 1961 to the year 1942 when the Allies were suffering defeats across the globe, and he warned Kennedy that "to turn the tide" the United States must "win" in Vietnam. If Vietnam could be held, Thailand, Laos, and Cambodia could be saved, and "we shall have

[13] Johnson to Kennedy, May 23, 1961, Kennedy Papers, Office File, Box 30.

[14] U.S. Congress, Senate, Subcommittee on Public Buildings and Grounds, *The Pentagon Papers* (*The Senator Gravel Edition*) (4 vols.; Boston, 1971), II, 60. Hereafter cited as *Pentagon Papers* (*Gravel*).

demonstrated that the Communist technique of guerrilla warfare can be dealt with."[15]

Preoccupied with more urgent matters such as Berlin, Kennedy fended off his more belligerent advisers and approved only small additional increments of aid until a dramatic worsening of conditions in the fall of 1961 compelled him to act. Infiltration into South Vietnam doubled to nearly 4,000 men in 1961. The Vietcong drastically stepped up their operations in September and for a brief period even seized a provincial capital just fifty-five miles from Saigon. Intelligence analysts reported a substantial increase in the size of Vietcong regular forces. The journalist Theodore H. White noted a "political breakdown of formidable proportions" in South Vietnam,[16] and in September, Diem urgently requested additional economic assistance. By early October, both the Joint Chiefs of Staff and the National Security Council were considering the introduction of sizable American combat forces into Vietnam.

Kennedy remained cautious. He expressed to Krock a profound reluctance to send American troops to the Asian mainland. He noted grave doubts that the United States should interfere in "civil disturbances caused by guerrillas," adding that "it was hard to prove that this wasn't largely the situation in Vietnam."[17] Increasingly concerned by the military and political deterioration in South Vietnam, but fearful of expanding the American commitment, he ordered Rostow and his personal military adviser General Maxwell D. Taylor to go to Vietnam to assess conditions firsthand and weigh the necessity of sending American forces.

Taylor and Rostow confirmed the pessimistic reports that had been coming out of Saigon for the past month. The South Vietnamese Army was suffering from what Taylor described as a "defensive outlook." The Diem government was disorganized, inefficient, and increasingly unpopular. The basic problem, they noted, was a "deep and pervasive crisis of confidence and a serious loss in national morale," stemming from developments in Laos, the intensification of Vietcong activity, and a devastating flood in the Mekong Delta. "No one felt the situation was hopeless," Taylor later re-

[15] Rostow to Kennedy, March 29, 1961, Kennedy Papers, National Security File, Box 192, and June 17, 1961, Kennedy Papers, Office File, Box 65.

[16] Quoted in *Pentagon Papers (Gravel)*, II, 70.

[17] Krock memorandum of conversation with Kennedy, October 11, 1961, Krock Papers, Box 59.

called, but all agreed that it was "serious" and demanded "urgent measures."[18]

Taylor and Rostow recommended a significant expansion of American aid to arrest the deterioration in South Vietnam. They emphasized that the Vietnamese themselves must win the war; the United States could not do it for them. They concluded, however, that the provision of American equipment and skilled American advisers working closely with the government at all levels could result in a "much better, aggressive, more confident performance from the Vietnamese military and civilian establishment."[19] Highly trained advisory groups, strategically placed throughout the South Vietnamese bureaucracy, could help to identify and correct major political, economic, and military problems. Improved training for the Civil Guard and the Village Self-Defense Corps would free the army for offensive operations, and equipment such as helicopters would give the army the mobility required to execute such operations effectively.

The most novel—and ultimately most controversial—of the Taylor-Rostow proposals was the dispatch of an 8,000-man "logistic task force," comprised of engineers, medical groups, and the infantry to support them. The ostensible purpose of the force would be to assist in repairing the massive flood damage in the Mekong Delta, but Taylor had other, more important motives in mind. Diem continued to resist the introduction of U.S. combat troops, but many government officials and many Americans in Saigon believed that troops were desperately needed. Taylor himself felt a "pressing need to do something to restore Vietnamese morale and to shore up confidence in the United States." The task force would serve as a "visible symbol of the seriousness of American intentions," he advised Kennedy, and would constitute an invaluable military reserve should the situation in South Vietnam suddenly worsen.[20] The humanitarian purpose of the force would provide a convenient pretext for its introduction into Vietnam, and it could be removed without embarrassment when its job was completed. Taylor and Rostow emphasized that their proposals constituted minimum steps, and, if they were not enough to save South Vietnam, the United States might have to take more drastic measures

[18] Maxwell D. Taylor, *Swords and Ploughshares* (New York, 1972), p. 241.

[19] Rostow, *Diffusion of Power*, p. 275.

[20] Taylor, *Swords and Ploughshares*, p. 239.

such as the dispatch of combat troops or the launching of offensive operations against North Vietnam.

While the Taylor-Rostow report was circulating in Washington, Undersecretary of State Chester Bowles and the veteran diplomat W. Averell Harriman, the chief American negotiator on Laos, were promoting a very different course. Harriman expressed grave doubt that Diem's "repressive, dictatorial and unpopular regime" could survive under any circumstances, and warned that the United States should not "stake its prestige in Vietnam." Bowles admonished that the United States was "headed full blast up a dead end street." The two men thus proposed that Kennedy defer any major commitment to Diem. If the Laos negotiations proceeded smoothly, the United States could then expand the conference to include Vietnam and seek an overall settlement based on the 1954 Geneva Agreements.[21] The Taylor report and the Bowles-Harriman proposals for the first time posed a clear-cut choice in Vietnam.

Kennedy flatly rejected a negotiated settlement. The administration had vowed to wage the Cold War vigorously, but in its first months it suffered apparent setbacks in Cuba and Laos, and in August the Russians, without warning, had constructed a steel and concrete wall sealing off East Berlin from the Western zone. Throughout the year, Republicans and right-wing Democrats had charged the administration with weakness, and Kennedy seems to have feared that a decision to negotiate on Vietnam would unleash domestic political attacks on him as rancorous and destructive as those which had followed the fall of China in 1949.

The President was equally concerned with the international implications, however. Administration strategists felt that it was essential in a divided and dangerous world to establish the credibility of America's commitments. Should the nation appear weak, its allies would lose faith and its enemies would be emboldened to further aggression, a process which, if unchecked, could at some point leave it with the awesome choice of a complete erosion of its position in the world or nuclear war. By late 1961, Kennedy and many of his advisers were convinced that they must prove their toughness to Khrushchev. "That son of a bitch won't pay any attention to

---

[21] Harriman to Kennedy, November 11, 1961, Kennedy Papers, National Security File, Box 195; Chester Bowles, *Promises to Keep* (New York, 1971), p. 409; Pelz, "Kennedy's Decisions," 378.

words," the President remarked during the Berlin crisis. "He has to see you move."[22] The "gut issue," Kennedy told his staff on November 14, was not whether Diem was a good ruler but whether the United States could continue to accept with impunity Communist "aggression" in South Vietnam. The moves the United States now made would be "examined on both sides of the Iron Curtain . . . as a measure of the administration's intentions and determination," and if it chose to negotiate it might "in fact be judged weaker than in Laos." Admitting the dangers of an expanded commitment in Vietnam, Kennedy nevertheless concluded that in cases where the United States had shown "strength and determination," it had "come home free."[23]

The President refused to go as far as Taylor advocated, however. Kennedy's advisers feared that the introduction of American combat troops into Vietnam might jeopardize the Laos negotiations or provoke an escalation of the conflict in Vietnam itself. They questioned whether the force proposed by Taylor would be large enough or, given its announced purpose of flood relief, whether it was capable of restoring morale. The force might come under attack, and the United States would then face the more difficult choice of backing it up with additional forces or withdrawing it altogether. "If we commit 6–8,000 troops and then pull them out when the going gets rough we will be finished in Vietnam and probably all of Southeast Asia," one National Security Council staff member warned.[24] Kennedy himself questioned the psychological value of the force and expressed fear that it would only lead to requests for more men. "The troops will march in; the bands will play; the crowds will cheer," he told Arthur Schlesinger, Jr., "and in four days everyone will have forgotten. Then we will be told we have to send in more troops. It's like taking a drink. The effect wears off, and you have to take another."[25]

Faced with the difficult choice of negotiating or sending combat troops, Kennedy opted for a middle-of-the-road approach. He

[22] Quoted in Paterson, "Bearing the Burden," 206.

[23] Kennedy memorandum, November 14, 1961, Kennedy Papers, Office File, Box 128.

[24] Robert Johnson to Bundy, October 31, 1961, Kennedy Papers, National Security File, Box 194.

[25] Quoted in Arthur M. Schlesinger, Jr., *A Thousand Days* (Boston, 1965), p. 547.

approved Taylor's recommendations to increase significantly the volume of American assistance and the number of advisers in the hope that this would be enough to arrest the military and political deterioration in South Vietnam. The administration took these steps in full recognition that it was violating the Geneva Accords of 1954, and on December 15 it released a "white paper" detailing North Vietnamese breaches of the Geneva Agreements and charging that Hanoi's renewal of aggression in South Vietnam justified the American response.[26]

In undertaking what Taylor described as a "limited partnership" with South Vietnam, the Kennedy administration at first took a hard line. American officials had long agreed that Diem's repressive and inefficient government constituted a major obstacle to defeating the insurgency. Reluctant to commit American men, money, and prestige to a "losing horse," as Secretary of State Dean Rusk put it, the administration instructed the Embassy in Saigon to inform the President that approval of the new aid program would be contingent on specific promises to reorganize and reform the government and to permit the United States a share in the decision-making process.[27]

The American demands provoked an immediate crisis in Saigon, however, and the administration quickly retreated. Diem angrily protested the limited nature of the American commitments and lashed out at the proposals for a new relationship, bluntly informing Ambassador Frederick Nolting that South Vietnam "did not want to be a protectorate."[28] The administration at first responded firmly, holding up shipments of military equipment and instituting a quiet search for a possible replacement for Diem. Ambassador Nolting strongly questioned the new policy, however, advising that a "cool and unhurried approach is our best chance of success."[29] And the State Department could identify no South Vietnamese politician who appeared capable of filling Diem's shoes.

[26] Department of State, *A Threat to the Peace: North Viet Nam's Effort to Conquer South Viet Nam* (Washington, D.C., 1961).

[27] Rusk to State Department, November 1, 1961, Kennedy Papers, National Security File, Box 194; *Pentagon Papers (Gravel)*, II, 120.

[28] Nolting to State Department, November 18, 1961, Kennedy Papers, National Security File, Box 165.

[29] Nolting to State Department, November 29, 1961, Kennedy Papers, National Security File, Box 195.

Convinced, as Kennedy put it, that "Diem is Diem and the best we've got," the administration backed down.[30] The new relationship was redefined to mean simply that one party would not take action without consulting the other, and the emphasis was shifted from reform to efficiency. The two governments agreed on an innocuous statement of principles affirming these points and the crisis passed.

The Kennedy decisions of 1961 mark yet another critical turning point in American involvement in Vietnam. Rejecting the extremes of negotiations on the one hand and the dispatch of combat troops on the other, Kennedy settled on a limited commitment of aid and advisers. He recognized from the start, however, that this might not be enough to save South Vietnam, and events would demonstrate that the commitment, once made, could not easily be kept limited. By giving in to Diem, moreover, the administration seriously compromised its own criteria for a successful counterinsurgency program. American firmness at this point would probably not have compelled Diem to change his ways, but it would at least have forced the issue before American prestige became more deeply involved. By deferring to Diem, the United States encouraged his intransigence and opened the way for conflicts that would make a mockery of the word "partnership" and would have tragic consequences for all concerned.[31]

Their differences resolved, at least for the moment, the United States and South Vietnam in early 1962 launched a two-pronged plan to contain the Vietcong insurgency. Supported by a vast increase in American equipment and advisers, the South Vietnamese Army took the offensive against the Vietcong. At the same time, the Diem government adopted the so-called strategic hamlet program, developed by the British counterinsurgency expert Sir Robert Thompson on the basis of experiences in Malaya and the Philippines, and designed to isolate the Vietcong from its principal source of support, the people of South Vietnam. According to Thompson's plan, peasants from scattered villages would be

---

[30] Quoted in Benjamin Bradlee, *Conversations with Kennedy* (New York, 1976), p. 59.

[31] Kennedy sought to solidify the middle course in Vietnam and in other areas through what became known as the "Thanksgiving Day Massacre" in which the "dovish" Bowles was removed as Undersecretary of State and the "hawkish" Rostow was sent to the State Department.

brought together into hamlets surrounded by moats and bamboo stake fences and protected by military forces. The hamlets were regarded not only as a means of protecting the people against Vietcong terror but also as the instrument of a social and economic revolution that would bind the people closely to the government. The reinstitution of village elections, the establishment of land reform programs, and the creation of schools and medical services would persuade the people that life under the government offered more than under the Vietcong. The ultimate objective, as Kennedy adviser Roger Hilsman put it, was to reduce the Vietcong to "hungry, marauding bands of outlaws devoting all their energies to remaining alive," and to force them out of their hideouts where they would have to fight the Army of the Republic of Vietnam (ARVN) on its terms.[32]

To support the counterinsurgency program, the United States, in what was called "Project Beefup," drastically expanded its role in Vietnam. The Military Assistance and Advisory Group was replaced by an enlarged and reorganized Military Assistance Command, Vietnam, located in Saigon and headed by General Paul Harkins. American military assistance more than doubled between 1961 and 1962, and included such major items as armored personnel carriers and more than 300 military aircraft. Kennedy authorized the use of defoliants to deny the Vietcong cover and to secure major roads, and on a limited basis the use of herbicides to destroy Vietcong food supplies.

The number of American "advisers" was increased from 3,205 in December 1961 to more than 9,000 by the end of 1962. Highly trained professionals, in many cases veterans of World War II and Korea, the American advisers epitomized the global commitment and "can-do" spirit of the Kennedy era. Their casual dress— brightly colored caps, shoulder holsters, and bandoleers—reflected their unusual mission. They stoically endured the harsh climate and the dysentery (promptly dubbed "Ho Chi Minh's revenge"), confident that they were not only defending Vietnam against a Communist takeover but were also preparing themselves for the wars of the future. "It's as important for us to train as the Vietnamese," a helicopter pilot informed an American journalist.[33] The advisers performed varied, ever-widening tasks. Special Forces units conducted

[32] Roger Hilsman, *To Move a Nation* (New York, 1967), p. 432.
[33] Quoted in Richard Tregaskis, *Vietnam Diary* (New York, 1963), p. 149.

Civic Action programs among the primitive Montagnards of the Central Highlands. Marine and Air Force helicopter pilots dropped detachments of ARVN troops into battle zones deep in the swamplands, and picked up the dead and wounded after engagements. Americans went with Vietnamese trainees on bombing and strafing missions, and when the Vietnamese ran short of pilots, they flew the planes themselves. Army officers and enlisted men conducted expanded training programs for the ARVN and the Civil Guard, and advisers down to the battalion level accompanied ARVN units on combat missions.

The massive infusion of American men and weapons provided an immediate boost to South Vietnamese morale. The helicopters proved a particularly formidable weapon and seemed almost by themselves to turn the war around. They gave the ARVN a "fantastic mobility," Hilsman later recalled. "Roaring in over the treetops, they were a terrifying sight to the superstitious Viet Cong peasant. In those first few months, the Viet Cong simply turned and ran—and, flushed from their foxholes and hiding places, and running in the open, they were easy targets."[34] Buoyed by the new weapons and by a new aggressive spirit, the ARVN conducted extensive operations against Vietcong strongholds in the spring and summer of 1962, and for the first time appeared to seize the initiative from the insurgents.

The advantage proved to be of short duration, however. Even with aircraft and sophisticated electronic equipment, it proved nearly impossible to locate Vietcong bases amidst the dense forests and swampy paddylands of South Vietnam. The very nature of the "air-phibious" operations—an air strike followed by the landing of troops—gave advance warning of an impending attack and permitted the insurgents to slip away. "You have to land right on top of them or they disappear," a frustrated American adviser complained, and one senior U.S. officer contemptuously dismissed the helicopter operations as "rattle-assing around the country."[35] Government forces would often bomb and strafe large areas and land sizable detachments of troops with little result, and when they withdrew, the Vietcong would reoccupy the region. The insurgents

---

[34] Hilsman, *To Move a Nation*, p. 444.

[35] Tregaskis, *Vietnam Diary*, p. 155; Malcolm W. Browne, *The New Face of War* (Indianapolis, 1968), p. 76.

quickly adapted to the helicopters, moreover. Sometimes they would stand and fight, and they learned to bring down the slow, clumsy aircraft with small arms. On other occasions, they would lie in hiding until the helicopters had departed and would then ambush the landing force.

By late 1962, the Vietcong had regained the initiative. While the ARVN and its U.S. advisers were chasing enemy main force units, the front concentrated on the villages. Combining superior organization and great skill in political indoctrination with the highly effective use of selective violence, the Vietcong enjoyed marked success mobilizing the peasants. By late 1962, it had gained an estimated 300,000 members and a passive following of more than one million. In some areas, the Vietcong even initiated land reform programs. Militarily, the NLF units became increasingly bold and began to inflict heavy losses on ARVN forces. As operations became more costly, ARVN commanders, apparently under orders from Diem, reverted to their old caution, relying more and more on airpower and refusing to risk their troops in battle. The shift in the fortunes of war was dramatically revealed in January 1963 when an ARVN force with vast superiority in numbers and firepower was ambushed near the village of Ap Bac, losing five helicopters and suffering heavy casualties.

The political implications of techniques employed in military operations increasingly disturbed some Americans in the field and civilians in Washington. It was difficult to distinguish between Vietcong and innocent civilians, and ARVN soldiers, their lives constantly under threat, were not inclined to make fine distinctions. Civilians, even women and children, were gunned down, giving the Vietcong a powerful propaganda weapon. The bombing and strafing of villages suspected of harboring Vietcong and the use of napalm and defoliants turned villagers against the government, and critics argued that they did more harm than good. American and South Vietnamese military officials insisted that air cover was essential to ground operations, however, and Diem and General Harkins vigorously promoted the use of napalm. It "really puts the fear of God into the Vietcong," Harkins exclaimed. "And that is what counts."[36]

The much ballyhooed strategic hamlet program also produced

[36] Quoted in Hilsman, *To Move a Nation*, p. 442.

meager results. "In its very conception," Frances FitzGerald has observed, "the program was a study in misplaced analogy."[37] A similar plan had worked well in Malaya, where Malay villages were fortified against Chinese insurgents, but in Vietnam the hamlets were to be erected against Vietnamese, many of whom had lived among the villagers for years, and the issuance of more than seven million laminated identification cards proved a less than adequate safeguard against infiltration. In theory, the program was to avoid the massive relocation of peasants from sacred ancestral lands, the flaw of the ill-fated agroville plan, but in the delta region where villagers lived in scattered settlements, the hamlets could not be established without displacement. The large-scale uprooting of the peasantry added to the discontent that had pervaded the rural population since Diem's ascent to power.

In addition, the plan was poorly implemented. By the end of 1962, the government claimed to have established 3,500 hamlets with 2,000 more under construction. In many cases, however, Diem and Nhu moved too far too fast, establishing hamlets in areas where no real security existed, and the vulnerable settlements were quickly overrun or infiltrated by the Vietcong. Many of the hamlets lacked adequate defenses. In a visit to Vietnam in 1963, Hilsman encountered several hamlets spread over such large areas that a full division would have been required to defend them. "But the defenders," he recalled, "were only a few old men, armed with swords, a flintlock, and half a dozen American carbines."[38]

In the hands of Diem and Nhu, moreover, the program did nothing to bind the people to the government. Land reform was not incorporated into the plan, and many peasants were left landless. The United States allocated substantial funds for the institution of services in the hamlets, but as a result of inefficiency or corruption much of the money never reached its destination. The government lacked qualified people to staff the program, and many incompetent and corrupt officials represented it at the village level. In any event, Diem and Nhu regarded the program primarily as a means of extending their control over the rural population, and the heavy-handed tactics of their lieutenants further alienated the people.

---

[37] Frances FitzGerald, *Fire in the Lake: The Vietnamese and the Americans in Vietnam* (Boston, 1972), p. 123.

[38] Hilsman, *To Move a Nation*, p. 456.

The strategic hamlet program did not accomplish its goal of winning the war at the "rice roots." As a means of protecting the villagers from direct Vietcong attack, the program enjoyed some limited, short-term success, and among the Montagnards in the Central Highlands, where the United States assumed a major role in "pacification," it played a constructive role. By early 1963, however, it was clear even to many of the program's most ardent supporters that it had basic flaws which if not corrected could be the source of great problems. In addition, fearing that even limited success on the part of the government would deprive it of its base among the rural population and leave its members as "fish on the chopping block," the NLF launched a systematic and effective campaign against key hamlets, creating specially trained units to destroy them by direct attack or infiltration.[39]

Some Kennedy advisers continued to insist that an effective counterinsurgency program required sweeping political reforms, but Diem stubbornly resisted such advice. To appease his American "partners," he instituted some token reforms, such as the creation of a council of economic advisers. Instead of broadening his government, as the Americans urged, he retreated more and more into isolation, relying almost exclusively on Nhu, a frail and sinister man who at least tended toward paranoia and delusions of grandeur. The two men personally controlled military operations in the field and directed the strategic hamlet program, and they brooked no interference from their American advisers. Nhu's wife, the beautiful, ambitious, and acid-tongued "Dragon Lady" (so called after a popular cartoon character to whom she bore at least a faint resemblance), increasingly assumed the role of spokesperson for what by 1962 had become a narrow family oligarchy.

The suspicious and beleaguered Ngos tightened rather than relaxed the controls. The National Assembly pliantly approved laws prohibiting all types of public gatherings, weddings and funerals included, unless approved by the government in advance. The regime imposed on Americans as well as Vietnamese the most rigor-

---

[39] William J. Duiker, *The Communist Road to Power in Vietnam* (Boulder, Colo., 1981), p. 214. "Second Informal Appreciation of the Status of the Strategic Hamlet Program," September 1, 1963, Kennedy Papers, National Security File, Box 202. For a full and balanced discussion of the program, see Douglas S. Blaufarb, *The Counterinsurgency Era: U.S. Doctrines and Performance* (New York, 1977), pp. 89–127.

ous censorship of all written material. Diem angrily terminated the contract of the Michigan State University advisory group when several of its members, upon returning to the United States, wrote articles which he branded "untrue, unfair, and tendentious."[40] The veteran *Newsweek* correspondent Francois Sully was expelled from Saigon for critical remarks about Madame Nhu.

Throughout 1962, Vietnam remained an operational, rather than a policy, problem. Preoccupied with more pressing matters such as the Soviet military buildup in Cuba, top American officials devoted little attention to Vietnam. Having decided the hard questions of policy in 1961, they were content to leave the implementation of that policy to the men in the field and did not consider any fundamental changes in approach. Kennedy flatly rejected Rostow's proposal to put pressure on the Russians to stop the infiltration of men and supplies from North Vietnam. He ignored Galbraith's warnings that the United States was becoming entrapped in a "long drawn out indecisive involvement" and might "bleed as the French did," as well as Bowles's proposal for an "agonizing reappraisal" of America's Vietnam policy.[41]

As late as the end of 1962, a reappraisal appeared unnecessary, for the Embassy and military command in Saigon exuded great optimism about the progress of the counterinsurgency program. Their confidence was clearly misplaced, and in time they appeared at best fools, at worst dissemblers. But the flaws in the program were more apparent later than at the time. Strangers in an unfamiliar country, the Americans were to a large extent dependent for their information on the South Vietnamese government, which produced impressive statistics to back its claims of progress. Nolting and Harkins erred badly in accepting these figures at face value, but the conflict did not lend itself to easy analysis; they, like other observers, were impressed by the change of climate since 1961, when the Diem government had appeared on the verge of collapse. American policy was working, they argued, and with time and patience victory was attainable.

In late 1962, the American press corps in Saigon began to chal-

---

[40] Wesley Fishel to John Hannah, February 17, 1962, Kennedy Papers, National Security File, Box 196.

[41] Galbraith to Kennedy, April 4, 1962, Kennedy Papers, National Security File, Box 196.

lenge the official optimism. Correspondents such as David Halberstam of the *New York Times* and Neil Sheehan of United Press International did not question the importance of containing
Communism in Vietnam, but they argued, with increasing bitterness, that the war was being lost. They denounced the Diem government as corrupt, repressive, and unpopular, and the strategic
hamlet program as a sham. They questioned official reports of military progress, arguing that the government's statistics were grossly
inflated and that the ARVN was conducting "office-hours warfare,"
launching perfunctory operations during the day and returning to
its bases in the evening. Blaming most of the problems on Diem,
they suggested that the war could not be won as long as the United
States persisted in its policy of "sink or swim with Ngo Dinh
Diem." The angry, defensive response of the Embassy and the military command ("Get on the team!" a top military official demanded of one dissident journalist) only enraged the newsmen and
provoked charges that the government was deliberately deceiving
the American people about the war.[42]

Other observers raised even more troublesome questions. Kennedy's old friend and former Senate colleague Mike Mansfield visited Vietnam at the President's request and returned in December
1962 with a highly pessimistic appraisal. In a formal, published
statement, Mansfield noted that he could find little progress since
he had last visited Vietnam in 1955, and in a private report to the
President he was even more blunt, comparing the role being assumed by the United States with that of France during the First
Indochina War and warning that the nation might be sucked into a
large-scale and futile conflict. "It wasn't a pleasant picture I depicted for him," Mansfield later recalled.[43]

Mounting criticism of American policy in Vietnam aroused
grave concern in Washington. The administration had attempted
to keep its involvement under wraps, but the rising toll of American deaths in combat and the critical newspaper reports raised
troublesome questions. State and Defense Department officials
spent hours investigating the journalists' reports and answering
their allegations, and Kennedy himself attempted unsuccessfully to

---

[42] The attitudes of the dissident journalists and their experiences are chronicled
in David Halberstam, *The Making of a Quagmire* (New York, 1964).

[43] Mike Mansfield oral history interview, Kennedy Papers.

get the *New York Times* to recall Halberstam. Highly sensitive to criticism, the President was apparently enraged by Mansfield's report. But he could not ignore the warnings of an old and valued friend, and he immediately dispatched Hilsman and Michael Forrestal, a member of the White House staff, on a fact-finding mission to Vietnam.

Delivered to the President in early 1963, the Hilsman-Forrestal report struck a middle ground between the harsh criticism of the journalists and the rosy optimism of the Embassy. The two men expressed serious reservations about the effectiveness of ARVN military operations, found flaws in the implementation of the strategic hamlet program, and advised that Diem had become increasingly isolated from the people. They concluded that the United States and South Vietnam were "probably winning," but quickly added that the war would "probably last longer than we would like" and "cost more in terms of both lives and money than we had anticipated."[44] Despite a generally pessimistic appraisal and cautiously optimistic conclusions, Hilsman and Forrestal found American policy to be sound in its conception and recommended only tactical changes to ensure more effective implementation. Their report reinforced doubts about the reliability of official estimates of progress, but it kept alive hopes that the United States might yet achieve what it had set out to do in Vietnam.

Throughout the spring of 1963, optimism and uncertainty coexisted uneasily in both Saigon and Washington. The Embassy and the military command persisted in their optimism, and General Harkins even informed a gathering of top officials in Honolulu in April that the war might be over by Christmas. Intelligence analyses were much more cautious, warning that the military situation remained fragile and unpredictable. In the White House, in the lower echelons of the Washington bureaucracy, and among some Americans in Vietnam, there was a gnawing uncertainty as to how the war was really going and severe doubt, if it were not going well, about which way to turn.

Growing evidence of Vietnamese-American tension compounded the uncertainty. The tension existed at all levels, and it was probably inevitable given the rapid American buildup in Vietnam and the vastly different approaches of the two peoples. Rest-

[44] Quoted in Hilsman, *To Move a Nation*, p. 464.

less and impatient by nature, the Americans were eager to get on with the job and were frustrated by the inertia that pervaded the government and army of South Vietnam. Their arrogance was frequently manifested, one U.S. adviser conceded, by an attitude of "Get out of my way, I'd rather do it myself!"[45] Proud and sensitive, having only recently emerged from Western rule, the Vietnamese bristled at the presumptuousness of the newcomers who sought to tell them how to run their country.

By the spring of 1963, relations at the top levels had become particularly tense. The Americans urged "democratic" reforms, in order, they said, to bring the government popular support, but Diem feared that such reforms might undermine, rather than strengthen, his position. Trapped in the dilemma he had feared from the start, he recognized that the American presence, although necessary to hold the line against the Vietcong, had introduced another—perhaps pivotal—element into the already unstable Vietnamese political situation, and he became more and more sensitive to American criticism. His growing uneasiness was clearly revealed in May 1963 when Nhu publicly questioned whether the United States knew what it was doing in Vietnam and opposed the further expansion of American advisers. Sometime in the early summer of 1963, Diem and Nhu began to explore the possibility of a settlement with Hanoi which would result in an American withdrawal from Vietnam.[46]

Kennedy appears to have been thinking along the same lines. The Joint Chiefs of Staff had initiated long-range planning on troop levels in 1962 to ensure a balance between the Vietnam commitment and America's other global requirements, and in 1963 had produced a plan calling for a phased withdrawal of American advisers to begin later in the year and to end in 1965. The plan seems to have reflected the Pentagon's persisting optimism about progress in containing the insurgency. Some members of Kennedy's staff have since argued, however, that the President's approval of it indicated his determination to avoid an open-ended commitment. Indeed, Hilsman and White House staff member Kenneth O'Don-

[45] Quoted in Chester Cooper, *The Lost Crusade: America in Vietnam* (New York, 1970), p. 207.

[46] For a discussion of the north-south contacts of 1963, see King C. Chen, "Hanoi's Three Decisions and the Escalation of the Vietnam War," *Political Science Quarterly*, 90 (Summer 1975), 254–255.

nell claim that by the summer of 1963 Kennedy had recognized the futility of American involvement and was prepared to liquidate it as soon as he had been reelected. "If I tried to pull out completely now from Vietnam," he reportedly explained to Mansfield, "we would have another Joe McCarthy red scare on our hands."[47] The extent to which Kennedy had committed himself remains unclear, but the plan for a phased withdrawal does seem to reflect his growing concern about Vietnam and the increasingly strained relationship with Diem.

At the very time Kennedy and Diem were having sober second thoughts about their fateful partnership, an upheaval among Buddhists in the major cities of South Vietnam suddenly introduced a dramatic new threat to the Diem regime and new complications for an already faltering American policy. The affair began on May 8, seemingly inadvertently, when government troops fired into crowds gathered in Hue to protest orders forbidding the display of flags on the anniversary of Buddha's birth. The May 8 incident stirred new and vigorous protest. Buddhist leaders accused the government of religious persecution and demanded complete religious freedom. Unable or unwilling to conciliate his new opponents, Diem heatedly denied the existence of persecution and blamed the disorders on the Vietcong. Diem's response stimulated additional protest. Buddhist priests conducted well-publicized hunger strikes, and meetings in Hue and Saigon drew large crowds. The uprising attained new proportions on June 11 when a monk immolated himself in front of large, shrieking crowds at a major intersection in downtown Saigon. Sensitive to the potential value of drawing international attention to their cause, the Buddhist leadership had tipped foreign newsmen to the event, and an American photographer's candid and poignant picture of the monk engulfed in flames soon appeared in newspapers and on television screens across the world.

From that fiery moment in June 1963, the Buddhist protest emerged into a powerful, apparently deeply rooted political movement that threatened the very survival of the Diem government. Quiescent in periods of stability, the Buddhists throughout Vietnamese history had assumed a role of political and moral leadership in times of crisis. The immolation of the elderly monk was a "call to

[47] Quoted in Kenneth P. O'Donnell and David F. Powers, *"Johnny, We Hardly Knew Ye": Memories of John Fitzgerald Kennedy* (New York, 1973), p. 16.

rebellion," Frances FitzGerald has written, and the disaffected urban population of South Vietnam responded.[48] Students in the universities and high schools, including some Catholics, joined in mass protests, and discontent quickly spread to the army. The government's response spurred additional anger. While Diem did nothing, Madame Nhu publicly and with seeming glee dismissed the immolations as "barbecues" and offered to furnish the gasoline and matches for more. By midsummer, South Vietnamese society appeared on the verge of disruption.

The crisis brought consternation to a Washington already uneasy over its Vietnam policy. The administration was caught off guard by the protest, surprised by the response it touched off and shocked by the immolation of the monk. Fearing that these ominous new developments might undercut American support for the war and further endanger a counterinsurgency program which many suspected was already failing, the administration frantically attempted to reconcile the two sides, sending numerous emissaries to talk with Buddhist leaders and pressing Diem to take conciliatory measures. The Americans could never really determine what the Buddhists wanted, however, and in any event Diem would agree only to token concessions. The demonstrations and immolations continued; in all, seven monks met fiery deaths. While Madame Nhu and the government-controlled Saigon press issued shrill tirades against the Buddhists and the United States, Nhu's police carted off hundreds of protesters to South Vietnam's already bulging jails.

By the late summer, the Kennedy administration was increasingly troubled and deeply divided. The Buddhist mind remained *"terra incognita,"* one Kennedy adviser later conceded, but most Americans agreed that Diem's response had been provocative.[49] The fear persisted that there was no real alternative to Diem and that a change in government might bring even greater chaos to South Vietnam. Some administration officials retained confidence in the President himself, blaming the problems on Nhu and his wife and arguing that the damage might yet be repaired if they could be removed. But others began to view the Buddhist crisis as symbolic of basic, incorrectable defects in the regime and concluded that the United States must face up to the possibility of a change.

[48] FitzGerald, *Fire in the Lake,* p. 134.
[49] Cooper, *Lost Crusade,* p. 210.

An incident in late August clinched the issue as far as Diem's opponents in Washington were concerned. Nolting's appointment as Ambassador expired in the summer of 1963, and during his farewell visit, Diem had assured him, as a personal favor, that no further repressive action would be taken against the Buddhists. But on August 21, Nhu's American-trained Special Forces carried out massive raids in Hue, Saigon, and other cities, ransacking the pagodas and arresting more than 1,400 Buddhists. Whether Diem approved the raid in advance remains unclear, but in the eyes of most Americans, his subsequent refusal to disavow Nhu's actions placed the onus of responsibility squarely upon him. This latest repressive action, just days after the solemn pledges to Nolting, appeared to the anti-Diemists a "deliberate affront" which demanded a firm response. "We could not sit still and be the puppets of Diem's anti-Buddhist policies," Roger Hilsman later recalled.[50]

Within several days after the raid on the pagodas, moreover, a group of South Vietnamese Army generals opened secret contacts with the United States. The most recent incident made clear, they warned, that Nhu would stop at nothing. Reporting evidence that he was not only planning their execution but was also discussing with Hanoi a deal that would sell out the independence of South Vietnam, the generals inquired how the United States might respond should they move against the government. The anti-Diem group in Washington was undoubtedly alarmed by the reports that Nhu was making overtures to Hanoi, reinforcing their conviction that something must be done. More important, perhaps, the generals' inquiries suggested that there was, after all, an alternative to Diem.

The generals' overtures arrived in Washington on a Saturday, when many top officials were out of town, and Hilsman, Forrestal, and Harriman seized the opportunity to execute what Taylor later described as an "egregious end run."[51] They prepared a tough, if somewhat ambiguous, cable, instructing the newly appointed Ambassador, Henry Cabot Lodge, to give Diem an opportunity to rid himself of Nhu but adding that if he refused, the United States must "face the possibility that Diem himself cannot be preserved." They

---

[50] Hilsman, *To Move a Nation*, p. 482; Hilsman oral history interview, Kennedy Papers. The best account of the abortive August coup is Geoffrey Warner, "The United States and the Fall of Diem," Part I: "The Coup That Never Was," *Australian Outlook*, 28 (December 1974), 245–258.

[51] Taylor, *Swords and Ploughshares*, p. 292.

also instructed Lodge to make clear to the generals that the United States would not continue to support Diem if he refused to cooperate and that it would provide them "direct support in any interim period of breakdown of central government mechanism."[52] These last words left deliberately vague what the United States might do and under what circumstances, but the thrust of the message was unmistakable: if Diem remained obdurate, the United States was prepared to abandon him. The cable was cleared with Kennedy, who was then vacationing on Cape Cod, and the President's endorsement was apparently used to secure the acquiescence of responsible officials in the Defense Department.

Lodge wasted no time implementing his instructions. The Ambassador shared Hilsman's outrage at the August 21 incident. There was no doubt in his mind, he later recalled, that the raid on the pagodas "marked the beginning of the end of the Diem regime."[53] His convictions were reinforced by his first meeting with Diem. When he warned that the regime's handling of the Buddhists was endangering American support for South Vietnam, Diem gave him a long lecture on the difficulties of governing a nation with a "dearth of educated people."[54] The Embassy subsequently contacted the generals through a CIA agent—"so the official American hand would not show"—offering them assurances of American support should they succeed in overthrowing the government but warning that the United States would not assist them in undertaking a coup or "bail them out" if they got into trouble.[55]

By the time Kennedy met with his advisers on Monday, August 26, the United States was deeply committed to a coup. The meeting was tense and marked by sometimes bitter exchanges. Taylor and Secretary of Defense Robert McNamara protested that instructions for a basic change in policy had been sent to Lodge behind their backs, and the President himself was apparently un-

[52] Telegram, August 24, 1963, U.S. Congress, House, Committee on Armed Services, *United States–Vietnam Relations, 1945–1967: A Study Prepared by the Department of Defense* (Washington, D.C., 1971), Book 12, 536–537.

[53] Lodge oral history interview, Kennedy Papers.

[54] Forrestal to Kennedy, August 26, 1963, Kennedy Papers, Office File, Box 128.

[55] Neil Sheehan et al., *The Pentagon Papers as Published by the New York Times* (New York, 1971), pp. 195–196. Hereafter cited as *Pentagon Papers (NYT)*. See also memorandum, "Contacts with Vietnamese Generals," October 23, 1963, Lyndon B. Johnson Papers, Lyndon B. Johnson Library, DSDUF, Box 2.

happy, feeling, as one of his advisers later put it, "that he had been painted into a corner and . . . would have preferred to give an even more ambivalent answer to the generals."[56] Significantly, however, Kennedy did not retreat from the policy that had been established. In subsequent messages, he advised Lodge to proceed cautiously, but he reaffirmed the instructions of August 24 and gave the Ambassador unusually broad discretion in their implementation. Lodge was authorized to repeat to the generals assurances that the United States would not assist a coup but that it would support a new government that appeared to have a good chance of success. And he was authorized, at his own discretion, to announce publicly a reduction in American aid to Diem, the signal the generals had requested as an indication of U.S. support.

While American officials in Washington and Saigon nervously awaited the generals' response, the plans for a coup gradually came unraveled. The leaders of the plot were unable to secure the support of key army units in the Saigon area and, despite the assurances given by the CIA go-between, they remained uncertain of American support. On August 31, they informed Harkins that the coup had been called off. "There is neither the will nor the organization among the generals to accomplish anything," Lodge cabled Washington with obvious disappointment.[57] Although the plot of August 1963 came to nothing, it nevertheless marked another major turning point in American policy in Vietnam. Many officials had grave reservations about the desirability, feasibility, and possible consequences of a coup, but the anti-Diemists were able to commit the administration to their point of view. By making such a commitment, the administration encouraged opponents of the regime and made difficult, if not impossible, any real reconciliation with Diem. As Lodge put it, the United States was "launched on a course from which there is no respectable turning back."[58]

Over the next four weeks, the Kennedy administration heatedly debated the choices open to it. Nhu sent his wife out of the country, perhaps as much out of concern for her personal safety as to appease the United States, but he stubbornly refused to resign, and the regime made no real effort to conciliate the Buddhists. Hilsman

[56] Cooper, *Lost Crusade*, p. 212.
[57] Quoted in *Pentagon Papers (Gravel)*, II, 240.
[58] Lodge to Rusk, August 29, 1963, *ibid.*, 738.

and others argued that there was no chance of stabilizing South Vietnam as long as Nhu remained, and warned that Nhu might already be committed to a deal with Hanoi that would force the United States out of Vietnam. They concluded that the administration must therefore apply firm pressure on Diem, including aid cuts, to compel him to remove Nhu and adopt the changes in policy necessary to defeat the Vietcong. Others, such as Nolting, advocated a final attempt at reconciliation. The failure of the August coup made clear, they argued, that there was no real alternative to Diem. The President was unlikely to remove Nhu, even under the most severe American pressure, and cuts in aid would only hurt the war against the Vietcong, antagonize the South Vietnamese people, and further destabilize the country. There was still a chance, they concluded, that if the United States repaired its relations with the government, the war might be won.

A "fact-finding" mission to South Vietnam only added to the uncertainty. General Victor Krulak of the Defense Department played down the possibilities of a coup and advised that the war could be won if the United States firmly supported Diem. In contrast, Joseph Mendenhall of the State Department reported a "virtual breakdown of the civil government in Saigon," warned of a possible religious war between Catholics and Buddhists, and concluded that there was no chance of defeating the Vietcong unless, "as a minimum, Nhu withdrew or was removed from the government." "You two did visit the same country, didn't you?" Kennedy remarked with obvious exasperation.[59]

The administration by this time was more divided on Vietnam than it had been on any other issue. Such was the confusion that at one point Attorney General Robert Kennedy raised the ultimate question, wondering aloud whether any South Vietnamese government was capable of winning the war and whether the United States should not begin to extricate itself from an impossible tangle.

The Attorney General's question was both appropriate and timely. The disarray in South Vietnam had reached a point that both factions in the administration may have been right—the country could not have been stabilized with or without Diem. Moreover, important new developments for the first time raised a glimmer of hope for a negotiated settlement. In the aftermath of

[59] Hilsman, *To Move a Nation*, p. 502.

the Cuban Missile Crisis of October 1962, the long-simmering feud between the Soviet Union and China burst out into the open, and the United States and Russia took the first halting steps toward a relaxation of Cold War tensions. The new and more complex international environment of 1963 may have provided the last real opportunity for a negotiated settlement in Vietnam. Much remains unknown about the north-south overtures of 1963. President Charles de Gaulle of France seems to have taken the initiative, proposing the removal of U.S. troops, the neutralization of South Vietnam, and economic and cultural exchanges between north and south preliminary to a political settlement. When Diem and Nhu seemed receptive, de Gaulle used a Polish diplomat to explore the prospects with Hanoi. Whether the de Gaulle initiative offered any possibility of a settlement remains unclear. Given the past record of hostility between Diem and Hanoi and the conflicting ambitions of each, it seems unlikely. Still, each had good reason to avoid the full-scale war that seemed increasingly possible if not likely, and de Gaulle's scheme, with great power support, might have produced a temporary settlement, giving the United States a graceful means to extricate itself from a situation that was fast becoming untenable. One of Kennedy's advisers was thinking along just such lines in proposing an imaginative, if highly complex, "triple diplomatic play" by which the United States would pull out of South Vietnam in return for a complete Soviet withdrawal from Cuba and would encourage France to work for a Vietnam free of all foreign influence. The United States and Russia could thereby liquidate unprofitable and potentially dangerous ventures without losing face, the more conciliatory Soviets would get the edge over the more aggressive Chinese, and de Gaulle would get the "glory of a solution in Viet Nam along with the headaches."[60]

Hindsight makes clear that such an approach had much to commend it, but the administration gave it no consideration. Kennedy was increasingly frustrated by a situation which was rapidly becoming unmanageable, but he was not yet ready to abandon a policy that had been set for more than a decade. The President and his advisers seem to have been so preoccupied with day-to-day events that they found it difficult to think in terms of a long-range solution. Perhaps they were captives of their own rhetoric and

[60] "Observations on Viet Nam and Cuba," n.d., Kennedy Papers, Office File, Box 128.

could not seriously consider a settlement which required an American withdrawal. Some American experts on Vietnam minimized the possibility of a reconciliation between north and south, arguing that Nhu was merely raising the specter to gain "some maneuverability in the face of US pressures."[61] Others took the possibility seriously but saw it as a good reason to get rid of Nhu and possibly Diem. For whatever reason, Robert Kennedy's question was not raised again. The administration drifted along, divided against itself, with no clear idea where it was going.

After more than a month of debate, Kennedy in early October settled on a short-run policy that, characteristically, split the difference between the two extremes promoted by his advisers. Still quite uncertain what was going on in South Vietnam, he dispatched Taylor and McNamara to Saigon to get the "best possible on the spot appraisal" of the military and political situation.[62] Probably on the basis of discussions with Lodge, the two men quickly rejected any notion of conciliating Diem, arguing that it would merely reinforce his belief that he could bend the United States to his will. To assess the prospects of a coup, a tennis match was arranged between Taylor and General Duong Van Minh, one of the leaders of the August plot, at the Saigon Officers Club. Minh's "sole interest that afternoon seemed to be tennis," Taylor later recalled, and the Americans surmised that the generals had "little stomach" for another attempt to overthrow the government.[63] Taylor and McNamara therefore concluded that the only practicable course was to apply "selective pressures," including cuts in foreign aid, to the regime. Such an approach would probably not force Diem to remove Nhu, but it might at least persuade him to stop oppressing political dissenters. Generally optimistic about the progress of the counterinsurgency program, McNamara and Taylor concluded that if Diem could be brought around, the insurgency might be reduced to "something little more than organized banditry" by the end of 1965.[64]

[61] Chester Cooper to Director, CIA, September 19, 1963, Kennedy Papers, National Security File, Box 200.

[62] Kennedy to McNamara, September 19, 1963, Kennedy Papers, National Security File, Box 200.

[63] Taylor, *Swords and Ploughshares*, p. 297.

[64] Taylor-McNamara Report, October 2, 1963, *Pentagon Papers (Gravel)*, II, 751–766.

Although it badly misjudged the actual conditions in South Vietnam, the Taylor-McNamara report formed the basis of subsequent U.S. policy. The relative quiet in the countryside in late 1963 resulted from a deliberate North Vietnamese-Vietcong attempt to encourage negotiations rather than from the effectiveness of the counterinsurgency program. Taylor and McNamara underestimated the prospects of a coup and overestimated the efficacy of applying pressure to Diem. Apparently seeing no other route to take, Kennedy approved their recommendations on October 5, and over the next few weeks, the administration gradually implemented the policy of "selective pressures." Lodge remained away from the presidential palace, insisting that Diem must come to him. In the meantime, the administration recalled the CIA station chief in Saigon, John Richardson, known among Vietnamese and Americans as a close friend of Nhu, cut off funds to Nhu's Special Forces, and suspended shipments of tobacco, rice, and milk, under the commodity import program.

A number of Kennedy advisers later emphatically denied that these measures were designed to stimulate a coup, and in the most literal sense they were correct. The McNamara-Taylor report had explicitly rejected encouragement of a coup, and the aid cuts were designed to pressure Diem. The administration was not as innocent as some of its defenders have maintained, however. Hilsman later conceded that "some of the things that we did encouraged the coup, some we intended as pressure on Diem, although we knew it [*sic*] would encourage a coup."[65] Kennedy and his advisers would have been naive indeed if they did not recognize that the recall of Richardson, whom the generals had feared would tip off the August plot, and the cuts in aid, the very signal of support the generals had requested earlier, would influence Diem's opponents. And the timing is significant. The aid cuts were instituted *after* the generals had once again inquired how the United States would respond to a coup. Whatever their intent, the measures taken during October probably encouraged the generals to step up their planning and seek further assurances from the United States.

Once aware that the generals were again planning a coup, the administration did nothing to discourage them. The response to their inquiry was sufficiently vague to salve the consciences of those

[65] Hilsman oral history interview, Kennedy Papers.

who preferred a coup but hesitated to accept direct responsibility for it and to satisfy the reservations of those who remained wary of dumping Diem. But the instructions offered the assurances the generals sought. Lodge was authorized to inform the plotters that although the United States did not "wish to stimulate a coup," it would not "thwart a change of government or deny economic and military assistance to a new regime if it appeared capable of increasing [the] effectiveness of the military effort, ensuring popular support to win [the] war and improving working relations with the U.S."[66]

With his administration sharply divided to the very end, Kennedy stuck by his compromise policy. Harriman, Hilsman, and others felt that Diem should go. Vice President Johnson, top CIA and Pentagon officials, and Harkins continued to insist that there was no real alternative and that Diem's removal would bring chaos to South Vietnam. They also felt, as Harkins put it, that it was "incongruous" after nine years of supporting Diem "to get him down, kick him around and get rid of him."[67] Kennedy himself vacillated, adhering to the policy of not overtly supporting a coup but not discouraging one either. In this case, however, not to decide was to decide, and by leaving matters in the hands of Lodge, whose views were well known, the President virtually assured the outcome. The major fear among Kennedy and some of his advisers in the anxious days of late October seems to have been that the coup might fail, leaving the United States in an untenable and embarrassing position. Yet, even here the President was content to leave in Lodge's hands a final judgment as to the likelihood of success and a decision whether to try to call off or delay the coup.

Throughout the last week of October, Saigon was gripped with tension and deluged with rumors as the various actors played out their complicated—and ultimately tragic—drama. Determined to avoid the mistakes of 1960 and August 1963, the generals lined up their forces with the closest attention to every detail. In the meantime, Nhu had concocted an elaborate scheme to keep himself and his brother in power by staging a fake coup and using it as an excuse for eliminating suspected opponents. To complicate matters

[66] CIA to Lodge, October 6, 1963, *Pentagon Papers (Gravel)*, II, 769. See also Geoffrey Warner, "The United States and the Fall of Diem," Part II: "The Death of Diem," *Australian Outlook*, 29 (March 1975), 3–17.

[67] Quoted in *Pentagon Papers (Gravel)*, II, 785.

still further, in the last hours before the real coup, Diem suddenly turned conciliatory toward the United States, inquiring of Lodge at their last meeting what the United States wanted of him. Whether he was merely trying to buy time or had concluded that he must place himself in the hands of the United States is unclear. In any event, Diem's apparent concession came too late.

While Diem was talking with Lodge in the early afternoon of November 1, the generals seized key military installations and communications systems in Saigon, secured the surrender of Nhu's Special Forces, and demanded the resignation of Diem and Nhu. Stubbornly resistant to the end, the brothers requested that the generals come to the palace for consultation, the ploy that had worked in 1960, and Diem phoned Lodge to determine the official American attitude toward the coup. Finding support nowhere, they escaped through a secret underground passage to a Catholic church in the Chinese district, where they went to confession and received communion. They were subsequently captured and, despite promises of safe conduct, were brutally murdered in the back of an armored personnel carrier.

Throughout the coup, the United States followed to the letter its promises "not to thwart a change of government." American officials later insisted that they knew nothing of the timing or exact plans for a coup. In fact, CIA agent Lucien Conein maintained close touch with the generals in the planning stages through clandestine meetings at a dentist's office, and he had telephone contact with them while the coup was actually taking place. The United States refused even to intervene to ensure the personal safety of Diem and Nhu. Kennedy did send an old crony to try to persuade Diem to get rid of Nhu and seek refuge in the Embassy. When Diem refused, however, the administration all but abandoned him. Lodge was considerably less than candid in the telephone conversation with Diem when he pretended ignorance of Washington's attitudes. During the last pathetic phone call, he offered to help, but he then went off to bed, leaving matters entirely in the hands of the coup forces. Perhaps he accepted at face value the generals' pledges to spare Diem and Nhu, or he may have feared that any action taken on behalf of the brothers would be interpreted as a violation of the earlier U.S. assurances not to interfere.

The news of the coup and the bloody deaths of the Ngos evoked mixed reactions. In Saigon, jubilant crowds smashed statues of

Diem, danced in the streets, and covered ARVN soldiers with gar-
lands of flowers. In the ancient Vietnamese tradition, the mandate
of heaven had passed. In Washington, some of Kennedy's advisers
accepted the news as a matter of course. "Revolutions are rough.
People get hurt," Roger Hilsman told a reporter.[68] Nolting, Richardson, and others held what one of the participants described as
the "only Washington wake" for the Ngo brothers. By all accounts,
Kennedy himself was deeply troubled. When he learned of the
slaying of Diem and Nhu, Taylor later recalled, "he leaped to his
feet and rushed from the room with a look of shock and dismay on
his face which I had never seen before."[69] Others noted that the
President was more depressed than at any time since the Bay of
Pigs, and they speculated that he realized that Vietnam had been
his greatest failure in foreign policy.[70]

Just three weeks later, Kennedy himself was assassinated in Dal-
las. His defenders, many of whom would become outspoken opponents of the war, would later argue that at the time of his death he
was planning to extricate the United States from what he had perceived to be a quagmire. The record suggests otherwise. In a
speech to have been given on the day of his death, he conceded that
commitments in third-world nations could be "painful, risky and
costly," but warned that "we dare not weary of the test."[71] In any
event, what Kennedy might have done can never be known, and his
administration must be judged on what it actually did during its
brief tenure. Kennedy and most of his advisers accepted, without
critical analysis, the assumption that a non-Communist Vietnam
was vital to America's global interests, and their rhetoric in fact
strengthened the hold of that assumption. That the President himself never devoted his full attention to Vietnam, as his defenders
claim, seems clear. He reacted to crises and improvised responses
on a day-to-day basis, seldom examining the implications of his actions. Nevertheless, his cautious middle course significantly enlarged the American role and commitment in Vietnam, and with
the coup, the United States assumed direct responsibility for the

[68] Quoted in Marguerite Higgins, *Our Vietnam Nightmare* (New York, 1965), p.
225.

[69] Taylor, *Swords and Ploughshares*, p. 301.

[70] Schlesinger, *A Thousand Days*, pp. 997–998.

[71] Quoted in Herbert S. Parmet, *JFK: The Presidency of John F. Kennedy* (New
York, 1984), p. 336.

South Vietnamese government. Although apparently troubled by growing doubts, Kennedy refused, even after the problems with Diem had reached the crisis point, to face the hard questions. Perhaps in concealing from the nation the dangers of the growing American involvement, he deluded himself. Whatever his fears or his ultimate intentions, he bequeathed to his successor a problem eminently more dangerous than the one he had inherited from Eisenhower.

CHAPTER 4

Enough, But Not Too Much: Johnson's Decisions for War, 1963–1965

Between November 1963 and July 1965, Lyndon Baines Johnson transformed a limited commitment to assist the South Vietnamese government into an open-ended commitment to preserve an independent, non-Communist South Vietnam. Johnson inherited from Kennedy a rapidly deteriorating situation in South Vietnam. Fearing that large-scale American involvement might jeopardize his chances of election in 1964 and threaten his beloved Great Society domestic programs, he temporized for over a year, expanding American assistance and increasing the number of advisers in hopes that a beefed-up version of his predecessor's policy might somehow stave off disaster. South Vietnam's survival appeared more in doubt than ever in early 1965, however, and over the next six months Johnson made his fateful decisions, authorizing a sustained air offensive against North Vietnam and dispatching American ground forces to stem the tide in the south. By July 1965, the United States was engaged in a major war on the Asian mainland.

In late 1963, North Vietnam significantly escalated the war. The overthrow of Diem had been at best a mixed blessing for Hanoi. It eliminated a potentially dangerous anti-Communist leader, but it also removed the rallying point of the opposition in South Vietnam, and for a time the revolutionary spirit ebbed in the south. Desertions from the NLF increased and recruitment stalled, and even where the government lost ground the Vietcong did not always gain. North Vietnam attempted to negotiate with the junta the sort of deal discussed with Diem, but it seems to have gotten

North and South Vietnam

nowhere and it saw no weakening of U.S. resolve. Determined to attain the goal that had eluded them in 1954, the North Vietnamese leaders increasingly recognized that they could not succeed without a major commitment of their own resources. At the Central Committee's Ninth Plenum in December 1963, the party leadership decided to instruct the Vietcong to step up its political agitation and military operations against the South Vietnamese government. More important, Hanoi decided to expand infiltration into the south and even to send its own regular units into the war. The North Vietnamese at this point seem to have been unsure of Soviet support and they recognized the possibility of war with the United States. In what turned out to be a colossal miscalculation, they gambled that rapid escalation might force the disintegration of South Vietnam, leaving the United States no choice but to disengage.

For Johnson and the United States, the road to war was longer and more torturous. After listening to Ambassador Lodge's gloomy assessment of the post-coup prospects of the Saigon government on November 24, 1963, Johnson claimed to feel like a catfish that had just "grabbed a big juicy worm with a right sharp hook in the middle of it." The new President expressed his determination to meet the Communist challenge, however, and he vowed not to let Vietnam go the way of China. He instructed Lodge to "go back and tell those generals in Saigon that Lyndon Johnson intends to stand by our word. . . ." Two days later, National Security Council Action Memorandum (NSAM) 273 incorporated his pledge into policy, affirming that it was "the central objective of the United States" to assist the "people and Government" of South Vietnam "to win their contest against the externally directed and supported communist conspiracy."[1]

During the first three months of Johnson's presidency, the situation in South Vietnam got steadily worse. Some Americans had assumed that the removal of Diem and Nhu would restore domestic harmony and promote political unity, but the effect was quite the opposite. Diem had systematically destroyed the opposition, and his death left a gaping political vacuum. Buddhists and Catholics

---

[1] Bill Moyers, "Flashbacks," *Newsweek* (February 10, 1975), 76; U.S. Congress, Senate, Subcommittee on Public Buildings and Grounds, *The Pentagon Papers* (*The Senator Gravel Edition*) (4 vols.; Boston, 1971), III, 17–20. Hereafter cited as *Pentagon Papers* (*Gravel*).

comprised the most coherent groups in the cities, but their hatred of each other was implacable and neither represented a viable political force. The Buddhists were splintered into a bewildering array of factions. Although tightly disciplined, the Catholics had no political program or mass appeal. The coup released long pent-up forces, and in the months that followed new groups proliferated, but they were leaderless and hopelessly fragmented. In the countryside, decay was also the norm. The removal of Diemist controls over information made clear that the statistics compiled by the government to demonstrate progress had been grossly in error. U.S. officials were alarmed to discover that the insurgents controlled more people and territory than had been assumed. The strategic hamlet program was in shambles, many of the key hamlets in the critical Mekong Delta having been torn down either by the Vietcong or their own occupants. The situation was "very disturbing," McNamara warned Johnson in late December, and unless the trend could be reversed within the next few months, South Vietnam might be lost.[2]

The junta that assumed power after the coup did little to arrest the decline. The twelve army officers who formed the Military Revolutionary Council had been educated in France and had spent most of their careers in French service. They lacked experience, had no program, and found little support among the various groups that had opposed Diem. Suspicious of each other and of competing groups within the army, uncertain which way to move, they isolated themselves in their headquarters near Saigon's Tan Son Nhut Airport and did little. The few actions they took merely added to the confusion. The removal of Diem's province chiefs brought paralysis to local administration, and Harkins was alarmed by the junta's efforts to limit the role of U.S. advisers.

On January 29, 1964, a group of younger officers headed by General Nguyen Khanh overthrew the divided, ineffectual junta. Khanh appears to have doubted, with good reason, the capacity of the junta to govern, and he justified the coup on the grounds that several members of the Council had secretly endorsed de Gaulle's proposals for a neutral South Vietnam. It seems clear, however, that the general resented being shunted aside by the junta and that he acted primarily out of personal ambition. The U.S. role in the

[2] McNamara to Johnson, December 21, 1963, Declassified Documents Reference System (R)88E. Hereafter cited as DDRS.

coup remains unclear. Harkins and his aides were disturbed by the junta's lack of aggressiveness and its independence, and they may have encouraged and even helped to implement Khanh's schemes. At the very least, the United States knew of the coup plot and did nothing to stop it.[3]

The coup reinforced Washington's growing doubts about its client state. Khanh was known as a militant anti-Communist and an able military commander. In his checkered career, however, he had supported the Vietminh and the French and had worked for and against Diem, and he could not have been judged reliable. Putting the best face on a bad situation, Lodge speculated that one-man rule might be preferable to a divided junta, and he was encouraged by Khanh's pledges to take bold and decisive action. Nothing would please the United States more, he informed the general, than "the sight of an oriental chief of state who wanted to go fast and did not hesitate to kick people in the rear end." Khanh's response—he hoped he would "pick the right rear ends to kick"—could not have offered much reassurance, however, and Lodge conceded that it would be premature to predict a long life for the new government.[4] The United States quickly recognized Khanh, but with little enthusiasm and even less confidence.

The Khanh government faced truly staggering problems. Military operations and the strategic hamlet program had come to a complete standstill. The government's authority was nonexistent throughout much of the countryside, and near anarchy prevailed in the cities. In Saigon the "atmosphere fairly smelled of discontent," General William Westmoreland later observed, with "workers on strike, students demonstrating, the local press pursuing a persistent campaign of criticism of the new government."[5] As Vietcong incidents increased in number and in boldness, the capital took on all the appearances of an armed camp. Government buildings, stores, even cafés, were surrounded by barbed wire, while soldiers stood guard in concrete sentry boxes reinforced with sandbags. Khanh himself took up residence in a house on the Saigon River where he could flee by boat if necessary. American intelligence warned that

[3] George McT. Kahin, "Political Polarization in South Vietnam: U.S. Policy in the Post-Diem Period," *Pacific Affairs*, 52 (Winter 1979–1980), 647–673; Paul Harkins Oral History Interview, U.S. Army Military History Institute, Carlisle Barracks, Pa.

[4] Lodge to Secretary of State, February 5, 1964, DDRS(75)215A.

[5] William C. Westmoreland, *A Soldier Reports* (Garden City, N.Y., 1976), p. 63.

unless the new government took charge immediately and dealt with its problems effectively, South Vietnam had, "at best, an even chance of withstanding the insurgency menace during the next few weeks or months."[6]

To Johnson and the men around him, the crisis of early 1964 could not have been more unwelcome. The new President had assumed office in a moment of great national tragedy and had set as his foremost task conducting an orderly transition and restoring calm. He attached great importance to passage of Kennedy's legislative program, long stalemated in Congress, both as a memorial to the fallen leader and as a springboard from which he could launch a campaign for election in his own right. From this standpoint, the emergence of a crisis in Vietnam could only be regarded as an intrusion.

But it was an intrusion that had to be handled effectively. Johnson viewed the American commitment in Vietnam as part of the Kennedy program he was sworn to uphold. From the moment he took office, moreover, questions had been raised about his capacity to handle complex problems of foreign policy, and he saw that Vietnam might be a test case for him in an election year. Recognizing his inexperience in foreign policy, Johnson retained Kennedy's top advisers and relied heavily on them. Secretary of State Rusk, Secretary of Defense McNamara, and National Security Adviser McGeorge Bundy had all played prominent roles in shaping Kennedy's Vietnam policy, and they had a deep personal stake in upholding that policy. Indeed, they felt very strongly that expansion of the American commitment since 1961 had itself significantly increased the importance of holding the line there.

By 1964, policymakers perceived the extent to which changes in world politics had challenged old assumptions. Americans differed in their assessment of the Sino-Soviet conflict. Some argued that it was only superficial, a question of tactics, and that in any contest with the West the two rivals would be drawn back together. Many felt by 1964 that the split was irreparable and that in time the two Communist giants might be at war with each other. Johnson's advisers also recognized that the Sino-Soviet conflict had significantly affected the struggle in Vietnam. Hanoi had sided with Peking, and Soviet influence in Vietnam was negligible. Some American policymakers further calculated that, although China

[6] Quoted in *Pentagon Papers* (*Gravel*), III, 42.

had provided North Vietnam verbal and material support, its assistance was not yet decisive, and in view of traditional Vietnamese fears of Chinese domination, Hanoi probably preferred it that way. These important developments thus undermined the old idea that, in Vietnam, as elsewhere, the United States confronted a monolithic Communism united in its drive for world domination.

In the eyes of administration foreign policy experts, however, the Vietnam conflict still had vital international implications. The Soviet Union appeared to be in a conciliatory phase, and some Americans entertained long-range hopes of détente. Nonetheless, no one could be absolutely certain that the Russians had abandoned their expansionist goals, and there was always the chance, as McNamara warned, that the "very keenness" of the competition with China might increase Soviet "aggressiveness."[7] Whatever the Soviet intent, many Americans agreed, as Ambassador to the United Nations Adlai E. Stevenson put it, that henceforth an "arrogant, aggressive, resourceful and resolute" China might assume leadership of the forces of world revolution.[8]

Southeast Asia appeared to offer abundant opportunities for Chinese troublemaking. While Vietnam teetered on the brink of disaster, the Laos agreement of 1962 was under fire from both right and left, and Cambodia's Prince Sihanouk had renounced American aid and called for an international conference to guarantee his nation's neutrality. In the meantime, Indonesia's flamboyant and mercurial Sukarno had initiated an intense flirtation with China and launched open warfare against the pro-Western government of Malaysia. American policymakers perceived that historic ethnic and national conflicts were as much the source of instability in Southeast Asia as Communism. But they feared that any sudden change in the status quo could have a far-reaching effect on that troubled region. China had suffered from chronic agricultural shortages and might, "as an act of desperation, attempt to overrun Southeast Asia" to get the food it needed. At the very least, the Chinese could be counted upon to exploit the political turmoil in the countries around their periphery.[9]

An outburst of "polycentrism" across the world aroused even

[7] McNamara statement to House Subcommittee on Appropriations, February 6, 1963, DDRS(75)150D.

[8] Stevenson to Johnson, November 18, 1964, DDRS(75)212B.

[9] McNamara statement to Senate Armed Services Committee, February 8, 1964, DDRS(75)151B.

greater concern in Washington. De Gaulle's France was directly challenging American leadership in Southeast Asia as well as in Europe. Rioting in Panama underscored the explosiveness of anti-Americanism in the Western Hemisphere, creating opportunities which Cuba's Fidel Castro might exploit. Long-range intelligence estimates warned that "revolution and disorder" had become "epidemic" throughout the emerging nations and posed a serious threat to a stable world order. The Communist powers, acting together or separately, might attempt to exploit the rising unrest in the underdeveloped countries, or they might be drawn into local conflicts against their will. The "disorderly character of so much of the world," the CIA warned, posed great obstacles to any real détente with the Soviet Union and increased the danger of confrontations which might lead to nuclear war.[10]

Johnson and his advisers thus found compelling reasons to hold the line in Vietnam. The immediate objective, the President explained, was to deter Chinese aggression in Southeast Asia and "give the people on the periphery of Asian Communism in time, the confidence, and the help they needed to marshal their own resources in order eventually to live in peace and stability with their powerful neighbors." Johnson and his advisers felt very strongly, however, that the way they responded to "Communist provocations" in Vietnam would have "profound consequences everywhere." They flatly rejected the notion advanced by many Europeans and some Americans that Asia was an area of secondary importance. When a French diplomat observed that the "stakes in Europe were enormous" but that if South Vietnam fell "we would not be losing much," Secretary of State Rusk hotly retorted that if the United States did not protect Vietnam, "our guarantees with regard to Berlin would lose their credibility." It was all "part of the same struggle." A firm stand in Vietnam would discourage any Soviet tendencies toward adventurism and encourage the trend toward détente. More important, it would ensure order and stability in a strife-torn world by demonstrating that violent challenges to the status quo would be resisted. "Our strength imposes on us an obligation to assure that this type of aggression does not succeed," Johnson affirmed.[11] The President and his advisers thus dismissed out of hand any thought of an American withdrawal from Vietnam

[10] CIA, "Trends in the World Situation," June 9, 1964, DDRS(75)251A.

[11] Johnson to Charles Bohlen, February 28, 1964, DDRS(75)97C; memorandum of conversation, Rusk and French Ambassador, July 1, 1964, DDRS(75)105A.

and rejected without serious consideration the neutralization scheme proposed by de Gaulle and endorsed by Senator Mike Mansfield and the columnist Walter Lippmann.

Despite his concern for Vietnam, the President was not prepared to employ American military power on a large scale in early 1964. Like Kennedy and Eisenhower before him, he had no enthusiasm for a massive engagement of American forces on the Asian mainland. Moreover, he and his advisers feared that Americanization of the war would further undercut the self-reliance of the Vietnamese. The introduction of large-scale American forces in Vietnam would provoke much hostile propaganda throughout the world. It might cause major disruptions at home, threatening Johnson's legislative program and his campaign for the presidency. Johnson therefore flatly rejected proposals developed by the Joint Chiefs of Staff to undertake major air and ground operations against North Vietnam.

After a major policy review in mid-March, the President concluded that the "only realistic alternative" was "to do more of the same and do it more efficiently."[12] NSAM 288, approved March 17, did state U.S. objectives in more sweeping terms than before, emphasizing as the essential U.S. goal the preservation of an independent, non-Communist South Vietnam. The administration still hoped that its program of military and economic assistance would be workable, however, and at this point merely attempted to provide the means to make it more effective. Aware that the most urgent problem was the weakness of the South Vietnamese government, Washington publicly made clear its support for Khanh and privately advised the U.S. mission to do everything possible to avert further coups. NSAM 288 also called for a national mobilization plan to put South Vietnam on a war footing and for significant increases in the size of the South Vietnamese armed forces. The President appointed General William Westmoreland, a capable paratrooper and veteran of World War II and Korea, to replace the ineffectual and perennially optimistic Harkins. Over the next nine months, the United States increased the number of its "advisers" from 16,300 to 23,300 and expanded its economic assistance by $50 million. "As far as I am concerned," Johnson advised

[12] Doris Kearns, *Lyndon Johnson and the American Dream* (New York, 1976), p. 196.

Lodge in April, "you must have whatever you need to help the Vietnamese do the job, and I assure you that I will act at once to eliminate obstacles or restraints wherever they may appear."[13]

Although the administration did little more than reaffirm existing policy in the spring of 1964, the attention of Washington planners was shifting increasingly toward North Vietnam. The change reflected a growing American concern over the infiltration of men and supplies from the north and mounting frustration with ground rules that permitted Hanoi to support the insurgency with impunity. Some U.S. officials seem also to have concluded that action against the north might somehow compensate for the lack of progress in the south. Others wished to signal Hanoi that it would have to pay a heavy price for its continued intervention. Although covert operations in North Vietnam had been notably unsuccessful, they were expanded in early 1964 to include intelligence overflights, the dropping of propaganda leaflets, and OPLAN 34A commando raids along the North Vietnamese coast. The administration also intensified its planning to prepare U.S. forces for possible "border control" operations into Cambodia and Laos, "tit-for-tat" retaliatory bombing raids into North Vietnam, and a series of "graduated overt pressures" against North Vietnam, including air attacks against military and industrial targets. Firm warnings were delivered to Hanoi through Canadian intermediaries that continued support for the insurgency could bring great devastation to North Vietnam itself. At an NSC meeting on March 17, top administration officials expressed confidence that increased military and economic aid would be enough to stem the tide in South Vietnam. They also agreed, however, that failure of the program outlined in NSAM 288 might leave them no choice but to take the war to North Vietnam.[14]

The spring of 1964 program, like the programs before it, produced meager results. Under American supervision, Khanh developed ambitious plans for bringing the government down to the village level, but there remained a vast gap between planning and implementation. By U.S. estimates, the Vietcong controlled more than 40 percent of the territory and more than 50 percent of the

[13] Johnson to Lodge, April 4, 1964, Johnson Papers, National Security File, Country File: Vietnam, Box 3.

[14] Summary record of NSC meeting, March 17, 1964, Johnson Papers, National Security File, NSC Meetings File, Box 1.

population of South Vietnam, and in many areas it was so firmly entrenched that it could not be dislodged without the application of massive force. Where it could function freely, the government was hampered by a shortage of skilled officials and by what one American described as "outmoded concepts, directives and practices, bureaucratic constipation, [and] insufficient on-the-spot resources."[15] As a result of spiraling desertion rates, the ARVN's strength remained well below the figure authorized before the projected increase. The army won a few minor engagements in the early summer, but it was never able to gain the initiative. American officials publicly lavished praise on Khanh's "able and energetic leadership," and Khanh dutifully followed American suggestions for gaining popular support, visiting numerous villages and cities and even making a series of "fireside chats." But while a word from well-placed Americans could topple governments in Vietnam, it could not induce stability, and mere speeches were inadequate to bring together South Vietnam's disparate political forces. Catholics and Buddhists mobilized against each other and agitated against a government neither trusted. After a period of quiescence, the students began to stir again. The government itself was rent by internal dissension, and a coup plot in July failed only because the United States made known its opposition. Maxwell Taylor, who replaced Lodge as Ambassador in midsummer, advised Washington in August that "the best thing that can be said about Khanh's government is that it has lasted six months and has about a 50-50 chance of lasting out the year."[16]

In the meantime, Hanoi had responded defiantly to American warnings. There is no reason to suppose that the North Vietnamese leaders wanted war with the United States. Rather, they seem to have remained hopeful that intensification of aid to the Vietcong would force the collapse of the South Vietnamese government, leaving the United States no choice but to abandon its ally. They may have dismissed the various U.S. "signals" as mere bluff. In any event, they were not prepared to abandon their goal in the face of American threats. In the spring and summer of 1964, North Vietnam mobilized its own forces for war, speeded up the transforma-

[15] William Colby memorandum, May 11, 1964, Johnson Papers, National Security File, Country File: Vietnam, Box 3.

[16] Quoted in *Pentagon Papers (Gravel)*, III, 82.

tion of the Ho Chi Minh Trail into a modern logistical network capable of handling large trucks, and began to prepare units of its own regular army for infiltration into South Vietnam intact. Premier Pham Van Dong bluntly informed Canadian Blair Seaborn in June that the stakes were high for North Vietnam as well as for the United States and that the NLF and its supporters were prepared to endure regardless of the cost. If the United States forced war upon North Vietnam, he concluded with a ringing declaration, "We shall win!"[17]

Under these circumstances, Americans increasingly looked north for a solution they could not find in the south. Alarmed by the persistent lack of progress in South Vietnam, annoyed by Hanoi's defiant response, and fearful that the North Vietnamese might seek to exploit the administration's presumed immobility in an election year, some of Johnson's advisers by the midsummer of 1964 had developed a full "scenario" of graduated overt pressures against the north, according to which the President, after securing a Congressional resolution, would authorize air strikes against selected North Vietnamese targets. Secretaries Rusk and McNamara finally rejected the program for fear that it would "raise a whole series of disagreeable questions" which might jeopardize passage of the administration's civil rights legislation, but the proposals clearly indicate the drift of official attitudes during this period.[18]

The administration implemented much of the proposed "scenario" in response to a series of incidents in the Gulf of Tonkin in early August. While engaged in electronic espionage off the coast of North Vietnam on the morning of August 1, the destroyer *Maddox* encountered a group of North Vietnamese torpedo boats. South Vietnamese gunboats involved in OPLAN 34A operations had bombarded the nearby island of Hon Me the preceding evening, and the North Vietnamese, apparently assuming that the *Maddox* had been supporting the covert attacks, closed in on the destroyer. In a brief and frenzied engagement, the *Maddox* opened fire, the patrol boats launched torpedoes, and aircraft from the *USS Ticonderoga* joined the fighting. The torpedo boats were driven away, and one was badly damaged.

[17] George C. Herring, ed., *The Secret Diplomacy of the Vietnam War: The Negotiating Volumes of the Pentagon Papers* (Austin, Tex., 1983), p. 8.

[18] McNamara-Rusk memorandum, June 11, 1964, Johnson Papers, National Security File, Country File: Vietnam, Box 4.

Johnson was reportedly enraged when he learned of the encounter, but no retaliation was ordered. "The other side got a sting out of this," Secretary of State Rusk remarked. "If they do it again, they'll get another sting."[19] To avoid any appearance of weakness and to assert traditional claims to freedom of the seas, the Navy ordered the *Maddox* to resume operations in the Gulf of Tonkin and sent the destroyer *C. Turner Joy* to support it. The United States was not seeking to provoke another attack, but it did not go out of its way to avoid one either. The administration kept the destroyers close to North Vietnamese shores, where they were vulnerable to attack. Eager for "open season" on the North Vietnamese, responsible military officials in the area were choosing targets for retaliatory raids before reports of a second attack began to come in.

On the night of August 4, while operating in heavy seas some sixty miles off the North Vietnamese coast, the *Maddox* and *Turner Joy* suddenly reported that they were under attack. The initial reports were based on sonar and radar contacts, both of which were admittedly unreliable under the adverse weather conditions, and on visual sightings of torpedoes and enemy searchlights on a night which one seaman described as "darker than the hubs of Hell." The captain of the *Maddox* later conceded that evidence of an attack was less than conclusive. North Vietnamese gunboats were probably operating in the area, but no evidence has ever been produced to demonstrate that they committed hostile acts.

This time, Washington was poised to strike back. Reports of an impending attack began to arrive in the capital early on the morning of August 4, and the Joint Chiefs immediately insisted that the United States must "clobber" the attackers. Throughout the morning, while the destroyers reported being under continuous attack, the Joint Chiefs worked out a series of retaliatory options ranging from limited air strikes against North Vietnamese naval installations to mining of parts of the coastline. When the President met with his advisers in the early afternoon, there was no doubt that an attack had taken place. The CIA pointed out quite logically that the North Vietnamese might be responding defensively to the commando raids on their territory, but the administration concluded that Hanoi was trying to make the United States appear a

---

[19] Quoted in John Galloway, *The Gulf of Tonkin Resolution* (Rutherford, N.J., 1970), p. 52. For a good short account, see "The 'Phantom Battle' That Led to War," *U.S. News & World Report* (July 23, 1984), pp. 56–67.

"paper tiger." Johnson and his advisers agreed, as McNamara put it, that "we cannot sit still as a nation and let them attack us on the high seas and get away with it." They quickly decided on a "firm, swift retaliatory [air] strike" against North Vietnamese torpedo boat bases.[20]

Although serious questions were subsequently raised about the nature and even existence of the alleged attacks, the administration stuck by its decision. "FLASH" messages from the *Maddox* arriving in Washington early in the afternoon indicated that "freak weather effects" on the radar and sonar, as well as "overeager" sonarmen, may have accounted for many of the reported torpedo attacks and enemy contacts. Contradicting earlier messages, the commander of the *Maddox* also reported that there had been no "visual sightings" and that a "complete evaluation" of all the evidence should be made before retaliation was ordered. McNamara postponed implementation of the air strikes temporarily to make "damned sure that the attacks had taken place." By late afternoon, however, he was convinced, on the basis of evidence which appears suspect. Ignoring the belated uncertainty of the men on the scene, the Secretary of Defense accepted at face value the judgment of the Commander-in-Chief, Pacific Fleet, Admiral U.S. Grant Sharp, in Honolulu, whose certainty was based on the first reports from the *Maddox* and intercepts of North Vietnamese messages indicating that two patrol boats had been "sacrificed." McNamara and his military advisers did not knowingly lie about the alleged attacks, but they were obviously in a mood to retaliate and they seem to have selected from the evidence available to them those parts that confirmed what they wanted to believe. Accepting McNamara's conclusions without question, Johnson in the late afternoon authorized retaliatory air strikes against North Vietnamese torpedo boat bases and nearby oil storage dumps. Described by the Joint Chiefs as a "pretty good effort," the strikes destroyed or damaged twenty-five patrol boats and 90 percent of the oil storage facilities at Vinh.[21]

The President also seized the opportunity to secure passage of

[20] "Chronology of Events, Tuesday, August 4 and Wednesday, August 5, 1964, Tonkin Gulf Strike," Johnson Papers, National Security File, Country File: Vietnam, Box 18; summary notes of 538th NSC meeting, August 4, 1964, Johnson Papers, National Security File, NSC Meetings File, Box 1; Rusk to Taylor, August 8, 1964, DDRS(75)845-H.

[21] "Chronology of Events," Johnson Papers, National Security File, Country File: Vietnam, Box 18; "Transcripts of Telephone Conversations, 4–5 August," Johnson Papers, National Security File, Country File: Vietnam, Box 228.

a Congressional resolution authorizing him to take "all necessary measures to repel any armed attacks against the forces of the United States and to prevent further aggression." Johnson did not seek the resolution as a blank check for a later expansion of the war to which he was already committed. At this point, he still hoped that American objectives in Vietnam could be achieved by limited means. His main purpose rather was to indicate to North Vietnam that the nation was united in its determination to stand firm in Vietnam. The resolution also served immediate domestic political needs. The show of force and the appeal for national support permitted him to disarm his Republican challenger, Senator Barry Goldwater, who had vigorously urged escalation of the war, and to demonstrate that he could be firm in defending American interests without recklessly expanding the war. In presenting its case, however, the administration deliberately misled Congress and the American people. Nothing was said about the covert raids. Official reports indicated that the *Maddox* was engaged in routine patrols in international waters. The incidents were portrayed as "deliberate attacks" and "open aggression on the high seas."

Congress responded quickly and pliantly. Senator Wayne Morse of Oregon raised some embarrassing questions about the covert raids and the mission of the American destroyers. Senator Ernest Gruening of Alaska attacked the resolution as a "predated declaration of war," and Senator Gaylord Nelson of Wisconsin attempted to limit the grant of authority to the executive. During a period when America's national interests seemed constantly in peril, however, Congress had grown accustomed to approving executive initiatives without serious question, and the crisis atmosphere seemed to leave no time for debate. "The American flag has been fired upon," Representative Ross Adair of Indiana exclaimed. "We will not and cannot tolerate such things."[22] The Senate debated the resolution less than ten hours, during much of which time the chamber was less than one-third full. By his own admission more concerned with the challenge posed by Goldwater than with giving a blank check to Johnson, Senator J. William Fulbright carefully shepherded the resolution through, choking off debate and amendments. The vote in the Senate was an overwhelming 88 to 2, with only Morse and Gruening dissenting. Consideration

[22] Quoted in Anthony Austin, *The President's War* (Philadelphia, 1971), p. 98.

in the House was even more perfunctory, passage taking a mere forty minutes and the vote unanimous.

From a domestic political standpoint, Johnson's handling of the Tonkin Gulf incident was masterly. His firm but restrained response to the alleged North Vietnamese attacks won broad popular support, his rating in the Louis Harris poll skyrocketing from 42 to 72 percent overnight. He effectively neutralized Goldwater on Vietnam, a fact which contributed to his overwhelming electoral victory in November. Moreover, this first formal Congressional debate on Vietnam brought a near-unanimous endorsement of the President's policies and provided him an apparently solid foundation on which to construct future policy.

In time, Johnson would pay a heavy price for his easy victory. U.S. prestige was now publicly and more firmly committed not merely to defending South Vietnam but also to responding to North Vietnamese provocations. By attacking North Vietnamese targets, the President temporarily silenced his hawkish critics inside and outside of government, but in doing so he had broken a long-standing barrier against taking the war to the north. The first steps having been taken, the next ones would be easier. Johnson's victory in Congress probably encouraged him to take the legislators lightly in making future policy decisions on Vietnam. And when the administration's case for reprisals later turned out to be less than overwhelming, many members of Congress correctly concluded that they had been deceived. The President's resounding triumph in the Tonkin Gulf affair brought with it enormous, if still unforeseen, costs.

The Johnson administration did not follow up the Tonkin Gulf reprisals with additional attacks against North Vietnam. The President preferred not to jeopardize his political fortunes by escalating the war. Having established his determination to defend American interests with force if necessary, in the final months of the campaign he emphasized his wish to limit American involvement if possible. "We seek no wider war," he stated in numerous speeches.

At the same time, political turmoil in South Vietnam made caution essential. Attempting to exploit the Tonkin Gulf affair to save his political skin, Khanh on August 6 assumed near-dictatorial powers and imposed severe restrictions on civil liberties. Thousands of Saigonese immediately took to the streets, and when an angry mob forced Khanh to stand atop a tank and shout "Down with dictatorships," the humiliated General resigned. For days, near anarchy reigned in Saigon, mobs rampaging through the streets, Buddhists and Catholics waging open warfare, and gangs of thugs fighting and pillaging with hatchets and machetes. Behind the scenes, politicians and generals, Khanh included, jockeyed for power.

Under these circumstances, the administration concluded that it would be unwise to escalate the war. By early September, the Air Force and Marine Corps were vigorously pressing for extended air attacks against North Vietnam. Ambassador Taylor and others conceded that such steps would have to be taken in time, but they argued that it would be too risky to "overstrain the currently weakened GVN [Government of Vietnam] by drastic action in the immediate future." Johnson concurred, stating that he did not wish to "enter the patient in a 10-round bout, when he was in no shape to hold out for one round. We should get him ready to face 3 or 4 rounds at least," the President concluded. While holding other options in reserve, the administration decided merely to continue its covert operations against North Vietnam and to be ready to respond to North Vietnamese provocations on a "tit for tat basis."[23] Johnson remained sufficiently concerned about the internal situation in South Vietnam that he refused to retaliate when the Vietcong on November 1 attacked the U.S. air base at Bien Hoa, killing four Americans and destroying five aircraft.

By the end of November, however, a firm consensus had emerged that the United States must soon undertake what Taylor described as a "carefully orchestrated bombing attack" against North Vietnam.[24] American officials disagreed among themselves as to the reasons for the bombing, some viewing it as a way of boosting morale in South Vietnam, others as a means of cutting down on infiltration from the north, and still others as a weapon to force Hanoi to stop its support of the insurgency. They also disagreed on the type of bombing campaign that should be mounted. The Joint Chiefs pressed for a "fast and full squeeze"—massive attacks against major industries and military targets. Civilians in the Pentagon and State Department advocated a "slow squeeze," a graduated series of attacks beginning with infiltration routes in Laos

[23] McGeorge Bundy memorandum for the record, September 14, 1964, Johnson Papers, National Security File, Country File: Vietnam, Box 6.

[24] Taylor to State Department, August 18, 1964, *Pentagon Papers (Gravel)*, III, 547.

and slowly extending to targets in North Vietnam. Despite warnings from the intelligence community that bombing would probably not have a decisive impact on the war in the south, the great majority of Johnson's advisers endorsed the use of air power in some form.

Only Undersecretary of State George Ball vigorously dissented. An experienced diplomat who as Counsel to the French Embassy had observed firsthand the French defeat in Indochina, Ball forcefully argued that an air offensive would not solve the American dilemma in Vietnam. The contention that bombing North Vietnam would improve morale in the south was at best unproven, he warned. There was good reason to doubt, moreover, whether air power would compel Hanoi to stop its support of the insurgency, and if it did whether the south would be able to defeat the Vietcong. In Ball's view, the risks of escalation outweighed the possible gains. Hanoi might retaliate by pouring its virtually unlimited manpower into the south, forcing the United States to respond in kind and raising the possibility of a drawn-out and bloody conflict. American escalation might provoke Chinese intervention or even force the Soviet Union and China to put aside their differences. Most important, the United States could not be certain of controlling events after the process of escalation had been initiated. "Once on the tiger's back," Ball concluded, "we cannot be sure of picking the place to dismount."[25]

Ball's argument had little impact in Washington. Johnson's advisers conceded that the bombing might not achieve its objectives, but they were prepared to take the chance. At the very least, they argued, it would give the government of Vietnam a "breathing spell and opportunity to improve." They were confident, moreover, that they could control the risks of escalation. Moscow's role in Vietnam was "likely to remain a relatively minor one." A limited bombing campaign that did not threaten the survival of North Vietnam would give China no pretext for intervention, and Vietnam's historic fears of Chinese domination would lead Hanoi to discourage large-scale Chinese involvement. Most important, the consequences of a possible defeat in Vietnam made the risks acceptable. China had just exploded a nuclear weapon, increasing its prestige and its potential for troublemaking in the Far East, and

[25] George W. Ball, "Top Secret: The Prophecy the President Rejected," *The Atlantic,* 230 (July 1972), 35–49. See also George W. Ball, *The Past Has Another Pattern* (New York, 1982), especially pp. 380–385.

American officials concluded that it was more urgent than ever to hold the line in Vietnam. "We should delay China's swallowing up Southeast Asia until (a) she develops better table manners and (b) the food is somewhat more indigestible," Michael Forrestal observed.[26] Convinced that something must be done to avert a total collapse in South Vietnam and that bombing was less risky than the introduction of ground forces, the administration turned to air power as the only acceptable solution to an urgent problem.

By the end of November, Johnson's senior advisers had formulated concrete proposals for the use of American air power in Vietnam. Rejecting the more extreme program of the Joint Chiefs of Staff, they advocated a two-phase plan of gradually intensifying air attacks. The first phase, to last roughly a month, consisted of limited bombing raids against infiltration routes in Laos, along with reprisal strikes against North Vietnamese targets in response to any provocative acts. In the meantime, Taylor would use the promise of direct strikes against North Vietnam to persuade the South Vietnamese leadership to put its house in order. Once the Saigon government had reached an acceptable level of stability, the United States would move into phase two, a large-scale air offensive, lasting from two to six months, to be followed, if necessary, by a naval blockade of North Vietnam.

Persisting instability in Saigon delayed implementation of the program for more than two months. On December 1, Johnson approved immediate initiation of phase one bombing operations in Laos, but he would go no further. Insisting that it was "easy to get in or out" but "hard to be patient," he ordered Taylor to do what was necessary to get the South Vietnamese to pull together. He would not send American boys "out to die" while the South Vietnamese were "acting as they are." Moreover, if the United States was going to "slap" North Vietnam, the South Vietnamese and Americans must be prepared to "take a slap back." "We don't want to send a widow woman to slap Jack Dempsey." The President and his advisers agreed that there would be reprisals, but they deferred a decision on the timing and the form these should take.[27] Johnson would not even retaliate when the Vietcong on Christmas Eve

[26] Forrestal to William Bundy, November 23, 1964, *Pentagon Papers (Gravel)*, III, 644.

[27] Meeting on Vietnam, December 1, 1964, Johnson Papers, Meeting Notes File, Box 1.

bombed an American officers' billet in Saigon, killing two Americans and injuring thirty-eight. The President later justified his inaction on the grounds that reprisals might have provoked further Vietcong attacks at a time when "the political base in the South . . . was probably too shaky to withstand a major assault by the Communists."[28]

By the end of January 1965, however, the major argument against escalation had become the most compelling argument for it. After Khanh's resignation, a civilian government had been formed, but it was never able to consolidate its position. Upon his return to Saigon, Taylor called together the top political and military leaders and informed them that the United States would consider escalating the war if they could work together and stabilize the government. The answer came within several days when a group of younger military officers headed by Vice Air Marshal Nguyen Cao Ky and General Nguyen Chanh Thi executed a "purge" that amounted to a coup. Outraged, Taylor called the officers together and lectured them as a drill instructor might talk to a group of recruits. Perhaps something was wrong with his French, he asked sarcastically, for the officers had obviously not understood his injunction for stability. "Now you have made a real mess," he added angrily. "We cannot carry you forever if you do things like this."[29]

The harsh reprimand produced some "shame-faced grins," Taylor later recalled, but no results.[30] The military finally agreed to cooperate with civilian politicians in forming a new government, but Buddhist leaders refused to participate and launched a new round of demonstrations, hunger strikes, and immolations which took on increasingly anti-American tones. Protesters publicly demanded the resignation of Taylor, and in late January 5,000 students sacked the United States Information Service library in Hue. Rumors of coup plots abounded throughout the month, and American officials began to fear that there might emerge out of the chaos a new government willing to negotiate with the Vietcong and North Vietnam on the basis of a U.S. withdrawal. In the meantime,

---

[28] Lyndon B. Johnson, *The Vantage Point* (New York, 1971), p. 121.

[29] Quoted in Neil Sheehan et al., *The Pentagon Papers as Published by the New York Times* (New York, 1971), pp. 371–381.

[30] Maxwell D. Taylor, *Swords and Ploughshares* (New York, 1972), p. 330.

the Vietcong had decimated two elite South Vietnamese units in major battles. Combined with reports that North Vietnamese regular units were now entering the south, the defeats aroused growing fears that the enemy had decided to launch an all-out attack which the ARVN could not withstand. "To take no positive action now," Taylor ominously warned, "is to accept defeat in the fairly near future."[31]

By the end of January, most of Johnson's advisers agreed that persisting instability in the south required the United States to bomb the north. The bombing might not have a decisive impact on the war, William Bundy advised, but it offered "at least a faint hope of really improving the Vietnamese situation." More important, the impending collapse in South Vietnam made clear that a continuation of existing policies could "only lead to a disastrous defeat." Even if the United States could not hold South Vietnam, Assistant Secretary of Defense John McNaughton argued, it would appear stronger to allies and adversaries alike if it "kept slugging away" rather than meekly accepting defeat. No formal policy decision was made, but by the end of January most administration officials agreed that the United States should seize the first opportunity to launch air strikes and should then "feel its way" into a sustained bombing campaign against North Vietnam.[32]

The opportunity was not long in coming. On February 6, Vietcong units attacked a U.S. Army barracks in Pleiku and a nearby helicopter base, killing nine Americans and destroying five aircraft. That evening, after a meeting of less than two hours, the administration decided to strike back. Only Senator Mansfield dissented, arguing that the United States might provoke Chinese intervention, but Johnson brusquely dismissed Mansfield's argument. "We have kept our guns over the mantel and our shells in the cupboard for a long time now," he exclaimed with obvious impatience. "I can't ask our American soldiers out there to continue to fight with one hand behind their backs."[33] The President ordered the immediate implementation of FLAMING DART, a plan of reprisal strikes already drawn up by the Joint Chiefs of Staff. Later that day and again the following day American aircraft struck North Vietnamese military installations just across the seventeenth parallel. When the

[31] Johnson, *Vantage Point*, p. 122.
[32] Bundy to Rusk, January 6, 1965, *Pentagon Papers* (*Gravel*), III, 685.
[33] Johnson, *Vantage Point*, p. 125.

Vietcong on February 10 attacked an American enlisted men's quarters at Qui Nhon, the President ordered another, even heavier series of air strikes.

Within less than forty-eight hours, the administration had moved from reprisals to a continuing, graduated program of air attacks against North Vietnam. McGeorge Bundy returned from a visit to South Vietnam the day after the Pleiku raids and warned that "without new U.S. action defeat appears inevitable—probably not in a matter of weeks or perhaps even months, but within the next year or so." Bundy and McNaughton, who had accompanied him to Vietnam, urged the immediate implementation of a policy of "sustained reprisal" against the north. McNaughton conceded the risks but argued that "measured against the cost of defeat" the program would be "cheap," and even if it failed to turn the tide "the value of the effort" would "exceed the costs."[34] The next day, apparently without extended debate, the administration initiated ROLLING THUNDER, the policy of gradually intensified air attacks which Bundy and McNaughton had advocated.

The administration was considerably less than candid in explaining to the American public the reasons for and significance of its decision to bomb North Vietnam. Spokesmen from the President down justified the air strikes as a response to the Pleiku attack and emphatically denied implementing any basic change of policy. It is abundantly clear, however, that Pleiku was the pretext rather than the cause of the February decision. The possibility of a South Vietnamese collapse appeared to make essential the adoption of a policy American officials had been advocating for more than two months. It was, therefore, simply a matter of finding the right opportunity to justify measures to which the administration was already committed. Pleiku provided such an opportunity, although it could as easily have been something else. "Pleikus are like streetcars," McGeorge Bundy later remarked.[35] And despite the administration's disclaimers, the February decisions marked an important watershed in the war. The initiation of regular bombing attacks advanced well beyond the limited "tit-for-tat" reprisal strikes of Tonkin Gulf and provided a built-in argument for further escalation should that become necessary.

Indeed, almost as soon as ROLLING THUNDER got under

[34] *Ibid.*, pp. 127–128.

[35] Quoted in Anthony Lake, ed., *The Vietnam Legacy* (New York, 1976), p. 183.

way, there were pressures to expand it. The initial attacks achieved
meager results, provoking Taylor to complain that ROLLING
THUNDER had constituted but a "few isolated thunder claps" and
to call for a "mounting crescendo" of air strikes against North
Vietnam.[36] Intelligence reports ominously warned that the military
situation in South Vietnam was steadily deteriorating and that at
the present rate the government within six months might be reduced to a series of islands surrounding the provincial capitals.
From the outset, Johnson had insisted on maintaining tight personal control over the air war; "they can't even bomb an outhouse
without my approval," he is said to have boasted.[37] But in response
to these urgent warnings, the President permitted a gradual expansion of the bombing and a relaxation of the restrictions under
which it was carried out. The use of napalm was authorized to ensure greater destructiveness, and pilots were given the authority to
strike alternative targets without prior authorization if the original
targets were inaccessible. In April, American and South Vietnamese pilots flew a total of 3,600 sorties against North Vietnamese
targets. The air war quickly grew from a sporadic, halting effort
into a regular, determined program.

The expanded air war also provided the pretext for the introduction of the first U.S ground forces into Vietnam. Anticipating
Vietcong attacks against U.S. air bases in retaliation for ROLLING
THUNDER, General Westmoreland in late February urgently requested two Marine landing teams to protect the air base at Danang. Although he conceded the importance of protecting the base,
Taylor expressed grave concern about the long-range implications
of Westmoreland's request. He questioned whether American
combat forces were adequately trained for guerrilla warfare in the
Asian jungles, and he warned that the introduction of such forces
would encourage the ARVN to pass military responsibility to the
United States. Most important, the introduction of even small numbers of combat troops with a specific and limited mission would
violate a ground rule the United States had rigorously adhered to
since the beginning of the Indochina wars, and once the first step
had been taken it would be "very difficult to hold [the] line."[38]

Taylor's objections were in many ways prophetic, but they

---

[36] *Pentagon Papers (Gravel)*, III, 335.

[37] Westmoreland, *Soldier Reports*, p. 119.

[38] *Pentagon Papers (Gravel)*, III, 418.

were ignored. The need appears to have been so pressing and immediate, the commitment so small, that the decision was made routinely, with little discussion of its long-range consequences. After less than a week of apparently perfunctory debate, the President approved Westmoreland's request, and on March 8, two battalions of Marines, fitted out in full battle regalia, with tanks and 8-inch howitzers, splashed ashore near Danang where they were welcomed by South Vietnamese officials and by pretty Vietnamese girls passing out leis of flowers. It was an ironically happy beginning for what would be a wrenching experience for the two nations.

As Taylor had predicted, once the first step had been taken it was very difficult to hold the line. Alarmed by the slow pace of the ARVN buildup and fearful of a major Vietcong offensive in the Central Highlands, Westmoreland concluded by mid-March that if the United States was to avert disaster in Vietnam there was "no solution . . . other than to put our own finger in the dike."[39] He therefore advocated the immediate commitment of two U.S Army divisions, one to the highlands and the other to the Saigon area. The Joint Chiefs forcefully endorsed Westmoreland's request. Long impatient with the administration's caution and eager to assume full responsibility for the war, they even went beyond Westmoreland, pressing for the deployment of as many as three divisions to be used in offensive operations against the enemy.

The administration now found itself on what McNaughton called "the horns of a trilemma." The options of withdrawal and a massive air war against North Vietnam had been firmly rejected. It was apparent by mid-March, however, that the limited bombing campaign undertaken in February would not produce immediate results, and Westmoreland's urgent warnings raised fears that further inaction might lead to a South Vietnamese collapse. Many administration officials therefore reluctantly concluded that there was no alternative but to introduce American ground forces into Vietnam. They fully appreciated, on the other hand, the possible domestic political consequences of the sort of commitment Westmoreland proposed. And Taylor ominously warned that to place major increments of American forces in the highlands would invite heavy losses, even the possibility of an American Dienbienphu.

The administration resolved its "trilemma" with a compromise,

---

[39] Westmoreland, *Soldier Reports*, p. 126.

rejecting the proposals of Westmoreland and the Joint Chiefs but still approving a significant commitment of ground forces and an enlargement of their mission. At a conference in Honolulu in late April, McNamara, Taylor, and the Joint Chiefs put aside their differences and agreed upon a hastily improvised strategy, the object of which was to "break the will of the DRV/VC by depriving them of victory." The bombing would be maintained at its "present tempo" for six months to a year. But the conferees agreed, as McNamara put it, that bombing "would not do the job alone."[40] They therefore decided that some 40,000 additional U.S. ground combat forces should be sent to Vietnam. These forces were not to be used in the highlands or given an unrestricted mission, as Westmoreland and the Joint Chiefs had advocated, but would be used in the more cautious "enclave strategy" devised by Taylor. Deployed in enclaves around the major U.S. bases, their backs to the sea, they would be authorized to undertake operations within fifty miles of their base areas. The administration hoped that this limited commitment of forces would be adequate to deny the enemy a knockout blow, thus allowing time for the South Vietnamese buildup and for the bombing to take its toll on Hanoi. Although the April decisions stopped short of the commitment urged by the military, they advanced well beyond the original objective of base security and marked a major step toward a large-scale involvement in the ground war. The new strategy shifted emphasis from the air war against North Vietnam to the war in the south, and by adopting it, the administration at least tacitly committed itself to expand its forces as the military situation required.

By this time Johnson recognized that achievement of American objectives in Vietnam would require a sustained and costly commitment, but he refused to submit his policies to public or Congressional debate. Many administration officials shared a view widely accepted at the height of the Cold War that foreign policy issues were too complex and too important to be left to an indifferent and ignorant public and a divided and unwieldly Congress. Johnson seems to have feared that a declaration of war might trigger a Chinese or Soviet response or increase domestic pressures for an unlimited conflict in Vietnam. He particularly feared, as he later

---

[40] McNamara to Johnson, April 21, 1965, Johnson Papers, National Security File, Country File: Vietnam, Box 13.

put it, that a Congressional debate on "that bitch of a war" would destroy "the woman I really loved—the Great Society."[41] The President's unparalleled knowledge of Congress and his confidence in his renowned powers of persuasion encouraged him to believe that he could expand the war without provoking a backlash, and the repeated deference of the Congress to executive initiatives gave him no reason to anticipate a major challenge.

Johnson thus took the nation into war in Vietnam by indirection and dissimulation. The bombing was publicly justified as a response to the Pleiku attack and the broader pattern of North Vietnamese "aggression," rather than as a desperate attempt to halt the military and political deterioration in South Vietnam. The administration never publicly acknowledged the shift from reprisals to "sustained pressures." The dispatch of ground troops was explained solely in terms of the need to protect U.S. military installations, and not until June, when it crept out by accident in a press release, did administration spokesmen concede that American troops were authorized to undertake offensive operations.

Although the administration effectively concealed the direction of its policy, the obvious expansion of the war, particularly the bombing, attracted growing criticism. White House mail ran heavily against the bombing. A few newspapers joined the *New York Times* in warning of the cost of "lives lost, blood spilt and treasure wasted, of fighting a war on a jungle front 7,000 miles from the coast of California." Prominent Democratic Senators such as Frank Church, Mike Mansfield, and George McGovern called upon the President to search for a negotiated settlement. Professors at the University of Michigan, Harvard, and Syracuse conducted all-night "teach-ins," students on various campuses held small protest meetings and distributed petitions against the bombing, and in April 12,000 students gathered in Washington to march in protest against the war.

Escalation also aroused widespread criticism abroad and brought forth, even from some of America's staunchest allies, appeals for restraint. United Nations Secretary General U Thant of Burma had been trying for months to arrange private talks between the United States and North Vietnam, and when the administration responded coolly to his overtures and initiated the bombing he

[41] Quoted in Kearns, *Johnson*, p. 251.

publicly charged that Washington was withholding the truth from the American people. In early April, seventeen nonaligned nations issued an "urgent appeal" for negotiations without precondition. Great Britain as co-chairman of the Geneva Conference called upon the parties to the conflict to state their terms for a settlement. And in a move that particularly galled Johnson, Canadian Prime Minister Lester Pearson, speaking on American soil, appealed to Washington to stop the bombing and work for a peaceful settlement.

The administration moved quickly to counter its critics. White House aides organized "Target: College Campuses," sending their "best young troops," to speak at universities and bringing professors and student leaders to Washington for "seminars."[42] The President invited dissident Congressmen and newspaper editors and representatives of foreign governments in for sessions that sometimes lasted for three hours, vigorously defending his policies and reminding his visitors of past favors. Administration spokesmen publicly replied to their critics, revealing from the start an abrasiveness and arrogance that would steadily widen the gap between Washington and opponents of the war. Addressing the American Society for International Law, Secretary of State Rusk expressed incredulity at the "stubborn disregard of plain facts by men who are supposed to be helping our young to learn . . . how to think."[43]

The administration also sought to disarm its critics by several dramatic peace initiatives. In a speech at Johns Hopkins University on April 7, Johnson affirmed that the United States was prepared to enter into "unconditional discussions" and even held out the offer of a billion-dollar economic development program for the Mekong River Valley region, a program "on a scale even to dwarf our TVA."[44] In early May, the President, with considerable reluctance, approved a five-day bombing pause, accompanied by private messages to Hanoi indicating that a diminution of North Vietnamese and Vietcong military activity could lead to a scaling down of U.S. air attacks.

The President was unquestionably sincere in his desire for peace, but the spring 1965 initiatives were designed primarily to

[42] Jack Valenti to McGeorge Bundy, April 23, 1965, Johnson Papers, National Security File, Country File: Vietnam, Box 13.

[43] Quoted in *Time* (April 30, 1965), 29.

[44] *Public Papers of the Presidents of the United States, Lyndon B. Johnson, 1965* (Washington, D.C., 1966), I, 394–399.

silence domestic and international critics rather than to set in motion determined efforts to find a peace settlement. Despite Johnson's offer to participate in "unconditional discussions," the United States had no real desire to begin serious negotiations at a time when its bargaining position was so weak. Indeed, it had not even begun internal discussions to formulate a program for negotiations. The President made clear in his Johns Hopkins speech, moreover, that the United States would not compromise its fundamental objective of an independent South Vietnam, which, by implication, meant a non-Communist South Vietnam. And administration officials were certain that the North Vietnamese would not negotiate on this basis.

As expected, the peace moves brought the two nations no closer to negotiations. No more inclined than the United States to make concessions under duress, Hanoi denounced the bombing pause as a "worn-out trick of deceit and threat," and refused to curb its military activities. The extent to which North Vietnam was willing to negotiate at this point is unclear, but in any event the United States offered little inducement for negotiations. On April 8, Pham Van Dong did release a four-point program for negotiations. In theory at least, much of the program did not conflict with basic U.S. objectives, and some American officials urged further contacts to explore Hanoi's position in greater depth. But the President and his top advisers interpreted the statement that a settlement must be in "accordance with the program of the National Liberation Front" as only a thinly disguised cover for Communist domination of South Vietnam and saw no reason to discuss it further.

The peace moves did help still domestic and foreign criticism, at least temporarily, and the administration used the respite to solidify Congressional support. On May 4, Johnson presented Congress with a request for $700 million to support military operations in Vietnam and made clear that he would regard a vote for the appropriation as an endorsement of his policies. The basic decisions had already been made, of course, and the President did nothing to clarify the policy he was actually pursuing. It was very difficult for the legislators to vote against funds for troops already in the field, and Congress approved the request quickly and without dissent. Johnson would later cite this vote, along with that on the Tonkin Gulf Resolution, to refute those critics who said he had not given Congress an opportunity to pass on his policy in Vietnam.

In the three months after the May bombing pause, the Johnson administration edged inexorably toward its decision for war in Vietnam. Despite the bombing, continued increases in U.S. aid, and the small infusion of American ground forces, the military situation deteriorated drastically. At this most critical phase of the war, the ARVN was on the verge of disintegration. The desertion rate among draftees in training centers ran as high as 50 percent. Discouraged by the failure of the bombing to turn the war around and displaying a growing tendency to "let the Americans do it," the officer corps grew more cautious than usual. The high command was "close to anarchy" from internal squabbling and intrigue.[45] Bolstered by as many as four regiments of North Vietnamese regulars, the Vietcong took the offensive in May, and in major engagements in the highlands and just north of Saigon mauled ARVN forces and inflicted huge casualties. The defeats increased Westmoreland's already pronounced doubts about the ARVN's capabilities, and the heavy losses completely upset his plans for building up the South Vietnamese Army. By the end of May, he had concluded that major increments of U.S. forces would be required to avert defeat in Vietnam.

The political situation showed no signs of improvement. Khanh had continued to play a dominant political role after his resignation in August 1964, resuming the premiership for a brief period and then taking command of the armed forces. After more than a year at or near the center of power, during which time he had sharply exacerbated the divisions in South Vietnam, the embattled general finally withdrew from politics in February 1965 and to the relief of the Americans accepted an appointment as "roving ambassador." Following an impossibly confusing series of coups and countercoups, a civilian government was formed headed by Phan Huy Quat, and relative quiet prevailed for a time. When Quat attempted to shake up his cabinet in May, however, another crisis developed and the so-called Young Turks, Air Marshal Nguyen Cao Ky and General Nguyen Van Thieu, finally emerged from the shadows, dissolving the Quat government and assuming power. The new government, the fifth since the death of Diem, would survive far longer than any of its predecessors, but at the outset its future seemed uncertain. Thieu, who assumed the posi-

---

[45] William Depuy memorandum for the record, March 9, 1965, and memorandum to Westmoreland, April 13, 1965, William Depuy Papers, U.S. Army Military History Institute, Carlisle Barracks, Pa., Folder D(65).

tion of Commander-in-Chief of the armed forces, was respected by the Americans as a capable military leader, and Taylor regarded him as a man of "considerable poise and judgment."[46] The Prime Minister, Ky, was another matter entirely. Customarily attired in a flashy flying suit with a bright purple scarf and an ivory-handled pistol hanging ostentatiously on his hip, the flamboyant, musta-chioed Air Marshal had a well-earned reputation for "drinking, gambling and chasing women," as well as for speaking out of turn and using the air force for personal political intrigue.[47] The Ameri-cans found it hard to take Ky seriously and saw little cause for op-timism in his accession to power. The Ky-Thieu directorate "seemed to all of us the bottom of the barrel, absolutely the bottom of the barrel," William Bundy later recalled.[48]

Under these circumstances, Johnson's advisers again began pressing for vigorous action to stave off what appeared to be cer-tain defeat. Long frustrated by the restrictions on the bombing, Westmoreland, the Joint Chiefs, and Walt Rostow of the State De-partment urged intensification of the air war. The present level of bombing, they contended, was merely inconveniencing Hanoi, and the restraints had given North Vietnam the freedom to strengthen both its offensive and defensive capabilities. Rostow, in particular, argued that military victory was within grasp if the United States would strike directly against North Vietnam's industrial base.

At the same time, Westmoreland and the Joint Chiefs advo-cated a drastic expansion of American ground forces and the adop-tion of an offensive strategy in the south. More certain than ever that South Vietnam lacked sufficient manpower to hold the line on its own, Westmoreland, with the support of the Joint Chiefs, re-quested an additional 150,000 U.S. troops in early June. Tradi-tionalists in their attitude toward the use of military power, West-moreland and the Joint Chiefs had opposed the enclave strategy from the start and now insisted that it be abandoned in favor of an aggressive, offensive strategy. "You must take the fight to the enemy," General Earle Wheeler, the Chairman of the Joint Chiefs affirmed. "No one ever won a battle sitting on his ass."[49] Indeed, by

[46] Taylor, *Swords and Ploughshares*, p. 345.

[47] CIA memorandum, October 8, 1964, Johnson Papers, National Security File, Country File: Vietnam, Box 7.

[48] William Bundy oral history interview, Johnson Papers.

[49] Graff, *Tuesday Cabinet*, p. 138.

the summer of 1965, even Ambassador Taylor conceded, as he later put it, that "the strength of the enemy offensive had completely overcome my former reluctance to use American ground troops in general combat."[50]

Only George Ball and Washington attorney Clark Clifford, a frequent personal adviser to Johnson, vigorously opposed a major commitment of American ground forces. Ball expressed profound doubt that the United States could defeat the Vietcong "or even force them to the conference table on our terms, no matter how many hundred thousand *white, foreign* (U.S.) troops we deploy." He expressed grave concern that approval of Westmoreland's proposals would lead to a "protracted war involving an open-ended commitment of U.S. forces, mounting U.S. casualties, no assurances of a satisfactory solution, and a serious danger of escalation at the end of the road." Once committed, he warned, there could be no turning back. "Our involvement will be so great that we cannot—without national humiliation—stop short of achieving our complete objectives." Clifford concurred, urging the President to keep U.S. forces to a minimum and to probe "every serious avenue leading to a possible settlement." "It won't be what we want," he concluded, "but we can learn to live with it."[51]

The clinching argument was provided by McNamara after another of his whirlwind visits to Saigon in early July. The Secretary of Defense underscored the pessimistic reports from Westmoreland and Taylor, and warned that to continue "holding on and playing for the breaks" would only defer the choice between escalation and withdrawal, perhaps until it was "too late to do any good." McNamara conceded that the expansion of American involvement would make a later decision to withdraw "even more difficult and costly than would be the case today." On the other hand, it might "stave off defeat in the short run and offer a good chance of producing a favorable settlement in the longer run." The Secretary recommended the gradual deployment of an additional 100,000 American combat forces.[52]

In late July, Johnson made his fateful decisions, setting the

[50] Taylor, *Swords and Ploughshares,* p. 347.

[51] Ball to Johnson, July 1, 1965, in Sheehan, *Pentagon Papers (NYT),* pp. 449–454; Clifford to Johnson, May 17, 1965, Johnson Papers, National Security File, Country File: Vietnam, Box 16.

[52] Johnson, *Vantage Point,* pp. 145–146.

United States on a course from which it would not deviate for nearly three years and opening the way for seven years of bloody warfare in Vietnam. The President did not approve the all-out bombing campaign urged by Westmoreland and the Joint Chiefs. He and his civilian advisers continued to fear that a direct, full-scale attack on North Vietnam might provoke Chinese intervention. They also felt that the industrial base around Hanoi was a major trump card held by the United States and that the threat of its destruction might be more useful than destruction itself. The administration approved Westmoreland's request to use B-52s for saturation bombing in South Vietnam and permitted a gradual intensification of the bombing of North Vietnam; sorties increased from 3,600 in April to 4,800 in June and would continue to increase thereafter. Johnson kept tight control over the bombing, personally approving the targets in advance of each strike and restricting air attacks to the area south of the twentieth parallel.

At the same time, the President approved a major new commitment of ground forces and a new strategy to govern their deployment. Determined to prevail in Vietnam and increasingly alarmed by the reports of steady military and political decline, in July he approved the immediate deployment of 50,000 troops to South Vietnam. Recognizing that this would not be enough, however, he privately agreed to commit another 50,000 before the end of the year, and implicitly, at least, he committed himself to furnish whatever additional forces might be needed later. Johnson also authorized Westmoreland to "commit U.S. troops to combat independent of or in conjunction with GVN forces in any situation . . . when . . . their use is necessary to strengthen the relative position of GVN forces."[53] These decisions rank among the most important in the history of American involvement in Vietnam. In July 1965, Johnson made an open-ended commitment to employ American military forces as the situation demanded. And by giving Westmoreland a free hand, he cleared the way for the United States to assume the burden of fighting in South Vietnam.

Some of Johnson's advisers strongly recommended that he place the July decisions squarely before the nation. The Joint Chiefs pressed for mobilization of the reserves and calling up the National Guard to make clear, as Wheeler later put it, that the United States

---

[53] Sheehan, *Pentagon Papers* (*NYT*), p. 412.

was not becoming engaged in "some two-penny military adventure."[54] McNamara was sufficiently concerned with the domestic political implications of the decisions to urge Johnson to declare a state of national emergency and to ask Congress for an increase in taxes—in short, without seeking a declaration of war, to put the nation on a war footing. The President himself apparently toyed with the idea of securing another Congressional resolution explicitly endorsing his policies.

After extensive deliberation, Johnson decided against any such steps. He continued to fear that anything resembling a declaration of war might provoke the Soviet Union and China. His attorney general assured him that he had the power to commit large-scale forces without going to Congress.[55] Perhaps most important, the civil rights and Medicare bills were then at crucial stages in the legislative process, and Congressional approval was pending on numerous other administration proposals. The President was determined to establish his place in history through the achievement of sweeping domestic reforms, and he feared that going to Congress for authority to wage war in Vietnam would destroy his dream of creating the Great Society at home. Johnson thus rejected the advice of the Joint Chiefs and McNamara, informing his staff that he wished the decisions implemented in a "low-keyed manner in order (a) to avoid an abrupt challenge to the Communists, and (b) to avoid undue concern and excitement in the Congress and in domestic public opinion."[56]

To avoid "undue excitement," the President continued to mislead Congress and the public as to the significance of the steps he was taking. To make his decisions more palatable to potential waverers, he and his aides issued dire warnings that a failure to act decisively would play into the hands of those who wanted to take drastic measures, the "Goldwater crowd," who were "more numerous, more powerful and more dangerous than the fleabite professors. . . ."[57] To appease skeptics such as Senate Majority Leader

[54] Earle Wheeler oral history interview, Johnson Papers.

[55] Nicholas Katzenbach to Johnson, June 10, 1965, Johnson Papers, National Security File, Country File: Vietnam, Box 17.

[56] Benjamin Read memorandum, July 23, 1965, Johnson Papers, National Security File, Country File: Vietnam, Box 16.

[57] McGeorge Bundy to Johnson, July 14, 1965, Johnson Papers, Diary Backup File, Box 19.

Mike Mansfield, Johnson implied that he would give equal priority to seeking a diplomatic settlement of the conflict, without divulging his certainty that such efforts were doomed to failure. In meetings with Congressional leaders and in a televised speech on July 28, he indicated that he was sending 50,000 troops to Vietnam and that more would be required later. But he emphatically denied that he had authorized any change in policy and he did not give a clear indication—even in the sense that he understood it at the time—of what lay ahead. His tactics reflected his continuing determination to achieve his goals in Vietnam without sacrificing the Great Society and his certainty that he could accomplish both things at once.

The July decisions—the closest thing to a formal decision for war in Vietnam—represented the culmination of a year and a half of agonizing on America's Vietnam policy and stemmed logically from the administration's refusal to accept the consequences of withdrawal. Johnson and Rusk had been at the center of the political upheaval that had followed the fall of China in 1949, and they were certain that the "loss" of Vietnam would produce an even more explosive debate, "a mean and destructive debate," Johnson once commented, "that would shatter my Presidency, kill my administration, and damage our democracy."[58] They also deeply feared the international consequences of withdrawal. The decision-makers of 1965 felt that they were upholding policies the United States had pursued since the late 1940s, policies that still had validity despite the enormous changes that had taken place in the world. They were frequently vague as to what they were containing; sometimes they stressed China, other times Communism, and still other times wars of liberation in general. In any case, they believed that to withdraw from Vietnam would encourage disorder throughout the world and drastically weaken American influence. Men of action and achievement, leaders of a nation with an unbroken record of success, they were unwilling to face the prospect of failure. If the United States pulled out of Vietnam, Johnson warned on one occasion, "it might as well give up everywhere else—pull out of Berlin, Japan, South America."[59]

In making the July commitments, the administration saw itself

[58] Kearns, *Johnson*, p. 252.

[59] John D. Pomfret memorandum of conversation with Johnson, June 24, 1965, Krock Papers, Box 59.

moving cautiously between the two extremes of withdrawal and total war; it sought, in Johnson's words, to do "what will be enough, but not too much." The President and his advisers did not seek the defeat of North Vietnam. They did not "speak of conquest on the battlefield . . . as men from time immemorial had talked of victory," the historian Henry Graff recorded. Their objective rather was to inflict sufficient pain on the North Vietnamese and Vietcong to force them to negotiate on terms acceptable to the United States—in Johnson's Texas metaphor, to apply sufficient force until the enemy "sobers up and unloads his pistol."[60]

Displaying the consummate political skill that had become his trademark, Johnson in the last week of July shaped a consensus for his Vietnam policy in his administration, in Congress, and in the country. He appears to have been committed from the outset to a policy that would give the United States "the maximum protection at the least cost."[61] During the week of July 21–28, however, he gave the Joint Chiefs and George Ball their days in court, listening carefully to their arguments and raising numerous probing questions before rejecting their proposals for large-scale escalation and withdrawal.[62] In meetings with the Congressional leadership, he emphasized to conservatives his determination to hold the line in Vietnam, while reassuring liberals that he would not permit the war to get out of hand. "I'm going up old Ho Chi Minh's leg an inch at a time," he told Senator George McGovern.[63] Johnson's middle course probably reflected the aspirations of the American public and Congress, and the President went to war with support that appeared to be solid.

Getting into war would turn out to be much easier for Johnson than getting out. The administration's decisions of July 1965 proved to be based on two crucial miscalculations. In seeking to do what would be "enough, but not too much," the President and his advisers never explored with any real precision how much would be enough. They had no illusions that success could be achieved painlessly, but they grossly underestimated the determination of

[60] Graff, *Tuesday Cabinet*, pp. 54, 59.

[61] Summary notes of National Security Council meeting, June 11, 1965, Johnson Papers, National Security File, NSC Meetings, Box 1.

[62] Larry Berman, *Planning a Tragedy: The Americanization of the War in Vietnam* (New York, 1982).

[63] George McGovern, *Grassroots* (New York, 1977), pp. 104–105.

the enemy to resist and they did not foresee the cost the war would bring the United States. When Ball warned that it might take as many as a half million troops, McNamara dismissed the argument as "dirty pool" and called the figure "outrageous."[64] Leaders of the most powerful nation in the history of the world, U.S. officials simply could not conceive that a small, backward country could stand up against them. It would be like a filibuster, Johnson speculated, "enormous resistance at first, then a steady whittling away, then Ho hurrying to get it over with."[65]

Miscalculating the costs that the United States would incur in Vietnam, the administration could not help but overestimate the willingness of the nation to pay. On July 27, 1965, Senator Mike Mansfield penned a long, eloquent, and prophetic warning to his old friend and political mentor. He advised Johnson that Congress and the nation supported him because he was President, not because they understood or were deeply committed to his policy in Vietnam, and that there lingered beneath the surface a confusion and uncertainty that could in time explode into outright opposition.[66] Mansfield correctly perceived the flimsiness of Johnson's backing. As long as U.S. objectives could be obtained at minimal cost, Americans were willing to stay in Vietnam. When the war turned out to last much longer and cost much more than had been anticipated, however, the President's support began to wither away and the advocates of escalation and withdrawal whom he had parried so skillfully in July 1965 became less manageable.

Johnson disregarded Mansfield's admonitions. After months of uncertainty, he had finally set his course, and in July 1965, quietly and without fanfare, he launched the United States on what would become its longest, most frustrating, and most divisive war.

[64] Benjamin Read oral history interview, Johnson Papers.

[65] Kearns, *Johnson,* p. 266.

[66] Mansfield to Johnson, July 27, 1965, Johnson Papers, National Security File, National Security Council Histories: Deployment of Major U.S. Forces to Vietnam, July 1965, Box 40.

CHAPTER 5

On the Tiger's Back: The United States at War, 1965–1967

While visiting the aircraft carrier *Ranger* off the coast of Vietnam in 1965, Robert Shaplen overheard a fellow journalist remark: "They just ought to show this ship to the Vietcong—that would make them give up."[1] From Lyndon Johnson in the White House to the GI in the field, the United States went to war in 1965 in much this frame of mind. The President had staked everything on the casual assumption that the enemy could be quickly brought to bay by the application of American military might. The first combat troops to enter Vietnam shared similar views. When "we marched into the rice paddies on that damp March afternoon," Marine Lieutenant Philip Caputo later wrote, "we carried, along with our packs and rifles, the implicit conviction that the Viet Cong would be quickly beaten."[2] Although by no means unique to the Vietnam War, this optimism does much to explain the form taken by American participation in that struggle. The United States never developed a strategy appropriate for the war it was fighting, in part because it was assumed that the mere application of its vast military power would be sufficient. The failure of one level of force led quickly to the next and then the next, until the war attained a degree of destructiveness no one would have thought possible in 1965. Most important, the optimism with which the nation went to war more than anything else accounts for the great frustration that sub-

[1] Robert Shaplen, *The Lost Revolution: The U.S. in Vietnam, 1946–1966* (New York, 1966), p. 186.

[2] Philip Caputo, *A Rumor of War* (New York, 1977), p. xii.

sequently developed in and out of government. Failure never comes easily, but it comes especially hard when success is anticipated at little cost.

Within two years, the optimism of 1965 had given way to deep and painful frustration. By 1967, the United States had nearly a half million combat troops in Vietnam. It had dropped more bombs than in all theaters in World War II and was spending more than $2 billion per month on the war. Some American officials persuaded themselves that progress had been made, but the undeniable fact was that the war continued. Lyndon Johnson thus faced an agonizing dilemma. Unable to end the war by military means and unwilling to make the concessions necessary to secure a negotiated settlement, he discovered belatedly what George Ball had warned in 1964: "once on the tiger's back we cannot be sure of picking the place to dismount."

American strategy in Vietnam was improvised rather than carefully designed and contained numerous inconsistencies. The United States went to war in 1965 to prevent the collapse of South Vietnam, but it was never able to relate its tremendous military power to the fundamental task of establishing a viable government in Saigon. The administration insisted that the war must be kept limited—the Soviet Union and China must not be provoked to intervene—but the President counted on a quick and relatively painless victory to avert unrest at home. That these goals might not be compatible apparently never occurred to Johnson and his civilian advisers. The United States injected its military power directly into the struggle to cripple the Vietcong and persuade North Vietnam to stop its "aggression." The administration vastly underestimated the enemy's capacity to resist, however, and did not confront the crucial question of what would be required to achieve its goals until it was bogged down in a bloody stalemate.

While the President and his civilian advisers set limits on the conduct of the war, they did not provide firm strategic guidelines for the use of American power. Left on its own to frame a strategy, the military fought the conventional war for which it was prepared without reference to the peculiar conditions in Vietnam. Westmoreland and the Joint Chiefs chafed under the restraints imposed by the civilians. Sensitive to MacArthur's fate in Korea, however, they would not challenge the President directly or air their case in public. On the other hand, they refused to develop a strategy that accommodated to the restrictions imposed by the White House, but rather attempted to break them down one by one until they got what they wanted. The result was considerable ambiguity in purpose and method, growing civil-military tension, and a steady escalation that brought increasing costs and uncertain gain.

The United States relied heavily on airpower. Military doctrine taught that bombing could destroy an enemy's warmaking capacity, thereby forcing him to come to terms. The limited success of airpower as applied on a large scale in World War II and on a more restricted scale in Korea raised serious questions about the validity of this assumption, and the conditions prevailing in Vietnam, a primitive country with few crucial targets, might have suggested even more. The Air Force and Navy advanced unrealistic expectations about what airpower might accomplish, however, and clung to them long after experience had proven them unjustified. The civilian leadership accepted the military's arguments, at least to a point, because the bombing was cheaper in lives lost and therefore more palatable at home, and because it seemed to offer a quick and comparatively easy solution to a complex problem.[3] Initiated in early 1965 as much from the lack of alternatives as anything else, the bombing of North Vietnam was expanded over the next two years in the vain hope that it would check infiltration into the south and force North Vietnam to the conference table.

The air war gradually assumed massive proportions. The President firmly resisted the Joint Chiefs' proposal for a knockout blow, but as each phase of the bombing failed to produce results, he expanded the list of targets and the number of strikes. Sorties against North Vietnam increased from 25,000 in 1965 to 79,000 in 1966 and 108,000 in 1967; the tonnage of bombs dropped increased from 63,000 to 136,000 to 226,000. Throughout 1965, ROLLING THUNDER concentrated on military bases, supply depots, and infiltration routes in the southern part of the country. From early 1966 on, air strikes were increasingly directed against the North Vietnamese industrial and transportation system and moved steadily northward. In the summer of 1966, Johnson authorized massive strikes against petroleum storage facilities and transportation networks. A year later, he permitted attacks on steel factories, power plants,

[3] Robert L. Gallucci, *Neither Peace Nor Honor: The Politics of American Military Policy in Vietnam* (Baltimore, 1975), pp. 74–80.

and other approved targets around Hanoi and Haiphong, as well as on previously restricted areas along the Chinese border.

The bombing inflicted an estimated $600 million damage on a nation still struggling to develop a viable, modern economy. The air attacks crippled North Vietnam's industrial productivity and disrupted its agriculture. Some cities were virtually leveled, others severely damaged. Giant B-52s, carrying payloads of 58,000 pounds, relentlessly attacked the areas leading to the Ho Chi Minh Trail, leaving the countryside scarred with huge craters and littered with debris. The bombing was not directed against the civilian population, and the administration publicly maintained that civilian casualties were minimal. But the CIA estimated that in 1967 total casualties ran as high as 2,800 per month and admitted that these figures were heavily weighted with civilians; McNamara privately conceded that civilian casualties were as high as 1,000 per month during periods of intensive bombing. A British diplomat later recalled that by the fall of 1967 there were signs among the civilian population of the major cities of widespread malnutrition and declining morale.[4]

The manner in which airpower was used in Vietnam virtually ensured that it would not achieve its objectives, however. Whether, as the Joint Chiefs argued, a massive, unrestricted air war would have worked remains much in doubt. In fact, the United States had destroyed many major targets by 1967 with no demonstrable effect on the war. Nevertheless, the administration's gradualist approach gave Hanoi time to construct an air defense system, protect its vital resources, and develop alternative modes of transportation. Gradualism probably encouraged the North Vietnamese to persist despite the damage inflicted upon them.

North Vietnam demonstrated great ingenuity and dogged perseverance in coping with the bombing. Civilians were evacuated from the cities and dispersed across the countryside; industries and storage facilities were scattered and in many cases concealed in caves and under the ground. The government claimed to have dug over 30,000 miles of tunnels, and in heavily bombed areas the people spent much of their lives underground. An estimated 90,000 North Vietnamese, many of them women and children, worked

[4] Raphael Littauer and Norman Uphoff, eds., *The Air War in Indochina* (Boston, 1972), pp. 39–43. For a firsthand account of the impact of the bombing, see John Colvin, "Hanoi in My Time," *Washington Quarterly* (Spring 1981), 138–154.

full-time keeping transportation routes open, and piles of gravel were kept along the major roadways, enabling "Youth Shock Brigades" to fill craters within hours after the bombs fell. Concrete and steel bridges were replaced by ferries and pontoon bridges made of bamboo stalks which were sunk during the day to avoid detection. Truck drivers covered their vehicles with palm fronds, and banana leaves and traveled at night, without headlights, guided only by white markers along the roads. B-52s devastated the narrow roads through the Mu Gia Pass leading to the Ho Chi Minh Trail, but, to the amazement of the Americans, trucks moved back through the pass within several days. "Caucasians cannot really imagine what ant labor can do," one American remarked with a mixture of frustration and admiration.[5]

Losses in military equipment, raw materials, and vehicles were more than offset by increased aid from the Soviet Union and China. Until 1965, Russia had remained detached from the conflict, but the new leaders who succeeded Khrushchev in October 1964 took much greater interest in the Vietnam conflict, and U.S. escalation presented opportunities and challenges they could not pass up. The bombing created a need for sophisticated military equipment that only the Soviet Union could provide, giving Moscow a chance to wean North Vietnam away from China. At a time when the Chinese were loudly proclaiming Soviet indifference to the fate of revolutions across the world, the direct threat to a Communist state posed by the air strikes required the Russians to prove their credibility. American escalation did not force the two Communist rivals back together, as George Ball had predicted. Fearful of Soviet intrusion in Vietnam, the Chinese angrily rejected Moscow's call for "united action" (a phrase borrowed, perhaps consciously, from Dulles) and even obstructed Russian aid to North Vietnam. The increasingly heated Sino-Soviet rivalry over Vietnam did, however, enable Hanoi to play off one power against the other to get increased aid and prevent either from securing predominant influence. The Chinese continued to supply large quantities of rice, small arms and ammunition, and vehicles. Soviet aid increased dramatically after 1965, and included such modern weaponry as fighter planes, surface-to-air missiles, and tanks. Total assistance

[5] Quoted in Townsend Hoopes, *The Limits of Intervention* (New York, 1970), p. 79. For North Vietnam's response to the air war, see Jon M. Van Dyke, *North Vietnam's Strategy for Survival* (Palo Alto, Calif., 1972).

from Russia and China has been estimated in excess of $2 billion between 1965 and 1968.

Various other factors reduced the effectiveness of the bombing. Heavy rains and impenetrable fog forced sharp curtailment of missions during the long monsoon season from September to May. Airmen claimed to be able to bomb with "surgical" precision, but the weather and techniques which had not advanced much beyond World War II made for considerable inaccuracy, and many targets had to be bombed repeatedly before they were finally destroyed. As they approached closer to Hanoi and Haiphong, moreover, American aircraft ran up against a highly effective air defense system. Anti-aircraft missiles and MiG fighters provided by the Soviet Union did not score a high kill rate, but they threw off bombing patterns and forced the pilots down to altitudes where they confronted heavy flak and deadly small-arms fire.

Despite the extensive damage inflicted on North Vietnam, the bombing did not achieve its goals. It absorbed a great deal of manpower and resources that might have been diverted to other military uses. It hampered the movement of men and supplies to the south, and its proponents argued that infiltration would have been much greater without it. Official American estimates nevertheless conceded that infiltration increased from about 35,000 men in 1965 to as many as 90,000 in 1967 even as the bombing grew heavier and more destructive. It is impossible to gauge with any accuracy the psychological impact of the bombing on North Vietnam, but it did not affect Hanoi's determination to prevail and it may have enabled the leadership to mobilize the civilian population more effectively in support of the war.

By 1967, the United States was paying a heavy price for no more than marginal gains. The cost of a B-52 mission ran to $30,000 per sortie in bombs. The direct cost of the air war, including operation of the aircraft, munitions, and replacement of planes lost, was estimated at more than $1.7 billion during 1965 and 1966, a period when aircraft losses exceeded 500. Overall, the United States between 1965 and 1968 lost 950 aircraft costing roughly $6 billion. According to one estimate, for each $1 of damage inflicted on North Vietnam, the United States spent $9.60. The costs cannot be measured in dollars alone, however. Captured American airmen gave Hanoi a hostage which would assume increasing importance in the stalemated war. The continued pounding of a small, backward country by the world's wealthiest and most advanced nation gave the North Vietnamese a propaganda advantage they exploited quite effectively. Opposition to the war at home increasingly focused on the bombing, which, in the eyes of many critics was at best inefficient, at worst immoral.

American ground operations in the south also escalated dramatically between 1965 and 1967. Even before he had significant numbers of combat forces at his disposal, Westmoreland had formulated the strategy he would employ until early 1968. It was a strategy of attrition, the major objective of which was to locate and eliminate the Vietcong and North Vietnamese regular units. Westmoreland has vigorously denied that he was motivated by any "Napoleonic impulse to maneuver units and hark to the sound of cannon," but "search and destroy," as it came to be called, did reflect traditional U.S. Army doctrines of warfare. In Westmoreland's view, North Vietnam's decision to commit large units to the war left him no choice but to proceed along these lines. He did not have sufficient forces to police the entire country, nor was it enough simply to contain the enemy's main units. "They had to be pounded with artillery and bombs and eventually brought to battle on the ground if they were not forever to remain a threat." Once the enemy's regulars had been destroyed, Westmoreland reasoned, the South Vietnamese government would be able to stabilize its position and pacify the countryside, and the adversary would have no choice but to negotiate on terms acceptable to the United States.[6]

Westmoreland's aggressive strategy required steadily increasing commitments of American manpower. Even before the 1965 buildup had been completed, the General requested sufficient additional forces to bring the total to 450,000 by the end of 1966. In contrast to the air war, over which it retained tight control, the administration gave Westmoreland broad discretion in developing and executing the ground strategy, and it saw no choice but to give him most of the troops he asked for. In June 1966, the President approved a force level of 431,000 to be reached by mid-1967. While these deployments were being approved, Westmoreland was developing requests for an increase to 542,000 troops by the end of 1967.

[6] William C. Westmoreland, *A Soldier Reports* (Garden City, N.Y., 1976), pp. 149–150.

Furnished thousands of fresh American troops and a massive arsenal of modern weaponry, Westmoreland took the war to the enemy. He accomplished what has properly been called a "logistical miracle," constructing virtually overnight the facilities to handle huge numbers of U.S. troops and enormous volumes of equipment. The Americans who fought in Vietnam were the best fed, best clothed, and best equipped army the nation had ever sent to war. In what Westmoreland described as the "most sophisticated war in history," the United States attempted to exploit its technological superiority to cope with the peculiar problems of a guerrilla war. To locate an ever elusive enemy, the military used small, portable radar units and "people sniffers" which picked up the odor of human urine. IBM 1430 computers were programmed to predict likely times and places of enemy attacks. Herbicides were used on a wide scale and with devastating ecological consequences to deprive the Vietcong of natural cover. C-123 "RANCHHAND" crews, with the sardonic motto "Only You Can Prevent Forests," sprayed more than 100 million pounds of chemicals such as Agent Orange over millions of acres of forests, destroying an estimated one-half of South Vietnam's timberlands and leaving human costs yet to be determined. C-47 transports were converted into awesome gunships (called "Puff the Magic Dragon") that could fire 18,000 rounds a minute.

The United States relied heavily on artillery and airpower to dislodge the enemy at minimal cost, and waged a furious war against Vietcong and North Vietnamese base areas. "The solution in Vietnam is more bombs, more shells, more napalm . . . till the other side cracks and gives up," observed General William Depuy, one of the principal architects of "search and destroy."[7] From 1965 to 1967, South Vietnamese and U.S. airmen dropped over a million tons of bombs on South Vietnam, more than twice the tonnage dropped on the north. Retaliatory bombing was employed against some villages suspected of harboring Vietcong. Airpower was used to support forces in battle according to the "pile-on concept," in which U.S. troops encircled enemy units and called in the aircraft. "Blow the hell out of him and police up," one officer described it.[8] A much greater proportion of the air strikes comprised what was

[7] Quoted in Daniel Ellsberg, *Papers on the War* (New York, 1972), p. 234.
[8] Quoted in Littauer and Uphoff, *Air War*, p. 52.

loosely called interdiction—massive, indiscriminate raids, primarily by B-52s, against enemy base areas and logistics networks. Entire areas of South Vietnam were designated Free Fire Zones which could be pulverized without regard for the inhabitants.

North Vietnam matched the U.S. escalation of the war. Although surprised by the American willingness to fight for South Vietnam and keenly aware of the enormous cost of a full-scale war, Hanoi had invested so much in the struggle that it saw no choice but to meet the challenge. In late 1965, North Vietnamese leaders mobilized the entire nation to "foil the war of aggression of the U.S. imperialists." Recognizing that the South Vietnamese government and army and American public opinion were their enemies' most vulnerable points, they attempted through intensive guerrilla and main unit operations to put maximum military pressure on the South Vietnamese and keep U.S. casualties as high as possible in hopes that the Americans might weary of the war. Infiltration increased sharply, and during peak periods in the mid-1960s North Vietnam was able to move an estimated 400 tons of supplies per week and as many as 5,000 men per month on the three-month, more than 600-mile journey along the Ho Chi Minh Trail into South Vietnam.

Throughout 1965 and 1966, the North Vietnamese and Vietcong attempted to keep U.S. units off balance, thereby disrupting search-and-destroy operations. In 1967, they engaged U.S. forces in major actions around the demilitarized zone, giving themselves short supply lines and convenient sanctuary and hoping to draw the Americans away from the populated areas and leave the countryside vulnerable to the Vietcong. Tactically, the North Vietnamese relied on ambushes and hit-and-run operations and sought to "cling to the belts" of the Americans in close-quarter fighting that would minimize the impact of the vastly superior U.S. firepower. Like their Vietcong counterparts, the North Vietnamese were capable fighters. "Damn, give me two hundred men that well disciplined and I'll capture this whole country," one U.S. adviser commented after a major battle in the Central Highlands in late 1965.[9]

---

[9] Quoted in the *New York Times*, October 28, 1965. William J. Duiker, *The Communist Road to Power in Vietnam* (Boulder, Colo., 1981), pp. 240–256, contains a persuasive assessment of North Vietnamese strategy. The story of the Ho Chi Minh Trail is well told in Douglas Pike, "Road to Victory," *War and Peace*, 5 (Issue 60, 1984), 1196–1199.

Throughout 1966 and 1967, intensive fighting took place across much of South Vietnam. Along the demilitarized zone, Marines and North Vietnamese regulars were dug in like the armies of World War I, pounding each other relentlessly with artillery. In the jungle areas, small American units probed for the hidden enemy in a manner comparable to the Pacific island campaigns of World War II. Increasingly, however, Westmoreland concentrated on large-scale search-and-destroy operations against enemy base areas. Operation CEDAR FALLS, a major campaign of early 1967, sent some 30,000 U.S. troops against the Iron Triangle, a Vietcong stronghold just north of Saigon. After B-52s saturated the area, U.S. troops surrounded it and helicopters dropped large numbers of specially trained combat forces into the villages. Following removal of the population, giant Rome plows with huge spikes on the front leveled the area, destroying what remained of the vegetation and leaving the guerrillas no place to hide. The region was then burned and bombed again to destroy the miles of underground tunnels dug by the insurgents.

It remains difficult to assess the results of U.S. ground operations from 1965 to 1967. American troops fought well, despite the miserable conditions under which the war was waged—dense jungles and deep swamps, fire ants and leeches, booby traps and ambushes, an elusive but deadly enemy. In those instances where main units were actually engaged, the Americans usually prevailed, and there was no place in South Vietnam where the enemy enjoyed security from American firepower. It was clear by 1967 that the infusion of American forces had staved off what had appeared to be certain defeat in 1965.

In a war without front lines and territorial objectives, where "attriting the enemy" was the major goal, the "body count" became the index of progress. Most authorities agree that the figures were notoriously unreliable. The sheer destructiveness of combat made it difficult to produce an accurate count of enemy killed in action. It was impossible to distinguish between Vietcong and non-combatants, and in the heat of battle American "statisticians" made little effort. "If it's dead and Vietnamese, its VC, was a rule of thumb in the bush," Philip Caputo has recalled.[10] Throughout the chain of command there was heavy pressure to produce favorable

---

[10] Caputo, *Rumor of War*, p. xviii.

figures, and padding occurred at each level until by the time the numbers reached Washington they bore little resemblance to reality. Even with an inflated body count—and estimates of padding range as high as 30 percent—it is clear that the United States inflicted huge losses on the enemy. Official estimates placed the number as high as 220,000 by late 1967. Largely on the basis of these figures, the American military command insisted that the United States was "winning" the war.

As with the air war, the strategy of attrition had serious flaws. It assumed that the United States could inflict intolerable losses on the enemy while keeping its own losses within acceptable bounds, an assumption that flew in the face of past experience with land wars on the Asian continent and the realities in Vietnam. An estimated 200,000 North Vietnamese reached draft age each year, and Hanoi was able to replace its losses and match each American escalation. Moreover, the conditions under which the war was fought permitted the enemy to control its losses. The North Vietnamese and Vietcong remained extraordinarily elusive and were generally able to avoid contact when it suited them. They fought at times and places of their own choosing and on ground favorable to them. If losses reached unacceptable levels, they could simply melt away into the jungle or retreat into sanctuaries in North Vietnam, Laos, and Cambodia.

Thus, the United States could gain no more than a stalemate. The North Vietnamese and Vietcong had been hurt, in some cases badly, but their main forces had not been destroyed. They retained the strategic initiative, and could strike sharply and quickly when and where they chose. Westmoreland did not have sufficient forces to wage war against the enemy's regulars and control the countryside. The Vietcong political structure thus remained largely untouched, and even in areas such as the Iron Triangle, when American forces moved on to fight elsewhere, the Vietcong quietly slipped back in. It all added up to a "state of irresolution," Robert Shaplen observed in 1967.[11]

Skeptics increasingly questioned whether the progress made was not more than offset by the consequences of large-scale American military operations. In 1966 alone, unexploded American bombs and shells provided the Vietcong enough explosives to kill

[11] Robert Shaplen, *The Road from War: Vietnam, 1965–1970* (New York, 1970), p. 167.

as many as 1,000 men. The massive bombing and artillery fire disrupted the agriculture upon which the South Vietnamese economy depended, produced huge numbers of civilian casualties, and drove millions of noncombatants into hastily constructed refugee camps or into the already overcrowded cities. American military operations further undermined the social fabric of an already fragile nation and alienated the people from a government which had never had a firm base of popular support. "It was as if we were trying to build a house with a bulldozer and wrecking crane," one American official later observed.[12]

Americanization of the war also had a debilitating effect on the South Vietnamese Army. Westmoreland had called for American forces because he doubted the ARVN's battle-worthiness, and once he had them he relied primarily on them. During the period of American military preponderance, the ARVN was largely shunted aside, relegated to lesser operations and population control, chores its officers considered demeaning and took on with considerable reluctance. The sense of inferiority thus engendered did nothing to resolve the problems of morale and leadership which had always been the ARVN's curse. Much time and money were spent training and equipping the South Vietnamese from 1965 to 1967, but it was all in the American mold, preparing the ARVN to fight the kind of war the Americans were waging. The ARVN thus became more than ever dependent on the United States and was ill prepared to assume the burden of the fighting at some later, unspecified date.

The United States paid a heavy price for limited gains. In many operations vast quantities of firepower were expended, sometimes with negligible results. The ammunition costs of the war were "astronomical," Army Chief of Staff Harold Johnson later recalled, and some surveys revealed that as much as 85 percent of the ammunition used was unobserved fire, "a staggering volume."[13] Although the United States killed 700 Vietcong in the CEDAR FALLS operation, the enemy main force escaped. American casualties were small compared to Vietnamese, but the number killed in action rose to 13,500 by late 1967, and swelling draft calls and mounting casualties brought rising opposition to the war at home.

Thus, despite the impressive body count figures, it was clear to

[12] Stephen Young, quoted in W. Scott Thompson and Donaldson D. Frizzell, *The Lessons of Vietnam* (New York, 1977), p. 225.

[13] Harold Johnson oral history interview, U.S. Army Military History Institute, Carlisle Barracks, Pa.

many observers by mid-1967 that the hopes of a quick and relatively inexpensive military victory had been misplaced. Each American blow "was like a sledgehammer on a floating cork," the journalist Malcolm Browne observed. "Somehow the cork refused to stay down."[14] By this point the United States had nearly 450,000 troops in Vietnam. Westmoreland conceded that if his request for an additional 200,000 men was granted, the war might go on for as long as two years. If not, he warned, it could last five years or even longer.

While drastically expanding its military operations in Vietnam, the United States also grappled with what many had always regarded as the central problem—construction of a viable South Vietnamese nation. Ky surprised the skeptics by surviving in office for more than six months. Persuaded that it had found a solid foundation upon which to build, in early 1966 the administration decided to make clear its commitment and to press Ky to reform his government. At a hastily arranged "summit" meeting in Honolulu, Johnson publicly embraced a somewhat embarrassed Ky, symbolizing the new commitment, and secured his agreement to a sweeping program of reform. The President left no doubt of the importance he attached to the program. The Honolulu communiqué was a "kind of bible," he declared. He would not be content with promises or "high-sounding words," but must have "coonskins on the wall."[15]

No sooner had Ky returned to Saigon than he faced a stiff internal challenge. Quiescent for nearly a year, the Buddhists viewed Honolulu as a clear sign that Ky, with American support, would attempt to maintain absolute power, and they again took to the streets. As in 1963, the demonstrations began in Hue and were led by Buddhist monks, but they quickly spread to Saigon and drew together the many groups dissatisfied with the regime: students, labor unions, Catholics, even factions within the army. The demonstrations took on an increasingly anti-American tone. Signs reading "END FOREIGN DOMINATION OF OUR COUNTRY" appeared in Hue and Danang. An angry mob burned the U.S. Consulate in Hue, and firemen refused to extinguish the blaze.

---

[14] Malcolm W. Browne, *The New Face of War* (Indianapolis, Ind., 1968), p. ix.

[15] Transcript of Johnson briefing, February 8, 1966, Johnson Papers, National Security File, International Meetings File: Honolulu, Box 2.

The Buddhist crisis exposed the fragility of the Saigon government and the weakness of the American position in Vietnam. The existence of a virtual civil war within an insurrection dampened the hopes that had begun to develop for Ky's government. The protesters advocated the holding of elections and the restoration of civilian government, goals to which the United States could hardly take exception. The State Department nevertheless feared that giving in to the Buddhists would "take us more rapidly than we had envisaged down a road with many pitfalls," and Rusk instructed the Embassy to persuade moderate Buddhist leaders to drop their "unrealistic demands" because of the "grave danger of simply handing the country over to the Viet Cong."[16] When American "mediation" failed and the crisis worsened, some administration officials proposed abandoning Ky in order to save South Vietnam, and others began to develop plans for a face-saving American withdrawal. Acting without prior approval from Washington, the embattled Premier eventually solved the American dilemma and saved his own skin by dispatching 1,000 South Vietnamese marines to Danang to suppress the rebellion. The Buddhists gave way in the face of superior force and withdrew in sullen protest. Although deeply annoyed by Ky's independence, the administration was more than satisfied with the outcome. The President "categorically thrust aside the withdrawal option," William Bundy recalled, and "we all relaxed."[17]

In the aftermath of the Buddhist crisis, Americans and Vietnamese struggled to live up to the lofty promises of Honolulu. From Washington's standpoint, pacification was a top-priority item. Improving the South Vietnamese standard of living was the one area of the war that struck a responsive chord in Johnson. He identified with the people of South Vietnam and deeply sympathized with their presumed desire for political freedom and economic progress. Like most of his colleagues, he believed that it was necessary to win the support of the people in order to defeat the Vietcong, and he felt a keen personal need to endow the war with some higher purpose. He could wax eloquent about such things as inoculation programs, educational reform, and use of American expertise to teach

[16] Rusk to Embassy Saigon, March 16, 1966, Johnson Papers, National Security File, Country File: Vietnam, Box 28; Rusk to Embassy Saigon, April 5, 1966, Johnson Papers, National Security File, Country File: Vietnam, Box 29.

[17] William Bundy oral history interview, Johnson Papers.

the Vietnamese to raise larger hogs and grow more sweet potatoes. "Dammit," he exploded on one occasion, "we need to exhibit more compassion for these Vietnamese plain people. . . . We've got to see that the South Vietnamese government wins the battle . . . of crops and hearts and caring."[18] Under intensive prodding from Washington, the Americans and South Vietnamese devised an ambitious Revolutionary Development Program (RD), consciously imitative of Vietcong techniques, in which fifty-nine-man teams, trained in propaganda and social services, would go into the villages, live with the people, and carry out hundreds of tasks to build popular support for the government and undermine the Vietcong.

Revolutionary Development ran afoul of many of the problems that had frustrated earlier pacification programs. The creaking Saigon bureaucracy and poor coordination between Americans and Vietnamese hampered administration of the plan. It was impossible to recruit sufficient personnel in a country short of manpower, and less than half the cadres needed actually went into training. Candidates were trained on a mass-production basis for a mere three months and in most cases were inadequately prepared for the formidable task that lay ahead. Once in the field, the RD teams were frustrated by local officials who regarded them as a threat. Funds promised for many projects never reached their destination. Having seen so many other programs come and go, the villagers greeted the arrivals with a mixture of apathy and caution. Because of the chronic manpower shortage, many cadres were often shifted to new areas before their work was completed, and any gains were quickly erased. Good performance by RD teams was sometimes undercut by the behavior of ARVN units that extorted taxes and fees from the villagers and stole chickens and pigs. When asked what would most help pacification in his area, one U.S. adviser responded: "Get the 22nd [ARVN] Division out of the province."[19]

The fundamental problem was the absence of security. The U.S. military was preoccupied with the shooting war and gave little attention to what became known as "the other war" (the term itself suggested the absence of coordination between pacification and military operations). In most cases the ARVN was incapable of providing security, and in some areas it was part of the problem.

[18] Jack Valenti, *A Very Human President* (New York, 1973), p. 133; Lady Bird Johnson, *A White House Diary* (New York, 1970), pp. 370–371.

[19] Daniel Ellsberg memorandum, March 30, 1966, John P. Vann Papers, U.S. Army Military History Institute, Carlisle Barracks, Pa.

Sometimes, RD teams would make some progress, only to have it nullified when American aircraft bombed their villages. Cadres were frequently sent into insecure areas where they were harassed and terrorized by the Vietcong. Many fled. Those who stayed and worked effectively with the people were often found with their throats slit. During a seven-month period in 1966, 3,015 Revolutionary Development personnel were murdered or kidnapped.[20]

Under these circumstances, pacification achieved little. Roads were repaired, schools built, and village elections held, but even on the basis of the highly inaccurate methods used to measure progress, the number of "pacified" villages increased by a mere 5 percent in the first year. In an attempt to revive the program, in the spring of 1967 Johnson placed it under the immediate authority of the U.S. Military Command, and Westmoreland persuaded a reluctant ARVN to commit the bulk of its forces to rural security. These changes would eventually produce better results, but at a time when the vast American military effort had attained nothing better than a stalemate, the failure of pacification was especially discouraging.

In at least one area, the two nations did live up to the goals of the Honolulu communiqué: a new constitution was drafted and national elections were held. The Americans did not presume that the export of democracy would solve South Vietnam's problems. On the contrary, many agreed with Lodge (who had returned for a second tour as Ambassador) that the establishment of real democracy in a land with no Western democratic traditions was "clearly an impossible task," and some feared that a genuinely open political process would lead to chaos. The Americans nevertheless felt that a new constitution and elections would give South Vietnam a better image and might, in Lodge's words, "substitute a certain legitimacy for the hurly-burly of unending coups."[21]

The Ky regime dutifully followed American advice but in a way that ensured its own perpetuation. Elections for a constituent assembly were so tightly circumscribed that the Buddhists boycotted them. The assembly met in early 1967 and turned out a polished document, based on American and French models and including a

[20] Douglas A. Blaufarb, *The Counterinsurgency Era: U.S Doctrines and Performance* (New York, 1977), pp. 205–242, contains a full discussion of the Revolutionary Development Program.

[21] Henry Cabot Lodge, Jr., *The Storm Has Many Eyes* (New York, 1973), p. 215.

Bill of Rights. The government nevertheless insisted on a strong executive and on provisions permitting the President to assume near-dictatorial powers in an emergency, which could be declared at his discretion. Those branded Communists or "neutralist sympathizers" were disqualified from office. The President was to be elected by a plurality, ensuring that opposition candidates did not band together in a runoff.

Throughout the preelection maneuvering, the United States quietly but firmly supported the government's efforts to remain in power. The State Department expressed concern about the wholesale disqualification of opposition candidates, but Lodge's argument that the "GVN should not be discouraged from taking moderate measures to prevent [the] elections from being used as a vehicle for a Communist takeover" prevailed.[22] The most serious challenge to the government came from bitter internal squabbling which was resolved only under intense pressure from the United States and after a long meeting, filled with histrionics, in which Ky tearfully gave way and agreed to run for the vice presidency on a ticket headed by Thieu.

The September 1967 elections were neither as corrupt as critics charged nor as pure as Johnson claimed. The regime conducted them under conditions which made defeat unlikely, and there was evidence of considerable last-minute fraud. But the large turnout and the fact that elections had been held in the midst of war were cited by Americans as evidence of growing political maturity. What stands out in retrospect is the narrowness of the government's victory. The Thieu-Ky ticket won 35 percent of the vote, but Truong Dinh Dzu, an unknown lawyer who had run on a platform of negotiations with the Vietcong, won 17 percent. The elections may have provided the regime a measure of respectability, but they also underscored its continued weakness. In a nation where political authority derived from the will of heaven and popular support was an obligation, the narrowness of the victory could only appear ludicrous. Many Vietnamese cynically regarded the entire process as "an American-directed performance with a Vietnamese cast."[23]

While the United States and South Vietnam struggled to resolve

[22] U.S. Congress, Senate, Subcommittee on Public Buildings and Grounds, *The Pentagon Papers (The Senator Gravel Edition)* (4 vols., Boston, 1971), II, 384.
[23] Shaplen, *Road from War,* p. 151.

old problems, Americanization of the war created new and equally formidable problems. Among these, the most serious—and most tragic—was that of the refugees. The expansion of American and enemy military operations drove an estimated four million South Vietnamese, roughly 25 percent of the population, from their native villages. Some drifted into the already teeming cities; others were herded into shabby refugee camps. The United States furnished the government some $30 million a year for the care of the refugees, but much of the money never reached them. Resettlement programs were initiated from time to time, but the problem was so complex that it would have taxed the ingenuity of the most imaginative officials. In any event, nothing could have compensated the refugees for the loss of their homes and lands. A large portion of South Vietnam's population was left rootless and hostile, and the refugee camps became fertile breeding grounds for Vietcong fifth columns.

The sudden infusion of a half million American troops, hundreds of civilian advisers, and billions of dollars had a profoundly disruptive effect on a weak and divided nation. The buildup was so rapid and so vast that it threatened to overwhelm South Vietnam. Saigon's ports were congested with ships and goods, and vessels awaiting unloading were backed up far out to sea. The city itself became a "thorough-going boom town," Shaplen remarked, its streets clogged with traffic, its restaurants "bursting with boisterous soldiers," its bars as "crowded as New York subway cars in the rush hour."[24] Signs of the American presence appeared everywhere. Long strips of seedy bars and brothels sprang up overnight around base areas. In a remote village near Danang, Caputo encountered houses made of discarded beer cans: "red and white Budweiser, gold Miller, cream and brown Schlitz, blue and gold Hamm's from the land of sky-blue waters."[25]

American spending had a devastating effect on the vulnerable South Vietnamese economy. Prices increased by as much as 170 percent during the first two years of the buildup. The United States eventually controlled the rate of inflation by paying its own soldiers in scrip and by flooding the country with consumer goods, but the corrective measures themselves had harmful side effects. Instead of

[24] *Ibid.*, pp. 20–21.
[25] Caputo, *Rumor of War*, p. 107.

using American aid to promote economic development, South Vietnamese importers bought watches, transistor radios, and Hondas to sell to people employed by the United States. The vast influx of American goods destroyed South Vietnam's few native industries and made the economy even more dependent on continued outside aid. By 1967, much of the urban population was employed providing services to the Americans.

In the bonanza atmosphere, crime and corruption flourished. Corruption was not new to South Vietnam or unusual in a nation at war, but by 1966 it operated on an incredible scale. Government officials rented land to the United States at inflated prices, required bribes for driver's licenses, passports, visas, and work permits, extorted kickbacks for contracts to build and service facilities, and took part in the illicit importation of opium. The black market in scrip, dollars, and stolen American goods became a major enterprise. On Saigon's PX Alley, an open-air market covering two city blocks and comprised of more than 100 stalls, purchasers could buy everything from hand grenades to scotch whiskey at markups as high as 300 percent. Americans and Vietnamese reaped handsome profits from the illegal exchange of currencies. International swindlers and "monetary camp followers" quickly got into the act, and the currency-manipulation racket developed into a "massive financial international network" extending from Saigon to Wall Street with connections to Swiss banks and Arab sheikdoms. The pervasive corruption undermined the U.S. aid program and severely handicapped American efforts to stabilize the economy of South Vietnam.[26]

American officials perceived the problem, but they could not find solutions. Ky candidly admitted that "most of the generals are corrupt. Most of the senior officials in the provinces are corrupt." But, he would add calmly, "corruption exists everywhere, and people can live with some of it. You live with it in Chicago and New York."[27] The Embassy pressed the government to remove officials known to be corrupt, but with little result. "You fight like hell to get someone removed and most times you fail and you just make it

[26] *New York Times*, November 16, 1966; Abraham Ribicoff to Robert McLellan, January 15, 1969, and memorandum, January 15, 1970, Abraham Ribicoff Papers, Library of Congress, Washington, D.C., Box 432.

[27] Harry McPherson to Johnson, June 13, 1967, Johnson Papers, McPherson File, Box 29.

worse," a frustrated American explained to David Halberstam. "And then on occasions you win, why hell, they give you someone just as bad."[28] The United States found to its chagrin that as its commitment increased, its leverage diminished. Concern with corruption and inefficiency was always balanced by fear that tough action might alienate the government or bring about its collapse. Lodge and Westmoreland were inclined to accept the situation and deal with other problems.

Tensions between Americans and South Vietnamese increased as the American presence grew. Because of chronic security leaks, the United States kept Vietnamese off its major bases, and Vietcong infiltration of the ARVN's top ranks compelled U.S. officers to keep from their Vietnamese counterparts the details of major military operations. Americans were openly cynical toward their ally. "I wish the southern members of the clan would display the fighting qualities of their northern brethren," a senior U.S. officer observed with obvious scorn.[29] The ARVN indeed became an object of ridicule, its mode of attack best depicted, according to a standard American joke, by the statue of a seated soldier in the National Military Cemetery. Vietnamese slowness to accept American methods exasperated U.S. advisers. "I am sure that if Saigon were left to fend for itself . . . in 20 years this place would be all rice paddies again," one American acidly observed.[30] The seeming indifference of many Vietnamese, while Americans were dying in the field, provoked growing resentment and hatred. The unerring ability of the villagers to avoid mines and booby traps that killed and maimed GIs led to charges of collusion with the enemy.

The Vietnamese attitude toward the foreigner was at best ambivalent. The Vietnamese undoubtedly appreciated American generosity, but they came to resent American ways of doing things. They complained that American soldiers "acted despicably" toward the villagers, tearing up roads and endangering the lives of noncombatants by reckless handling of vehicles and firearms. An ARVN major protested that Americans trusted only those Vietnamese who accepted without question their way of doing things and

[28] David Halberstam, "Return to Vietnam," *Harpers*, 235 (December 1967), 52.

[29] General A. S. Collins to Edward F. Smith, November 15, 1966, A. S. Collins Papers, U.S. Army Military History Institute, Carlisle Barracks, Pa.

[30] Curtis Herrick diary, January 13, 1965, Curtis Herrick Papers, U.S. Army Military History Institute, Carlisle Barracks, Pa.

that they doled out their aid "in the same way as that given to beg-
gars."[31] The Vietnamese recognized their need for U.S. help, and
some were probably quite content to let the United States assume
complete responsibility for the war. On the other hand, many Vietnamese resented the domineering manner of the Americans and
came to consider the U.S. "occupation" a "demoralizing scourge."
Thoughtful Vietnamese recognized that Americans were not "colonialists," Shaplen observed. But, he added, "there has evolved here
a colonial ambiance that can sometimes be worse than colonialism
itself."[32]

Progress in the critical area of nation-building was thus even
more limited than on the battlefield. To be sure, the government
survived, and after the chronic instability of the Khanh era, that in
itself appeared evidence of progress. Survival was primarily a result
of the formidable American military presence, however, and did not
reflect increased popular support or intrinsic strength. Returning to
South Vietnam after an absence of several years, Halberstam was
haunted by a sense of déjà vu. There were new faces, new programs, an abundance of resources, and the Americans continued to
speak optimistically. But the old problems persisted, and the "new"
solutions appeared little more than recycled versions of old ones.
"What finally struck me," he concluded, "was how little had really
changed here."[33]

The steady expansion of the war spurred strong international
and domestic pressures for negotiations, but the military stalemate
produced an equally firm diplomatic impasse. American officials
later tallied as many as 2,000 attempts to initiate peace talks between 1965 and 1967. Neither side could afford to appear indifferent to such efforts, but neither was willing to make the concessions
necessary to make negotiations a reality. Although the North Vietnamese attempted to exploit the various peace initiatives for propaganda advantage, they counted on the American people to tire of
the war and they remained certain that they could achieve their
goals if they persisted. Hanoi adamantly refused to negotiate without first securing major concessions from the United States. Johnson
and his advisers could not ignore the various proposals for negotia-

---

[31] Weekly Psyops Field Operation Report, December 2, 1967, Vann Papers.
[32] Shaplen, *Road from War*, p. 154.
[33] Halberstam, "Return to Vietnam," p. 50.

tions, but they doubted that anything would come of them and suspected, not without reason, that Hanoi was expressing interest merely to get the bombing stopped. Despite any firm evidence of results, the President remained confident at least until 1967 that North Vietnam would eventually bend to American pressure, and he feared that if he were too conciliatory it would undercut his strategy. To defuse international and domestic criticism, Johnson repeatedly insisted that he was ready to negotiate, but he refused to make the concessions Hanoi demanded. As each side invested more in the struggle, the likelihood of serious negotiations diminished.[34]

The positions of the two sides left little room for compromise. The North Vietnamese denounced American involvement in Vietnam as a blatant violation of the Geneva Accords, and as a precondition to negotiations, insisted that the United States withdraw its troops, dismantle its bases, and stop all acts of war against their country. Hanoi stressed that the internal affairs of South Vietnam must be resolved by the South Vietnamese themselves "in accordance with the program of the National Liberation Front." North Vietnam was apparently flexible in regard to the timing and mechanism for political change in the south, but on the fundamental issues it was adamant. The "puppet" Saigon regime must be replaced by a government representative of the "people" in which the front would play a prominent role. Hanoi made clear, moreover, that the "unity of our country is no more a matter for negotiations than our independence."[35]

The United States formally set forth its position in early 1966. Persuaded that he would soon have to expand the bombing and increase the level of American forces, Johnson, with some reluctance, agreed to initiate a bombing pause over the Christmas holiday. The pause was partially designed, in McNamara's words, to "lay a foundation in the minds of the American public and world opinion . . . for an enlarged phase of the war."[36] The President accordingly decided to combine it with a well-publicized "peace offensive." With great fanfare, he dispatched such luminaries as Averell Har-

[34] Allan E. Goodman, *The Lost Peace: America's Search for a Negotiated Settlement of the Vietnam War* (Stanford, Calif., 1978), pp. 23–60, contains a detailed and generally persuasive account of the 1965–1967 peace initiatives.

[35] Quoted in Gareth Porter, *A Peace Denied: The United States, Vietnam, and the Paris Agreements* (Bloomington, Ind., 1975), p. 29.

[36] *Pentagon Papers (Gravel)*, IV, 33.

riman and Vice President Hubert Humphrey across the world to deliver the message that the United States was prepared to negotiate without condition.

Simultaneously, the State Department revealed American terms for a settlement. "We put everything into the basket but the surrender of South Vietnam," Rusk later claimed, but in fact the administration's Fourteen Points offered few concessions.[37] The United States indicated that it was willing to stop the bombing, but only after Hanoi took reciprocal steps of deescalation. It would withdraw its troops from the south, but only after a satisfactory political settlement had been reached. The administration accepted the principle that the future of South Vietnam must be worked out by the South Vietnamese. At the same time, it made clear that it would not admit the Vietcong to the government, a move that would be like "putting the fox in a chicken coop," Humphrey declared publicly.[38] The Fourteen Points conceded merely that the views of the Vietcong "would have no difficulty being represented," and this only after Hanoi had "ceased its aggression." Beneath these ambiguous words rested a firm determination to maintain an independent, non-Communist South Vietnam.

The fate of Johnson's peace offensive underscored the great gulf between the two nations. Ho Chi Minh's formal response was uncompromising. The North Vietnamese made a sharp distinction between American interference in a foreign country and their own involvement in matters that concerned Vietnamese, and they firmly refused to perform reciprocal acts in exchange for a cessation of the bombing. Denouncing the bombing pause as a "sham peace trick," Ho demanded that the United States "end unconditionally and for good all bombing raids and other attacks against the DRV" and accept Hanoi's position as the basis for a political settlement.[39] Some administration officials urged Johnson to extend the bombing pause, but the President angrily refused. Ho's response seemed to say, "All right, damn you! Forget it!" William Bundy recalled, and Johnson was infuriated by its tone. After a thirty-seven-day pause, the President on January 31 resumed and greatly expanded the bombing. He was never enthusiastic about

[37] Quoted in Chester Cooper, *The Lost Crusade: America in Vietnam* (New York, 1970), p. 294.

[38] Quoted in Henry Graff, *The Tuesday Cabinet* (Englewood Cliffs, N.J., 1970), p. 67.

[39] Quoted in Cooper, *Lost Crusade*, p. 294.

the pause, and from this point on his attitude toward conciliatory gestures hardened. "It was a new and tougher ball game," according to Bundy.[40]

To silence domestic and international critics and to test the diplomatic winds in Hanoi once again, the administration modified its position a bit in late 1966. Throughout the summer and fall, various third parties struggled to find a common ground for negotiations, and after a series of frenzied trips back and forth between Hanoi and Saigon, the Polish diplomat Januscz Lewandowski drafted a ten-point plan for settlement of the conflict. Johnson and his advisers were highly skeptical of the peace moves, which they dismissed as "Nobel Prize fever." They felt that the Lewandowski draft was vague on many critical points and that it gave away too much. The administration could not afford to appear intransigent, however, and it eventually accepted Lewandowski's proposals as a basis for negotiations with the qualification that "several specific points are subject to important differences of interpretation." Responding to Lewandowski's entreaties, the United States also advanced a two-track proposal to provide a face-saving way around Hanoi's opposition to mutual deescalation. The United States would stop the air strikes in return for confidential assurance that North Vietnam would stop infiltration into key areas of South Vietnam within a reasonable period. Once Hanoi had acted, the United States would freeze its combat forces at existing levels and peace talks could begin.[41]

Code-named MARIGOLD, the Polish initiative ended in fiasco. Spokesmen for Hanoi later claimed that a North Vietnamese delegate was en route to Warsaw, where talks were slated to begin in early December, but the extent to which North Vietnam had committed itself to the ten-point plan and was willing to compromise on the basic issues remains unclear. In any case, the initiative aborted. Several days before the scheduled opening of the talks, U.S. aircraft struck railroad yards within five miles of the center of Hanoi, causing heavy damage to residential areas and numerous civilian casualties. Frequently explained away as the product of poor coordination within the American government—the right hand did

---

[40] William Bundy oral history interview, Johnson Papers.

[41] George C. Herring (ed.), *The Secret Diplomacy of the Vietnam War: The Negotiating Volumes of the Pentagon Papers* (Austin, Tex., 1983), pp. 211–370, contains a full account of the Polish initiative along with many of the major American documents.

not know what the left was doing—the bombing in fact resulted
from a conscious decision. Lodge, McNamara, and Undersecretary
of State Nicholas Katzenbach all urged Johnson to refrain from
bombing near Hanoi during the most delicate stage of Lewandowski's diplomacy, but the President would have none of it. Like
many other American officials, he suspected that the entire arrangement was "phoney," and he insisted that a bombing halt had
not been specified as a precondition for the Warsaw talks.[42] Johnson's assessment of North Vietnamese intentions may have been
correct, but the December bombings, which came after a long lull
forced by bad weather, must have appeared to Hanoi as a major
escalation of the air war timed to coincide with the peace moves.
The North Vietnamese had always insisted that they would not negotiate under duress, and they quickly broke off the contact. The
Poles felt betrayed and MARIGOLD withered.

An initiative sponsored by British Prime Minister Harold Wilson met a similar fate in early 1967. Wilson persuaded a cautious
Soviet premier Alexei Kosygin, then in London, to try to bring the
North Vietnamese to formal peace negotiations on the basis of the
two-track proposal unveiled during MARIGOLD. By the time Kosygin had agreed to Wilson's ploy, however, the American position
had hardened. The administration had initiated another bombing
pause to coincide with the Tet holiday, but North Vietnam had
seized the opportunity to drastically step up the infiltration of men
and supplies into South Vietnam. An enraged Johnson now retreated to his original position that Hanoi must stop infiltration before he would end the bombing. This change was not made clear to
Wilson, and when he learned of the actual American stand he was
furious, feeling, justifiably, that he had been put in a "hell of a situation." The tenacious Prime Minister hastily concocted a compromise which Kosygin agreed to present to Hanoi, but Washington
gave him only fifteen hours to complete the transaction before it
resumed the bombing. What Wilson later described as a "historic opportunity" broke down under this "utterly unrealistic timetable."[43]

[42] William Bundy and Nicholas Katzenbach oral history interviews, Johnson
Papers.

[43] Harold Wilson, *The Labour Government, 1964–1970: A Personal Record* (London, 1971), pp. 359–365. Benjamin Read, executive secretary to Dean Rusk, later
claimed that the misunderstanding had been caused by sloppy phraseology in a
cable to London. The message explaining the American position was prepared
"with midnight oil and without the presence of a lawyer," according to Read,
and the "tense slipped." Read oral history interview, Johnson Papers.

Wilson exaggerated the likelihood of productive negotiations. Kosygin's apparent willingness to serve as an intermediary may have represented an important shift in Russian policy. As long as the war diverted American attention and resources from other areas and enabled them to undercut Chinese influence in Hanoi, the Soviets had been willing for it to go on. But continued American escalation, the upheaval that had accompanied the Cultural Revolution in China, and the increasingly bitter rhetoric employed by the Chinese may have aroused Soviet fears that the situation in Southeast Asia was getting out of hand. The Russians seem also to have been alarmed by the opening of Chinese-American contacts in Warsaw, angrily charging the two nations with conspiring to impose terms on North Vietnam. Kosygin may have concluded by early 1967 that it was desirable to end the war, and that a negotiated settlement might isolate China and solidify Russia's position with North Vietnam and the United States. His capacity to bring about a settlement was very limited, however. He could not press Hanoi too hard lest he play into the hands of the Chinese, who were accusing the Soviet "scabs and renegades" of collusion with the United States at Hanoi's expense. He could agree to nothing less than a settlement that met North Vietnam's basic goals.

Peace hinged, therefore, not on the influence of third parties but on the willingness of the belligerents to compromise. In response to international, and, in the case of the United States, domestic, pressures, each side by 1967 had inched cautiously away from the rigid positions assumed two years earlier. North Vietnam no longer insisted on acceptance of its four points, including a complete American military withdrawal, as a precondition to negotiations, demanding only that the bombing must be ended without condition. Hanoi had also relaxed its terms for a settlement, indicating, among other things, that reunification could take place over a long period of time. The United States had retreated from its original position that North Vietnam must withdraw its forces from the south in return for cessation of the bombing, insisting merely that further infiltration must be stopped. Despite these concessions, the two nations remained far apart on the means of getting negotiations started. And although their bargaining positions had changed slightly, they had not abandoned their basic goals. Each had met with frustration and had incurred heavy losses on the battlefield, but each still retained hope that it could force the other to accept its terms. Thus the two sides remained unwilling to compromise on the central issue—the future of South Vietnam—to the extent that their objectives would be jeopardized. The Wilson-Kosygin initiative was badly handled by the Johnson administration, but there is little reason to assume that even the most skillful and patient diplomacy could have achieved a breakthrough in the absence of concessions neither nation was prepared to make. The story of the 1965–1967 peace initiatives, one scholar has concluded, marks "one of the most fruitless chapters in U.S. diplomacy."[44]

By mid-1967, Johnson was snared in a trap he had unknowingly set for himself. His hopes of a quick and relatively painless victory had been frustrated. He was desperately anxious to end the war, but he had been unable to do so by force, and in the absence of a clear-cut military advantage, or a stronger political position in South Vietnam, he could not do so by negotiations. As the conflict increased in cost, moreover, he found himself caught in the midst of an increasingly angry and divisive debate at home, a debate which by 1967 seemed capable of wrecking his presidency and tearing the country apart.

At one extreme were the "hawks," largely right-wing Republicans and conservative Democrats, who viewed the conflict in Vietnam as an essential element in the global struggle with Communism. Should the United States not hold the line, they argued, the Communists would be encouraged to further aggression, allies and neutrals would succumb to Communist pressures, and the United States would be left alone to face a powerful and merciless enemy. Strong nationalists, certain of America's invincibility, and deeply frustrated by the stalemate in Vietnam, the hawks bitterly protested the restraints imposed on the military and demanded that the administration do whatever was necessary to attain victory. "Win or get out," Representative Mendel Rivers (D–S.C.) advised President Johnson in early 1966.[45]

At the other extreme were the "doves," a vast, sprawling, extremely heterogeneous and fractious group, which opposed the war with increasing bitterness and force. The antiwar movement grew almost in proportion to the escalation of the conflict. It included such diverse individuals as the pediatrician Dr. Benjamin Spock,

[44] Goodman, *Lost Peace,* p. 24.

[45] Notes on meeting with Congressional leadership, January 25, 1966, Johnson Papers, Meeting Notes File, Box 1.

heavyweight boxing champion Muhammad Ali, actress Jane Fonda and author Norman Mailer, old-line pacifists such as A. J. Muste and new radicals such as Tom Hayden, the black civil rights leader Dr. Martin Luther King, Jr., and Arkansas Senator J. William Fulbright. The doves comprised only a small percentage of the population, but they were an unusually visible and articulate group. Their attack on American foreign policy was vicious and unrelenting. In time, their movement became inextricably linked with the cultural revolution that swept the United States in the late 1960s and challenged the most basic of American values and institutions.

Although it defies precise categorization, the antiwar movement tended to group along three principal lines.[46] For pacifists such as Muste, who opposed all wars as immoral, Vietnam was but another phase of a lifelong crusade. For the burgeoning radical movement of the 1960s, opposition to the war extended beyond questions of morality. Spawned by the civil rights movement, drawing its largest following among upper-middle-class youth on college campuses, the "New Left" joined older leftist organizations in viewing the war as a classic example of the way the American ruling class exploited helpless people to sustain a decadent capitalist system.[47] Antiwar liberals far exceeded in numbers the pacifists and radicals. Although they did not generally question "the system," they increasingly questioned the war on both moral and practical grounds. Many liberal internationalists who had supported World War II, Korea, and the Cold War found Vietnam morally repugnant. By backing a corrupt, authoritarian government, they contended, the United States was betraying its own principles. In the absence of any direct threat to American security, the devastation wreaked on North and South Vietnam was indefensible. Many more liberals questioned the war on practical grounds. It was essentially an internal struggle, they argued, whose connection with the Cold War was at best indirect. Liberals questioned the validity of the domino theory, especially after the Indonesian army threw out Sukarno and crushed the Indonesian Communist party. They agreed that Vietnam was of no more than marginal significance to the security of the United States. Indeed,

---

[46] See Charles DeBenedetti, *The Peace Reform in American History* (Bloomington, Ind., 1984), pp. 171–178.

[47] Irwin Unger, *The Movement* (New York, 1974), pp. 35–93.

they insisted that the huge investment there was diverting attention from more urgent problems at home and abroad, damaging
America's relations with its allies, and inhibiting the development
of a more constructive relationship with the Soviet Union. The liberal critique quickly broadened into an indictment of American
"globalism." The United States had fallen victim to the "arrogance
of power," Fulbright claimed, and was showing "signs of that fatal
presumption, that over-extension of power and mission, which
brought ruin to ancient Athens, to Napoleonic France and to Nazi
Germany."[48]

The various groups that made up "the movement" disagreed
with each other and among themselves on goals and methods. For
some pacifists and liberals, terminating the war was an end in itself;
for radicals it was merely a means to the ultimate end—the overthrow of American capitalism. Many New Left radicals indeed
feared that a premature end to the war might sap the revolutionary
spirit and hinder achievement of their principal goal. Most liberals
stopped short of advocating withdrawal from Vietnam, much less
domestic revolution, proposing merely an end to the bombing,
gradual deescalation, and negotiations. Disagreement on methods
was even sharper. Liberals generally preferred nonviolent protest
and political action within the system and sought to exclude the
Communists from demonstrations. Radicals and some pacifists increasingly pressed for a shift from protest to resistance, and some
openly advocated the use of violence to bring down a system that
was itself violent.

Opposition to the war took many different forms. Fulbright
conducted a series of nationally televised hearings, bringing before
the viewing public critics of administration policies. There were
hundreds of acts of individual defiance. The folk singer Joan Baez
refused to pay that portion of her income tax that went to the defense budget. Muhammad Ali declared himself a conscientious ob-
jector and refused induction orders. Three army enlisted men—the
Fort Hood Three—challenged the constitutionality of the conflict
by refusing to fight in what they labeled an "unjust, immoral, and
illegal war." Army Captain Howard Levy used the doctrine of individual responsibility set forth in the Nuremberg war crimes trials to
justify his refusal to train combat teams for action in Vietnam.
Thousands of young Americans exploited legal loopholes, even

[48] Quoted in Thomas Powers, *Vietnam: The War at Home* (Boston, 1984), p. 118.

mutilated themselves, to evade the draft; others fled to Canada or served jail sentences rather than to go to Vietnam. A handful of Americans adopted the method of protest of South Vietnam's Buddhists, publicly immolating themselves. Antiwar rallies and demonstrations drew larger crowds in 1966 and 1967, and the participants became more outspoken in their opposition. Protesters marched daily around the White House chanting "Hey, hey, LBJ, how many kids have you killed today?" and "Ho, Ho, Ho Chi Minh, NLF is going to win." Antiwar forces attempted "lie-ins" in front of troop trains, collected blood for the Vietcong, and tried to disrupt the work of draft boards, Army recruiters, and the Dow Chemical Company, one of the makers of the napalm used in Vietnam. The most dramatic single act of protest came on October 21, 1967, when as many as 100,000 foes of the war gathered in Washington and an estimated 35,000 demonstrated at the entrance to the Pentagon, the "nerve center of American militarism."

The impact of the antiwar protests remains one of the most controversial issues raised by the war. The obvious manifestations of dissent in the United States probably encouraged Hanoi's will to hold out for victory, although there is nothing to suggest that the North Vietnamese would have been more compromising in the absence of the movement. Antiwar protest did not turn the American people against the war, as some critics have argued. The effectiveness of the movement was limited by the divisions within its own ranks. Public opinion polls make abundantly clear, moreover, that a majority of Americans found the antiwar movement, particularly its radical and "hippie" elements, more obnoxious than the war itself. In a perverse sort of way, the protest may even have strengthened support for a war that was not in itself popular. The impact of the movement was much more limited and subtle. It forced Vietnam onto the public consciousness and challenged the rationale of the war and indeed of a generation of Cold War foreign policies. It limited Johnson's military options and may have headed off any tendency toward more drastic escalation. Perhaps most important, the disturbances and divisions set off by the antiwar movement caused fatigue and anxiety among the policymakers and the public, and thus eventually encouraged efforts to find a way out of the war.[49]

[49] DeBenedetti, *Peace Reform,* pp. 174–182; Melvin Small, "The Impact of the Antiwar Movement on Lyndon Johnson, 1965–1968: A Preliminary Report," *Peace and Change,* X (Spring 1984), 1–17.

The majority of Americans appear to have rejected both the hawk and dove positions, but as the war dragged on and the debate became more divisive, public concern increased significantly. Expansion of the war in 1965 had been followed by a surge of popular support—the usual rally-round-the-flag phenomenon. But the failure of escalation to produce any discernible result and indications that more troops and higher taxes would be required to sustain a prolonged and perhaps inconclusive war combined to produce growing frustration and impatience.[50] If any bird symbolized the growing public disenchantment with Vietnam, opinion analyst Samuel Lubell observed, it was the albatross, with many Americans sharing a "fervent desire to shake free of an unwanted burden." The public mood was probably best expressed by a housewife who told Lubell: "I want to get out but I don't want to give up."[51]

Support for the war dropped sharply during 1967. By the summer of that year, draft calls exceeded 30,000 per month, and more than 13,000 Americans had died in Vietnam. In early August, the President recommended a 10 percent surtax to cover the steadily increasing costs of the war. Polls taken shortly after indicated that for 'the first time a majority of Americans felt the United States had been mistaken in intervening in Vietnam, and a substantial majority concluded that despite a growing investment, the United States was not "doing any better." Public approval of Johnson's handling of the war plummeted to 28 percent by October. Waning public confidence was mirrored in the press and in Congress. A number of major metropolitan dailies shifted from support of the war to opposition in 1967, and the influential *Time-Life* publications, fervently hawkish at the outset, began to raise serious questions about the administration's policies. Members of Congress found it impossible to vote against funds for American forces in the field and hesitated to challenge the President directly, but many who had firmly backed him at first came out openly against him. Admitting that he had once been an "all-out hawk," Republican Senator Thruston B.

[50] Sidney Verba et al., "Public Opinion and the War in Vietnam," *American Political Science Review*, 61 (June 1967), 317–333; John E. Mueller, "Trends in Popular Support for the Wars in Korea and Vietnam," *ibid.*, 65 (June 1971), 358–375; and Peter W. Sperlich and William L. Lunch, "American Public Opinion and the War in Vietnam," *Western Political Quarterly*, 32 (March 1979), 21–44.

[51] Samuel Lubell, *The Hidden Crisis in American Politics* (New York, 1971), pp. 254–260.

Morton of Kentucky spoke for the converts when he complained that the United States had been "planted into a corner out there" and insisted that there would "have to be a change."[52] White House aides nervously warned of further defections in Congress and major electoral setbacks in 1968 in the absence of dramatic changes in the war.[53]

By late 1967, for many observers the war had become the most visible symbol of a malaise that had afflicted all of American society. Not all would have agreed with Fulbright's assertion that the Great Society was a "sick society," but many did feel that the United States was going through a kind of national nervous breakdown. The "credibility gap"—the difference between what the administration said and what it did—had produced a pervasive distrust of government. Rioting in the cities, a spiraling crime rate, and noisy demonstrations in the streets suggested that violence abroad had produced violence at home. Increasingly divided against itself, the nation appeared on the verge of an internal crisis as severe as the Great Depression of the 1930s. Anxiety about the war had not translated into a firm consensus for either escalation or withdrawal, but the public mood—tired, angry, and frustrated—perhaps posed a more serious threat to the administration than the antiwar movement.

The public debate on Vietnam was paralleled by increasingly sharp divisions within the government. Rejecting CIA estimates that played down the impact of U.S. military operations on the enemy, Westmoreland insisted that progress was being made and that the war could be won if the United States used its military power effectively. Although they had beaten down many of the restrictions on the bombing by 1967, the Joint Chiefs remained deeply dissatisfied with the conduct of the air war, and they were angered by the President's continuing refusal to mobilize the reserves. Westmoreland had been given considerable leeway in implementing ground operations, but he keenly resented what he later described as the "naive, gratuitous advice" he constantly re-

[52] For the shift of 1967, see Don Oberdorfer, *Tet!* (Garden City, N.Y., 1971), pp. 83–92, and Louis Harris, *The Anguish of Change* (New York, 1973), pp. 60–61.

[53] Rostow to Johnson, August 1, 1967, Johnson Papers, Declassified and Sanitized Documents from Unprocessed Files (DSDUF), Box 2; Harry McPherson to Johnson, August 25, 1967, Harry McPherson Files, Lyndon Baines Johnson Library, Austin, Tex., Box 32.

ceived from the "self-appointed field marshals" in the State and Defense Departments, and he was greatly frustrated by the restrictions which forbade him from pursuing the enemy into its sanctuaries.[54]

Westmoreland and the Joint Chiefs joined forces in the spring of 1967 to try to secure a commitment to all-out war. Still confident that search and destroy could succeed, Westmoreland requested an additional 200,000 troops to step up ground operations against the enemy. The Joint Chiefs strongly supported him and urged a limited mobilization of the reserves to secure the new increments. To deny the enemy its sanctuaries, the military pressed for intensive ground and air operations in Cambodia and Laos, as well as for an amphibious "hook" across the demilitarized zone into North Vietnam. Conceding that the bombing of North Vietnam had reached the point of "target saturation," the Joint Chiefs nevertheless advocated intensified bombing of the Hanoi-Haiphong area and the mining of North Vietnamese ports. Presenting a united front, the military urged further escalation and expansion of the war to force a North Vietnamese defeat.[55]

By the time the military presented its proposals, some of Johnson's civilian advisers were openly advocating the abandonment of policies they had come to regard as bankrupt. Throughout 1966, opposition to escalation of the war increased within the administration. Some internal critics, including Bill Moyers of the White House staff and George Ball, quietly resigned, feeling, as James Thomson later put it, "totally alienated from the policy, but helpless as to how to change it."[56] The opposition continued to grow and increasingly centered among the civilians in the Defense Department. The major proponent of change by the spring of 1967 was, ironically, the Secretary of Defense, a man who had been so closely associated with escalation that the war had for a time been called "McNamara's war." As early as the summer of 1966, McNamara began to fear that the vast expansion of the war was endan-

---

[54] Westmoreland, *Soldier Reports*, p. 161.

[55] Westmoreland to Joint Chiefs of Staff, March 28, 1967, in Neil Sheehan et al., *The Pentagon Papers as Published by the New York Times* (New York, 1971), pp. 560–565; Joint Chiefs of Staff to McNamara, April 20, 1967, *ibid.*, pp. 565–567.

[56] James C. Thomson, "Getting Out and Speaking Out," *Foreign Policy*, 13 (Winter 1973–1974), 57.

gering the global security position he had labored so diligently to construct since taking office in 1961. He was troubled by the destructiveness of the war, particularly the civilian casualties, and by the growing domestic opposition, brought home to him time and again in public appearances when he had to shove his way through and shout down protesters. McNamara's reputation as a businessman and public servant had been based on his ability to attain maximum results at minimal cost. By early 1967, however, he was forced to admit that escalation of the war had not produced results in the major "end products—broken enemy morale and political effectiveness." The South Vietnamese government seemed no more stable than before; pacification had "if anything, gone backward." The air war had brought heavy costs but no results. "Ho Chi Minh is a tough old S.O.B.," McNamara conceded to his staff. "And he won't quit no matter how much bombing we do."[57] Moreover, the Secretary of Defense admitted that the bombing had cost the United States heavily in terms of domestic and world opinion. "The picture of the world's greatest superpower killing or seriously injuring 1,000 non-combatants a week, while trying to pound a tiny, backward nation into submission on an issue whose merits are hotly disputed, is not a pretty one," he advised Johnson in early 1967.[58] McNamara and his advisers were also disillusioned with the ground war in South Vietnam. Increases in U.S. troops had not produced correspondingly large enemy losses, and there was nothing to indicate that further expansion of the war would place any real strains on North Vietnamese manpower.

Throughout 1967, McNamara quietly and somewhat hesitantly pressed for basic changes in policy. Arguing that the major military targets in North Vietnam had already been destroyed, he proposed either an unconditional bombing halt or the restriction of the bombing to the area south of the twentieth parallel. Such a move, he added, would help to appease critics of the war at home and might lead to serious negotiations. The Secretary of Defense also advocated placing a ceiling on American troop levels, and shifting from search and destroy to a more limited ground strategy based on providing security for the population of South Vietnam. In somewhat ambiguous terms, he further proposed a scaling down of

[57] Quoted in Henry Trewhitt, *McNamara* (New York, 1971), p. 235.

[58] McNamara to Johnson, May 18, 1967, in Sheehan, *Pentagon Papers* (*NYT*), p. 580.

American political objectives. Inasmuch as the United States had gone to war to contain China, he argued, it had succeeded: the Communist defeat in Indonesia, as well as rampant political turmoil within China itself, suggested that trends in Asia were now running against China and in favor of the United States. The administration might therefore adopt a more flexible bargaining position. It could still hope for an independent, non-Communist South Vietnam, but it should not obligate itself to "guarantee and insist upon these conditions." Obliquely at least, McNamara appears to have been suggesting that the United States modify its military strategy and diplomatic stance in order to find a face-saving way out of its dilemma in Vietnam.[59]

By the summer of 1967, Lyndon Johnson was a deeply troubled man, physically and emotionally exhausted, frustrated by his lack of success, torn between his advisers, uncertain which way to turn. He seems to have shared many of McNamara's reservations, and he flatly rejected the view of the military that the solution was expansion of the war. He was disenchanted by the Joint Chiefs. "Bomb, bomb, bomb, that's all you know," he is said to have complained on several occasions.[60] He was worried by the implications of Westmoreland's ground strategy and his request for more troops. "When we add divisions, can't the enemy add divisions," he asked the General pointedly in April. "If so, where does it all end?"[61] He remained firmly opposed to mobilizing the reserves and expanding the war. Such measures would heighten the domestic opposition. They would not satisfy the military but would only lead to pressures for further escalation, perhaps even for the use of nuclear weapons. He continued to fear a confrontation with the Soviet Union or China. "I am not going to spit in China's face," he insisted.[62]

Johnson could not accept McNamara's recommendations, however. He had gradually lost confidence in his Secretary of Defense, whose dovishness he incorrectly attributed to the pernicious influ-

[59] *Ibid.*, pp. 584–585.

[60] Quoted in Lawrence J. Korb, *The Joint Chiefs of Staff: The First Twenty-Five Years* (Bloomington, Ind., 1976), p. 181.

[61] Excerpt from Johnson-Westmoreland conversation, April 20, 1967, in Sheehan, *Pentagon Papers (NYT)*, p. 567.

[62] Quoted in C. L. Sulzberger, *Seven Continents and Forty Years* (New York, 1977), p. 435.

ence of his arch-rival Robert Kennedy. The relationship between Johnson and McNamara had so soured by late 1967 that the Secretary gladly accepted an appointment to head the World Bank. Westmoreland continued to report steady progress, moreover, and the President was not ready to concede defeat. He would not consider a return to the enclave strategy—"We can't hunker down like a jackass in a hailstorm," he said—or even a ceiling on the troop level.[63] Although he seems to have agreed that the bombing had accomplished nothing, he was not prepared to stop or even limit it. Denouncing McNamara's proposals as an "aerial Dienbienphu," the Joint Chiefs had threatened to resign en masse if Johnson approved them, and the hawkish Mississippi Senator John Stennis was planning an investigation into the conduct of the air war.[64] The President was not prepared to risk a major confrontation with the hawks or a potentially explosive public debate on the bombing. Moreover, many of those to whom Johnson turned for advice posed strong arguments against McNamara's recommendations. Dean Rusk, Walt Rostow, Maxwell Taylor, Clark Clifford, and McGeorge Bundy all agreed that domestic critics would not be appeased by a bombing halt. Doves, like hawks, had "insatiable appetites," Bundy warned, and if concessions were made to them they would merely demand more. "To stop the bombing today would give the Communists something for nothing," Bundy added, and would be seen by Hanoi as a sign of weakness.[65]

Johnson thus continued to hold the middle ground between the extremes offered by his advisers. He rejected the military's proposals to expand the war and Westmoreland's request for 200,000 additional men, approving an increase of only 55,000. No ceilings were set, however, and there was no reassessment of the search-and-destroy strategy. Johnson also turned down McNamara's proposals to limit or stop the bombing. Indeed, to placate the Joint Chiefs and Congressional hawks, he significantly expanded the list of targets, authorizing strikes against bridges, railyards, and barracks within the Hanoi-Haiphong "donut" and formerly restricted areas along the Chinese border.

---

[63] *Ibid.*, p. 436.

[64] Korb, *Joint Chiefs of Staff*, p. 166.

[65] Bundy to Johnson, ca. May 4, 1967, in Sheehan, *Pentagon Papers (NYT)*, pp. 569–572.

Johnson's decisions of 1967, even more than those of 1965, were improvisations that defied military logic and did not face, much less resolve, the contradictions in American strategy. The bombing was sustained not because anyone thought it would work but because Johnson deemed it necessary to pacify certain domestic factions and because stopping it might be regarded as a sign of weakness. The President refused to give his field commander the troops he considered necessary to make his strategy work, but he did not confront the inconsistencies in the strategy itself.

The administration did modify its negotiating position again in late 1967. The so-called San Antonio formula, first conveyed secretly to the North Vietnamese by the Harvard political scientist Henry Kissinger through French intermediaries and then announced publicly in September, backed away from a firm prior agreement on mutual deescalation. The United States would stop the bombing "with the understanding" that this would lead "promptly to productive discussions"; it would "assume" that North Vietnam would not "take advantage" of the cessation of air strikes. As later explained, this meant that Hanoi would not significantly increase the infiltration of men and supplies across the seventeenth parallel.[66] The administration also indicated its willingness to admit the Vietcong to political participation in South Vietnam, a major step away from its earlier stance. This softening of the American bargaining position did not reflect the change of goals which McNamara had recommended, however. The commitment to the Thieu regime remained firm, and the willingness to deal with the Vietcong appears to have been based on a hope that it could be co-opted or defeated by political means.

By the end of the year, moreover, Johnson recognized that additional steps would be necessary to hold off disaster. After months of uncertainty, the administration finally concluded in the late summer that slow but steady progress was in fact being made in Vietnam. Officials in Saigon optimistically reported that U.S. operations were keeping the enemy off balance and inflicting enormous losses. The Vietcong was encountering increasingly difficult problems in recruiting. The ARVN's desertion rate had declined noticeably, and the performance of some units in combat had improved. After months of floundering, the pacification program seemed at

[66] Herring, *Secret Diplomacy*, pp. 538–544.

last to be getting off the ground. Even the generally pessimistic McNamara was moved to comment in July that "There is no military stalemate."[67]

By this time, however, the home front was obviously collapsing. The consensus which Johnson had so carefully woven in 1964 was in tatters, the nation more divided than at any time since the Civil War. Opposition in Congress, as well as inattention and mismanagement resulting at least partially from the administration's preoccupation with Vietnam, had brought his cherished Great Society programs to a standstill. The President himself was a man under siege in the White House, his popularity steadily waning, the target of vicious personal attacks. His top aides had to be brought surreptitiously into public forums to deliver speeches.

Johnson was alarmed by the position he found himself in, stung by his critics, and deeply hurt by the desertion of trusted aides such as McNamara. He angrily dismissed much of the criticism as unfair, and he repeatedly emphasized that his critics offered no alternatives. He had accomplished great things at home, he insisted. But the press could only whine "Veetnam, Veetnam, Veetnam, Veetnam," he would add, savagely mimicking a baby crying.[68] The harsher the criticism became, the more Johnson chose to disregard it by discrediting the source. Fulbright was a "frustrated old woman" because he had never been appointed Secretary of State. The dissent of the young sprang from ignorance. They had not lived through World War II. They would not "know a Communist if they tripped over one." The President cited with undisguised satisfaction an FBI report indicating that a large number of draft-card burners had spent time in mental institutions.[69]

Johnson recognized that he could not ignore the opposition, however. From the beginning of the war he had perceived that "the weakest chink in our armor is public opinion." During the early years, he seems to have feared the hawks more than the doves, but by late 1967 he had changed his mind. "The major threat we have is from the doves," he told his advisers in September

[67] Notes on meeting, July 12, 1967, Johnson Papers, Tom Johnson Notes on Meetings, Box 1.

[68] Quoted in Sulzberger, *Seven Continents*, p. 443.

[69] Quoted in Doris Kearns, *Lyndon Johnson and the American Dream* (New York, 1976), pp. 312–313; Graff, *Tuesday Cabinet*, pp. 99–100; notes on meeting with Congressional leaders, October 31, 1967, Johnson Papers, Diary Backup.

1967.[70] Increasingly fearful that the war might be lost in the United States, the President launched a two-pronged offensive to silence his most outspoken enemies and win public support for his policies.

Mistakenly believing that the peace movement was turning the public against the war, he set out to destroy it. He instructed the CIA to institute a program of surveillance of antiwar leaders to prove his suspicions that they were Communists operating on orders from foreign governments. This program, later institutionalized as Operation CHAOS, violated the CIA's charter. It eventually led to the compilation of files on more than 7,000 Americans. Johnson repeatedly expressed his unwillingness to indulge in McCarthyite methods, but when the CIA was unable to prove the links he suspected, he leaked information to right-wing Congressmen that he had such proof, leaving it to them to issue public charges that the peace movement was "being cranked up in Hanoi." The war against the peace movement soon shifted from surveillance to harassment and disruption. Law enforcement agencies began to indict antiwar leaders like Dr. Spock for such things as counseling draft resistance. The FBI infiltrated the peace movement with the object of disrupting its work and causing its members to do things that would further discredit them in the eyes of the public.[71]

At the same time, the administration mounted an intensive public relations campaign to shore up popular support for the war. From behind the scenes, administration officials helped to organize the Committee for Peace with Freedom in Vietnam, an ostensibly private organization headed by former Illinois Senator Paul Douglas, the principal aim of which was to mobilize the "silent center" in American politics. Johnson's advisers supplied to friendly senators, including some Republicans, information to help answer the charges of Congressional doves. A Vietnam Information Group was set up in the White House to monitor public reactions to the war and deal with problems as soon as they surfaced.[72] Recognizing that the major obstacle he faced was the widespread per-

[70] Jim Jones notes on meeting, September 5, 1967, Johnson Papers, Meeting Notes File, Box 2.

[71] Charles DeBenedetti, "A CIA Analysis of the Anti-Vietnam War Movement: October 1967," *Peace and Change*, 9 (Spring 1983), 31–35.

[72] See the extensive correspondence in Johnson Papers, Marvin Watson File, Box 32.

ception that the war was a stalemate, the President ordered the
embassy and military command in Saigon to "search urgently for
occasions to present sound evidence of progress in Viet Nam." U.S.
officials dutifully responded, producing reams of statistics to show a
steady rise in enemy body counts and the number of villages pacified, and publishing captured documents that supported these
claims. The White House even helped to make arrangements for
influential citizens to go to Vietnam and observe the progress that
was being made.[73]

As part of the public relations offensive, Westmoreland was
brought home in November, ostensibly for top-level consultations,
in fact to reassure a troubled nation. Upon arriving in Washington,
he told reporters, "I am very, very encouraged. . . . We are making
real progress." In a speech to Congress, he offered a generally optimistic appraisal of the war, advising that although the enemy had
not been defeated, it had been badly hurt. "We have reached an
important point where the end begins to come into view," he concluded, and he even hinted that the United States might begin
troop withdrawals within two years.[74]

Although his public relations offensive began to show immediate results, Johnson seems to have concluded by the end of the year
that a change of strategy in Vietnam might also be necessary to win
the war at home. Pressures for abandoning Westmoreland's search-
and-destroy operations mounted throughout 1967. Increasingly
disillusioned with the high cost and lack of results, McNamara's civilian advisers pressed for a shift to small unit patrols that would be
more "cost-effective" and would reduce U.S. casualties.[75] In his last
major policy memorandum to Johnson, the Secretary of Defense
endorsed their views, proposing a study of military operations in
the south to find ways of reducing U.S. casualties and forcing the
South Vietnamese to assume a greater burden of the fighting. Recognizing that public disillusionment threatened not only success in
Vietnam but also the internationalist foreign policy the nation had
pursued since World War II, a group of leading "establishment"

---

[73] Rostow to Bunker, September 27, 1967, Johnson Papers, DSDUF, Box 4; Eugene Locke to Johnson, October 7, 1967, Johnson Papers, National Security File,
Country File: Vietnam, Box 99.

[74] Quoted in Richard P. Stebbins; *The United States in World Affairs, 1967* (New
York, 1968), p. 68.

[75] Depuy to Westmoreland, October 19, 1967, Depuy Papers, Folder WXYZ(67).

figures, meeting under the auspices of the Carnegie Endowment, proposed adoption of a "clear and hold" strategy that would stabilize the war at a "politically tolerable level" and save South Vietnam "without surrender and without risking a wider war."[76]

The major impetus for change came from the so-called Wise Men, a distinguished group of former government officials whom Johnson occasionally called upon for guidance. Admitting that he was "deeply concerned about the deterioration of public support," he appealed to them in early November to advise him on how to unite the country behind the war. The Wise Men generally endorsed existing policies. They did warn, however, that "endless inconclusive fighting" was "the most serious single cause of domestic disquiet." To counter this, they proposed adopting a ground strategy that would be less expensive in lives and funds, and they advised shifting to the South Vietnamese greater responsibility for the fighting. Acting as a spokesman for the Wise Men, former presidential assistant McGeorge Bundy went a step further. Conceding that it was a serious matter to challenge the field commander in time of war, Bundy advised the President that since Vietnam had now become a critical issue at home, he had an obligation to do so. He urged Johnson to "visibly take command of a contest that is more political in its character than any other in our history except the Civil War" and to find a strategy that would be tolerable in cost to the American people for the five to ten years that might be required to stabilize the situation in Vietnam.[77] Johnson did not initiate a change in strategy before the end of the year. He did, however, privately commit himself to "review" the conduct of ground operations with an eye toward reducing U.S. casualties and transferring greater responsibility to the South Vietnamese.[78] Even before the Tet Offensive of 1968, he was moving in the direction of what would later be called Vietnamization.

Although he began to consider a change in strategy, Johnson did not reevaluate his essential goals in Vietnam. To take such a

[76] "Carnegie Endowment Proposals," December 5, 1967, Matthew B. Ridgway Papers, U.S. Army Military History Institute, Carlisle Barracks, Pa., Box 34A.

[77] Jim Jones notes on meeting, November 2, 1967, Johnson Papers, Meeting Notes File, Box 2; Bundy to Johnson, November 10, 1967, Johnson Papers, Diary Backup, Box 81.

[78] Johnson memorandum for the record, December 18, 1967, in Lyndon B. Johnson, *The Vantage Point* (New York, 1971), pp. 600–601.

step would have been difficult for anyone as long as there was hope of eventual success. It would have been especially difficult for Lyndon Johnson. Enormously ambitious, he had set high goals for his presidency, and he was unwilling to abandon them even in the face of frustration and massive unrest at home. It was not a matter of courage, for by persisting in the face of declining popularity Johnson displayed courage as well as stubbornness. It was primarily a matter of pride. The President had not wanted the war in Vietnam, but once committed to it he had invested his personal prestige to a degree that made it impossible for him to back off. He chose to stay the course in 1967 for the same reasons he had gone to war in the first place—because he saw no alternative that did not require him to admit failure or defeat.

While quietly contemplating a change in strategy, the President publicly made clear his determination to see the war through to a successful conclusion. "We are not going to yield," he stated repeatedly. "We are not going to shimmy. We are going to wind up with a peace with honor which all Americans seek." At a White House dinner for the Prime Minister of Singapore, the President expressed his commitment in different terms. "Mr. Prime Minister," he said, "you have a phrase in your part of the world that puts our determination very well. You call it 'riding the tiger.' You rode the tiger. We shall!" The words would take on a bitterly ironic ring in the climactic year 1968.[79]

---

[79] Quoted in Stebbins, *United States in World Affairs, 1967*, pp. 397–398.

CHAPTER 6

A Very Near Thing: The Tet Offensive and After, 1968

At 2:45 A.M. on January 30, 1968, a team of Vietcong sappers blasted a large hole in the wall surrounding the United States Embassy in Saigon and dashed into the courtyard of the compound. For the next six hours, the most important symbol of the American presence in Vietnam was the scene of one of the most dramatic episodes of the war. Unable to get through the heavy door at the main entrance of the Embassy building, the attackers retreated to the courtyard and took cover behind large concrete flower pots, pounding the building with rockets and exchanging gunfire with a small detachment of military police. They held their positions until 9:15 A.M., when they were finally overpowered. All nineteen of the Vietcong were killed or severely wounded.

The attack on the Embassy was but a small part of the Tet Offensive, a massive, coordinated Vietcong assault against the major urban areas of South Vietnam. In most other locales, the result was the same: the attackers were repulsed and incurred heavy losses. Later that morning, standing in the Embassy courtyard amidst the debris and fallen bodies in a scene one reporter described as a "butcher shop in Eden," Westmoreland rendered his initial assessment of Tet. The "well-laid plans" of the North Vietnamese and Vietcong had failed, he observed. "The enemy exposed himself by virtue of his strategy and he suffered heavy casualties." Although his comments brought moans of disbelief from the assembled journalists, from a short-term tactical standpoint Westmoreland was correct: Tet represented a defeat for the enemy.[1] As Bernard Brodie has observed, however, the Tet Offensive was "probably unique in that the side that lost completely in the tactical sense came away with an overwhelming psychological and hence political victory."[2] Tet had a tremendous impact in the United States and ushered in a new phase of a seemingly endless war.

In the spring or summer of 1967, the North Vietnamese decided upon a change in strategy. Some Americans have depicted the Tet Offensive as a last-gasp, desperation move, comparable to the Battle of the Bulge, in which a beleaguered North Vietnam attempted to snatch victory from the jaws of defeat. This seems quite doubtful, although Hanoi's decision to take the offensive probably did reflect growing concern with the heavy casualties in the south and fear of the costs of a prolonged war of attrition with the United States. It seems more likely that the offensive was born of excessive optimism, a growing perception that the urban areas of South Vietnam were ripe for revolution. There are no indications that Hanoi thought the offensive would be decisive, however. Certainly its leaders would have been pleased to force the collapse of the South Vietnamese government and bring about an American withdrawal. Most probably, they viewed the offensive as an essential part of a complex, multifaceted, long-term strategy of "fighting while negotiating." There is no evidence that the North Vietnamese timed the offensive to coincide with the first stages of the American presidential election campaign, although they certainly hoped to exploit the rising discontent with the war in the United States.

Sometime in 1967, Hanoi began developing specific plans to implement the new strategy. To lure American troops away from the major population centers and maintain a high level of U.S. casualties, a series of large-scale diversionary attacks were to be launched in remote areas. These would be followed by coordinated Vietcong assaults against the major cities and towns of South Vietnam designed to weaken the government and ignite a "general uprising" among the population. Simultaneously, new efforts would be made to open negotiations with the United States. The North Vietnamese most probably hoped through these coordinated ac-

[1] Quoted in Don Oberdorfer, *Tet!* (Garden City, N.Y., 1973), p. 34.

[2] Bernard Brodie, "The Tet Offensive," in Noble Frankland and Christopher Dowling, eds., *Decisive Battles of the Twentieth Century* (London, 1976), p. 321.

tions to get the bombing stopped, weaken the Saigon regime, exacerbate differences between the United States and its South Vietnamese ally, and intensify pressures for a change in policy in the United States. Their ultimate objective was to secure an acceptable negotiated settlement, the minimum ingredients of which would have been a coalition government and a U.S. withdrawal.

Hanoi began executing its plan in late 1967. In October and November, North Vietnamese regulars attacked the Marine base at Con Thien across the Laotian border, and the towns of Loc Ninh and Song Be near Saigon and Dak To in the Central Highlands. Shortly after, two North Vietnamese divisions laid siege to the Marine garrison at Khe Sanh near the Laotian border. In the meantime, crack Vietcong units moved into the cities and towns, accumulating supplies and laying final plans. To undermine the Saigon government, the National Liberation Front encouraged the formation of a "popular front" of neutralists, and attempted to entice government officials and troops to defect by offering generous pardons and positions in a coalition government. To spread dissension between the United States and Thieu, the front opened secret contacts with the American Embassy in Saigon and disseminated rumors of peace talks. Hanoi followed in December 1967 by stating categorically that it would negotiate with the United States if Johnson stopped the bombing.

The first phase of the North Vietnamese plan worked to perfection. Westmoreland quickly dispatched reinforcements to Con Thien, Loc Ninh, Song Be, and Dak To, in each case driving back the North Vietnamese and inflicting heavy losses but dispersing U.S. forces and leaving the cities vulnerable. By the end of 1967, moreover, the attention of Westmoreland, the President, and indeed much of the nation, was riveted on Khe Sanh, which many Americans assumed was Giap's play for a repetition of Dienbienphu. The press and television carried daily reports of the action. Johnson, insisting that the fortress must be held at all costs, kept close watch on the battle with a terrain map in the White House "war room." Westmoreland sent 6,000 men to defend the garrison, and American B-52s carried out the heaviest air raids in the history of warfare, eventually dropping more than 100,000 tons of explosives on a five-square-mile battlefield.[3]

[3] Robert Pisor, *The End of the Line: The Siege of Khe Sanh* (New York, 1982).

While the United States was preoccupied with Khe Sanh, the North Vietnamese and Vietcong prepared for the second phase of the operation. The offensive against the cities was timed to coincide with the beginning of Tet, the lunar new year and the most festive of Vietnamese holidays. Throughout the war, both sides had traditionally observed a cease-fire during Tet, and Hanoi correctly assumed that South Vietnam would be relaxing and celebrating, soldiers visiting their families, government officials away from their offices. While the Americans and South Vietnamese prepared for the holidays, Vietcong units readied themselves for the bloodiest battles of the war. Mingling with the heavy holiday traffic, guerrillas disguised as ARVN soldiers or civilians moved into the cities and towns, some audaciously hitching rides on American vehicles. Weapons were smuggled in on vegetable carts and even in mock funeral processions.

Within twenty-four hours after the beginning of Tet, January 30, 1968, the Vietcong launched a series of attacks extending from the demilitarized zone to the Ca Mau Peninsula on the southern tip of Vietnam. In all, they struck thirty-six of forty-four provincial capitals, five of the six major cities, sixty-four district capitals, and fifty hamlets. In addition to the daring raid on the Embassy, Vietcong units assaulted Saigon's Tan Son Nhut Airport, the presidential palace, and the headquarters of South Vietnam's general staff. In Hue, 7,500 Vietcong and North Vietnamese troops stormed and eventually took control of the ancient Citadel, the interior town which had been the seat of the Emperors of the Kingdom of Annam.

The offensive caught the United States and South Vietnam off guard. American intelligence had picked up signs of intensive Vietcong activity in and around the cities and had even translated captured documents which, without giving dates, outlined the plan in some detail. The U.S. command was so preoccupied with Khe Sanh, however, that it viewed evidence pointing to the cities as a diversion to distract it from the main battlefield. As had happened so often before, the United States underestimated the capability of the enemy. The North Vietnamese appeared so bloodied by the campaigns of 1967 that the Americans could not conceive that they could bounce back and deliver a blow of the magnitude of Tet. "Even had I known exactly what was to take place," Westmoreland's intelligence officer later conceded, "it was so preposterous that I probably would have been unable to sell it to anybody."[4]

Although taken by surprise, the United States and South Vietnam recovered quickly. The timing of the offensive was poorly coordinated, and premature attacks in some towns sounded a warning which enabled Westmoreland to get reinforcements to vulnerable areas. In addition, the Vietcong was slow to capitalize on its initial successes, giving the United States time to mount a strong defense. In Saigon, American and ARVN forces held off the initial attacks and within several days had cleared the city, inflicting huge casualties, taking large numbers of prisoners, and forcing the remnants to melt into the countryside. Elsewhere the result was much the same. The ARVN fought better under pressure than any American would have dared predict, and the United States and South Vietnam used their superior mobility and firepower to devastating advantage. The Vietcong launched a second round of attacks on February 18, but these were confined largely to rocket and mortar barrages against U.S. and South Vietnamese military installations and steadily diminished in intensity.

Hue was the only exception to the general pattern. The liberation of that city took nearly three weeks, required heavy bombing and intensive artillery fire, and ranks among the bloodiest and most destructive battles of the war. The United States and South Vietnam lost an estimated 500 killed while enemy killed in action have been estimated as high as 5,000. The savage fighting caused huge numbers of civilian casualties and created an estimated 100,000 refugees. The bodies of 2,800 South Vietnamese were found in mass graves in and around Hue, the product of Vietcong and North Vietnamese executions, and another 2,000 citizens of Hue were unaccounted for and presumed murdered. The beautiful city, with its many architectural treasures, was left, in the words of one observer, a "shattered, stinking hulk, its streets choked with rubble and rotting bodies."[5]

It remains difficult to assess the impact of the battles of Tet. The North Vietnamese and Vietcong did not force the collapse of South Vietnam. They were unable to establish any firm positions in the urban areas, and the South Vietnamese people did not rise up to

[4] Quoted in William C. Westmoreland, *A Soldier Reports* (Garden City, N.Y., 1976), p. 321.

[5] Dave Richard Palmer, *Summons of the Trumpet* (San Rafael, Calif., 1978), p. 194.

welcome them as "liberators." Vietcong and North Vietnamese battle deaths have been estimated as high as 40,000, and although this figure may be inflated, the losses were huge. The Vietcong bore the brunt of the fighting; its regular units were decimated and would never completely recover, and its political infrastructure suffered crippling losses.

If, in these terms, Tet represented a "defeat" for the enemy, it was still a costly "victory" for the United States and South Vietnam. ARVN forces had to be withdrawn from the country-side to defend the cities, and the pacification program incurred another major setback. The destruction visited upon the cities heaped formidable new problems on a government that had shown limited capacity to deal with the routine. American and South Vietnamese losses did not approach those of the enemy, but they were still high: in the first two weeks of the Tet campaigns, the United States lost 1,100 killed in action and South Vietnam 2,300. An estimated 12,500 civilians were killed, and Tet created as many as one million new refugees. As with much of the war, there was a great deal of destruction and suffering, but no clear-cut winner or loser.

To the extent that the North Vietnamese designed the Tet Offensive to influence the United States, they succeeded, for it sent instant shock waves across the nation. Early wire service reports exaggerated the success of the raid on the Embassy, some even indicating that the Vietcong had occupied several floors of the building. Although these initial reports were in time corrected, the reaction was still one of disbelief. "What the hell is going on?" the venerable newscaster Walter Cronkite is said to have snapped. "I thought we were winning the war!"[6] Televised accounts of the bloody fighting in Saigon and Hue made a mockery of Johnson and of Westmoreland's optimistic year-end reports, widening the credibility gap, and cynical journalists openly mocked Westmoreland's claims of victory. The humorist Art Buchwald parodied the general's statements in terms of Custer at Little Big Horn. "We have the Sioux on the run," Buchwald had Custer saying. "Of course we still have some cleaning up to do, but the Redskins are hurting badly and it will only be a matter of time before they give in."[7] The

[6] Quoted in Oberdorfer, *Tet!* p. 158.
[7] *Washington Post*, February 6, 1968.

battles of Tet raised to a new level of public consciousness basic questions about the war which had long lurked just beneath the surface. The offhand remark of a U.S. Army officer who had participated in the liberation of the delta village of Ben Tre—"We had to destroy the town to save it"—seemed to epitomize the purposeless destruction of the war. Candid photographs of the police chief of Saigon holding a pistol to the head of a Vietcong captive—and then firing—starkly symbolized the way in which violence had triumphed over morality and law.[8]

The Tet Offensive left Washington in a state of "troubled confusion and uncertainty."[9] Westmoreland insisted that the attacks had been repulsed and that there was no need to fear a major setback, and administration officials publicly echoed his statements. Johnson and his advisers were shocked by the suddenness and magnitude of the offensive, however, and intelligence estimates were much more pessimistic than Westmoreland. Many officials feared that Tet was only the opening phase of a larger Communist offensive. Some felt that Khe Sanh was still the primary objective, a fear that seemed to be borne out when the besieging forces renewed their attack on the Marine base in early February. Others feared a major offensive in the northern provinces or a second wave of attacks on the cities. An "air of gloom" hung over White House discussions, Taylor later observed, and General Wheeler likened the mood to that following the first Battle of Bull Run.[10]

The President responded with a stubborn determination to hold the line at any cost. He insisted that Khe Sanh must be held and advised Westmoreland that he was prepared to send whatever reinforcements were needed to defend the threatened fortress or meet any other threat. "The United States is not prepared to accept a defeat in South Vietnam," Wheeler advised Saigon, ". . . if you need more troops, ask for them." When Westmoreland indicated that he would appreciate any help he could get, Johnson immediately ordered an additional 10,500 men to Vietnam. In the first few weeks after Tet, the President's main concern seemed to be to "get on with the war as quickly as possible," not only by sending rein-

---

[8] Oberdorfer, *Tet!* pp. 164–171, 184–185; George A. Bailey and Lawrence W. Lichty, "Rough Justice on a Saigon Street: A Gatekeeper Study of NBC's Tet Execution Film," *Journalism Quarterly,* 49 (Summer 1972), 221–229.

[9] Townsend Hoopes, *The Limits of Intervention* (New York, 1970), p. 145

[10] Earle Wheeler oral history interview, Johnson Papers.

forcements but also by stepping up the air attacks against North Vietnam.[11]

From the standpoint of the military, the new mood of urgency in Washington provided a timely opportunity to force decisions that had been deferred for too long. Wheeler and the Joint Chiefs had been pressing for mobilization of the reserves since 1965, and by February 1968 they were certain this step must be taken at once. The Tet Offensive raised the distinct possibility that significant reinforcements would have to be sent to Vietnam. North Korea's seizure of the American warship *Pueblo* in January and a new flareup in Berlin aroused fears that additional troops might have to be dispatched to these perennial Cold War trouble spots. Available forces were nearly exhausted, and Wheeler feared that unless the United States mobilized the reserves immediately it could not meet its global commitments.

Confident that he could exploit the enemy's defeat at Tet and buoyed by the President's apparent willingness to send substantial reinforcements, Westmoreland revived his 1967 proposals to expand the war. The enemy's decision to throw in "all his military chips and go for broke," the General advised Washington, provided the United States a "great opportunity." The North Vietnamese and Vietcong could not afford the heavy losses sustained in the Tet Offensive, and with large numbers of additional troops Westmoreland was certain he could gain the upper hand. His "two-fisted" strategy envisioned an "amphibious hook" against North Vietnamese bases and staging areas across the demilitarized zone, attacks on the sanctuaries in Laos and Cambodia, and an intensified bombing campaign against North Vietnam. By taking the offensive at a time when the enemy was overextended, the General was confident that he could significantly shorten the war.[12]

Wheeler and Westmoreland conferred in Saigon in late February and devised an approach to force the President's hand. Wheeler appears to have been considerably less optimistic about the immediate prospects in Vietnam than Westmoreland, but he agreed that whether Tet provided new opportunities or posed increased dan-

[11] Herbert Schandler, *The Unmaking of a President: Lyndon Johnson and Vietnam* (Princeton, N.J., 1977), p. 91; "March 31 Speech," Johnson Papers, National Security File, National Security Council Histories: March 31, 1968 Speech, Box 47.

[12] John B. Henry, "February 1968," *Foreign Policy*, 4 (Fall 1971), 17.

gers, it justified a call for major reinforcements. The two men settled on the figure of 206,000 men, a number large enough to meet any contingency in Vietnam and to force mobilization of the reserves. Roughly half of the men would be deployed in Vietnam by the end of the year; the rest would constitute a strategic reserve. Wheeler raised no objections to Westmoreland's proposed changes in strategy, but he persuaded the field commander that it would be best to defer such recommendations until the President had approved the new troop level. He was keenly aware of Johnson's opposition to widening the war, and he apparently feared that if he presented the case for additional troops on the basis of an optimistic assessment and an offensive strategy, he would be turned down again. Troops, not strategy, offered the "stronger talking point."[13]

Wheeler's report to Washington was deeply pessimistic. Describing the Tet Offensive as a "very near thing," he warned that the initial enemy attacks had almost succeeded in numerous places and had been turned back only by the "timely reaction of the United States forces." The North Vietnamese and Vietcong had suffered heavily, but they had repeatedly demonstrated a capacity for quick recovery, and they would probably attempt to sustain the offensive with renewed attacks. Without additional troops, he concluded, the United States must be "prepared to accept some reverses," a line calculated to sway a President who had already made clear he was not willing to accept defeat. Wheeler insisted that large-scale reinforcements were necessary to protect the cities, drive the enemy from the northern provinces, and pacify the countryside. His pessimism may have been sincere; he had never been as confident as Westmoreland. It seems clear, however, that by presenting a gloomy assessment he hoped to stampede the administration into providing the troops needed to rebuild a depleted strategic reserve and meet any contingency in Vietnam. His proposal reopened in even more vigorous fashion the debate that had raged in Washington throughout 1967.[14]

Wheeler's report shocked a government already in a state of deep alarm. In terms of policy choices, it posed a hard dilemma. The General suggested that denial of the request for 206,000 troops

[13] *Ibid.*, 21.

[14] Wheeler Report, February 27, 1968, excerpted in Neil Sheehan et al., *The Pentagon Papers as Published by the New York Times* (New York, 1971), pp. 615–621.

could result in a military defeat, or at least in an indefinite continuation of the war. Acceptance of his recommendations, on the
other hand, would force a major escalation of the war and the im-
position of heavy new demands on the American people in an election year and at a time when public anxiety about Vietnam was
already pronounced. Not inclined to make a hasty decision on a
matter fraught with such grave implications, Johnson turned the
problem over to Clark Clifford, who had just replaced McNamara
as Secretary of Defense, with the grim instruction: "Give me the
lesser of evils."[15]

Whether Johnson instructed Clifford to initiate a full reevalua-
tion of Vietnam policy or whether the Secretary of Defense acted
on his own is not clear. The magnitude of the request was such that
it demanded careful study, a point Johnson perceived even if he did
not explicitly instruct Clifford along these lines. Clifford had consistently defended the President's policies in Vietnam, but his new-
ness to the job and his need to clarify many fundamental issues led
him naturally in the direction of a full reassessment. He was encouraged in this regard by the senior civilians in the Pentagon, men
such as Paul Warnke, Townsend Hoopes, and Paul Nitze, who had
long been disenchanted with American strategy and had been partially responsible for McNamara's conversion. Thus, Clifford immediately began raising at the highest levels questions that had been
avoided for years. He demanded of Wheeler and Westmoreland
precise information on how the additional troops might be deployed and what results could be expected. He instructed his civilian advisers to study all the implications of the request and to
review possible alternatives.[16]

Seizing the opportunity, the civilians in the Pentagon responded with a vigorous indictment of prevailing policy. Alain
Enthoven of Systems Analysis attacked the request for more troops
as another "payment on an open-ended commitment" and challenged the argument that it would shorten the war.[17] North Viet-

[15] Lyndon B. Johnson, *The Vantage Point* (New York, 1971), pp. 392–393.

[16] For differing views on this issue, see *ibid.*, p. 397; Clark Clifford, "A Viet Nam
Reappraisal," *Foreign Affairs*, 47 (July 1969), 609; and Schandler, *Johnson and
Vietnam*, pp. 134–137.

[17] Quoted in U.S. Congress, Senate, Subcommittee on Public Buildings and
Grounds, *The Pentagon Papers* (*The Senator Gravel Edition*) (4 vols.; Boston,
1971), IV, 558.

nam had already demonstrated that it could match American increases with increases of its own and that it could limit its losses if it chose. Even with 206,000 additional troops, Enthoven and others concluded, the current strategy could "promise no early end to the conflict, nor any success in attriting the enemy or eroding Hanoi's will to fight." The costs would be heavy, moreover. The provision of substantial additional troops could lead to "total Americanization of the war," encouraging the ARVN's tendency to do nothing and reinforcing the belief of South Vietnam's "ruling elite that the U.S. will continue to fight while it engages in backroom politics and permits widespread corruption." Expansion of the war would bring increased American casualties and require new taxes, risking a "domestic crisis of unprecedented proportions." Clifford's advisers thus agreed that the administration should maintain existing limits on the war and give Westmoreland no more than a token increase in troops.[18]

The Pentagon civilians went further, however, proposing major changes in American policy. In their final report, they urged a shift from search and destroy, with its goal of "attriting" the enemy, to a strategy based on the principle of "population security." The bulk of American forces would be deployed along the "demographic frontier," an imaginary line just north of the major population centers, where they could defend against a major North Vietnamese thrust and, by engaging in limited offensive operations, keep the enemy's main forces off balance. At the same time, the United States should force the ARVN to assume greater responsibility for the war and compel the Saigon government to "end its internal bickering, purge corrupt officers and officials and move to develop efficient and effective forces." The goal of the new approach would be a negotiated settlement rather than military victory, and in this regard the civilians urged the scaling down of American objectives to a "peace which will leave the people of SVN free to fashion their own political institutions." The plan closely resembled McNamara's proposals of 1967, but it was stated more emphatically and it went further in outlining specific alternatives.[19]

The military bitterly opposed the Defense Department recom-

---

[18] *Ibid.*, 563–564.
[19] *Ibid.*, 564–568.

mendations. Recognizing the threat to his request for additional troops—indeed, to his entire strategy—Westmoreland, with the support of Wheeler, warned that rejection of his proposals would deny the United States a splendid opportunity to take advantage of an altered strategic situation. Wheeler found "fatal flaws" in the population security strategy, admonishing that it would lead to increased fighting near the population centers, and hence to expanded civilian casualties, and that it would leave the initiative with the enemy.[20] The United States was at a "cross-road," Admiral U.S. Grant Sharp, Commander-in-Chief, Pacific Forces, warned. It must choose between using its power without restriction to achieve victory, accepting a "campaign of gradualism" and a "long drawn-out contest," or retreating "in defeat from Southeast Asia," leaving its "allies to face the Communists alone." Along with Westmoreland, the Joint Chiefs continued to advocate that the military be permitted to pursue enemy forces into Laos and Cambodia, "beat up" North Vietnam from the sea and air, and, after an Inchon-type landing, take and occupy parts of North Vietnam as far as thirty miles north of the demilitarized zone.[21]

As had happened so often before, Clifford recommended against the military's proposals without resolving the debate on strategy. The Secretary seems to have leaned toward the population security strategy and a scaling down of American objectives. "I see more and more fighting with more and more casualties on the U.S. side and no end in sight to the action," he complained on March 4.[22] He seems to have felt, however, that the proposed change, with its implicit assumption that American policy had failed, would be more than the President could accept and he may have wished to prepare Johnson for change gradually rather than confront him immediately. Clifford's formal report attempted to keep the strategic issue alive by calling for continued study of possible alternatives, but it did not address itself to the issues raised by the civilians in the Pentagon. The Secretary of Defense merely recommended the immediate deployment to Vietnam of 22,000

[20] *Ibid.*, 568.

[21] Sharp is quoted in Schandler, *Johnson and Vietnam*, pp. 166–167. For the views of the Joint Chiefs, see Clifford notes on meeting, March 18, 1968, Clark Clifford Papers, Lyndon Baines Johnson Library, Austin, Tex.

[22] Notes on meeting, March 4, 1968, Johnson Papers, Tom Johnson Notes on Meetings, Box 1.

troops, a reserve call-up of unspecified magnitude, and a "highly forceful approach" to Thieu and Ky to get the South Vietnamese to assume greater responsibility for the war.[23]

The administration accepted Clifford's recommendations without serious debate. The President and his top civilian advisers had long opposed expansion of the war, and they seem to have agreed as early as November 1967 that American forces should not be enlarged above prevailing levels. In the immediate aftermath of the Tet attacks, Johnson had been ready to send additional troops if they were required to hold the line, but by the time he received Clifford's report, the military situation in South Vietnam seemed well in hand. Westmoreland and Ambassador Ellsworth Bunker reported that American and South Vietnamese forces had fully recovered from the initial shock of the enemy offensive and were ready to mount a major counteroffensive. Under these circumstances, there seemed to be no need for immediate large-scale reinforcements, and although Johnson did not formally approve Clifford's recommendations at this time, he agreed with them and was prepared to act upon them.

The administration also accepted the principle that South Vietnam should do more to defend itself. Johnson's advisers agreed that from a long-range standpoint the key to achieving American objectives was South Vietnam's ability to stand on its own, and they had concluded in late 1967 that more should be done to promote self-sufficiency. The ARVN's quick recovery from the initial panic of Tet and its surprising effectiveness in the subsequent battles reinforced this notion by suggesting that "Vietnamization" might in fact work. Indeed, in the discussions of late February and early March 1968, some of the strongest arguments against sending massive American reinforcements were that it would encourage the South Vietnamese to do less at a time when they should be doing more and that it would take equipment which might better be used by the ARVN. The administration thus agreed in early March that Thieu and Ky should be bluntly informed that the United States was willing to send limited reinforcements and substantial quantities of equipment but that continued American assistance would depend upon South Vietnam's ability to put its own affairs in order

---

[23] Draft presidential memorandum, March 4, 1968, in *Pentagon Papers* (*Gravel*), IV, 575–576.

and assume a greater burden of the fighting.[24] The decision represented a significant shift in American policy—a return, at least in part, to the principle that had governed its involvement before 1965 and adoption, at least in rudimentary fashion, of the concept of Vietnamization, which would be introduced with much fanfare by the Nixon administration a year later.

While agreeing in principle to Clifford's recommendations, the administration also began serious consideration of a cutback in the bombing and a new peace initiative. The Secretary of Defense had recommended against further peace moves in his report and, perhaps as a sop to the military, had even urged intensification of the bombing. The initiative came from Secretary of State Rusk. Rusk had felt for some time that the bombing had produced only marginal gains at heavy cost, and he proposed that the administration seriously consider the possibility of limiting it, without condition, to those areas "which are integrally related to the battlefield," namely, the supply routes and staging areas just north of the demilitarized zone. Such a move would cost the United States nothing, he argued, since inclement weather in the next few months would severely restrict raids over the northern part of North Vietnam. Bunker had speculated that Hanoi's purpose in launching the Tet Offensive may have been to establish a favorable position for negotiations, and in late February neutral intermediaries had brought several peace feelers to the State Department. Rusk was inclined to believe that the chances for productive negotiations remained "bleak," but relaxation of the ambiguous San Antonio formula might entice Hanoi to the conference table and at least would test its intentions. Even if North Vietnam did not respond positively, domestic critics would be persuaded that the administration was taking important steps to get negotiations under way. The United States could resume air attacks on Hanoi and Haiphong later, if necessary, the Secretary pointed out, probably with increased public support.[25]

Since the abortive "peace offensive" of 1965, Johnson had stubbornly opposed any reduction of the bombing, but he was attracted to Rusk's proposal. The President was certain that North Vietnam had suffered heavy losses in the Tet Offensive, and he appears to

---

[24] Schandler, *Johnson and Vietnam*, p. 179.
[25] *Ibid.*, pp. 181–193.

have concluded that the United States could undertake negotiations from a vastly strengthened position. He recognized the need to do something to still the growing outcry against the war at home. And he was responsive to the idea because it came from Rusk, a man whose loyalty, caution, and measured judgment he had come to respect deeply.[26] Johnson later claimed to have accepted the idea of a reduction of the bombing and a new peace initiative as early as March 7, but he was not inclined to move hastily and he remained outwardly noncommittal for several weeks. He urged his advisers merely to study the matter carefully and to develop specific proposals that might be included in a major speech he was scheduled to deliver at the end of the month.

The administration's inclination to move in new directions was strengthened by mounting evidence of public dissatisfaction with the war. Discussion of Vietnam during February and March 1968 took place in an atmosphere of gloom and futility. The media continued to depict events in highly unfavorable and sometimes distorted terms. Early reports of a smashing enemy victory went largely uncorrected. The fact that the United States and South Vietnam had hurled back the attacks and quickly stabilized their position was completely lost in the image of chaos and defeat.[27] For those television and newspaper commentators who had long opposed the conflict, Tet provided compelling evidence of its folly. "The war in Vietnam is unwinnable," the columnist Joseph Kraft reported, "and the longer it goes on the more the Americans . . . will be subjected to losses and humiliation." Many opinion-makers who had supported the President or had been only mildly critical now came out forcefully against the war. Tet made clear, *Newsweek* commented, that "a strategy of more of the same is intolerable." In a much-publicized broadcast on February 27, Walter Cronkite eloquently summed up the prevailing mood. "To say that we are closer to victory today is to believe, in the face of the evidence, the optimists who have been wrong in the past. To suggest that we are on the edge of defeat is to yield to unreasonable pessi-

---

[26] Of Rusk, Johnson once said: "He has the compassion of a preacher and the courage of a Georgia cracker. When you're going in with the marines, he's the kind you want at your side." Max Frankel notes of conversation with Johnson, July 8, 1965, Krock Papers, Box 1.

[27] For a critical analysis of press and television coverage of Tet, see Peter Braestrup, *Big Story* (2 vols.; Westview, Colo., 1977).

mism. To say that we are mired in stalemate seems the only reasonable, yet unsatisfactory conclusion."[28]

A *New York Times* story of March 10, reporting that the administration was considering sending another 206,000 men to Vietnam, added to the furor. By this time, Johnson had decided to turn down Westmoreland's request, but he had not revealed his intentions publicly and the story set off a barrage of protest.[29] Critics asked why so many troops were needed and whether more would follow. Skeptics questioned the results of further escalation, warning that the North Vietnamese would be able to match any American increase. The only thing that would change, NBC's Frank McGee observed, would be the "capacity for destruction." The time had come, McGee concluded, "when we must decide whether it is futile to destroy Vietnam in the effort to save it."[30]

The possibility of another major troop increase provoked a stormy reaction in Congress. Democrats and Republicans, hawks and doves, demanded an explanation and insisted that Congress must share in any decision to expand the war. On March 11 and 12, the Senate Foreign Relations Committee grilled Rusk for a total of eleven hours, dramatically revealing a growing discontent with the administration's policies and a determination to exercise some voice in future decisions. A week later, 139 members of the House of Representatives sponsored a resolution calling for a full review of American policy in Vietnam. The Congressional outcry reinforced the administration's conviction that it could not escalate the war without setting off a long and bitter debate, and persuaded some officials, Clifford among them, that major steps must be taken to scale down American involvement.[31]

Indexes of public opinion also revealed a sharp rise in disillusionment. Support for the war itself remained remarkably steady between November 1967 and March 1968, hovering around 45 percent.[32] But approval of Johnson's conduct of it, which had risen to 40 percent as a result of the 1967 public relations campaign,

[28] Quoted in Oberdorfer, *Tet!* p. 251.

[29] Schandler, *Johnson and Vietnam*, pp. 200–205.

[30] Oberdorfer, *Tet!* p. 273.

[31] Schandler, *Johnson and Vietnam*, pp. 207–217.

[32] Approval and disapproval of the war were measured by the question "Do you think the United States made a mistake sending troops to Vietnam?"—at best an imperfect way of judging a complex issue.

plummeted to an all-time low of 26 percent during Tet. By March, moreover, an overwhelming majority of Americans (78 percent) were certain that the United States was not making any progress in Vietnam. The polls indicated no consensus for either escalation or withdrawal, only a firm conviction that the United States was hopelessly bogged down and growing doubt that Johnson could break the stalemate.[33]

By mid-March, public discontent had assumed ominous political overtones. Senator Eugene McCarthy of Minnesota, an outspoken dove, had audaciously decided to challenge Johnson's renomination, and his surprisingly strong showing in the New Hampshire primary on March 12, suddenly transformed what had seemed a quixotic crusade into a major political challenge. Johnson's name had not been on the ballot, but the party organization had mounted a vigorous write-in campaign for him, and when McCarthy won 42 percent of the vote it was widely interpreted as a defeat for the President. Subsequent analysis revealed that hawks outnumbered doves by a wide majority among McCarthy supporters in New Hampshire. Early appraisals, however, emphasized that the vote reflected a growing sentiment for peace, and within several days a more formidable peace candidate had entered the field. After weeks of hesitation and soul-searching, Senator Robert Kennedy of New York announced on March 16 that he too would run against the President on a platform of opposition to the war. With his name, his glamor, and his connections in the party, Kennedy appeared a serious threat to Johnson's renomination. Worried party regulars urged the President to do "something exciting and dramatic to recapture the peace issue" and to shift the emphasis of his rhetoric from winning the war to securing "peace with honor."[34]

The impact of public opinion on the decision-making process in March 1968 is difficult to measure. Westmoreland and others have charged that a hostile and all-too-powerful media, especially the television networks, seized defeat from the jaws of victory by turning the public against the war and limiting the government's freedom of action just when the United States had a battered enemy on

[33] Louis Harris, *The Anguish of Change* (New York, 1973), pp. 63–64, and Burns W. Roper, "What Public Opinion Polls Said," in Braestrup, *Big Story*, I, 674–704.

[34] James Rowe to Johnson, March 19, 1968, Johnson Papers, Marvin Watson File, Box 32.

the ropes.[35] In fact, up to Tet, television coverage of the war tended overwhelmingly to be neutral or favorable to the government. The reporting during and after Tet was much more critical. A direct link between television reporting and public opinion cannot be established, however, and it seems more likely that the media's shift to a critical position reflected rather than caused the parallel shift in public opinion.[36] Vietnam was the first television war, to be sure, and it is possible that the nightly exposure to violence contributed to public war-weariness. Such an assertion can never be proven, however, and it can be argued as plausibly that television generated support for the war or even caused apathy.[37]

In addition, the Johnson administration itself was at least partially responsible for media and public disillusionment during Tet. Its unduly optimistic pronouncements of 1967 made the shock of Tet greater than it might have been otherwise and widened an already large credibility gap. The President and his advisers could have corrected the distortions of the media, but their public response to Tet was itself halting and confused, in part because they were uncertain what was happening and how to respond.

The stab-in-the-back thesis is suspect on more basic grounds. That victory was within grasp, even had Westmoreland been given all the troops he requested, remains quite doubtful. And the influence of public opinion does not appear to have been as great as Westmoreland alleges. None of Johnson's civilian advisers favored expansion of the war and another large troop increase, and the President had rejected Westmoreland's proposals before the public protest reached significant proportions. Evidence of growing popular discontent merely confirmed the view that it would be disastrous to escalate the war. Public anxiety persuaded some officials that the United States must move toward a withdrawal from Vietnam, but the President did not go this far. He eventually concluded that he must make additional conciliatory gestures, but he did not alter his policy in any fundamental way or abandon his goals.

On March 22, Johnson formally rejected Westmoreland's pro-

---

[35] Westmoreland, *Soldier Reports*, p. 410; also Robert Elegant, "How to Lose a War," *Encounter*, LVII (August 1981), 73–90.

[36] Michael Mandelbaum, "Vietnam: The Television War," *Daedalus*, III (Fall 1982), 157–168; Daniel C. Hallin, "The Media, the War in Vietnam, and Political Support: A Critique of the Thesis of an Oppositional Media," *Journal of Politics*, 46 (1984), 1–23.

[37] Michael J. Arlen, *The Living Room War* (New York, 1969).

posals to seek victory through an expanded war. He was undoubtedly influenced by public opinion, but the steadily improving situation in South Vietnam seems to have been decisive. The Saigon government was responding to American pressures. Stability and order had been restored to the cities, and in late March, Thieu announced a massive increase in draft calls that would raise the ARVN's strength by 135,000 men. The intensity of Vietcong rocket attacks was steadily diminishing. Enemy forces were withdrawing from the positions established before Tet and splitting into small groups to avoid destruction or capture. In mid-March, Westmoreland informed Johnson of plans for a major offensive in the northern provinces, the central objective of which was to relieve the siege of Khe Sanh.

Under these circumstances, Johnson saw no need for a major increase in American forces. Indeed, he did not even authorize the 22,000 men recommended by Clifford, agreeing merely to deploy 13,500 support troops to augment the emergency reinforcements sent in February. At the same time, he decided to bring Westmoreland back to Washington to assume the position of Chief of Staff of the Army. The General had come under heavy fire for his prophecies of victory and for his failure to anticipate the Tet Offensive, and Johnson wanted to spare him from becoming a scapegoat. The President may also have wished to remove him from the untenable position of fighting a war under conditions he did not approve. Whatever the precise purpose, the recall of Westmoreland seems to have signified the administration's determination to maintain the limits it had placed on the war and, tacitly at least, to check further escalation of the conflict.

During the last week of March, the internal debate on Vietnam policy reached a decisive stage, and it became increasingly sharp and emotional. Some of the President's advisers still insisted that the United States should do everything possible to "hang in there." At one time during the Tet crisis, Rostow had proposed sending to Congress a new Southeast Asia Resolution to rally the nation behind the war, and he continued to urge the President to stand firm at what could be a critical turning point. Rusk persisted in working for the partial bombing halt he had outlined in early March. He was concerned by the domestic protest, but he had not despaired of success in Vietnam nor was he disposed to capitulate to the administration's critics. He seems to have been certain that the North

Vietnamese would reject his proposal, but a conciliatory gesture would show the American people that the administration was doing everything possible to bring about negotiations, thus buying time to stabilize the home front and shore up South Vietnam.[38]

By this time, Clifford had moved significantly beyond his position of late February. He was concerned by the apparent damage Vietnam was doing to the nation's international financial position. He was alarmed by the growing domestic unrest, particularly the "tremendous erosion of support" among the nation's business and legal elite. These men felt the United States was in a "hopeless bog," he reported, and the idea of "going deeper into the bog" struck them as "mad." Although unclear precisely how to proceed, he had set his mind on a "winching down" strategy that would put the United States irreversibly on a course of step-by-step deescalation. U.S. forces should not be expanded above existing levels and should be used primarily to protect the South Vietnamese population from another enemy offensive. Thieu should be pressed to clean up and broaden his government. Clifford seems also to have been prepared to make major concessions to secure a negotiated settlement. He frankly conceded that the United States might have to settle for the best it could obtain. "Nothing required us to remain until the North had been ejected from the South and the Saigon government had established complete control of all South Viet Nam," he later wrote. At a meeting on March 28, he delivered a long, impassioned plea to initiate the process of deescalation. Working behind the scenes with White House aide Harry McPherson, he waged an unrelenting campaign to win the battle for the President's mind.[39]

While the debate raged about him, Johnson remained noncommittal. His instincts leaned toward the Rusk position. He was infuriated by the desertion of Clifford, on whose support he had counted, and he was deeply opposed to abandoning a policy in which he had invested so much, particularly in view of the improved situation in South Vietnam. Publicly, he continued to take a hard line, proclaiming that "We must meet our commitments in

[38] See Rostow to Johnson, March 15, 1968, Johnson Papers, Diary Backup, Box 95; Schandler, *Johnson and Vietnam*, p. 243.

[39] Clifford, "Viet Nam Reappraisal," 613; memorandum of conversation with Clifford, March 20, 1968, Krock Papers; Harry McPherson oral history interview, Johnson Papers.

Vietnam and the world. We shall and we are going to win!"[40] On
the other hand, he could not ignore the protest that was building
around him, inside and outside the government, and he concluded,
gradually and apparently with reluctance, that some additional
conciliatory steps must be taken.

Trusted advisers from outside the government seem to have
clinched it for Johnson. To move the President from his indecision,
Clifford suggested that he call his senior advisory group, the Wise
Men, back to Washington for another session on Vietnam. After a
series of briefings by diplomatic and military officials on March 26,
the group, in a mood of obvious gloom, reported its findings. A minority advocated holding the line militarily and even escalating if
necessary, but the majority favored immediate steps toward deescalation. After its last meeting in November, McGeorge Bundy reported, the group had expected slow and steady progress. This
appeared not to have happened, however, and the majority view,
as summed up by former Secretary of State Dean Acheson, was that
the United States could "no longer do the job we set out to do in
the time we have left and we must begin to take steps to disengage." The Wise Men disagreed among themselves on what needed
to be done, some proposing a total and unconditional bombing halt,
others a shift in the ground strategy. Most of them agreed that the
goal of an independent, non-Communist South Vietnam was probably
bly unattainable and that moves should be made toward eventual
disengagement. "Unless we do something quick, the mood in this
country may lead us to withdrawal," Cyrus Vance warned.[41] "The
establishment bastards have bailed out," an angry and dispirited
Johnson is said to have remarked after the meeting.[42]

Keeping his intentions under wraps until the very end, the Pres-

[40] Schandler, *Johnson and Vietnam*, p. 248.

[41] Summary of notes, March 26, 1968, Johnson Papers, Meeting Notes File, Box 2.
The "Wise Men" were Dean Acheson, George Ball, McGeorge Bundy, Douglas
Dillon, Cyrus Vance, Arthur Dean, John McCloy, Omar Bradley, Matthew Ridg-
way, Maxwell Taylor, Robert Murphy, Henry Cabot Lodge, Abe Fortas, and
Arthur Goldberg.

[42] Quoted in Roger Morris, *An Uncertain Greatness: Henry Kissinger and American Foreign Policy* (New York, 1977), p. 44. Johnson was furious with the nega-
tive tone of the March 26 briefings. The "first thing I do when you all leave is to
get those briefers . . . ," he told one of the Wise Men. Notes, March 26, 1968,
Johnson Papers, Diary Backup File, 95. See also Depuy oral history interview,
Depuy Papers.

ident in a televised address on March 31 dramatically revealed a series of major decisions. Accepting Rusk's proposal, he announced that the bombing of North Vietnam would henceforth be limited to the area just north of the demilitarized zone. Responding to the entreaties of Clifford and the Wise Men, however, he went further. "Even this limited bombing of the North could come to an early end," he stressed, "if our restraint is matched by restraint in Hanoi." He named the veteran diplomat Averell Harriman as his personal representative should peace talks materialize, and he made clear that the United States was ready to discuss peace, any time, any place. In a bombshell announcement that caught the nation by surprise, Johnson concluded by saying firmly: "I shall not seek, and I will not accept, the nomination of my party for another term as your President." He later revealed that for some time he had considered not running for reelection. He was exhausted physically and emotionally from the strains of office. He realized that he had spent most of his political capital and that another term would be conflict-ridden and barren of accomplishment. By removing himself from candidacy, he could emphasize the sincerity of his desire for negotiations and contribute to the restoration of national unity and domestic harmony.[43]

Johnson's speech is usually cited as a major turning point in American involvement in Vietnam, and in some ways it was. No ceiling was placed on American ground forces, and the President did not obligate himself to maintain the restrictions on the bombing. Indeed, in explaining the partial bombing halt to the Embassy in Saigon, the State Department indicated that Hanoi would probably "denounce" it and "thus free our hand after a short period."[44] Nevertheless, the circumstances in which the March decisions were made and the conciliatory tone of Johnson's speech made it difficult, if not impossible, for him to change course. March 31, 1968, marked an inglorious end to the policy of gradual escalation.

The President did not change his goals, however. The apparent American success in the battles of Tet reinforced the conviction of Johnson, Rusk, and Rostow that they could yet secure an indepen-

---

[43] *Public Papers of Lyndon B. Johnson, 1968–1969* (2 vols.; Washington D.C., 1970), I, 469–476. On Johnson's decision not to run, see also George Christian memorandum, March 31, 1968, Johnson Papers, Diary Backup File, Box 96

[44] "March 31 Speech," Johnson Papers, National Security File, National Security Council Histories: March 31, 1968 Speech, Box 47.

dent, non-Communist South Vietnam. "My biggest worry was not Vietnam itself," the President later conceded, "it was the divisiveness and pessimism at home.... I looked on my approaching speech as an opportunity to help right the balance and provide better perspective. For the collapse of the home front, I knew well, was just what Hanoi was counting on."[45] By rejecting major troop reinforcements, reducing the bombing, shifting some military responsibility to the Vietnamese, and withdrawing from the presidential race, Johnson hoped to salvage his policy at least to the end of his term, and he felt certain that history would vindicate him for standing firm under intense criticism. Johnson's speech did not represent a change of policy, therefore, but a shift of tactics to salvage a policy that had come under bitter attack.

The new tactics were even more vaguely defined and contradictory than the old, however. The March decisions marked a shift from the idea of graduated pressure to the pre-1965 concept of saving South Vietnam by denying the enemy victory. Precisely how this was to be achieved was not spelled out. The debate over ground strategy was not resolved, and Westmoreland's successor, General Creighton Abrams, was given no strategic guidance. Administration officials generally agreed that ground operations should be scaled down to reduce American casualties, but it was not clear how they would contribute to the achievement of American goals. The bombing was to be concentrated against North Vietnamese staging areas and supply lines, but it had not reduced infiltration significantly in the past and there was no reason to assume it would be more effective in the future. The exigencies of domestic politics required acceptance of the concept of Vietnamization, and the surprising response of the ARVN during Tet raised hopes that it would work. There was little in the past record of various South Vietnamese governments to suggest, however, that Thieu and his cohorts could conciliate their non-Communist opponents and pacify the countryside while effectively waging war against a weakened but still formidable enemy. Negotiations were also desirable from a domestic political standpoint, but in the absence of concessions the administration was not prepared to make, diplomacy could accomplish nothing and its failure might intensify the pressures the talks were designed to ease. In short, the tactics of

[45] Johnson, *Vantage Point*, p. 422.

1968 perpetuated the ambiguities and inconsistencies that had marked American policy from the start.

U.S. policy in the months after Tet makes clear that, although the Johnson administration spoke a more conciliatory language and altered its tactics, it had not retreated from its original goals. The President made good on his pledge to negotiate, accepting, after numerous delays, Hanoi's proposal to send representatives to Paris for direct talks. From the outset, however, he refused to compromise on the fundamental issues. In the meantime, the United States sought to keep maximum pressure on enemy forces in South Vietnam and assisted the South Vietnamese in a frantic drive to gain control of the countryside, while making plans for a gradual shift of the military burden to the ARVN. The result was to harden the stalemate, leaving resolution of the problem to the next administration.

Despite the accommodating tone of Johnson's March 31 speech, the administration approached the reality of negotiations with extreme caution. Hanoi's positive response caught Washington by surprise, and many U.S. officials suspected a clever North Vietnamese ploy to exploit antiwar sentiment in the United States. The administration had no choice but to accept the enemy's proposal for direct talks, but it was determined not to rush into negotiations. Although Johnson had vowed to send representatives "to any forum, at any time," he rejected Hanoi's proposed sites of Phnom Penh, Cambodia, and Warsaw, where, he said, the "deck would be stacked against us."[46]

The two nations finally agreed to meet in Paris, and the administration took a hard line from the outset. Harriman and Clifford advocated a generous initial offer to get negotiations moving and extricate the United States from Vietnam as quickly as possible. Johnson's other advisers were not persuaded, however. Westmoreland and Bunker claimed that the U.S. position in South Vietnam had improved significantly and that the administration would be negotiating from strength in Paris. Johnson and his advisers expressed grave doubts that the talks would lead to anything. They were certainly sincere in their desire for peace, but the terms for which they were prepared to hold out made virtually certain that nothing would be accomplished. Rusk insisted that the United

[46] *Ibid.*, pp. 505–506.

States should get North Vietnam "to make concessions" or "take responsibility for breaking off the talks." In return for a complete bombing halt, administration officials seemed inclined to back off from the San Antonio formula. Rusk even talked about holding out for North Vietnamese observance of the 1962 Geneva Accords on Laos and reestablishment of the demilitarized zone. The United States was opposed to a cease-fire that would tie its hands militarily in the south, and in terms of a political settlement Rusk spoke hopefully of restoration of the status quo antebellum.[47]

Formal talks opened in Paris on May 13 and immediately deadlocked. North Vietnam had agreed to talks as part of its broader strategy of fighting while negotiating. It probably had no interest in substantive negotiations while the military balance of forces was unfavorable, and it may have viewed the Paris talks primarily as a means of getting the bombing stopped, exacerbating differences between the United States and South Vietnam, and intensifying antiwar pressures in the United States. The North Vietnamese made clear that they were establishing contact with the United States to secure the "unconditional cessation of U.S. bombing raids and all other acts of war so that talks may start." The Johnson administration was willing to stop the bombing, but, as in the past, it insisted on reciprocal steps of deescalation. Hanoi continued to reject the American demand for reciprocity and refused any terms which limited its ability to support the war in the south while leaving the United States a free hand there.

The American delegation subsequently introduced a new proposal, actually a variant of the old two-track plan, in an attempt to break the impasse. The United States would stop the bombing "on the assumption that" North Vietnam would respect the demilitarized zone and refrain from further rocket attacks on Saigon and other cities, and that "prompt and serious talks" would follow. The offer brought no formal response or any indication that one might be forthcoming. American officials complained that the North Vietnamese seemed prepared to sit in Paris "and even read the telephone directory if necessary to keep non-productive talks going," and the Joint Chiefs pressed relentlessly for reescalation, including

[47] Notes on meeting, May 6, 1968, Johnson Papers, Meeting Notes File, Box 3; Harold Johnson notes on meetings, May 6, 8, 1968, Harold Johnson Papers, Box 127; Andrew Goodpaster oral history interview, U.S. Army Military History Institute, Carlisle Barracks, Pa.

B-52 strikes against North Vietnamese sanctuaries in Cambodia.[48]

Fearful that the talks might drag on inconclusively, perpetuating the war and exacerbating domestic divisions, the chief American negotiator, W. Averell Harriman, urged the President to compromise. Although North Vietnam had not responded formally to the American proposal, Vietcong rocket attacks had subsided and there were indications that significant numbers of North Vietnamese troops had been withdrawn from the south. Harriman argued that the military lull could be interpreted as the sign of deescalation the United States had sought, and he pressed Johnson to stop the bombing and reduce the level of American military activity while making clear the next move he expected from Hanoi. Clifford supported Harriman's proposal, but the military argued that the lull was simply a regroupment for the next offensive and warned that stopping the bombing would endanger American troops. Johnson flatly rejected Harriman's proposal. Indeed, at a press conference on July 31, he threatened that if there were no breakthrough in Paris, he might be compelled to undertake additional military measures. "Our most difficult negotiations were with Washington and not Hanoi . . . ," one U.S. diplomat later lamented, "we just couldn't convince the President that summer."[49]

While standing firm in Paris, the administration used every available means to strengthen its position in South Vietnam. The United States stepped up the pace of military operations in the spring of 1968. The air war in the south reached a new peak of intensity, as B-52s and fighter-bombers relentlessly attacked infiltration routes, lines of communication, and suspected enemy base camps. The number of B-52 missions tripled in 1968, and the bombs dropped on South Vietnam exceeded one millions tons. In March and April, the United States and South Vietnam conducted the largest search-and-destroy mission of the war, sending more than 100,000 troops against enemy forces in the provinces around Saigon. "Charlie [the Vietcong] is being relentlessly pursued night and

---

[48] Notes on National Security Council meeting, May 22, 1968, Johnson Papers, National Security File, NSC Meetings, Box 3; notes on meetings, May 25, 28, Johnson Papers, Meeting Notes File, Box 3.

[49] Quoted in Allan E. Goodman, *The Lost Peace: America's Search for a Negotiated Settlement of the Vietnam War* (Stanford, Calif., 1978), p. 69.

day and pounded to shreds whenever and wherever we catch him," one U.S. officer exclaimed.[50] The scale of American military operations diminished somewhat in the summer and fall as Abrams shifted to small-unit patrols and mobile spoiling attacks, but throughout the remainder of the year the United States kept intense pressure on enemy forces in South Vietnam.

The United States and South Vietnam also launched an Accelerated Pacification campaign to secure as much of the countryside as possible in the event serious negotiations should begin. Abrams committed a major proportion of American and ARVN manpower to the program, and local defense forces were enlarged and given modern military equipment. To use their resources more effectively, the United States and South Vietnam focused their pacification efforts in certain key areas. U.S. and South Vietnamese officials energetically applied both carrot and stick to cripple an already weakened Vietcong. The Chieu Hoi Program, which offered amnesty and "rehabilitation" to defectors, was intensified, as was the Phoenix Program, a direct attack on the Vietcong infrastructure through mass arrests. By late 1968, for the first time, the United States and South Vietnam had committed a major portion of their resources and manpower to the task of controlling the countryside.[51]

The United States also pressed forward with Vietnamization. American officials candidly admitted that the South Vietnamese were nowhere near ready to assume the burden of their own defense. "If you took out all the United States ... forces now," Abrams conceded, "the Government would have to settle for a piece of Vietnam."[52] New plans were nevertheless drawn up to expand and upgrade the South Vietnamese armed forces and to shift to them gradually the primary responsibility for military operations. The force level was increased from 685,000 to 850,000, training programs were drastically expanded, and ARVN units were given the newest equipment. To increase the combat-readiness of Vietnamese troops and to smooth the transition, Abrams employed

[50] Frank Clay to Mr. and Mrs. Lucius Clay, May 15, 1968, Frank Clay Papers, U.S. Army Military History Institute, Carlisle Barracks, Pa.

[51] Douglas S. Blaufarb, *The Counterinsurgency Era: U.S. Doctrines and Performance* (New York, 1977), pp. 264–265.

[52] A. J. Langguth, "General Abrams Listens to a Different Drummer," *New York Times Magazine* (May 5, 1968), 28.

ARVN and American units in combined operations.[53]

Pacification and Vietnamization were both long-range under-takings, however, and the frenzied efforts of 1968 could not make up for years of neglect. It was the end of the year before the pacifi-cation program got back to where it had been before Tet. The es-tablishment of a presence in the villages was not tantamount to gaining the active support of the people, something that could not be accomplished overnight. The ARVN was larger and better equipped, but its basic problems remained uncorrected. Desertions reached an all-time high in 1968; an acute shortage of qualified offi-cers persisted. At the end of the year, American advisers rated two ARVN divisions "outright poor," eight no better than "improving," and only one "excellent."[54] Americans detected among the Viet-namese a stubborn, if quiet, resistance to the whole notion of Viet-namization. Clifford returned from a visit to Saigon "oppressed" by the "pervasive Americanization" of the war. The United States was still doing most of the fighting and paying the cost. "Worst of all," he concluded, "the South Vietnamese leaders seemed content to have it that way."[55]

The crash programs of 1968 did not decisively alter the military or political balance in South Vietnam. The Vietcong's hold on the countryside was weaker than ever before, and defections increased significantly. The harsh methods used to rebuild the insurgents' de-pleted ranks alienated many villagers. The government was there-fore able to regain much of what had been lost in the early days of Tet and even extend its influence into new areas. The United States held the military initiative throughout much of South Vietnam during 1968, and its spoiling attacks on base areas and supply lines kept the enemy off balance. Americans detected a marked deterio-ration in the quality of the NVA soldiers they faced after Tet. The Vietcong clandestine organization and North Vietnamese main units remained intact, however, and the launching of major opera-tions in May and September, as well as sporadic rocket attacks on

[53] J. Lawton Collins, Jr., *The Development and Training of the South Vietnamese Army, 1950–1972* (Washington, D.C., 1975), pp. 85–88, 100–101, 104–105, 117–118.

[54] Robert Shaplen, *The Road from War: Vietnam, 1965–1970* (New York, 1970), p. 250.

[55] Clifford, "Viet Nam Reappraisal," pp. 614–615; also Clifford to Johnson, July 16, 18, 1968, Clifford Papers, Box 5.

the cities, made clear that the adversary retained significant strength and the will to fight on.

Although it improved markedly in the aftermath of Tet, the performance of the Government of Vietnam remained at best uneven, its stability uncertain. Government and people worked together effectively in implementing Operation Recovery, a massive crash program to repair the damage done the cities by the battles of Tet. At American urging, Thieu adopted a new economic program to combat inflation, and instituted an anti-corruption program to deal with one of South Vietnam's oldest and most pervasive problems. On the basis of these actions and others, some optimistic observers concluded by late in the year that the government was functioning more effectively than at any time since the mid-1950s. For every problem attacked, however, others remained unchallenged and new ones surfaced. Land reform moved forward at a snail's pace, if at all. Tet created thousands of new refugees, and American officials expressed grave concern at the government's apparent indifference to their plight. The prospect of negotiations made Thieu more reluctant than ever to broaden the base of his government. He made some cosmetic changes, appointing a civilian, Tran Van Huong, as Prime Minister and promising to increase civilian influence in the government. Increasingly, however, he withdrew into himself, trusting no one and making most decisions on his own. "He is his own Nhu," one American complained with more than a touch of resignation.[56]

The possibility of an American withdrawal exacerbated the fragmented political system of South Vietnam. "Divisiveness is still endemic," Robert Shaplen observed in late 1968, "and rivalries exist across the board, in politics, in the Army, among religious groups, and so on." The rivalry between Ky and Thieu intensified, factionalizing much of the government. The Buddhists remained more alienated than ever, issuing open demands for the foundation of a "peace cabinet" and urging the soldiers to lay down their arms. Both the Buddhists and the sects appeared to look forward to the collapse of the government so that they could pick up the pieces. New political groups proliferated after the peace negotiations

[56] Quoted in Shaplen, *Road from War*, p. 248. See also William Colby oral history interview, Johnson Papers, and James P. Grant to Ernest Lindley, September 21, 1968, Johnson Papers, National Security File, Country File: Vietnam, Box 101.

began, but they were dissension-ridden and could not work together. Much of the urban population persisted in its demeanor of watchful waiting. The South Vietnamese, Shaplen concluded, seem "more and more like men who know they are suffering from an incurable malady."[57]

Vietnamese-American tensions increased significantly in the period after Tet. The government and its supporters angrily protested that they had been railroaded into negotiations before they were ready. Those Vietnamese who had come to depend upon the United States expressed bitter fears that they would be left at the mercy of the Vietcong. The accumulated frustrations of fighting a war they could not "win" in a hostile environment were manifested more openly among American servicemen in 1968, and the savagery of the battles of Tet and the heavy losses sustained inflamed anti-Vietnamese feelings. A gallows' humor solution to the Vietnam dilemma that went the round of fire bases and GI bars typified the attitude. "What you do is, you load all the Friendlies onto ships and take them out to the South China Sea. Then you bomb the country flat. Then you sink the ship."[58] The murder of more than 200 civilians, including women and children, in the village of My Lai by an American company under the command of Lieutenant William Calley in March 1968 starkly reveals the hostility that some Americans had come to feel for all Vietnamese.

Divisions within the United States also increased dramatically in 1968, and although Vietnam was only one of numerous causes, it increasingly became the focal point. Campus unrest mounted significantly, with some 200 demonstrations erupting in the first half of the year. The most violent took place at Columbia University in New York, where 1,000 police wielding nightsticks forcefully broke up a mass sit-in. The assassination of Martin Luther King, Jr., in April brought latent racial unrest to the surface, provoking rioting, looting, and burning of urban areas throughout the country. U.S. Army units had to be brought into the nation's capital to maintain order. The assassination of presidential candidate Robert Kennedy in June seemed to indicate the extent to which violence had triumphed over reason. More than anything else, the Democratic convention in Chicago in August dramatized the reality of a nation

[57] Shaplen, *Road from War*, p. 208.
[58] Michael Herr, *Dispatches*, (New York, 1978), p. 59.

divided against itself. While delegates inside the convention hall bitterly debated the war, antiwar protesters engaged police in bloody battles in the streets of Chicago. The convention nominated Johnson's preferred candidate, Vice President Hubert H. Humphrey, and endorsed the President's policies, proving beyond doubt to some critics that the war could not be ended by working within the system. More important, the bloodshed in the streets of "nightstick city" was brought into the homes of Americans each night on television, and the nation "could no longer turn away from the fact that the war in Southeast Asia . . . was causing a kind of civil war in the United States."[59]

Largely in response to domestic pressures, Johnson in late 1968 made one last effort to get the peace talks off dead center. The convention in Chicago badly discredited the Democrats, and in its aftermath some party leaders pleaded for a dramatic peace move to assist Humphrey, who lagged well behind Republican candidate Richard M. Nixon in the early polls. The President had repeatedly insisted that he would not be swayed by political considerations, but he was sympathetic to the concerns of leading Democrats, and he was eventually persuaded that he might be able to break the deadlock in Paris without undue risk. Harriman continued to argue that the military lull in South Vietnam was a clear sign of North Vietnamese interest in substantive negotiations, and Abrams assured Johnson that a bombing halt would not pose a military threat. The North Vietnamese had been badly hurt by the spring campaigns. In any case, the approach of the monsoon season would severely limit the effectiveness of the bombing for several months. To appease the military and keep pressure on North Vietnam, Johnson agreed, in the event of a bombing halt, to redeploy American airpower against North Vietnamese supply lines in Laos. The President, with apparent reluctance, finally committed himself to stop the bombing altogether if some concessions could be obtained from the North Vietnamese.[60]

Over the next few weeks, Harriman diligently negotiated an "understanding." To meet Hanoi's continuing objections to reciprocity, he indicated that the bombing would be stopped unilat-

[59] Nancy Zaroulis and Gerald Sullivan, *Who Spoke Up? American Protest Against the War in Vietnam, 1963–1975* (New York, 1984), p. 200.

[60] Johnson, *Vantage Point,* pp. 514–515; memorandum for the record, October 23, 1968, Johnson Papers, Diary Backup, November 11, 1968, Box 115.

erally, and North Vietnam eventually dropped its insistence that the bombing halt be unconditional. The U.S. delegation made clear, however, that North Vietnam would be expected to stop rocket and mortar attacks on South Vietnamese cities and limit the infiltration of men and supplies across the demilitarized zone. In addition, the North Vietnamese informally agreed that serious peace talks would begin within four days after the bombing had been stopped. The administration was especially pleased to secure Hanoi's consent to the Saigon government's participation in the peace talks. To get around North Vietnam's repeated refusal to negotiate directly with the "puppet" Saigon government and Thieu's refusal to join in any negotiations in which the NLF participated, Harriman devised an ingenious "our side, your side" formula. The negotiations would be two-sided, but each side was free to work out its own composition and to interpret the makeup of the other as it chose. The NLF and the Saigon government could thus participate in the proceedings without recognizing the other as an independent entity. The North Vietnamese refused to commit themselves formally to these "understandings," but they gave numerous private assurances that they would "know what to do" once the bombing had stopped. Hesitant to the end, Johnson finally agreed to "go the last mile" for peace, although administration officials agreed that if the North Vietnamese took advantage of the bombing halt or appeared not to be negotiating seriously, the United States might resume air operations.[61]

No sooner had the arrangements been completed than the South Vietnamese balked. Thieu may have been responding to right-wing politicians in his own country, Ky included, who issued dire warnings of an American "sellout." His intransigence was encouraged by Republican leaders who feared a Democratic preelection "peace gimmick" that would undercut the Nixon campaign, and hence urged the South Vietnamese to hold out until after the election.[62] A wily, calculating politician, Thieu probably con-

---

[61] Johnson, *Vantage Point*, p. 518; notes on meetings, October 14, 31, 1968, Johnson Papers, Meeting Notes File, Box 3.

[62] The Nixon contact with Thieu comprises a story of "espionage" and intrigue worthy of a spy novel. Nixon's future National Security Adviser Henry Kissinger had excellent contacts in the Johnson administration, having served as an intermediary in a major peace move the preceding year. Eager to secure a top-level foreign policy position, Kissinger kept the Nixon camp informed as Johnson's secret negotiations for a bombing halt unfolded. Nixon used Madame Anna Chen-

cluded without any prompting that he would do better with the
Republicans than with the Democrats and that delay was advantageous. Proclaiming that his government was not a "car that can be
hitched to a locomotive and taken anywhere the locomotive wants
to go," he insisted that he would not meet with the Vietcong and
that the American-arranged understanding was a "clear admission
of defeat." Hanoi must issue formal assurances that it would dees-
calate the war and must negotiate directly with Saigon.[63]

Thieu's obstinacy posed a dilemma for the United States. Johnson recognized that to concede to Saigon's demands would "blow
the whole peace effort sky high," perhaps wrecking Humphrey's
chances as well.[64] On the other hand, he feared that to negotiate
without Saigon, as Harriman and even Rusk urged, offered little
prospect of an acceptable settlement and risked Republican
charges of a sellout. The President thus announced the bombing
halt on October 31 without South Vietnamese approval, but he delayed the opening of formal talks. In the meantime, the United
States combined renewed assurance that it would not recognize the
Vietcong or impose a coalition government on South Vietnam with
private pressures and eventually a public threat to begin talks
without Saigon if it did not give way. After a two-week delay, during which time Nixon won a precariously thin victory over Humphrey, Thieu agreed to send representatives to Paris.

Once in Paris, the South Vietnamese raised procedural objections which nullified any hope of a peace settlement. The United
States had originally proposed that the delegations be seated at two
long tables to emphasize the two-sided nature of the talks, but
North Vietnam had demanded a square table with one delegate on
each side to give force to its contention that the NLF was a separate
party to the talks. To get around this impasse, Harriman had proposed a round table and the North Vietnamese had acquiesced. But
Saigon refused to go along. Thieu may have felt that the issue was
of sufficient symbolic or even practical importance to merit resis-

nault, widow of the legendary founder of the World War II Flying Tigers, to
urge Thieu to sabotage the administration's diplomacy, suggesting that South
Vietnam might fare better with a Nixon administration in January than with a
Johnson administration in its last days. See Seymour M. Hersh, *The Price of
Power: Kissinger in the Nixon White House* (New York, 1983), pp. 15–22.

[63] Quoted in Shaplen, *Road from War*, p. 243.

[64] Johnson, *Vantage Point*, pp. 517–519.

tance, or he may simply have seized on it to stall the talks until a presumably more sympathetic Nixon took office. Harriman, outraged at what he later denounced as a "ridiculous performance" on the part of the South Vietnamese, again urged Johnson to negotiate without them, and Clifford raised the possibility of starting to withdraw U.S. troops.[65] The President upheld Thieu's objections, however, and with the assistance of the Soviet Union persuaded Hanoi to accept a compromise: two rectangular tables placed at opposite ends of a round table. By the time the battle of the tables had been resolved, the Johnson administration was in its last days and any chance of substantive negotiations had passed.[66]

It seems highly doubtful that South Vietnamese intransigence sabotaged an opportunity for a peace settlement. Hanoi's approach on procedural issues was more flexible in late 1968 than previously, probably because the North Vietnamese wanted to get the bombing stopped, possibly because they hoped to extract an acceptable settlement from Johnson before he left office. Hanoi's flexibility most likely did not extend to substantive issues, however. There is nothing to indicate that Hanoi would have accepted anything short of an American withdrawal and a coalition government. These terms would not have been acceptable to the United States. Although he had given in on the bombing halt and was deeply annoyed with Thieu, Johnson still clung to the goals he had pursued so doggedly since taking office. He made clear to Thieu that he would not recognize the NLF or accept a coalition government or some form of cosmetic settlement that would permit an American withdrawal. He seems to have felt that he could still achieve his original goals, and he was convinced that he had the enemy on the ropes.[67] On the day he ordered the bombing halt, he instructed Abrams to "use his manpower and resources in a maximum effort" to "keep the enemy on the run" and convince him "he could never win on the field of battle."[68] Thus, even if Thieu had gone along

---

[65] Clifford notes for meeting with Johnson, November 18, 1968, Clifford Papers, Box 6.

[66] *New York Times Magazine* (August 24, 1969), 72; Harriman oral history interview, Johnson Papers; Cooper, *Lost Crusade*, pp. 406–407.

[67] The enemy could "still knock out a window light," Johnson remarked in November, but "they have been out of it since September." Henry Graff, *The Tuesday Cabinet* (Englewood Cliffs, N.J., 1970), p. 163. Also notes on meeting with Nixon, November 11, 1968, Johnson Papers, Tom Johnson Notes, Box 1.

[68] Johnson, *Vantage Point*, p. 523.

from the start, it appears highly unlikely that any meaningful peace agreement could have been reached in 1968, particularly in view of the short timetable. Each side could claim "victory" in the campaigns of Tet, but the position of each was also significantly weakened and neither emerged with sufficient leverage to force a settlement. Tet merely hardened the deadlock, and it would take four more years of "fighting while negotiating" before it was finally broken.

CHAPTER 7

A War for Peace: Nixon, Kissinger, and Vietnam, 1969–1973

"We will not make the same old mistakes," Henry A. Kissinger proclaimed of Vietnam in 1969. "We will make our own."[1] Kissinger's remark underscored the Nixon administration's determination to find new solutions to an old problem, and the self-effacing humor, a Kissinger trademark, suggested a certainty of success. But the prediction turned out to be only partially correct. Kissinger and Nixon did try new approaches, some of which in time produced their own mistakes, but their policy suffered from the same flaws as those of their predecessors. Although disguising it in the rhetoric of "peace with honor," the Nixon administration persisted in the quixotic search for an independent, non-Communist Vietnam. This goal was to be achieved primarily by a massive buildup of South Vietnamese military strength and by the application of military pressure against North Vietnam, methods that had been tried before in various forms and had been found wanting. The result was four more years of bloody warfare in Indochina, a marked increase in domestic strife, and a peace settlement that permitted American extrication but was neither honorable nor lasting.

American foreign policy in the Nixon-Kissinger era bore the distinct personal imprint of its shapers. The Middle American professional politician and the German-born Harvard professor could hardly have been more different in background, but they shared a

[1] Quoted in Roger Morris, *An Uncertain Greatness: Henry Kissinger and American Foreign Policy* (New York, 1977), p. 4.

love of power and a burning ambition to mold a fluid world in a way that would establish their place in history. Loners and outsiders in their own professions, they were perhaps naturally drawn to each other, and at least in the first years, a lingering mutual suspicion was kept in check by mutual dependence, Kissinger viewing Nixon as a means to prominence and power, Nixon relying on Kissinger to shape and implement his broad designs. Although both men had reputations as rigid ideologues, they were pragmatic and flexible in their approach to problems, and they shared a penchant for secrecy and intrigue and a great flair for the unexpected move. Above all, they shared a contempt for bureaucracy. They took the controls of American foreign policy firmly in their own hands and jealously guarded them, using, but never relying on, the rest of the government. The result was a foreign policy that was sometimes bold and imaginative in conception, sometimes crude and improvised; sometimes brilliant in execution, sometimes bungling; a policy dedicated to the noble goal of a "generation of peace," but frequently ruthless and cynical in the use of military power.

Prior to taking office, Nixon and Kissinger had firmly defended the American commitment in Vietnam. At the height of the domestic debate in 1967, Nixon had vigorously argued that the presence of American troops in Southeast Asia had helped to contain an expansionist China and had given the "free" Asian nations time to develop stable institutions. "Whatever one may think of the 'domino theory,'" he asserted, "it is beyond question that without the American commitment in Vietnam, Asia would be a far different place today."[2] Kissinger was more equivocal, conceding that the United States may have exaggerated the significance of Vietnam in the early stages of its involvement. "But the commitment of five hundred thousand Americans has settled the issue of the importance of Vietnam," he quickly added. "For what is involved now is confidence in American promises."[3]

By 1969, Nixon and Kissinger recognized that the war must be ended. It had become, in the words of one of Nixon's speechwriters, a "bone in the nation's throat," a divisive force which had torn the country apart and hindered any constructive approach to domestic

[2] Richard M. Nixon, "Asia After Vietnam," *Foreign Affairs*, 46 (October 1967), 111.

[3] Henry A. Kissinger, "The Vietnam Negotiations," *Foreign Affairs*, 47 (January 1969), 219.

and foreign policy problems.[4] Nixon clearly perceived, moreover, that his ability to extricate the nation from Vietnam would decisively affect his political future and his place in history. "I'm not going to end up like LBJ," he once remarked, "holed up in the White House afraid to show my face on the street. I'm going to stop that war. Fast."[5]

The two men nevertheless insisted that the war must be ended "honorably." Simply to pull out of Vietnam would be a callous abandonment of those South Vietnamese who had depended upon American protection and would be unworthy of the actions of a great nation. As a young Congressman, Nixon had led the right-wing Republican attack on Truman for "losing" China, and, like Johnson before him, he feared the domestic upheaval that might accompany the fall of South Vietnam to Communism. The reaction would be "terrible," he told a journalist in May 1969, "... We would destroy ourselves if we pulled out in a way that wasn't really honorable."[6] Most important, Nixon and Kissinger feared the international consequences of a precipitous withdrawal. Even before taking office, they had begun sketching the outlines of a new world order based on American primacy. Their grand design included at least a limited accommodation with the Soviet Union and China, and they felt that they must extricate the United States from the war in a manner that would demonstrate to these old adversaries resoluteness of purpose and certainty of action, a manner that would earn the respect of friends and foes alike. "However we got into Vietnam," Kissinger observed, "whatever the judgment of our actions, ending the war honorably is essential for the peace of the world. Any other solution may unloose forces that would complicate the prospects of international order."[7] Nixon agreed. "The true objective of this war is peace," he affirmed shortly after taking office. "It is a war for peace."[8]

An "honorable" settlement had to meet several essential conditions. The American withdrawal from Vietnam must be conducted

---

[4] William Safire, *Before the Fall* (New York, 1975), p. 121.

[5] H. R. Haldeman, *The Ends of Power* (New York, 1978), p. 81.

[6] Quoted in C. L. Sulzberger, *Seven Continents and Forty Years* (New York, 1977), pp. 505–507.

[7] Kissinger, "Vietnam Negotiations," 234.

[8] Sulzberger, *Seven Continents*, p. 507.

in a way that avoided even the slightest appearance of defeat. There must be no face-saving political settlement designed merely to permit a graceful American exit from Vietnam. Kissinger explicitly rejected the idea of a coalition government, which, he said, would "destroy the existing political structure and thus lead to a Communist takeover." Nixon and Kissinger set as their optimum goal a "fair negotiated settlement that would preserve the independence of South Vietnam." At a minimum, they insisted on a settlement that would give South Vietnam a reasonable chance to survive.[9]

Although this objective had eluded the United States for more than a decade, Nixon and Kissinger were certain that they could succeed where others had failed. They perceived that the Saigon government could not survive an abrupt American withdrawal, but it appeared stronger than ever before in early 1969, and with continued U.S. backing Thieu might hold on indefinitely. The North Vietnamese must recognize, Kissinger reasoned, that they could not eject the United States from Vietnam by force. They might therefore be persuaded to exchange an American withdrawal for a political settlement that would leave Thieu firmly in control.

Nixon and Kissinger were confident, moreover, that they could compel Hanoi to accept the terms it had consistently rejected. The Soviet Union had made clear its strong interest in expanded trade with the United States and an agreement limiting strategic arms, and this leverage could be used to secure Russian assistance in getting North Vietnam to agree to a "fair" settlement. Great power diplomacy would be supplemented by the use of force. Nixon felt that military pressure had failed thus far because it had been employed in a limited, indecisive manner. A "fourth-rate power like North Vietnam" must have a "breaking point," Kissinger insisted, and he and Nixon were prepared to use maximum force, threatening the very survival of North Vietnam, to get what they wanted.[10] Nixon compared his situation to that faced by Eisenhower in Korea in 1953, and he was certain that the threat of "massive retaliation" would intimidate the North Vietnamese as it had the North Koreans. He counted on his image as a hard-line anti-Communist to make the threat credible. "They'll believe any threat of force

[9] Richard M. Nixon, *RN: The Memoirs of Richard Nixon* (New York, 1978), p. 349; Safire, *Before the Fall*, p. 134.

[10] Quoted in Morris, *Uncertain Greatness*, p. 164.

Nixon makes because it's Nixon," he told one of his advisers. "We'll just slip the word to them that, 'for God's sake, you know Nixon's obsessed about Communism . . . and he has his hand on the nuclear button.' "[11]

With that sublime self-confidence common among men new to power, Nixon and Kissinger set out to end the war. Through French intermediaries, the President conveyed a personal message to the North Vietnamese expressing his sincere desire for peace and proposing as a first step the mutual withdrawal of American and North Vietnamese troops from South Vietnam and the restoration of the demilitarized zone as a boundary between north and south. Kissinger informed Soviet Ambassador Anatoly Dobrynin that the administration was eager to negotiate with Russia on a variety of urgent topics but bluntly warned that a peace settlement in Vietnam must come first.

As a signal to both Hanoi and Moscow that the United States meant business, Nixon ordered intensive bombing attacks against North Vietnamese sanctuaries in neutral Cambodia, a step repeatedly advocated by the Joint Chiefs of Staff but rejected by the Johnson administration. The military objective of the bombing was to limit North Vietnam's capacity to launch an offensive against the south, but Nixon's primary motive was to indicate that he was prepared to take measures which Johnson had avoided, thus frightening Hanoi into negotiating on his terms. Over the next fifteen months, 3,630 B-52 raids were flown, dropping more than 100,000 tons of bombs on Cambodia. The operation was dubbed (with singular inappropriateness) MENU, its individual components BREAKFAST, LUNCH, SNACK, DESSERT. At Nixon's insistence, it was kept secret from the public—and indeed from much of the government—and elaborate methods of bookkeeping were devised to conceal its existence. The number of civilian deaths among Cambodians will never be known, and to avoid the American bombs, the North Vietnamese moved deeper into Cambodian territory.[12]

Recognizing that the success of his strategy hinged on his ability to maintain at least the appearance of unity at home, Nixon adopted a public strategy to parallel his secret diplomacy. In May

[11] Quoted in Haldeman, *Ends of Power*, p. 83.

[12] William Shawcross, *Sideshow: Kissinger, Nixon and the Destruction of Cambodia* (New York, 1979), pp. 26–35.

1969, he unveiled what he described as a "comprehensive peace plan," publicly revealing the proposals he had privately made to North Vietnam and adding his hope that all "foreign" troops might be removed from South Vietnam within a year after the signing of a peace agreement. To make plain his intention of terminating American involvement in the war, he initiated planning for the phased withdrawal of American combat troops, and after conferring with Thieu on Midway Island in June, he announced the immediate withdrawal of 25,000 American combat forces. To emphasize to the Russians, the North Vietnamese, and the right wing at home that he had not gone soft, Nixon delivered several tough speeches, attacking as "new isolationists" those doves who argued that the war was diverting the nation from more pressing problems at home and stressing that his administration intended to uphold America's international responsibilities.

Nixon's secret diplomacy and implied military threats failed to wrench any concessions from Hanoi. From the North Vietnamese standpoint, the President's proposals were no improvement over those of Johnson, and to have accepted them would have represented an abandonment of goals for which they had been fighting for nearly a quarter of a century. The North Vietnamese delegation to the peace talks publicly dismissed the American offer as a "farce" and indicated that, if necessary, they would sit in Paris "until the chairs rot."[13] They continued to insist on the total and unconditional withdrawal of all U.S. forces from Vietnam and called for the establishment of a provisional coalition government from which Thieu would be excluded. Still hurting from those losses suffered in the Tet Offensive but by no means ready to quit the fight, Hanoi in 1969 shifted to a defensive, protracted war strategy, sharply curtailing the level of military activity in the south and withdrawing some of its troops back across the demilitarized zone. Certain that American public opinion would eventually force Nixon to withdraw from Vietnam, the North Vietnamese were prepared to wait him out, no matter what additional suffering it might entail.

Nixon's peace moves also failed to contain the opposition at home. When it became apparent that there would be no break-

---

[13] Robert Shaplen, *The Road from War: Vietnam, 1965–1970* (New York, 1970), pp. 300–301.

through in the Paris talks, public approval of the President's handling of the war dropped sharply. Expressing the growing frustration of the hawks, Senator Richard Russell of Georgia insisted that if the Paris talks did not soon produce results, the United States must make a "meaningful move" against North Vietnam.[14] The organized peace movement, dormant since the Democratic Convention of 1968, began to stir again, announcing plans for massive demonstrations in the fall. Congressional doves had remained silent during the administration's first hundred days, giving the President an opportunity to end the war, but by June they began to speak out anew. Republican Senator Jacob Javits of New York charged Nixon with pursuing the same "sterile and unsuccessful approach" followed by Johnson, and Fulbright denounced the "new isolationism" speech as "demagogy and personally offensive." Senate doves were not satisfied with Nixon's peace offer and troop withdrawal, and many Democrats rallied behind Clark Clifford's call for the withdrawal of all American forces from Vietnam by the end of 1970. By midsummer, Nixon's brief honeymoon with the Democratic-controlled Congress had ended.

Fearful that the rising domestic protest might doom his efforts to pressure the North Vietnamese into a settlement, in July Nixon quickly improvised a "go-for-broke" strategy, an all-out attempt to "end the war one way or the other—either by negotiated agreement or by force." Again through French intermediaries, he sent a personal message to Ho Chi Minh, reiterating his desire for a "just peace," but adding an ultimatum: unless some progress toward a settlement were made by November 1, he would have no choice but to resort to "measures of great consequence and force." Kissinger again spoke with Dobrynin, warning that "as far as Vietnam is concerned, the train has just left the station and is now headed down the track."[15] On Nixon's orders, Kissinger convened a special, top-secret National Security Council study group to draw up plans for what he described as "savage, punishing blows" against North Vietnam, including massive bombing attacks on the major cities, a blockade of the ports, and even the possible use of tactical nuclear weapons in certain "controlled" situations. To give force to his

[14] Russell to L. M. Thacker, July 26, 1969, Richard M. Russell Papers, University of Georgia Library, Athens, Georgia, Dictation File, Box IJ7.

[15] Nixon, *RN*, pp. 393–394, 399.

warnings, Nixon leaked word to newsmen that he was considering such options, and he emphatically told a group of Congressmen that he would not be the first American President to lose a war.[16]

Nixon's ultimatum had no effect. Hanoi did agree to secret peace talks outside the Paris framework, and on August 4 in the first of a long series of secret meetings, Kissinger met privately with North Vietnamese diplomat Xuan Thuy. Kissinger reiterated Nixon's peace proposals and ultimatum, but Xuan Thuy responded with the standard North Vietnamese line that the United States would have to withdraw all its troops and abandon Thieu in order to secure an agreement. Ho Chi Minh's formal response, written shortly before his death, conveyed the same message and was, in Nixon's words, a "cold rebuff." From Nixon's standpoint, the North Vietnamese were not only intransigent but also deliberately provocative. Hanoi Radio tossed back at the President statements made by Senate doves that Nixon's policies were prolonging the war and expressed to the "American people" hope that their "fall [peace] offensive" would "succeed splendidly."[17]

Unable to intimidate Hanoi into making even the slightest concession, Nixon was forced to choose between a major escalation of the war and an embarrassing retreat. He was infuriated by North Vietnam's defiance and by the domestic criticism, which he felt, encouraged the enemy's intransigence. His natural inclination was to strike back. But Secretary of Defense Melvin Laird and Secretary of State William Rogers implored him not to take any action that would inflame the opposition at home. And after weeks of careful analysis, Kissinger's study group concluded that air strikes and a blockade might not force concessions from Hanoi or even significantly limit its capacity to continue the war in the south. Haunted throughout his political career by a near-obsessive fear of defeat and humiliation, Nixon abandoned the plan for "savage, punishing blows" with the greatest reluctance and only after being persuaded that it would not work. Having relied on military pressure to bring a quick and decisive end to the war, he suddenly found himself in November 1969 without a policy.

[16] The most complete discussion of this planning, code-named DUCK HOOK, is in Seymour Hersh, *The Price of Power: Kissinger in the Nixon White House* (New York, 1983), pp. 125–130.

[17] Nixon, *RN*, pp. 397–399.

Unwilling to make concessions and unable to end the war by force, Nixon again improvised, this time falling back on the Vietnamization policy he had inherited from Johnson. While he was still pondering escalation in October, the British counterinsurgency expert, Sir Robert Thompson, informed him that South Vietnam was daily growing stronger and that if the United States continued to furnish large-scale military and economic assistance, the Saigon government might be strong enough within two years to resist a Communist takeover without external help. With no place else to go, Nixon eagerly and uncritically embraced Thompson's conclusions as the foundation for a new approach to extricate the United States from the war. He seems to have reasoned that if he could mobilize American opinion behind him, persuade Hanoi that he would not abandon Thieu, and intensify the buildup of South Vietnamese military strength, the North Vietnamese might conclude that it would be better to negotiate with the United States now than with South Vietnam later, and he could extract from them the concessions necessary to secure peace with honor.

In a major speech on November 3, Nixon set out to isolate his critics and to mobilize popular backing for his policy. He firmly defended the American commitment in Vietnam, warning that a pullout would produce a bloodbath in South Vietnam and a crisis of confidence in American leadership at home and abroad. Spelling out his Vietnamization policy in some detail, he offered the alluring prospect that it would not only reduce American casualties but might also terminate American involvement in an honorable fashion regardless of what North Vietnam did. Although some members of his staff cautioned against a confrontation with the peace movement, Nixon rejected their advice. He dismissed the protesters as an irrational and irresponsible element, and accused them of sabotaging his diplomacy. He openly appealed for the support of those he labeled the "great silent majority," and he concluded with a dramatic warning: "North Vietnam cannot humiliate the United States. Only Americans can do that."[18]

Nixon's "silent majority" speech was a shrewd and, for the most part, successful political maneuver. He placed his opponents squarely on the defensive. By offering a policy which could achieve

---

[18] *Public Papers, Richard M. Nixon, 1969* (Washington, D.C., 1971), pp. 901–909.

an honorable peace with minimal American sacrifice, he appeared to have reconciled the contradictory elements of popular attitudes toward the war. He cleverly appealed to the patriotism of his listeners and to their reluctance to accept anything resembling defeat. By specifically identifying a "silent majority," he helped to mobilize a bloc of support where none had existed.

The "moratoriums" of October 15 and November 15 were spectacularly successful and signaled a new turn in the evolution of the antiwar movement. Organized by liberals, the demonstrations attracted millions of sober, middle-class citizens, comprising "the greatest outpouring of mass protest that the country had ever known" and making clear that the peace movement was becoming "respectable."[19] In contrast to the bedlam and violence of Chicago, the fall moratoriums were peaceful and dignified affairs with religious overtones. Across the nation, church bells tolled, the names of American war dead were called out at candlelight services, and participants quietly intoned the antiwar chant "Give Peace a Chance." In Washington's March of Death, thousands of protesters carrying candles marched through high winds and rain from Arlington Cemetery to the Capitol, where they placed signs bearing the names of GIs killed in Vietnam in wooden coffins.

The fall demonstrations did not produce a change in policy, however. Although alarmed and deeply angered by the protest, Nixon publicly feigned indifference, and his silent majority speech temporarily neutralized the effects of the protest. In the immediate aftermath of the moratoriums, the antiwar movement grew quiescent again. The polls indicated solid support for the administration, and in late November pro-Nixon rallies were held in a number of cities. "We've got those liberal bastards on the run now," the President exulted, "and we're going to keep them on the run."[20]

Making Vietnamization work proved a much more formidable task than manipulating American public opinion. By the time Nixon formally announced his "new" plan to end the war, the program had been in effect for more than a year and a half. While U.S. combat forces kept the North Vietnamese and Vietcong off balance by relentlessly attacking their supply lines and base areas,

[19] Charles DeBenedetti, *The Peace Reform in American History* (Bloomington, Ind., 1984), pp. 184–185.

[20] Quoted in Szulc, *Illusion of Peace*, p. 158.

American advisers worked frantically to build up and modernize the South Vietnamese armed forces. The force level, about 850,000 when Nixon took office, was increased to over one million, and the United States turned over to South Vietnam huge quantities of the newest weapons: more than a million M-16 rifles, 12,000 M-60 machine guns, 40,000 M-79 grenade launchers, and 2,000 heavy mortars and howitzers. The Vietnamese were also given ships, planes, helicopters, and so many vehicles that one Congressman wondered aloud whether the objective of Vietnamization was to "put every South Vietnamese soldier behind the wheel."[21] Military schools were expanded to a capacity of more than 100,000 students a year. To improve morale and check the desertion rate, the promotion system was modernized, pay scales increased, veterans' benefits expanded, and systematic efforts made to improve conditions in military camps.

The Accelerated Pacification Campaign, originally designed as a crash program to extend government control over the countryside prior to negotiations, was institutionalized and expanded in 1969 and 1970. To improve security in the villages, the major weakness of earlier programs, regular forces assigned to pacification were expanded to 500,000 men, armed with M-16 rifles, and supplemented by a hastily created militia numbering in the thousands. Americans and South Vietnamese also attempted to infuse new life into old programs of village development. Village elections were held, restoring the autonomy that had been taken away in the Diem era. Elected officials were trained in civic responsibilities at the Rural Development Center in Vung Tau and upon graduation were given black pajamas furnished by the American CIA. The government turned over to individual villages control over the militia and over funds to be used for local projects. Strenuous efforts were made to clear roads, repair bridges, establish schools and hospitals, and expand agricultural production. In March 1970, the government launched an ambitious land reform program through which nearly one million hectares were eventually redistributed.

Vietnamization was in full swing by early 1970, and most observers agreed that significant gains had been made. Literally overnight the South Vietnamese Army had become one of the largest

---

[21] Thomas Buckley, "The ARVN Is Bigger and Better, But—," *New York Times Magazine* (October 12, 1969), 132.

and best equipped in the world. When properly led, moreover, ARVN units fought well, and some American advisers began to detect that, perhaps out of necessity, their performance improved noticeably as U.S. support units were withdrawn. In some areas, improvement in the performance of the militia was even greater than that of the ARVN. American "spoiling" tactics, along with North Vietnam's decision to go on the defensive, left the countryside more secure than at any time since the war had begun. The ability of the Vietcong to tax and recruit had been sharply reduced, and NVA units in South Vietnam appeared to be suffering from serious personnel and materiel shortages. In former Vietcong strongholds, roads were passable at least by day and the number of terrorist incidents declined markedly. On the surface, at least, the insurgency appeared to be under control, and even long-time skeptics like pacification expert John Vann concluded that "we are now on the right road."[22]

Real progress in Vietnamization remained uncertain, however. American officials claimed to have "neutralized" as many as 20,000 members of the Vietcong infrastructure through the Phoenix Program, and the Communists later conceded that Phoenix caused them serious problems. The figures were grossly inflated, however, and although the insurgents' clandestine apparatus was severely damaged, it remained intact. American officials also conceded that the gains in security had resulted primarily from U.S. military operations and the enemy standdown, and they were unsure whether these could be sustained in the face of the withdrawal of U.S. forces and the renewal of enemy attacks. The biggest question mark remained the government itself. Despite the frenetic activity in the villages, there was nothing to indicate that the pacification program had generated any real enthusiasm for the Thieu government. One senior U.S. officer observed, moreover, that although significant progress had been made in numerous areas, the government had not yet "succeeded in mobilizing the will and energies of the people against the enemy and in support of national programs."[23]

Americans were also unsure whether the ARVN could fill the vacuum left by U.S. troop withdrawals. On paper, it was indeed a

[22] Vann to General Frederick Weyand, January 22, 1970, Vann Papers.

[23] Memorandum by General Arthur S. Collins, fall 1970, Collins Papers; see also Report by Vietnam Special Studies Group, January 10, 1970, and Charles S. Whitehouse to William Colby, September 22, 1970, both in Vann Papers.

formidable force, but many of its fundamental weaknesses remained uncorrected. Americans estimated that the practice of "ghosting"—keeping on the rosters the names of dead and deserted soldiers so the officer-in-charge could pocket the pay—ran as high as 20 percent. Desertion remained a chronic problem, and there was a severe shortage of qualified, competent, and honest officers at all levels. Even the better ARVN units repeatedly manifested an unwillingness to engage the enemy in sustained combat, provoking a senior U.S. officer to question whether the United States would ever "be able to create an army with the offensive and aggressive spirit that will be necessary to counter either the VC or the NVA."[24] Americans also began to realize belatedly the extent to which the South Vietnamese had come to depend on the United States. The "nagging question" in 1968–1969 was whether the ARVN could fend for itself after the United States withdrew, and many U.S. advisers conceded that, at best, much time would be required before the South Vietnamese would be able to stand on their own against Hanoi's seasoned and disciplined forces.[25]

By the spring of 1970, the contradictions in Nixon's Vietnamization strategy had become all too apparent. The silent majority speech had quieted the opposition temporarily, but Nixon realized that his success was only transient. In March he announced the phased withdrawal of 150,000 troops over the next year in order to "drop a bombshell on the gathering spring storm of anti-war protest."[26] However necessary from the standpoint of domestic politics, Nixon recognized that such a move would weaken his hand in other areas. Abrams had bitterly protested the new troop withdrawals, warning that they would leave South Vietnam vulnerable to enemy military pressure and could be devastating to the Vietnamization program. Nixon had rather naively hoped that his professed determination to remain in Vietnam indefinitely and the demonstrations of public support that had followed his November 3 speech would persuade the North Vietnamese to negotiate. But there had been no breakthrough in Paris, and he recognized that the announcement of additional troop withdrawals would probably

[24] Collins memorandum, April 25, 1970, Collins Papers.

[25] Collins memorandum, fall 1970, Collins Papers; William Rosson oral history interview, U.S. Army Military History Institute, Carlisle Barracks, Pa.

[26] Nixon, *RN*, p. 448.

encourage Hanoi to delay further. Increasingly impatient for results and still certain that he could end the war by a dramatic show
of force, he once more began looking about for "initiatives" that
might be undertaken to "show the enemy that we were still serious
about our commitment in Vietnam."[27]

The overthrow of Cambodia's neutralist Prince Sihanouk in
March by a pro-American clique headed by Prime Minister Lon
Nol posed new dangers to the Vietnamization policy and presented
enticing opportunities for the initiative Nixon sought. Kissinger has
vigorously denied American complicity in the coup, and no evidence has ever been produced to prove that the United States was
directly involved. The administration appears not to have been
surprised by Lon Nol's move, however, and Washington's long-
standing and obvious dislike for Sihanouk and its interest in attacking the North Vietnamese sanctuaries in Cambodia may have encouraged Lon Nol to believe that a successful coup would be
rewarded with U.S. support.[28]

Kissinger's later claim that the United States intervened in
Cambodia only hesitantly and belatedly, and only after being persuaded that the North Vietnamese were committed to the destruction of Lon Nol's government, appears at best misleading. Shortly
after the coup, presumably with U.S. authorization, South Vietnamese units conducted raids across the border into Cambodia, and
the United States quickly recognized the new Cambodian government and initiated covert military aid. That North Vietnam decided in the aftermath of the coup to take over Cambodia remains
unproven today and was open to serious question at the time. On
the other hand, from the outset, some U.S. officials were eager to
exploit developments in Cambodia. The military for years had been
anxious to attack the North Vietnamese sanctuaries in Cambodia.
The change of government in Phnom Penh removed the long-
standing concern about violating Cambodian neutrality, and attacks on the sanctuaries could now be justified in terms of sustain-
ing a friendly Cambodian government as well as easing the military
threat to South Vietnam. Nixon therefore quickly endorsed a Defense Department proposal that South Vietnamese units with

[27] *Ibid.*, p. 445.

[28] The controversy over Cambodia is one of the most bitter and emotional to
come out of the war. The respective positions are spelled out in Shawcross, *Sideshow*, especially pp. 112–127, and in Henry A. Kissinger, *White House Years*
(Boston, 1979), pp. 457–521.

American air support attack an enemy sanctuary on the Parrot's Beak, a strip of Cambodian territory thirty-three miles from Saigon. Even before plans for this operation had been completed, the President approved a more dramatic—and much more risky—move. After nearly a week of careful and apparently agonizing study and over the vigorous opposition of Laird and Rogers, he approved Abrams's proposal that American forces attack Fishhook, a North Vietnamese base area fifty-five miles northwest of Saigon. Kissinger appears to have muted his own reservations about the enterprise, at least in part to establish himself as Nixon's premier foreign policy adviser.

Nixon's decision to send American troops into Cambodia, one of the most important and controversial decisions of his tumultuous presidency, was motivated by a variety of considerations. He was swayed by the military's argument that the operation would buy time for Vietnamization and would help to sustain a friendly government in Cambodia. On the other hand, he realized that his decision would have a "shattering effect" at home.[29] Nixon's willingness to run this risk for uncertain gains reflects, in part, what he called his "big play philosophy," his belief that since the administration was "going to get unshirted hell for doing this at all," it might as well "go for all the marbles."[30] Rather than fearing the domestic backlash he was sure would come, Nixon seems to have welcomed it. By the spring of 1970, he was embattled at home as well as abroad. The Democratic-controlled Senate had just rejected for the second time his nominee for a Supreme Court vacancy, and he was determined to show "those Senators ... who's really tough."[31] Most important, he was still confident that he could make peace by threatening Hanoi. Embarrassed by backing down from the November ultimatum, a move which conveyed precisely the wrong message, he seems to have reasoned that widening the war into previously off-limits Cambodia would make clear that unlike his predecessor he would not be bound by restraints. The North Vietnamese would then have to decide "whether they want to take us on all over again," he explained to his staff, and in terms of pressures on them to negotiate "this was essential."[32] Preoccupied

[29] *Ibid.*, p. 449.

[30] Safire, *Before the Fall*, pp. 102–103.

[31] Morris, *Uncertain Greatness*, pp. 174–175.

[32] Safire, *Before the Fall*, p. 190.

throughout his career with the importance of responding to crises, Nixon appears to have eagerly grasped an opportunity to demonstrate his courage under fire and to show his domestic and foreign adversaries that he would not be intimidated.

The President explained his decision in a belligerent, provocative televised speech on April 30. He justified the Cambodian "incursion" as a response to North Vietnamese "aggression," although Hanoi's intentions remained unclear, and as necessary to protect American forces in Vietnam, although he did not explain why an old threat suddenly required such a vigorous response. The real target of the operation, he explained, was the Central Office for South Vietnam (COSVN), the "nerve center" of North Vietnamese military operations, although the Defense Department had made clear to him its uncertainty as to where COSVN was located or whether it even existed. Anticipating a furor at home, Nixon indicated that he would rather be a one-term President than preside over America's first defeat. He concluded with a bit of inflated rhetoric which appeared to make America's very survival hinge on his Cambodian venture. "If when the chips are down," he warned, "the world's most powerful nation acts like a pitiful helpless giant, the forces of totalitarianism and anarchy will threaten free nations and free institutions throughout the world."[33]

From a military standpoint, Nixon's Cambodian venture produced at best limited results. The American command claimed to have killed some 2,000 enemy troops, cleared over 1,600 acres of jungle, destroyed 8,000 bunkers, and captured large stocks of weapons, rendering the sanctuaries unusable for awhile and complicating North Vietnam's supply problems. By relieving any immediate threat from Cambodia, the operation may indeed have bought some time for Vietnamization. The incursion set back North Vietnam's offensive capabilities only temporarily, however, and instead of an Asian Pentagon, COSVN turned out to be little more than "a scattering of empty huts."[34] Whatever advantages the operation gained for Vietnamization may have been more than offset by enlargement of the theater of war. At a time when the United States was attempting to scale down its role in Vietnam, it had to divert

---

[33] *Public Papers, Richard M. Nixon, 1970* (Washington, D.C., 1971), pp. 405–410.

[34] Stanley Karnow, *Vietnam: A History* (New York, 1983), p. 610.

precious resources to support an even more fragile client state in Cambodia.

In Cambodia itself, U.S. actions contributed to one of the great tragedies of recent history. The United States was not exclusively responsible for Cambodia's misery. North Vietnam had violated Cambodia's precarious neutrality first, and Cambodians of all political factions inflicted their share of suffering on one another. The United States did encourage the Lon Nol government to initiate a war it could not win, however. The American invasion forced the North Vietnamese to move out of their sanctuaries and into the heartland of Cambodia. Whether as a direct or indirect consequence of the American invasion, North Vietnam initiated large-scale support for the Khmer Rouge insurgents fighting Lon Nol. In the particularly brutal civil war that followed, the United States lavishly supported the Cambodian government and unleashed thousands of tons of bombs on Cambodia. The ultimate tragedy was that from beginning to end, the Nixon administration viewed its new ally as little more than a pawn to be used to help salvage the U.S. position in Vietnam, showing scant regard for the consequences for Cambodia and its people.

The domestic reaction to Cambodia exceeded Nixon's worst expectations—in tragic ways. The unexpected expansion of a war which the President had promised to wind down enraged his critics, and his intemperate defense of his actions, including a statement indiscriminately branding protesters as "bums," added to the furor. Demonstrations broke out on campuses across the nation, and at Kent State University and Jackson State College six students were killed in angry confrontations with National Guardsmen and police. More than 100,000 demonstrators gathered in Washington the first week of May to protest Cambodia and Kent State. Students at hundreds of colleges went "on strike," and some campuses were closed down to avert further violence. The Kent State killings provoked outbreaks of violence even at normally conservative and placid institutions. At the University of Kentucky, a building was burned and student demonstrations were broken up by National Guardsmen using tear gas.[35]

The Cambodian incursion also provoked the most serious Con-

---

[35] Mitchell K. Hall, " 'A Crack in Time': The Response of Students at the University of Kentucky to the Tragedy at Kent State," *Kentucky Historical Register*, 83 (Winter 1985), 36–63.

gressional challenge to presidential authority since the beginning of the war. The President had consulted only with a handful of Congressmen, all known to be sympathetic. Many legislators, including Senate Minority Leader Hugh Scott, were outraged at having been kept in the dark by the administration, and others were infuriated by Nixon's broadening of the war.[36] In a symbolic act of defiance, the Senate voted overwhelmingly in June to terminate the Tonkin Gulf Resolution of 1964. An amendment sponsored by Senators John Sherman Cooper of Kentucky and Frank Church of Idaho proposed to cut off all funds for American military operations in Cambodia after June 30. An even more restrictive amendment sponsored by Senators George McGovern of South Dakota and Mark Hatfield of Oregon would have required the administration to withdraw all American forces from Vietnam by the end of 1971.

Enraged by the outpouring of criticism, Nixon struck back with a vengeance. There would be no more "screwing around" with Congressional foes, he instructed his staff. "Don't worry about divisiveness. Having drawn the sword, don't take it out—stick it in hard."[37] The President publicly blamed his domestic opponents for prolonging the war, and he bluntly warned Congressional leaders that if "Congress undertakes to restrict me, Congress will have to assume the consequences."[38] He approved one of the most blatant attacks on individual freedom and privacy in American history, the so-called Huston Plan, which authorized the intelligence agencies to open mail, use electronic surveillance methods, and even burglarize to spy on Americans. The agencies subsequently refused to implement this specific plan, but they did use many of its methods in the futile effort to verify suspected links between radical groups in the United States and foreign governments.[39]

The administration eventually rode out the Cambodian storm. Nixon removed American troops from Cambodia by the end of June, depriving his opponents of their most telling issue, and the protests gradually abated. Despite the flurry of activity, Congress

[36] Scott to Kissinger, May 21, 1970, Hugh Scott Papers, University of Virginia Library, Charlottesville, Va., Box 65.

[37] Safire, *Before the Fall*, p. 190.

[38] Henry Brandon, *The Retreat of American Power* (New York, 1974), pp. 146–147.

[39] Athan Theoharis, *Spying on Americans: Political Surveillance from Hoover to the Huston Plan* (Philadelphia, 1978), pp. 13–39.

was not yet ready to challenge the President directly or assume responsibility for ending the war. The more dovish Senate approved the Cooper-Church amendment, but the House rejected it, permitting the administration to continue air operations in Cambodia and send money and supplies to Lon Nol. The Hatfield-McGovern amendment could not even secure a majority of the Senate.

Although Nixon escaped with his power intact, the Cambodian episode tightened the trap he had set for himself. The domestic reaction reinforced his determination to achieve "peace with honor" while sharply limiting his options for attaining it. Cambodia may have bought some time for Vietnamization, but it also imposed clear-cut, if implicit, limits on the future use of American combat forces and increased the pressures for speeding up the pace of withdrawal. Divisiveness within the United States increased even beyond the level of 1968, with far-reaching, if still unforeseen, implications for Nixon's future. In the summer of 1970, an embittered President declared virtual warfare on those he considered his enemies: the "madmen" on the Hill, the "liberal" press, those who marched in protest. "Within the iron gates of the White House, quite unknowingly, a siege mentality was setting in," one of Nixon's aides later stated. "It was now 'us' against 'them.' Gradually, as we drew the circle closer around us, the ranks of 'them' began to swell."[40]

Hoping to break the diplomatic deadlock by going into Cambodia, Nixon seems merely to have hardened it. North Vietnamese and Vietcong delegates boycotted the formal Paris talks until American troops had been withdrawn from Cambodia, and the secret talks lapsed for months. Hanoi was content to bide its time, and the uproar in the United States probably reinforced its conviction that domestic pressures would eventually force an American withdrawal.

In an effort to resolve his foreign and domestic problems, in October 1970, Nixon launched what he described as a "major new initiative for peace." The proposals he made in a televised speech, while cleverly phrased, appear to have offered no concessions on the fundamental issues, and Hanoi promptly rejected his call for a cease-fire in place, which, it perceived, would restrict the Vietcong to areas they presently controlled without assuring them any role in

[40] Charles W. Colson, *Born Again* (Old Tappan, N.J., 1976), p. 41.

a political settlement. In any case, the speech appears to have been designed primarily for the upcoming Congressional elections. Nixon followed it up by touring ten states, angrily denouncing the antiwar protesters and urging the voters to elect men who would "stand with the President." Even here, the results were disappointing. Several doves were defeated, but the Republicans gained only two seats in the Senate and lost nine in the House.

After two years of continued heavy fighting, intensive secret diplomacy, and political maneuvering, Nixon's position was worse than when he had taken office. The negotiations with North Vietnam remained deadlocked, and a National Security Council study of late 1970 grimly concluded that the United States could neither persuade nor force Hanoi to remove its troops from the south. At home, Nixon had kept "one step ahead of the sheriff," as he would put it, narrowly managing to head off any restrictions on his warmaking powers. But he still faced a hostile and even more determined opposition in Congress and a revived antiwar movement which had seemed moribund just a year before. The situation in South Vietnam remained stable. By the end of the year, however, intelligence reported a sharp increase in the infiltration of men and supplies into Laos, Cambodia, and South Vietnam, posing an ominous threat to the northern provinces and Hue, where sizable American forces had been withdrawn.

Instead of rethinking a policy which had brought no results, Nixon clung stubbornly throughout much of 1971 to the approach he had improvised the preceding year. To appease critics at home, the timetable of American troop withdrawals was speeded up. Over the protests of General Abrams, the President ordered the removal of 100,000 troops by the end of the year, leaving 175,000 men in Vietnam of whom only 75,000 were combat forces. To make clear, at the same time, his continued determination to secure a "just" peace and to counter the threat to Vietnamization posed by increased North Vietnamese infiltration and American troop reductions, Nixon stepped up the military pressure against North Vietnam. U.S. aircraft mounted heavy attacks against supply lines and staging areas in Laos and Cambodia. Using as a pretext North Vietnamese firing upon American "reconnaissance" planes, the administration ordered "protective reaction" air strikes against bridges, base camps, and trails across the demilitarized zone and in the Hanoi-Haiphong area. In February 1971, Nixon again expanded the war, approving a major ground operation into Laos. The objective was the same as that of the Cambodian incursion—to buy time for Vietnamization by disrupting enemy supply lines—but this time the ARVN assumed the burden of the fighting, with only American air support.

The policy of troop withdrawals combined with military pressures brought limited success. The Laotian operation was at best a costly draw, at worst an unmitigated disaster. U.S. intelligence had anticipated only light resistance, but Giap apparently saw an opportunity to strike a body blow at Vietnamization and hurled some 36,000 troops, supported by the newest Russian-made tanks, against the two South Vietnamese divisions that crosssed the border. After six weeks of the bloodiest fighting of the war, the battered and exhausted ARVN forces retreated back into South Vietnam. Official spokesmen claimed to have killed as many as 15,000 enemy troops and to have destroyed North Vietnam's supply network in Laos, thus delaying a major offensive for a year. Even if these claims are true, however, the ARVN took a beating, suffering a casualty rate as high as 50 percent and an estimated 2,000 dead. The South Vietnamese performance was not what had been hoped, and it would have been much worse without the support of American aircraft, which dumped 48,000 tons of bombs during the operation. Administration assertions that the ARVN had conducted an "orderly retreat" appeared ludicrous amidst the haste and confusion which accompanied the withdrawal from Laos, and the sight of South Vietnamese soldiers clinging desperately to the skids of departing helicopters raised serious questions about the success of the Vietnamization program.

At home, the protests and demonstrations continued, drawing new faces and becoming more rancorous and unruly. In early 1971, the group Vietnam Veterans Against the War conducted its own "Winter Soldiers" investigation of U.S. war crimes in Indochina. In April, a group of Vietnam war veterans, clothed symbolically in faded uniforms adorned with combat ribbons and peace symbols, gathered in front of the Capitol, testified to their own war crimes, and ceremoniously tossed away their medals. Several days later, 30,000 self-styled members of the Mayday Tribe descended upon Washington with the avowed intention of "shutting the government down," and proceeded to conduct "lie-ins" on bridges and major thoroughfares and at the entrances of government buildings.

Mobs roamed the streets, stopping traffic and breaking windows, leading to one of the worst riots in Washington's history.

Many Americans would undoubtedly have preferred that the war simply go away, but by the summer of 1971 the history of a conflict in which the United States had been engaged for more than a decade had begun to come back to haunt the nation. After a long and much-publicized trial, a military court found Lieutenant William Calley guilty of at "least twenty-two murders" in the My Lai incident of 1968 and sentenced him to life imprisonment, once more bringing before public attention the brutality that had attended the war and setting off a brief but bitter debate on the question of responsibility for alleged war crimes. No sooner had the Calley furor abated than the *New York Times* began publication of the so-called *Pentagon Papers*, a history of decision-making in Vietnam based on secret Defense Department documents and leaked by a former Pentagon official, Daniel Ellsberg. The documents confirmed what critics of the war had long been arguing, among other things that Kennedy and Johnson had consistently misled the public about their intentions in Vietnam.

An increasingly isolated and embattled Nixon responded fiercely to what he perceived as sinister threats to his authority to govern. The Justice Department secured an injunction to prevent the veterans from sleeping on the Mall, and the government hauled off to jail some 12,000 Mayday protesters, often without bothering to charge them with any specific offense. Nixon personally intervened in the Calley case while it was still under appeal, ordering Calley released from prison and indicating that he would review the conviction. Obsessed with leaks since revelations of the secret bombing of Cambodia in 1969 and certain that critics would use the *Pentagon Papers* "to attack my goals and policies,"[41] the President took the extraordinary step of securing an injunction to prevent their publication. When the Supreme Court overturned the order, an enraged Nixon approved the creation of a clandestine group of "plumbers" to plug leaks within the government and instructed them to use any means necessary to discredit Ellsberg.

Neither Nixon's withdrawal policy nor his vigorous counterattacks against the opposition could stem the war-weariness and general demoralization which had enveloped the nation by the

[41] Nixon, *RN*, p. 509.

summer of 1971. Former Secretary of State Dean Acheson lamented the plight of "this floundering republic," and journalist Robert Shaplen labeled the United States "the sick man of the western hemisphere."[42] Disillusionment with the war reached an all-time high, with a whopping 71 percent agreeing that the United States had made a mistake by sending troops to Vietnam and 58 percent regarding the war as "immoral." Nixon's public approval rating on Vietnam had dropped to a low of 31 percent, and opposition to his policies had increased sharply. A near majority felt that the pace of troop withdrawals was too slow, and a substantial majority approved the removal of all troops by the end of the year even if the result was a Communist takeover of South Vietnam.[43] Congress reflected the growing public uneasiness, although it continued to stop short of decisive action. On two separate occasions, the Senate approved resolutions which would have set a specific deadline for the removal of all American troops pending Hanoi's release of the prisoners of war. Each time, the House removed the deadline and otherwise watered down the language.

The malaise that increasingly afflicted the nation quickly spread to the U.S. armed forces in Vietnam. Until 1969, American GIs had fought superbly. After the initiation of Nixon's troop-withdrawal policy, however, the purpose of the war became increasingly murky to those called upon to fight it, and many GIs became much more reluctant to put their lives on the line. Discipline broke down in some units, with enlisted men simply refusing to obey the orders given by officers. Attacks on officers in time of war were not unique to Vietnam, but "fragging" reached unprecedented proportions in the Vietnamization period, more than 2,000 incidents being reported in 1970 alone. The availability and high quality of drugs in Southeast Asia meant that the drug culture that attracted growing numbers of young Americans at home was easily transported to Vietnam. The U.S. command estimated in 1970 that as many as 65,-000 American servicemen were using drugs. Nor were the armed services immune from the racial tensions that tore America apart in the Vietnam era, and numerous outbreaks of racial conflict in units in Vietnam and elsewhere drew growing attention to the break-

---

[42] Acheson to Matthew B. Ridgway, July 5, 1971, and Shaplen to Robert Aspey, n.d., both in Ridgway Papers, Box 34B.

[43] Louis Harris, *The Anguish of Change* (New York, 1973), pp. 72–73.

down of morale and discipline. With obvious pain, old soldier Matthew Ridgway, who had restored the morale of the army in Korea after the firing of Douglas MacArthur, lamented the "grievous blows" that Vietnam had inflicted on his beloved army.[44]

Although determined not to be stampeded, Nixon and Kissinger were sufficiently concerned by their predicament to try once again to break the stalemate in Paris. Kissinger expressed repeated fear that the administration might not be able to get through the year without Congress "giving the farm away."[45] Nixon recognized that he would probably need a peace settlement in order to win reelection, but he hoped to get it far enough in advance to avoid the appearance of an act of desperation or a blatant political maneuver. As a consequence, in May Kissinger secretly presented to the North Vietnamese the most comprehensive peace offer yet advanced by the United States. In exchange for release of the American prisoners of war, he pledged to withdraw all troops within seven months after an agreement had been signed. The United States also abandoned the concept of mutual withdrawal, insisting only that North Vietnam stop further infiltration in return for the removal of American forces.

This offer initiated the most intensive peace discussions since the war had begun. The North Vietnamese quickly rejected Kissinger's proposal, perceiving that it would require them to give up the prisoners of war (their major bargaining weapon), to stop fighting, and to accept the Thieu regime in advance of any political settlement. Hanoi's delegate, Le Duc Tho, promptly made a counteroffer, however, agreeing to release the POWs simultaneous with the withdrawal of American forces, provided that the United States dropped its support for Thieu prior to a political settlement. Kissinger found the North Vietnamese offer unacceptable, but he was deeply impressed by Tho's serious and conciliatory demeanor and sensed "the shape of a deal" between the two offers. He could "almost taste peace," he remarked excitedly to friends.[46]

The discussions eventually broke down over the issue of the

---

[44] Ridgway to Westmoreland, April 25, 1970, Ridgway Papers, Box 34B. For a good brief account of the breakdown, see Karnow, *Vietnam*, pp. 631–632. For a more detailed, if polemical, study, see Cincinnatus, *Self-Destruction* (New York, 1978).

[45] Quoted in Vernon A. Walters, *Silent Missions* (New York, 1978), p. 516.

[46] Quoted in Marvin and Bernard Kalb, *Kissinger* (Boston, 1974), p. 180.

Thieu regime. From the start of the secret talks, the North Vietnamese had insisted that Thieu's removal was an essential precondition to any peace agreement, and on several occasions they even hinted that the United States might assassinate him. Elections were scheduled to be held in South Vietnam in September, and Tho now proposed that if the United States would withdraw its support from Thieu, permitting an open election, it could take the first step toward a settlement without losing face. Perhaps sensing just such a deal, Thieu vastly complicated matters by forcing the removal of the two opposition candidates, Nguyen Cao Ky and Duong Van Minh. Thieu's blatant interference in the political process so enraged the American Embassy that Ambassador Ellsworth Bunker urged Nixon to publicly disassociate himself from Thieu and privately force him to accept a contested election. Nixon and Kissinger were unwilling to run the risk of abandoning Thieu at this critical juncture, however, and so rejected both the North Vietnamese proposal and Bunker's advice. The administration would only declare its "neutrality," a position that was meaningless while Thieu was running unopposed.

After Thieu had been safely reelected, Kissinger attempted to keep the secret talks alive, offering a new proposal calling for elections to be held within sixty days after a cease-fire and providing that Thieu would withdraw one month in advance of the elections. From Hanoi's standpoint, this offer was undoubtedly an improvement over earlier ones, but it did not guarantee that Thieu would not be a candidate or prevent him from using the machinery of the government to rig the election. North Vietnam promptly rejected the American proposal. The secret talks once again broke off in late November, leaving a frustrated and discouraged Kissinger to ponder the thought of building a dam across the Mekong River and flooding all of Vietnam.[47]

Although the negotiations of late 1971 were the most serious yet undertaken, they eventually broke down for the same reason earlier efforts had failed. Having invested so much blood, treasure, and prestige in a struggle of more than ten years' duration, neither side was yet willing to make the sort of concessions necessary to produce peace. Perhaps more important, each side still felt that it could get what it wanted by means other than compromise. Since

[47] *Ibid.*, p. 185.

1968, North Vietnam had remained on the defensive, carefully husbanding its resources and manpower for a final military offensive it hoped would topple the Thieu regime and force the United States out of Vietnam. While attempting, without much success, to keep Vietnam on the back burner in 1971, Nixon and Kissinger had focused their attention and energy on negotiations designed to achieve a dramatic reversal in American relations with the Soviet Union and China, thus making good their promises of a "generation of peace." By the end of 1971, summit meetings had been scheduled for both Peking and Moscow, giving Nixon and Kissinger renewed hope that they could salvage the administration, ensure the President's reelection, and leave North Vietnam isolated with no choice but to come to terms. Neither side would achieve what it hoped with the dramatic military and diplomatic moves of 1972 and each would pay a high price trying, but they did bring the war into a final, devastating phase which would ultimately lead to a compromise peace.

In March 1972, North Vietnam launched a massive, conventional invasion of the south. At that time there were only 95,000 American forces there, of whom only 6,000 were combat troops, and Hanoi correctly assumed that domestic pressures would prevent Nixon from putting new forces into Vietnam. The invasion was probably timed to coincide with the beginning of the American presidential campaign in hopes that, as in 1968, a major escalation of the fighting would produce irresistible pressures for peace in the United States. The North Vietnamese aimed the offensive directly at the ARVN's main force units, hoping to discredit the Vietnamization policy and to tie down as many regular forces as possible, enabling the Vietcong to resume the offensive in the countryside, disrupt the pacification program, and strengthen its position prior to the final peace negotiations.

In its first stages, the offensive was an unqualified success. Spearheaded by Soviet tanks, 120,000 North Vietnamese troops struck across the demilitarized zone, in the Central Highlands, and across the Cambodian border northwest of Saigon. American intelligence completely misjudged the timing, magnitude, and location of the invasion. Achieving almost complete surprise, the North Vietnamese routed the thin lines of defending ARVN forces and quickly advanced toward the towns of Quang Tri in the north, Kontum in the highlands, and An Loc just sixty miles north of Saigon. Thieu was forced to commit most of his reserves to defend the threatened towns, thus freeing the Vietcong to mount an offensive in the Mekong Delta and in the heavily populated regions around Saigon.

Although stunned by the swiftness and magnitude of the invasion, Washington responded quickly and vigorously. Nixon refused to sit back and permit South Vietnam to fall. He was unwilling to send American ground forces back to Vietnam, but he was determined at the very least to give North Vietnam a "bloody nose," and he appears to have seen in the North Vietnamese invasion an opportunity to revive the end-the-war strategy he had been forced to discard in 1969.[48] He quickly approved B-52 strikes across the demilitarized zone and followed up with massive air attacks on fuel depots in the Hanoi-Haiphong area. In the meantime, Kissinger met secretly with Soviet Premier Leonid Brezhnev. For the first time Kissinger made explicit American willingness to permit North Vietnamese forces to remain in South Vietnam after a cease-fire. He also stated emphatically that the United States held the Soviet Union responsible for the invasion, and he warned that a continuation of the war could severely damage Soviet-American relations and have grave consequences for North Vietnam. The offer and the threats were repeated to Le Duc Tho on May 1.

Still confident of victory, the North Vietnamese flatly rejected Kissinger's offer, leaving Nixon a set of difficult choices. Warning that Hue and Kontum might soon fall and the "whole thing may be lost," Abrams on May 8 pressed for intensification of the bombing of North Vietnam and for the mining of Haiphong harbor.[49] On the other hand, Secretaries Laird and Rogers warned that drastic countermeasures could have disastrous domestic consequences, and Kissinger expressed concern that the Soviets might cancel Nixon's impending visit to Moscow, undoing months of tedious negotiations on strategic arms limitations and other major issues. Unwilling to risk defeat in South Vietnam and enraged by the North Vietnamese challenge, Nixon was determined to strike back. "The bastards have never been bombed like they're going to be bombed this time," he affirmed.[50] A number of Washington officials speculated that the Russians had too much at stake in their negotiations with

---

[48] Elmo R. Zumwalt, Jr., *On Watch* (New York, 1976), p. 379.

[49] Nixon, *RN*, p. 594.

[50] Nixon transcript, June 29, 1972, *New York Times*, June 30, 1974.

the United States to cancel the summit. Even should they decide to do so, Nixon was ready to take the risk for the sake of his credibility. "If we were to lose in Vietnam," he observed, "there would have been no respect for the American President . . . because we had the power and didn't use it. . . . We must be credible."[51] Thus on May 8, the President announced to a startled nation the most drastic escalation of the war since 1968: the mining of Haiphong harbor, a naval blockade of North Vietnam, and massive, sustained bombing attacks.

Nixon's gamble succeeded, at least up to a point. The Soviet leadership was unwilling to permit the war to interfere with détente, and the summit was not canceled. During Nixon's visit to Moscow in late May, Brezhnev and his colleagues went through the motions of protesting, complaining that American actions in Vietnam constituted "sheer aggression" and even comparing them to the policies of Nazi Germany.[52] But the negotiations proceeded in a cordial and businesslike manner, and major agreements were concluded. The Soviet Union continued to send economic assistance to North Vietnam, but it also sent a top-level diplomat to urge Hanoi to make peace. The Chinese issued perfunctory protests against Nixon's escalation of the war, but behind the scenes they also exerted pressure on Hanoi to settle with the United States. Both major Communist powers had apparently come to regard Vietnam as a sideshow which must not be allowed to jeopardize the major realignment of power then taking place in the world.

The domestic reaction was also manageable. A new round of protests and demonstrations erupted. Senate doves were "shocked," "mad," and "depressed," according to George Aiken of Vermont, and another flurry of end-the-war resolutions went into the Congressional hopper.[53] The American public had always considered bombing a more acceptable alternative than the use of ground forces, however, and many Americans felt that the North Vietnamese invasion justified Nixon's response. As on earlier occasions, both the public and Congress rallied around decisive presidential initiatives, and the success of the summit cut the ground from beneath those who argued that Nixon's rash action would un-

[51] Quoted in Raymond Price, *With Nixon* (New York, 1977), p. 112.

[52] Kissinger, *White House Years*, pp. 1226–1227.

[53] George Aiken, *Senate Diary* (Brattleboro, Vt., 1976), pp. 55–57.

dermine détente. Unwilling to leave anything to chance, zealous operatives in the Committee for the Reelection of the President forged thousands of letters and telegrams to the White House expressing approval of Nixon's policies, but even without such antics the President enjoyed broad support. His public approval rating shot up dramatically, Congress did nothing, and he emerged in a much stronger position at home than he had been before the North Vietnamese invasion.[54]

Nixon's decisive response appears also to have averted defeat in South Vietnam. Code-named LINEBACKER, the May operation vastly exceeded all previous attacks on North Vietnam. In June alone, American planes dropped 112,000 tons of bombs on North Vietnam, including new "smart" bombs precisely guided to their targets by computers receiving signals from television cameras and laser beams. The conventional military tactics employed by the North Vietnamese in the summer of 1972 depended heavily on vast quantities of fuel and ammunition, and the intensive bombing attacks, along with the blockade, made resupply extremely difficult. In South Vietnam itself, American bombers flew round-the-clock missions, pummeling North Vietnamese supply lines and encampments. With the vital assistance of American airpower, the ARVN managed to stabilize the lines in front of Saigon and Hue and even mounted a small counteroffensive.

In the final analysis, however, the furious campaigns of the summer of 1972 merely raised the stalemate to a new level of violence. Both sides suffered heavily, the North Vietnamese losing an estimated 100,000 men and the South Vietnamese 25,000, but neither emerged appreciably stronger than before. North Vietnam had demonstrated the continued vulnerability of the ARVN, and the Vietcong had scored some gains in the Delta, but Thieu remained in power and Nixon had not given in. Despite the heavy casualties suffered and the massive damage sustained from the American air attacks, the North Vietnamese retained significant forces in the south, and intelligence reports coming into Washington in late summer indicated that they had the capacity to fight on for at least two more years.[55]

Frustrated in their hopes of breaking the diplomatic stalemate

[54] Harris, *Anguish of Change*, p. 74.

[55] Szulc, *Illusion of Peace*, pp. 618–619.

by military means, by the fall of 1972 each side found compelling reasons to attempt to break the military deadlock by diplomacy. The Nixon administration was by no means desperate to get a settlement before the election. The Democrats had nominated George McGovern, an outspoken dove whose extreme views appeared to make him the easiest of the Democratic contenders to defeat and left Nixon a great deal of room to maneuver. Nonetheless, Nixon and Kissinger recognized that an indefinite continuation of the air war could cause problems at home. They were increasingly frustrated, moreover, by the persistence of a war they had come to regard as a major obstruction to their grand design for a generation of peace. They were eager to uphold their earlier promises to end the war, and they wanted a settlement before the election if it could be attained without embarrassment.

For North Vietnam, the pressures were equally, if not more, compelling. The policy of playing off Russia against China to secure aid and diplomatic support had exceeded the point of diminishing returns. The nation had suffered terribly from the latest round of American bombing, and although it was prepared to continue the war if necessary, it was anxious for peace if that could be accomplished without sacrificing its long-range goals. The North Vietnamese leaders had been disappointed in their hope that the offensive would force Nixon to compromise. They had at one time placed faith in the McGovern candidacy, but by September it seemed clear that Nixon would win in a landslide. Battered, exhausted, and isolated, the North Vietnamese appear to have concluded that they might get better terms from Nixon before the election.

From late summer on, the two nations began inching toward a compromise. Having already indicated its willingness to allow North Vietnamese troops to remain in the south after a cease-fire, the United States took a major step away from its absolute commitment to Thieu by agreeing to accept a tripartite electoral commission. This body, composed of the Saigon government, the Vietcong, and the neutralists, would be responsible for arranging a settlement after the cease-fire went into effect. In the meantime, the North Vietnamese dropped their insistence on the ouster of Thieu, accepting the principle of a cease-fire that would leave Thieu in control temporarily but would grant the PRG (the Provisional Revolutionary Government, the formal title assumed by the

National Liberation Front in 1969) status as a political entity in the south.

Serious discussions of a settlement along these lines began in late September, and during three weeks of intensive, sometimes frantic negotiations, Kissinger and Le Duc Tho hammered out the fundamentals of an agreement. Within sixty days after a cease-fire, the United States would withdraw its remaining troops, and North Vietnam would return the American POWs. A political settlement would then be arranged by the tripartite National Council of Reconciliation and Concord, which would administer elections and assume responsibility for implementing the agreement. By October 11, all but two issues had been resolved. Eager to wrap up the matter as quickly as possible, Kissinger and Tho agreed that these items could be left until later, and that after consulting with Nixon and Thieu, Kissinger would proceed on to Hanoi to initial the treaty on October 22.

In his haste to get an agreement, Kissinger badly miscalculated Thieu's willingness to do what the United States told him and Nixon's willingness to support Thieu. Kissinger spent five days in Saigon, going over the treaty item by item, patiently explaining its advantages for South Vietnam and issuing only slightly veiled warnings that a refusal to go along could mean the end of American support. Of all the parties concerned, however, Thieu had the least interest in an agreement providing for an American withdrawal, and he found the terms totally unacceptable. He bitterly protested that he had not been consulted in advance of the negotiations. He insisted that he would never accept an agreement which permitted North Vietnamese troops to remain in the south and accorded the Vietcong sovereignty. He brought to Kissinger's attention some notably careless phraseology in the text which accorded the tripartite commission the status of a coalition government. Demanding wholesale changes in the agreement, including establishment of the demilitarized zone as a boundary between two sovereign states, Thieu apparently gambled on driving a wedge between the United States and North Vietnam, blocking the treaty indefinitely and permitting a continuation of the war.

Thieu succeeded, at least for the short term. Furious at this unexpected threat to his handiwork, Kissinger urged Nixon to go ahead without Saigon's approval. Concerned primarily with getting the United States out of Vietnam, he seems to have been content to secure nothing more than a "decent interval" between an American withdrawal and the resolution of the conflict in Vietnam. Nixon, on the other hand, never abandoned the quest for "peace with honor." He seems to have shared some of Thieu's reservations about the October draft, and although he had approved it conditional upon Thieu's acquiescence, he seems to have sensed in Saigon's rejection an opportunity to achieve what he had sought from the start. Certain of an "enormous mandate" in the upcoming election, he decided to wait until after he had been reelected, at which point he could demand that North Vietnam settle or "face the consequences of what we could do to them."[56] He was not willing to let Thieu block an agreement indefinitely, but a brief delay would permit him to provide South Vietnam additional assistance, to patch up fundamental shortcomings in the treaty, and to weaken North Vietnam's ability to threaten the peace.

Kissinger attempted to keep alive hopes of an early settlement by stating publicly on October 31 that "peace is at hand," but Nixon's support of Thieu ensured the breakdown of the October agreement. When the secret discussions resumed in early November, the United States brought up for reconsideration some sixty points, many of them minor but others central to the compromise. Kissinger asked for at least a token withdrawal of North Vietnamese troops from the south and requested changes in the text which would have weakened the political status of the Vietcong, restricted the powers of the tripartite commission, and established the demilitarized zone as a virtual boundary. He added stern warnings that Nixon, having secured a landslide victory over McGovern, would not hesitate to "take whatever action he considers necessary to protect United States interests."[57] Certain that they had been betrayed and refusing to give way in the face of threats, the North Vietnamese angrily rejected Kissinger's proposals and raised numerous demands of their own, even reviving their old insistence upon the ouster of Thieu.

For weeks, Kissinger and Le Duc Tho sparred back and forth across the negotiating table in an atmosphere ridden with tension and marked by frequent outbursts of anger. Fearful that the peace that had seemed so close might yet slip away, each side made con-

---

[56] Nixon, *RN*, p. 701.
[57] *Ibid.*, p. 721.

cessions, and by mid-December they had returned to the essence of the original compromise with only the status of the demilitarized zone unresolved. By this time, however, Kissinger's patience had worn thin. Conveniently forgetting the American role in the breakdown, he complained bitterly that the North Vietnamese had "goaded us beyond endurance" and warned Nixon that they were deliberately stalling to force a break between the United States and Thieu.[58] Frustrated and impatient for results, the two men decided to break off the talks and resolve the issue by force.

Over the next few weeks, Nixon used every available means to impose a settlement on both South and North Vietnam. He ordered immediate delivery to South Vietnam of more than $1 billion worth of military hardware, leaving Thieu, among other things, with the fourth largest air force in the world. He gave the Saigon government "absolute assurances" that if the North Vietnamese violated a peace agreement he would order "swift and severe retaliatory action," and he ordered the Joint Chiefs of Staff to begin immediate planning for such a contingency.[59] At the same time, he warned Thieu that if he did not accept the best treaty that could be obtained, the United States would make peace without him. Thieu continued to hold out, refusing to give Nixon carte blanche to negotiate for him and defiantly informing the press that he had rejected an American ultimatum. Although infuriated by Thieu's intransigence, Nixon was not altogether displeased, perceiving that it gave him ample pretext for a break if it should come to that later.

While attempting to bludgeon Thieu into submission, Nixon employed what Kissinger described as "jugular diplomacy" against North Vietnam, ordering yet another massive dose of bombing. The ostensible motive was to force Hanoi to conclude an agreement, but the decision reflected the accumulated anger and frustration of four years and it may have been intended to weaken North Vietnam to the point where it would be incapable of threatening South Vietnam after a peace settlement had been concluded. Nixon made absolutely clear to the military his determination to inflict maximum damage on North Vietnam. "I don't want any more of this crap about the fact that we couldn't hit this target or that one," he lectured Admiral Thomas Moorer, Chairman of the Joint Chiefs of

---

[58] Sulzberger, *Seven Continents*, p. 593; Nixon, *RN*, pp. 725–726.

[59] Nixon, *RN*, p. 718; Zumwalt, *On Watch*, pp. 413–414.

Staff. "This is your chance to use military power to win this war, and if you don't, I'll consider you responsible."[60] Over the next twelve days, the United States unleashed the most intensive and devastating attacks of the war, dropping more than 36,000 tons of bombs and exceeding the tonnage during the entire period from 1969 to 1971.

Nixon and Kissinger's later claims that the so-called Christmas bombing compelled the North Vietnamese to accept a settlement satisfactory to the United States seem open to serious question. The bombing did not compare in terms of destructiveness to the bombing of Tokyo, Hiroshima, or Dresden in World War II, as critics charged. American pilots went to extraordinary lengths to avoid civilian casualties, and large numbers of civilians had already been evacuated from the major cities. Still, the destruction in parts of Hanoi and Haiphong was heavy, and as many as 1,600 civilians were killed. The bombing certainly gave the North Vietnamese reason to resume negotiations, especially since they had exhausted their stock of surface-to-air missiles by December 30.

The bombing may have given Nixon even more compelling reasons to return to the negotiating table. North Vietnamese air defenses exacted a heavy toll, bringing down fifteen B-52s and eleven other aircraft. The Christmas bombing also evoked cries of outrage across the world; the Soviets and the Chinese responded angrily, in marked contrast to their restraint of May. The reaction at home was one of shock and anger. Critics denounced Nixon as a "madman" and accused him of waging "war by tantrum."[61] Many of those who had accepted the May bombings questioned both the necessity and the unusual brutality of the December attacks, a "sorry Christmas present" for the American people, in the words of Senator Aiken.[62] Nixon's popular approval rating plummeted to 39 percent overnight, and Congressional doves made clear that when they returned to Washington after the Christmas recess they were ready to do battle with the President. "We took the threats from Congress seriously," one of Nixon's White House aides later observed; "we knew we were racing the clock" and if North Vietnam refused to negotiate "we faced stern action."[63] To keep his options

[60] Sulzberger, *Seven Continents*, p. 593; Nixon, *RN*, pp. 725–726.
[61] Nixon, *RN*, p. 738.
[62] Aiken, *Senate Diary*, p. 136.
[63] Colson, *Born Again*, p. 77–79.

open, Nixon had indicated to the North Vietnamese that he would stop the bombing if they agreed to resume the peace talks. Hanoi consented, and Nixon got himself off the hook.

Most important, the bombing did not produce a settlement markedly different from the one the United States had earlier rejected. The negotiations resumed in Paris on January 8. The atmosphere was grim and icy, but this time both parties were committed to a settlement, and after six days of marathon sessions, marked by compromise on both sides, Kissinger and Le Duc Tho resolved their differences. The changes from the October agreement were largely cosmetic, enabling each side to claim that nothing had been given up. On the major sticking point of December, the demilitarized zone, the North Vietnamese agreed to make explicit reference to it in the treaty, but the United States accepted its description as a "provisional and not a political and territorial boundary," preserving the substance of Hanoi's position. The question of civilian movement across the demilitarized zone was left to be resolved later in negotiations between North and South Vietnam.

This time, the United States imposed the agreement on Thieu. To sweeten the pill, Nixon indicated that if Thieu accepted the treaty he would provide South Vietnam continued support and would "respond with full force" if North Vietnam violated the agreement. At the same time, he made clear that if Thieu continued to resist he would cut off further assistance and he was prepared to sign the treaty alone, if necessary.[64] Thieu stalled for several days, but when it was apparent that he could do no better, he gave in, remarking with resignation, "I have done all that I can for my country." The Saigon government never formally endorsed the treaty, but Thieu let it be known in a cryptic way that he would not oppose it.

Only by the most narrow definition can the agreement be said to have constituted "peace with honor." It permitted American extrication from the war and secured the return of the POWs, while leaving the Thieu government intact, at least for the moment. On the other hand, North Vietnamese troops remained in the south and the PRG was accorded a position of status. The major question over which the war had been fought—the political future of South Vietnam—was left to be resolved later. The treaty of January 1973 presumed that it would be resolved by political means,

[64] Nixon, *RN*, p. 737; *New York Times*, May 1, 1975.

but the mechanism established for this purpose was vague and inherently unworkable, and all parties involved perceived that it would ultimately be settled by force. Indeed, at the very time Kissinger and Le Duc Tho emerged from the Hotel Majestic smiling broadly at their achievement, the combatants in South Vietnam were busily preparing for the final round. "Peace with honor" represented merely another phase in the thirty-year struggle for the control of Vietnam.

For all concerned, "peace with honor" came at a very high price. Official American estimates place the number of South Vietnamese battle deaths for the years 1969–1973 at 107,504, and North Vietnamese and Vietcong at more than a half million. There will probably never be an adequate accounting of civilian battle deaths and casualties. The tonnage of bombs dropped on Indochina during the Nixon era exceeded that of the Johnson years, wreaking untold devastation, causing permanent ecological damage to the countryside, and leaving millions of civilians homeless. The United States suffered much less than Vietnam, but the cost was nevertheless enormous. An additional 20,553 Americans were killed in the last four years of the war, bringing the total to more than 58,000. Continuation of the war fueled an inflation which neither Nixon nor his successors could control. The war polarized the American people and poisoned the political atmosphere as had no issue since slavery a century before. Although Nixon had held out for peace with honor in order to maintain America's position in the world, the United States emerged from the war with its image considerably tarnished abroad and its people weary of international involvement. For Nixon, too, the price was steep. By January 1973, he was exhausted and isolated, his administration reduced to a "small band of tired, dispirited, sometimes mean and petty men, bickering among themselves, wary and jealous of one another."[65] More than any other single issue, Vietnam brought a premature end to the Nixon presidency. The extreme measures he took to defend his Vietnam policy against enemies real and imagined led directly to the Watergate scandals which would eventually force his resignation. Thus, when the final Vietnam crisis came in 1975, the architect of peace with honor was no longer in the White House and the nation was in no mood to defend the agreement he had constructed at such great cost.

[65] Colson, *Born Again*, p. 80.

CHAPTER 8

The "Postwar War" and the Legacy of Vietnam

The "peace" agreements of January 1973 merely established a framework for continuing the war without direct American participation. North Vietnam still sought unification of the country on its terms; South Vietnam struggled to survive as an independent nation, and some U.S. officials, including President Nixon, continued to support its aspirations. The cease-fire thus existed only on paper. This last phase of the war was of remarkably short duration, however. Dependent on the United States from its birth, the Saigon government had great difficulty functioning on its own. Moreover, because of the Watergate scandals and American war-weariness, Nixon was not able to live up to the commitments he had made to Thieu, and indeed in August 1974 he was forced to resign. Congress drastically cut back aid to South Vietnam, further eroding the Saigon government's already faltering will to resist. When North Vietnam mounted a major offensive in the spring of 1975, South Vietnam collapsed with stunning rapidity, dramatically ending the thirty-year war and leaving the United States, on the eve of its third century, frustrated and bewildered.

The "postwar war" began the instant that peace was proclaimed. The United States had difficulty arranging with the North Vietnamese and Vietcong the return of its 587 prisoners of war, at one point threatening to delay further troop withdrawals in the absence of cooperation. By the end of March, the POWs had been released, returning home to receive the only heroes' welcome of the war, and all U.S. troops had been withdrawn. But these were the only tangible accomplishments of the teams assigned to implement the peace accords. From the start, efforts to effect a cease-fire were unavailing. None of the Vietnamese combatants had abandoned his goals, and each was willing to observe the agreements only to the extent that it suited his interests.[1]

Thieu took the offensive immediately. The Vietcong had launched a series of land-grabbing operations, immediately before the cease-fire was to go into effect, and Thieu undoubtedly wanted to retrieve as much of the lost territory as possible. Although he controlled an estimated 75 percent of the land and 85 percent of the people when the agreements were signed, he wanted to further solidify his position while U.S. support was still firm. To secure as much additional territory as possible, he resettled refugees and built forts in contested areas. ARVN units and South Vietnamese aircraft attacked North Vietnamese bases and supply lines and villages under PRG control. The ARVN lost more than 6,000 men, killed during the first three months of "peace," among the highest losses it suffered during the entire war.[2]

The North Vietnamese were more cautious but no less purposeful. Battered and exhausted from the bloody campaigns of 1972, short of food, manpower, and ammunition, they desperately needed time to regroup. They were also eager to secure a complete American withdrawal from Vietnam, and it was expedient to avoid blatant moves that might provoke the United States to reenter the conflict. During the first year after the cease-fire, the PRG sought primarily to consolidate the territory under its control and to undermine Thieu's position through political agitation. Military forces were instructed to attack South Vietnamese units only when they had clear-cut superiority. Meanwhile, the North Vietnamese quietly infiltrated troops and equipment into the south, built a system of modern highways linking staging areas to strategic zones in South Vietnam, and even constructed a pipeline to ensure adequate supplies of petroleum for forces in the field.

Although the Paris agreements provided that the future of South Vietnam would be settled by the Vietnamese, the United

---

[1] See Walter Scott Dillard, *Sixty Days to Peace: Implementing the Paris Peace Accords, Vietnam 1973* (Washington, D.C., 1982).

[2] The best account of the "postwar war" is Arnold R. Isaacs, *Without Honor: Defeat in Vietnam and Cambodia* (New York, 1984). See also Maynard Parker, "Vietnam: The War That Won't End," *Foreign Affairs*, 53 (January 1975), especially 365–366; and Gareth Porter, *A Peace Denied: The United States, Vietnam, and the Paris Agreements* (Bloomington, Ind., 1975), pp. 174–184, 188–196.

States persisted in its commitment to Thieu. Deeply frustrated by the months of tortuous negotiations and anxious to get on to other things, Kissinger appears to have sought nothing more than a "decent interval" between the signing of the agreements and a final settlement in Vietnam. Nixon, on the other hand, was no more willing in 1973 than he had been in 1969 to be the first American President to lose a war. The January accords gave the PRG political status in the south, but the President made clear that the United States would "continue to recognize the government of the Republic of Viet-Nam as the sole legitimate government of South Viet-Nam."[3]

Fully aware of the fragility of the agreements, Nixon and Kissinger used every available means to strengthen the Thieu government. To secure Saigon's acquiescence, Nixon had secretly promised to continue "full economic and military aid" and to "respond with full force" should North Vietnam violate the agreements.[4] In a meeting with Thieu at San Clemente in March, he reaffirmed his commitments and assured the South Vietnamese leader that "you can count on us."[5] Throughout the remainder of 1973, the administration employed various subterfuges to sustain its military aid at a high level without overtly violating the terms of the Paris accords. Instead of dismantling its bases, the United States transferred title to the South Vietnamese before the cease-fire went into effect. Supplies were designated "nonmilitary" and were rendered eligible for transfer. The military advisory group was replaced by a "civilian" team of some 9,000 men, many of them hastily discharged from military service and placed in the employ of the government of Vietnam.[6]

The administration attempted to use the leverage available to it to prevent North Vietnam from upsetting the delicate equilibrium in the south. As part of the Paris package, the United States had agreed to provide Hanoi $4.75 billion in aid for reconstruction. On several occasions in the spring of 1973, Nixon threatened to withhold the funds unless North Vietnam adhered to the letter of the

---

[3] Quoted in Porter, *Peace Denied*, p. 186.

[4] Nixon, *RN*, pp. 749–750; *New York Times*, May 1, 1975.

[5] Stephen T. Hosmer et al., *The Fall of South Vietnam* (Santa Monica, Calif., 1978), p. 11.

[6] Tad Szulc, *The Illusion of Peace: Foreign Policy in the Nixon Years* (New York, 1978), pp. 672–676.

agreements, and he eventually suspended talks on postwar aid in protest against continued infiltration into South Vietnam and intensification of the fighting in Cambodia. The President and Kissinger also sought to keep alive the threat of American military intervention. "The only way we will keep North Vietnam under control is not to say we are out forever," Kissinger observed. "We don't want to dissipate with them the reputation for fierceness that the President has earned."[7] The last American troops were withdrawn from Vietnam by the end of March, but the United States kept a formidable armada of naval and air power in the Gulf of Tonkin and in Thailand and Guam. The bombing of Cambodia was continued, in part to support Lon Nol against a determined Khmer Rouge offensive and in part to maintain Nixon's "reputation for fierceness." Several times, the President issued slightly veiled warnings that he might resume the bombing of North Vietnam, and in April he reinstituted reconnaissance flights north of the seventeenth parallel.

The North Vietnamese ignored the American warnings, however, and by early summer Nixon's ability to threaten was severely curtailed by a rebellious Congress. The Congressional challenge of 1973 reflected a war-weariness and a widespread feeling among the American people that once American troops had been safely removed, the nation should extricate itself entirely from the conflict. Mounting evidence of White House involvement in the Watergate scandal increased Nixon's vulnerability. Congress displayed no enthusiasm for aid to North Vietnam, doves protesting that it would not ensure peace and hawks denouncing it as "reparations." Republicans joined Democrats in condemning the bombing of Cambodia as illegal, and on May 10 the House voted to cut off funds for further air operations.

Perceiving the steady erosion of America's control over events in Indochina, Kissinger journeyed to Paris in May in a futile effort to persuade Le Duc Tho to observe the cease-fire. The North Vietnamese responded angrily to American charges of violations of the agreements with countercharges that South Vietnam and the United States were not upholding their commitments. More annoying to Kissinger, they dismissed his accusations as "attempts to deceive public opinion, as you have done with Watergate." The

[7] Quoted in William Safire, *Before the Fall* (New York, 1975), p. 673.

diplomats could agree on nothing more than an innocuous communiqué reaffirming the January accords. Upon returning to Washington, a weary Kissinger informed newsmen that he was going to reduce his involvement in Indochina affairs "in order to preserve my emotional stability."[8]

Kissinger's remark was more prophetic than he realized, for in June Congress deprived the administration of the little leverage it retained. By this time, the Watergate investigations had turned up sensational revelations of abuses of presidential power. Long-embittered Democrats were encouraged to take on the President, and Republicans were increasingly reluctant to stand behind him. Nixon and Kissinger vigorously defended the bombing of Cambodia as necessary to sustain Lon Nol and uphold the cease-fire. But an overwhelming majority of Congressmen agreed with Senator George Aiken that the bombing was "ill-advised and unwarranted," and many accepted Representative Norris Cotton's outspoken affirmation: "As far as I'm concerned, I want to get the hell out."[9] In late June, Congress approved an amendment requiring the immediate cessation of all military operations in and over Indochina. The House upheld Nixon's angry veto, but the President was eventually forced to accept a compromise extending the deadline to August 15. For the first time, Congress had taken decisive steps to curtail American involvement in the war. "It would be idle to say that the authority of the executive has not been impaired," Kissinger remarked with obvious understatement and disappointment.[10]

By the end of 1973, Nixon was virtually powerless. Watergate had reduced his popular approval ratings to an all-time low and left him fighting a desperate rearguard action to save his political life. In November, Congress passed over another veto the so-called War Powers Act, a direct response to the exercise of presidential authority in Vietnam. The legislation required the President to inform Congress within forty-eight hours of the deployment of American military forces abroad and obligated him to withdraw them in sixty days in the absence of explicit Congressional endorse-

---

[8] Quoted in Marvin and Bernard Kalb, *Kissinger* (Boston, 1974), p. 432.

[9] George Aiken, *Senate Diary* (Brattleboro, Vt., 1976), p. 198; Kalb and Kalb, *Kissinger*, p. 432.

[10] Kalb and Kalb, *Kissinger*, p. 434.

ment. Some Congressmen protested that the act conferred upon the President a more direct power to commit American troops to war than he had had before, but the circumstances under which the debate took place, combined with Watergate and the vote terminating operations in Indochina, made virtually certain the end of direct American involvement in the Vietnam War.

In the meantime, the Paris agreements had become a dead letter. Discussions of a political settlement had begun in early 1973 and continued sporadically throughout the year, but the basic issue—the future of South Vietnam—was nonnegotiable, and by early 1974 the talks had broken off. Apparently still confident of U.S support despite Watergate, Thieu formally proclaimed the start of the "Third Indochina War," and in late 1973 stepped up ground and air attacks on enemy bases and launched a series of land-grabbing operations in PRG-held territories along the eastern seaboard, in the Iron Triangle, and in the delta. This time, the North Vietnamese and PRG counterattacked, and over the next few months they scored success after success, mauling ARVN units in the Iron Triangle, retaking much of the territory that had been lost, and seizing additional territory formerly under Saigon's control.

By the fall of 1974, the military balance had shifted in favor of North Vietnam. More than half of South Vietnam's million-man army was tied down in static defense positions and scattered throughout the northern provinces. By this time, the North Vietnamese and PRG had mobilized large armies in the south. They had stockpiled vast quantities of supplies and built a highly sophisticated logistics system which permitted them to move regulars, along with tanks and artillery, to any battlefront within hours. At least in the Mekong Delta, they had regained most of the territory lost the preceding year.[11]

At the same time, South Vietnam's perennial economic and political problems had been sharply aggravated, in part as a result of the American withdrawal. Loss of the $400 million which the United States spent annually in South Vietnam, the reduction of American military aid from $2.3 billion in 1973 to about $1 billion in 1974, and a sharp rise in worldwide inflation combined to produce an annual inflation rate of 90 percent, massive unemployment, a drastic decline in morale in the armed forces and among

[11] Parker, "Vietnam," 366–367.

the urban population, and an increase in the ever present corruption. Scavengers stripped the American-built port at Camranh Bay to a bare skeleton, and pilots demanded bribes to fly missions in support of ground troops. The economic crisis of 1974 compounded Thieu's political woes. The Buddhists became more active than at any time since 1966, agitating for peace and reconciliation with the Communists. The Catholics, the government's most important base of support, organized an anti-corruption campaign, the major target of which was Thieu himself. A spirit of defeatism grew among those fence-sitters who had not supported the government but had not actively opposed it either.

The American abandonment of South Vietnam was manifest by the end of 1974. Nixon was forced to resign in August, removing from power the individual who had promised Thieu continued support. Throughout the year, Kissinger pleaded with an increasingly defiant Congress to expand American military aid to $1.5 billion, insisting that the United States had a moral obligation to South Vietnam and warning that failure to uphold it would have a "corrosive effect on our interests beyond Indochina." The arguments that had been accepted without challenge for nearly a quarter of a century now fell flat. Inflation in the United States evoked insistent demands for reducing expenditures, and many members of Congress agreed with Senator William Proxmire that there was less need for continued military aid to South Vietnam than for "any other single item" in the budget. Critics pointed out that the Thieu government was in no immediate peril and warned that much of the money would line the pockets of Saigon's corrupt bureaucrats. A continuation of massive American military aid would encourage Thieu to prolong the war, while a reduction might impress upon him the need to seek a political settlement. It was time to terminate America's "endless support for an endless war," Senator Edward Kennedy insisted. In September 1974, Congress approved an aid program of $700 million, half of which comprised shipping costs.[12]

The aid cuts of 1974 had a tremendous impact in South Vietnam. Without the continued large infusion of American funds and equipment, the armed forces could not fight the way the Americans had trained them. Air force operations had to be curtailed by as

[12] *Congressional Record*, 93rd Cong., 2d Sess., 29176–29180.

much as 50 percent because of shortages of gasoline and spare parts. Ammunition and other supplies had to be severely rationed. The inescapable signs of waning American support had a devastating effect on morale in an army already reeling under North Vietnamese blows, and desertions reached an all-time high of 240,000 in 1974. The aid cutbacks heightened Thieu's economic and political difficulties, spurring among many Vietnamese a "growing psychology of accommodation and retreat that sometimes approached despair."[13]

In early 1975, Hanoi concluded that the "opportune moment" was at hand. In December 1974, North Vietnamese main units and PRG regional forces attacked Phuoc Long, northeast of Saigon, and within three weeks had killed or captured 3,000 South Vietnamese troops, seized huge quantities of supplies, and "liberated" the entire province. The ease of the victory underscored the relative weakening of the ARVN during the past year and made clear, as North Vietnamese Chief of Staff Van Tien Dung later put it, that Thieu was now forced to fight a "poor-man's war." Aware from intelligence that Saigon was not expecting a major offensive in 1975, the North Vietnamese in January adopted a two-year plan, a series of large-scale offensives in 1975 to create the conditions for a "general offensive, general uprising" in 1976. The United States's failure to respond in any way to the fall of Phuoc Long confirmed what many North Vietnamese strategists had long suspected, that having pulled out of South Vietnam the Americans would not "jump back in." After days of sometimes heated debate, the leadership concluded that even if the United States responded with naval and air power, it could not "rescue the Saigon administration from its disastrous collapse."[14]

The collapse came with a suddenness which appears to have surprised even the North Vietnamese. Massing vastly superior forces against the stretched-out ARVN defenders, Dung attacked Ban Me Thuot in the Central Highlands on March 10 and took it within two days. To secure control of the highlands before the end of the dry season, he quickly moved north against Pleiku and Kontum. A panicky Thieu unwisely ordered his forces to withdraw from the highlands, but no plans had been drawn for retreat and

[13] Guenter Lewy, *America in Vietnam* (New York, 1978), p. 208.
[14] Van Tien Dung, *Our Great Spring Victory* (New York, 1977), pp. 17, 19–20.

the North Vietnamese had cut the major roads. The withdrawal turned into a rout. Hundreds of thousands of refugees fled with the departing soldiers, clogging the avenues of escape. Much of the army was captured or destroyed, and thousands of civilians died from enemy or ARVN gunfire and from starvation in what journalists called the "Convoy of Tears." Pleiku and Kontum fell within a week. The disastrous abandonment of the highlands cost Thieu six provinces, at least two divisions of soldiers, and the confidence of his army and people. It opened the way for even greater catastrophe in the coastal cities of South Vietnam.

Hanoi now sensed for the first time that total victory could be attained in 1975 and immediately put into effect contingency plans for the conquest of all of South Vietnam. When North Vietnamese forces advanced on Hue and Danang, the defending army along with hundreds of thousands of civilians fled for Saigon, duplicating on an even larger and more tragic scale the debacle in the highlands. Soldiers looted and money-hungry citizens charged refugees up to two dollars for a glass of water. Ten days after the attack had begun and almost ten years to the day after the U.S. Marines had splashed ashore at Danang, the two coastal cities were in North Vietnamese hands. South Vietnam had been cut in two, about half its army lost without putting up any resistance. Nha Trang and Camranh Bay were abandoned before they were even threatened by enemy troops. Dung now threw all his forces into the "Ho Chi Minh Campaign" to liberate Saigon.

The United States was stunned by the collapse of South Vietnam but was resigned to the outcome. American intelligence had correctly predicted that the major North Vietnamese thrust was not planned until 1976, but the capacity of the South Vietnamese to resist was again overestimated, and Washington was shocked by the sudden fall of the highlands. America's disinclination for further involvement was obvious; on the day Ban Me Thuot fell, Congress rejected President Gerald Ford's request for an additional $300 million in military aid for South Vietnam. The legislators' vote seems to have reflected the wishes of the American people. A few diehards issued one last appeal to honor the nation's commitments and to defend the cause of freedom, and some Americans raised the specter of a bloodbath in which hundreds of thousands of South Vietnamese would be slaughtered by the Communist conquerors. For the most part, however, such appeals fell on deaf ears.

Weary of the seemingly endless involvement in Vietnam and
pinched by an economic recession at home, Americans were not in
a generous mood. Why throw good money after bad, they asked. At
a time when they themselves were in "desperate financial straits,"
they saw no reason to continue to sacrifice for a government that
was "not only corrupt but grossly wasteful and inefficient." It was
about time that the South Vietnamese were made to stand on their
own feet, one "fed-up taxpayer" exclaimed. "My God, we're all
tired of it, we're sick to death of it," an Oregonian wrote. "55,000
dead and $100 billion spent and for what?"[15]

The fall of Danang and Hue and the imminent threat to Saigon
did nothing to change Americans' views. Ford apparently gave no
thought to the use of American naval and air power. To stiffen
South Vietnamese morale and perhaps to exculpate the United
States (and the executive branch) from responsibility, in early April
he asked Congress for $722 million in emergency military assis-
tance, reiterating the old argument that a failure to assist South
Vietnam in its hour of trial would weaken faith in American commitments across the world. Congressmen responded heatedly that
the South Vietnamese had abandoned more equipment in the
northern provinces than could be purchased with the additional
funds, and argued that no amount of money would be enough to
save an army that refused to fight. It was time for the United States
to end its involvement in "this horrid war."[16] The specter of Watergate and the Gulf of Tonkin hung over the debate, and revelations of Nixon's secret promises to Thieu provoked cries of outrage.
Congress eventually approved $300 million to be used for the evac-
uation of Americans and for "humanitarian" purposes, and endorsed Ford's request to use American troops to evacuate U.S.
citizens from South Vietnam. But it would go no further. "The
Vietnam debate has run its course," Kissinger commented with fi-
nality on April 17.[17]

The certainty that the United States would not intervene ended
whatever slim hope of survival South Vietnam may have had.
North Vietnamese forces advanced from Danang to the outskirts of

[15] Mrs. J. S. Mozzanini to James J. Kilpatrick, February 6, 1975, and numerous
other letters in James J. Kilpatrick Papers, University of Virginia Library, Charlottesville, Va., Box 5.

[16] *Congressional Record*, 94th Cong., 1st Sess., 10101–10108.

[17] *New York Times*, April 18, 1975.

the capital in less than a month, meeting strong resistance only at Xuan Loc, where a small contingent of ARVN forces fought desperately against superior numbers and firepower. With the fall of that town on April 21 and the Congressional rejection of Ford's request for aid, the intransigent Thieu finally and reluctantly resigned, bitterly blaming the debacle on the United States. He was replaced by the aged and inept Tran Van Huong, who vainly attempted to negotiate a settlement on the basis of the 1973 accords, and then by the pathetic Duong Van Minh, the architect of the 1963 coup, to whom was left the odious task of surrendering unconditionally. On May 1, 1975, Vietcong soldiers triumphantly ran up the flag over a renamed Ho Chi Minh City. Several days earlier, Gerald Ford formally proclaimed what had already become obvious: the Vietnam War is "finished as far as the United States is concerned."

The American withdrawal revealed in microcosm much of the delusion, the frustration, and the tragedy that had marked the American experience in Vietnam. U.S. officials persisted in the belief that South Vietnam would mount an effective defense until the North Vietnamese were at the gates of Saigon. Ambassador Graham Martin stubbornly supported Thieu long after it was evident the President had no backing within his own country: Martin headed off several coup attempts and encouraged Thieu's refusal to resign, resignation perhaps being the only chance of avoiding unconditional surrender. Fearful of spreading panic in Saigon, Martin delayed implementation of evacuation plans until the last minute. The United States managed to get its own people out, as well as 150,000 Vietnamese, but the operation was chaotic and fraught with human suffering. Corruption ran rampant, escape frequently going to the highest bidder, and the U.S. Embassy paid exorbitant fees to get exit visas for some of those seeking to flee. Because of the unavailability of adequate transport, many South Vietnamese who wished to leave could not. The spectacle of U.S. Marines using rifle butts to keep desperate Vietnamese from blocking escape routes and of angry ARVN soldiers firing on the departing Americans provided a tragic epitaph for twenty-five years of American involvement in Vietnam.[18]

The United States shared with the South Vietnamese leadership

[18] For a dramatic account of the fall of South Vietnam, see Alan Dawson, *55 Days* (New York, 1977).

responsibility for the debacle of April 1975. In the two years after the signing of the Paris agreements, the United States gave Thieu enough support to encourage his defiance but not enough to ensure his survival. Nixon's ill-advised promises tempted him to reject the admittedly risky choice of negotiations and to launch a war he could not win. The reduction of American involvement in the war and the cutbacks of American aid weakened South Vietnam's capacity and will to resist, and the refusal of the United States to intervene in the final crisis sealed its downfall. On the other hand, Thieu's intransigence, his gross tactical errors, and his desperate attempts to save himself while his nation was dying suggest that the outcome would probably have been the same regardless of what the United States had done. Without leadership from Thieu and the army's high command, the South Vietnamese people gave way to hysteria, each person doing only what he could to save his own skin. The nation simply collapsed.

The fall of South Vietnam just fifty-five days after the onset of the North Vietnamese offensive was symptomatic of the malaise which had afflicted the nation since its birth. Political fragmentation, the lack of able far-sighted leaders, and a tired and corrupt elite which could not adjust to the revolution that swept Vietnam after 1945 afforded a perilously weak basis for nationhood. Given these harsh realities, the American effort to create a bastion of anti-Communism south of the seventeenth parallel was probably doomed from the start. The United States could not effect the needed changes in South Vietnamese society without jeopardizing the order it sought, and there was no long-range hope of stability without revolutionary change. The Americans could provide money and weapons, but they could not furnish the ingredients necessary for political stability and military success. Despairing of the capacity of the South Vietnamese to save themselves, the United States had assumed the burden in 1965, only to toss it back in the laps of its clients when the American people tired of the war. The dependency of the early years persisted long after the United States had shifted to Vietnamization, however. To the very end and despite overwhelming evidence to the contrary, Thieu and his cohorts clung desperately to the belief that the United States would not abandon them.[19]

With the North Vietnamese victory, the "dominoes" in Indo-

[19] Hosmer et al., *Fall of South Vietnam*, pp. 118–120.

china quickly toppled. Cambodia in fact fell before South Vietnam, ending a peculiarly brutal war and initiating a period of unprecedented cruelty. Between 1970 and 1972, the United States had spent over $400 million in support of Lon Nol's government and army, and heavy bombing continued until Congress legislated its end in August 1973. In six months of 1973, the bombing exceeded 250,000 tons, more than was dropped on Japan in all of World War II. Lon Nol's government and army were ineffectual even by South Vietnamese standards, however, and with extensive support from North Vietnam and China, the Khmer Rouge pressed on toward Phnom Penh, using human-wave assaults in some areas. The government collapsed in mid-April, and the Khmer Rouge took over the capital on April 17. Thousands of lives were lost in the war, and over two million people were left refugees. The country as a whole faced starvation for the first time in its history. Upon taking over, the Khmer Rouge imposed the harshest form of totalitarianism and began the forced relocation of much of the population.

The end in Laos was less convulsive. The Laotian "settlement" of 1962 had been a dead letter from the start. A flimsy coalition government nominally upheld a precarious neutrality, while outsiders waged war up and down the land. The North Vietnamese used Laotian territory for their infiltration route into South Vietnam, and supported the insurgent Pathet Lao with supplies and as many as 20,000 "volunteers." While backing the "neutralist" government, the United States from 1962 to 1972 waged a "secret war" against North Vietnamese positions in Laos. When the bombing of North Vietnam was stopped at the end of 1968, Laos became the primary target. By 1973 the United States had dropped more than two million tons of bombs there, leaving many areas resembling a desert. At the same time, the CIA sponsored an army of Hmong or Meo tribesmen, led by General Vang Pao, which waged seasonal guerrilla warfare against the Ho Chi Minh Trail in Laos at enormous cost: more than 20,000 had been killed by the end of the war. The U.S. withdrawal from South Vietnam left the government without any chance of survival. An agreement of February 1973 created a coalition government in which the Pathet Lao held the upper hand. With the fall of Cambodia and South Vietnam, the Pathet Lao took over, making no effort to hide its subservience to North Vietnam.

The impact on world politics of America's failure in Vietnam was considerably less than U.S. policymakers had predicted. From

Thailand to the Philippines, there was obvious nervousness, even demands for the removal of U.S. bases. Outside of Indochina, however, the dominoes did not fall. On the contrary, in the ten years after the end of the war, the non-Communist nations of Southeast Asia prospered and attained an unprecedented level of stability. The Soviet Union continued to build up its military arsenal. Along with Cuba, it intervened in civil wars in Angola, Zaire, and Ethiopia, and in 1979 it invaded neighboring Afghanistan. The Soviets soon bogged down in Afghanistan themselves, however, and one of the most significant and ironic effects of the end of the Vietnam War was to heighten tension among the various Communist nations, especially in Southeast Asia. The brutal Pol Pot regime launched a grisly effort to rebuild Cambodia from the "Year Zero," resulting in the death of as many as two million people. More important from the Vietnamese standpoint, Cambodia established close ties with China. To preserve a "friendly" government next door, Vietnam invaded Cambodia in 1978, drove out Pol Pot and the Khmer Rouge, and established a puppet regime. China retaliated by invading Vietnam, provoking a short and inconclusive war. Sporadic border conflicts between Vietnam and China have persisted. The United States, which had gone to war in Vietnam in 1965 to contain China, found itself in the mid-1980s indirectly supporting China's efforts to contain Vietnam.

In Vietnam itself, the principal legacy of the war has been continued human suffering. The ultimate losers, of course, were the South Vietnamese. For those who remain in Vietnam there have been poverty, oppression, forced labor, and "reeducation" camps. More than 1.4 million South Vietnamese have fled the country since 1975. As many as 50,000 of these so-called boat people perished in flight, and some still languish in squalid refugee camps scattered throughout Southeast Asia. Nearly a million Vietnamese have resettled in other countries, over 725,000 of them in the United States. Most of them had to give up all their personal possessions merely to escape, and many left family behind.

Even for the ostensible winners, victory has been a bittersweet prize. The Hanoi regime has achieved what may have been its goal from the outset—hegemony in former French Indochina—but the cost has been enormous. An estimated 180,000 soldiers remain in Cambodia, facing stubborn resistance from a number of different guerrilla groups, a drain on an economy already strained to the breaking point. The task of maintaining hegemony in Laos and

Cambodia and defending against a hostile China requires one of the world's twelve poorest countries to maintain the world's fourth largest army. Vietnam's postwar aggressiveness has cost it much of the international good will it earned in the war against the United States.

Moreover, Hanoi's long-standing objective of unifying Vietnam under its control appears still to have been achieved in name only. Historic differences between north and south were sharpened during the war, and even the brutal and heavy-handed methods employed by the Hanoi regime have not forced the south into a northern-made mold. Just as it resisted American influence in the 1960s, southern Vietnam continues to resist outside influence today, making the task of consolidation quite difficult. There are also signs that in the classic tradition of the Far East, the ways of the conquered are rubbing off on the conqueror. The corruption and Western consumer culture that epitomized Saigon during the American war have carried over to postwar Ho Chi Minh City, where the black market still flourishes and bribery is necessary to accomplish anything. More significant, Saigon's mores appear to have afflicted the northern officials sent south to enforce revolutionary purity and even to have filtered north to Hanoi.

For all Vietnamese, the most pressing legacy has been economic deprivation. Thirty years of war left the country in shambles, and the regime's ill-conceived postwar efforts to promote industry and collectivize agriculture made things worse. The economic growth rate has hovered around 2 percent instead of the 14 percent optimistically projected in the five-year plan of 1975. Per capita income has averaged around $100. Inflation has run as high as 50 percent and unemployment is chronic, especially in the cities. Record rice crops in recent years have eased a severe postwar food shortage, but the food supply remains far below the needs of the population and most foods are rationed and expensive. The postwar economic crisis has forced Hanoi to abandon its central goal of socialization of southern Vietnam. New economic policies have been designed to increase production by such capitalist gimmicks as bonuses, piecework rates, and limited managerial autonomy. The collectivization of agriculture has been scrapped, at least temporarily.

A central goal of the thirty-year war was to rid Vietnam of foreign domination, and here again victory has been less than complete. Because of its poverty and its forced isolation from the

United States and China, Hanoi has been forced into a dependence on the Soviet Union that causes growing uneasiness and resentment. Some 6,000 Russians administer an aid program ranging between $1 and $2 billion per year. Russian aid bears a high price tag, moreover. To many Vietnamese, the Soviet presence is increasingly obnoxious, and some appear to regard their new ally as merely another in the long line of foreigners who have exploited their country. To a considerable degree, the legacy of victory for the Vietnamese has been one of disappointed dreams and continuing sacrifice and pain. The goals of the thirty-year war have been achieved only partially, if at all.

Ten years after the fall of Saigon, Vietnam appeared eager to break out of its diplomatic isolation from the West. Hanoi probably bungled an opportunity to establish relations with the United States in 1977 by demanding $3 billion in war reparations as a precondition. Relations between the two former enemies thereafter grew steadily worse. Vietnam's seeming indifference to the fate of some 2,500 U.S. servicemen still listed as missing in action in Southeast Asia deeply antagonized Americans. Its increasing closeness to the Soviet Union and its invasion of Cambodia widened an already large chasm. On the other side, Washington's reconciliation with China in 1979 reinforced Vietnam's already strong hostility toward the United States. The need for Western aid and technology and a wish to secure recognition of its position in Cambodia encouraged Hanoi in 1985 to seek an improvement of relations. It was more cooperative than at any time since the end of the war in dealing with MIA issues, and it eagerly sought a settlement on Cambodia. These approaches provided the United States an opportunity to wean Vietnam from its dependence on the Soviet Union and to resolve a number of issues left from the war, but lingering hostility toward the Vietnamese and fear of China's reaction posed major obstacles to an improvement in relations.

In the United States, the effects of the war have been more in the realm of the spirit than tangible. The fall of Saigon had a profound impact. Some Americans expressed hope that the nation could finally put aside a painful episode from its past and get on with the business of the future. Among a people accustomed to celebrating peace with ticker-tape parades, however, the end of the war left a deep residue of frustration, anger, and disillusionment. Americans generally agreed that the war had been a "senseless tragedy" and a "dark moment" in their nation's history. Some comforted themselves with the notion that the United States should never have become involved in Vietnam in the first place, but for others, particularly those who had lost loved ones, this was not enough. "Now it's all gone down the drain and it hurts. What did he die for?" asked a Pennsylvanian whose son had been killed in Vietnam. Many Americans expressed anger that the civilians did not permit the military to win the war. Others regarded the failure to win as a betrayal of American ideals and a sign of national weakness which boded poorly for the future. "It was the saddest day of my life when it sank in that we had lost the war," a Virginian lamented.[20] The fall of Vietnam came at the very time the nation was preparing to celebrate the bicentennial of its birth, and the irony was painfully obvious. "The high hopes and wishful idealism with which the American nation had been born had not been destroyed," *Newsweek* observed, "but they had been chastened by the failure of America to work its will in Indochina."[21]

In the immediate aftermath of the war, the nation experienced a self-conscious, collective amnesia. The angry debate over who lost Vietnam, so feared by Kennedy, Johnson, and Nixon, consisted of nothing more than a few sharp exchanges between the White House and Capitol Hill over responsibility for the April 1975 debacle. Perhaps because both parties were so deeply implicated in the war, Vietnam did not become a partisan political issue; because the memories were so painful, no one cared to dredge them up. On the contrary, many public figures called for restraint. "There is no profit at this time in hashing over the might-have-beens of the past," Mike Mansfield stated. "Nor is there any value in finger-pointing."[22] Vietnam was all but ignored by the media. It was scarcely mentioned in the presidential campaign of 1976. "Today it is almost as though the war had never happened," the columnist Joseph C. Harsch noted in late 1975. "Americans have somehow blocked it out of their consciousness. They don't talk about it. They don't talk about its consequences."[23]

Resentment and disillusionment nevertheless smoldered beneath the surface, provoking a sharp reaction against nearly three

---

[20] Jules Low, "The Mood of a Nation," AP Newsfeature, May 5, 1975.

[21] "An Irony of History," *Newsweek* (April 28, 1975), 17.

[22] Quoted in Joseph Siracusa, "Lessons of Viet Nam and the Future of American Foreign Policy," *Australian Outlook*, 30 (August 1976), 236.

[23] Joseph C. Harsch, "Do You Recall Vietnam—And What About the Dominoes?," Louisville *Courier-Journal*, October 2, 1975.

decades of crisis diplomacy and global intervention. Even before
the war had ended, the traumatic experience of Vietnam, combined with the apparent improvement of relations with the Soviet
Union and China and a growing preoccupation with domestic
problems, produced a drastic reordering of national priorities.
From the late 1940s to the 1960s, foreign policy had consistently
headed the list of national concerns, but by the mid-1970s, it
ranked well down the list. The public is "almost oblivious to foreign problems and foreign issues," opinion analyst Burns Roper remarked in late 1975.[24] The Vietnam experience also provoked
strong opposition to military intervention abroad, even in defense
of America's oldest and staunchest allies. Polls taken shortly before
the fall of Saigon indicated that only 36 percent of the American
people felt it was important for the United States to make and keep
commitments to other nations, and only 34 percent expressed willingness to send troops should the Russians attempt to take over
West Berlin. A majority of Americans endorsed military intervention only in defense of Canada. "Vietnam has left a rancid after-
taste that clings to almost every mention of direct military
intervention," the columnist David Broder observed.[25] The cyclical
theory of American foreign relations seemed confirmed. Having
passed through a stormy period of global involvement, the United
States appeared to be reverting to its more traditional role of ab-
stention.

Those Americans who fought in the war were the primary vic-
tims of the nation's desire to forget. Younger on the average by
seven years than their World War II counterparts, having endured
a war far more complex and confusing, Vietnam veterans by the
miracles of the jet age were whisked home virtually overnight to a
nation that was hostile to the war or indifferent to their plight.
Some were made to feel the guilt for the nation's moral transgres-
sions; others, responsibility for its failure. Most simply met silence.
Forced to turn inward, many veterans grew profoundly distrustful
of the government that had sent them to war and deeply resentful
of the nation's seeming ingratitude for their sacrifices. The great
majority adjusted, although often with difficulty, but many veterans

[24] Quoted in Charles W. Yost, "Why Americans Seem Disillusioned by Foreign
Affairs," Louisville *Courier-Journal*, October 26, 1975.

[25] David Broder, "Isolationist Sentiment Not Blind to Reality," *Washington Post*,
March 22, 1975.

experienced problems with drugs and alcohol, joblessness, and broken homes. Many also suffered from post-traumatic stress disorder, the modern term for what had earlier been called shell shock or battle fatigue. The popular image of the Vietnam veteran in the immediate postwar years was that of a drug-crazed, gun-toting, and violence-prone individual unable to adjust to civilized society. When America in 1981 gave a lavish welcome home to a group of hostages returned from a long and much-publicized captivity in Iran, Vietnam veterans poured out the rage that had been bottled up for more than half a decade. They themselves constructed a memorial in Washington to honor the memory of the more than 58,000 comrades who did not return.

Within a short time after the end of the war, Vietnam's place in the national consciousness changed dramatically. The amnesia of the immediate postwar years proved no more than a passing phenomenon, and by the mid-1980s the war was being discussed to a degree and in ways that would have once seemed impossible. Vietnam produced a large and in some cases distinguished literature, much of it the work of veterans. Hollywood had all but ignored the war while it was going on, but in its aftermath filmmakers took up the subject in a large way, producing works ranging from the haunting *Deer Hunter,* to the surreal and spectacular *Apocalypse Now,* to a series of trashy films in which American superheroes returned to Vietnam to take care of unfinished business. No television leading man was worth his salt unless he had served in Vietnam. The Vietnam veteran, sometimes branded a war criminal in the 1960s, became a popular culture hero in the 1980s, the sturdy and self-sufficient warrior who had prevailed despite being let down by his government and nation. Two million Americans a year visited the stark but moving V-shaped memorial on Washington's mall, making it the second leading tourist attraction in the nation's capital. The hoopla that accompanied the tenth anniversary of the fall of Saigon made abundantly clear how deeply embedded Vietnam was in the national psyche.

If they were more willing to talk about Vietnam, Americans remained confused and divided about its meaning, particularly its implications for U.S. foreign policy. The indifference and tendency toward withdrawal so manifest in 1975 declined sharply over the next ten years. Bitter memories of Vietnam combined with the frustration of the Iranian hostage crisis to produce a growing asser-

tiveness, a highly nationalistic impulse to defend perceived interests, even a yearning to restore the United States to its old position
in the world. The breakdown of détente, the steady growth of Soviet military power, and the use of that power in Afghanistan produced a heightened concern for American security. The defense
budget soared to record proportions in the early 1980s, and support
for military intervention in defense of traditional allies increased
significantly.[26]

The new nationalism was tempered by lingering memories of
Vietnam, however. Many Americans remained deeply skeptical of
1960s-style globalism and dubious of such internationalist mecha-
nisms as foreign aid or even the United Nations. Ten years after the
end of the war, a whopping majority still believed that intervention
in Vietnam had been a mistake. Recollection of Vietnam produced
strong opposition to intervention in third-world crises in Lebanon
and Central America. Thus, in the aftermath of Vietnam, the public mood consisted of a strange amalgam of nostalgia and realism,
assertiveness and caution.

The nation's foreign policy elite has been no more certain in its
judgments on Vietnam than the mass public. Indeed, systematic
polling of leadership groups makes clear that Vietnam was a "land-
mark event" that left "deep and profound" divisions. Americans
agree that to construct a viable foreign policy they must learn from
Vietnam. But they disagree sharply over what they should learn.[27]

The basic issue remains the morality and wisdom of intervention in Vietnam. In the light of Hanoi's postwar actions, Americans
are less likely to openly condemn their nation's intervention as immoral, an important sign of change in itself. Those who continue to
feel that intervention was wrong argue that it was unnecessary or
impractical or both, and most liberals still contend that at best it
represented overcommitment in an area of peripheral national interest, at worst an act of questionable morality.

The conservative point of view has been more vocal in recent
years and it takes two forms. Some, including President Ronald
Reagan, have found in postwar events in Indochina reason to speak
out anew on what they always felt was a fundamental reality—

---

[26] Adam Clymer, "What Americans Think Now," *New York Times Magazine*
(March 31, 1985), 34.

[27] Ole R. Holsti and James N. Rosenau, *American Leadership in World Affairs:
Vietnam and the Breakdown of Consensus* (Winchester, 1984).

that, as Reagan has repeatedly stated, Vietnam was "in truth a noble war," a selfless attempt on the part of the United States to save a free nation from outside aggression. Others concede that the United States might have erred in getting involved in Vietnam in the first place, but they go on to insist that over time an important interest was established that had to be defended for the sake of U.S. credibility throughout the world.

The second great issue, on which Americans also sharply disagree, concerns the reasons for U.S. failure in Vietnam. Many of the leading participants in the war have concluded that America's failure was essentially instrumental, a result of the improper use of available tools. General Westmoreland and others blame the "ill-considered" policy of "graduated response" imposed on the military by civilian leaders, arguing that had the United States employed its military power quickly, decisively, and without limit, the war could have been won.[28] Other critics view the fundamental mistake as the choice of tools rather than how they were used, and they blame an unimaginative military as much as civilians. Instead of trying to fight World War II and Korea over in Vietnam, these critics argue, the military should have adapted to the unconventional war in which it found itself and shaped an appropriate counterinsurgency strategy to meet it.[29] Still other commentators, including some military theorists, agree that military leaders were as responsible for the strategic failure as civilians. Critics such as Colonel Harry G. Summers, Jr., argue that instead of mounting costly and counterproductive search-and-destroy operations against guerrillas in South Vietnam, the United States should have used its own forces against North Vietnamese regulars along the seventeenth parallel to isolate the north from the south. Military leaders should also have insisted on a declaration of war to ensure that the war was not fought in "cold blood" and that popular support could be sustained.[30]

The lessons drawn are as divergent as the arguments advanced. Those who feel that the United States lost because it did not act decisively conclude that if the nation becomes involved in war again,

---

[28] William C. Westmoreland, *A Soldier Reports* (Garden City, N.Y., 1976), p. 410.

[29] Comments by Robert Komer in W. Scott Thompson and Donaldson Frizzell, *The Lessons of Vietnam* (New York, 1977), p. 223.

[30] Harry G. Summers, Jr., *On Strategy: The Vietnam War in Context* (Carlisle Barracks, Pa., 1981).

it must employ its military power with a view to winning quickly before public support erodes. Those who feel that the basic problem was the formulation rather than the execution of strategy insist that military and civilian leaders must think strategically, that they must examine more carefully the nature of the war and formulate more precisely the ways in which American power can best be used to attain clearly defined objectives.

Such lessons depend on the values and belief systems of those who pronounce them, of course, and those who opposed the war have reached quite different conclusions. To some former doves, the fundamental lesson is never to get involved in a land war in Asia; to others, it is to avoid intervention in international trouble spots unless the nation's vital interests are clearly at stake. Some commentators warn that policymakers must be wary of the sort of simplistic reasoning that produced the domino theory and the Munich analogy. Others point to the weaknesses of South Vietnam and admonish that "even a superpower can't save allies who are unable or unwilling to save themselves."[31] For still others, the key lessons are that American power has distinct limits and that in order to be effective, American foreign policy must be true to the nation's historic ideals.

The ghost of Vietnam hovered over an increasingly divisive debate on the proper American response to revolutions in Central America. Shortly after taking office in 1981, President Reagan committed U.S. prestige to defending the government of El Salvador against a leftist-led insurgency, in part in the expectation that success there might exorcise the so-called Vietnam syndrome—the perceived reluctance of the American public in the wake of Vietnam to take on responsibilities in third-world countries. When the quick victory did not materialize, the administration expanded U.S. military aid to El Salvador, created a huge military base in Honduras, and launched a not-so-covert war to overthrow the Sandinista government of Nicaragua. The administration insisted that the United States must support non-Communist forces to avert in Central America the bloodshed and misery that followed the end of the war in Vietnam. At the same time, the military and the Defense Department have made clear that they will not go to war under the conditions that prevailed in Vietnam. On the other side, dovish

[31] Louisville *Courier-Journal*, April 28, 1985.

critics ominously warn that U.S. intervention in Central America will lead straight into a quagmire like Vietnam.[32]

The ongoing debate over U.S. involvement in Vietnam leaves many questions unanswered. Whether a more decisive use of military power could have brought a satisfactory conclusion to the war without causing even more disastrous consequences remains highly doubtful. Whether the adoption of a more vigorous and imaginative counterinsurgency program at an earlier stage could have wrested control of the countryside from the Vietcong can never be known, and the ability of the United States to develop such a program in an alien environment is dubious. That the United States exaggerated the importance of Vietnam, as the liberals suggest, seems clear. But their argument begs the question of how one determines the significance of a given area and the even more difficult question of assessing the ultimate costs of intervention at an early stage.

The fundamental weakness of many of the lessons learned thus far is that they assume the continued necessity and practicability of the containment policy, at least in modified form, thereby evading or ignoring altogether the central questions raised by the war. The United States intervened in Vietnam to block the apparent march of a Soviet-directed Communism across Asia, enlarged its commitment to halt a presumably expansionist Communist China, and eventually made Vietnam a test of its determination to uphold world order. By wrongly attributing the Vietnamese conflict to external sources, the United States drastically misjudged its internal dynamics. By intervening in what was essentially a local struggle, it placed itself at the mercy of local forces, a weak client, and a determined adversary. It elevated into a major international conflict what might have remained a localized struggle. By raising the stakes into a test of its own credibility, it perilously narrowed its options. A policy so flawed in its premises cannot help but fail, and in this case the results were disastrous.

Vietnam made clear the inherent unworkability of a policy of global containment. In the 1940s the world seemed dangerous but manageable. The United States enjoyed a position of unprece-

---

[32] George C. Herring, "Vietnam, El Salvador, and the Uses of History," in Kenneth M. Coleman and George C. Herring, eds., *The Central American Crisis* (Wilmington, Del., 1985), pp. 97–110.

dented power and influence, and achieved some notable early successes in Europe. Much of America's power derived from the weakness of other nations rather than from its own intrinsic strength, however, and Vietnam demonstrated conclusively that its power, however great, had limits. The development of significant military capabilities by the Soviet Union and China made it extremely risky for the United States to use its military power in Vietnam on a scale necessary to achieve the desired results. Conditions in Vietnam itself and the constraints imposed by domestic opinion made it impossible to reach these goals with limited means. Vietnam makes clear that the United States cannot uphold its own concept of world order in the face of a stubborn and resolute, although much weaker, foe. The war did not bring about the decline of American power, as some have suggested, but was rather symptomatic of the limits of national power in an age of international diversity and nuclear weaponry.

To assume, therefore, that the United States can simply rouse itself from the nightmare of Vietnam and resume its accustomed role in a rapidly changing world would be to invite further disaster. The world of the 1980s is even more dangerous and much less manageable than that of the 1940s and 1950s. The proliferation of nuclear weapons, the emergence of a large number of new nations, the existence of a baffling array of regional and internal conflicts, have combined to produce a more confusing and disorderly world than at any time in the recent past. The ambiguous triangular relationship between the United States, the Soviet Union, and China has had a further destabilizing effect, creating enormous uncertainty and shifting tensions and giving lesser nations increased maneuverability and opportunity for mischief. A successful American adjustment to the new conditions requires the shedding of old approaches, most notably of the traditional oscillation between crusades to reform the world and angry withdrawal from it. To carry the "Never Again" syndrome to its logical conclusion and turn away from an ungrateful and hostile world could be calamitous. To regard Vietnam as an aberration, a unique experience from which nothing can be learned, would invite further frustration. To adapt to the new era, the United States must recognize its vulnerability, accept the limits to its power, and accommodate itself to many situations it does not like. Americans must understand that they will not be able to dictate solutions to world problems or to achieve all of their goals. Like it or not, Vietnam marked the end of an era in world history and of American foreign policy, an era marked by constructive achievements but blemished by ultimate, although not irreparable, failure.

Suggestions for Additional Reading

GENERAL

The best guide to the already massive literature on Vietnam is Richard Dean Burns and Milton Leitenberg, *The Wars in Vietnam, Cambodia, and Laos, 1945–1982* (Santa Barbara, Calif., 1983), a comprehensive bibliography of more than 6,000 items that is particularly valuable for its extensive list of periodical articles. For the manuscript and archival materials available as of August 1984, see George C. Herring, ed., "Sources for Understanding the Vietnam Conflict," *Society for Historians of American Foreign Relations Newsletter*, 16 (March 1985), 8–30. An excellent introduction to research on the war is Ronald H. Spector, *Researching the Vietnam Experience* (Washington, D.C., 1984).

There are numerous valuable collections of documents. William Appleman Williams et al., *America in Vietnam: A Documentary History* (New York, 1984), is a good brief collection. Gareth Porter, ed., *Vietnam: The Definitive Documentation of Human Decisions* (2 vols.; Stanfordville, N.Y., 1979), is scarcely definitive, but it contains Vietnamese as well as American documents.

The basic documentary source is the *Pentagon Papers*, a study prepared by the Department of Defense at the direction of Robert S. McNamara, subsequently leaked to the press by Daniel Ellsberg, and eventually published in several editions. The best introduction to the study is Neil Sheehan et al., *The Pentagon Papers as Published by the New York Times* (New York, 1971), which contains readable and generally reliable synopses of the original Defense Department analyses as well as many of the most important documents. U.S. Congress, Senate, Subcommittee on Public Buildings and Grounds, *The Pentagon Papers* (*The Senator Gravel Edition*) (4 vols.; Boston, 1971), is the most orderly and usable of the larger editions, containing much of the original text and a large collection of documents. A fifth volume includes an index and commentaries on the papers by a number of scholars. U.S. Congress, House, Committee on Armed Services, *United States–Vietnam Relations, 1945–1967: A Study Prepared by the Department of Defense* (12 books; Washington, D.C., 1971), has the largest collection of documents, but it is awkwardly arranged and poorly printed and contains numerous deletions. George C. Herring, ed., *The Secret Diplomacy of the Vietnam War: The Negotiating Volumes of the Pentagon Papers* (Austin, Tex., 1983), is an annotated edition of the previously unpublished section of the papers dealing with peace initiatives.

Although invaluable, the *Pentagon Papers* must be used with caution. The essays are of uneven quality and reflect the bias of McNamara's civilian advisers. They rely primarily on Defense Department records and do not always adequately treat the role of the White House and State Department. They emphasize military matters and devote only slight attention to such important things as the operation of the aid program and American involvement in South Vietnamese politics. George McT. Kahin, "The Pentagon Papers: A Critical Evaluation," *American Political Science Review,* LXIX (June 1975), 675–684, elaborates on the value and deficiencies of the various editions as historical sources.

Other useful collections of official documents include Department of State, *Foreign Relations of the United States,* still available only through 1957, although those volumes dealing with Vietnam will be published prior to the volumes in the regular series. *Public Papers of the Presidents of the United States* are annual volumes that contain the major speeches and press conferences.

There are a number of valuable studies of Vietnam during the thirty-year war. James Pinckney Harrison, *The Endless War* (New York, 1982), is scholarly and readable but tends to be uncritical of the Communist side. Much more balanced in interpretation and based heavily on Vietnamese sources is William Duiker's excellent study, *The Communist Road to Power in Vietnam* (Boulder, Colo., 1981). Also of value are Duiker's briefer survey, *Vietnam: Nation in Revolution* (Boulder, Colo., 1983), and Thomas L. Hodgkin, *Viet-*

nam: The Revolutionary Path (New York, 1981). Among the older works still useful are Donald Lancaster, *The Emancipation of French Indochina* (New York, 1961); Bernard Fall, *The Two Vietnams: A Political and Military Analysis* (New York, 1967), and *Last Reflections on a War* (New York, 1967), two invaluable studies by the distinguished French scholar who was killed while reporting on combat in Vietnam; and the several works by Joseph Buttinger: *The Smaller Dragon: A Political History of Vietnam* (New York, 1958), *Vietnam: A Dragon Embattled* (2 vols.; New York, 1967), and the survey *A Dragon Defiant: A Short History of Vietnam* (New York, 1972).

The literature on American involvement in Vietnam is already massive and its growth shows no sign of slacking. In a class by itself is Stanley Karnow, *Vietnam: A History* (New York, 1983), a balanced and immensely readable account based on the author's own wide-ranging experience as a journalist in Southeast Asia as well as a close reading of the sources. Michael Maclear, *The Ten Thousand Day War Vietnam: 1945–1975* (New York, 1981), is also worthwhile. The older surveys by Alexander Kendrick, *The Wound Within: America in the Vietnam Years, 1945–1974* (Boston, 1974), and Chester A. Cooper, *The Lost Crusade: America in Vietnam* (New York, 1970), are still useful, the latter especially so since it contains many insights from the author's experience as a second-level official in the Kennedy and Johnson years.

The war set off a vigorous and frequently bitter debate which quickly extended beyond Vietnam to the very wellsprings of American foreign policy. A frankly radical point of view is advanced in Gabriel Kolko, *The Roots of American Foreign Policy* (Boston, 1969). Richard J. Barnet, *Roots of War: The Men and Institutions Behind U.S. Foreign Policy* (New York, 1972), places less emphasis on economic factors but nevertheless indicts the "national security managers" whose sweeping definition of the national interest plunged the nation into a disastrous war. An early liberal critique, Arthur M. Schlesinger, Jr., *The Bitter Heritage: Vietnam and American Democracy* (Boston, 1966), argues that overly optimistic advisers misled reluctant Presidents step-by-step into the quagmire of Vietnam. Daniel Ellsberg, *Papers on the War* (New York, 1972), and Leslie H. Gelb and Richard K. Betts, *The Irony of Vietnam: The System Worked* (Washington, D.C., 1978) persuasively rebut the quagmire thesis, contending that Presidents from Truman to Johnson perceived the pitfalls of intervention but felt compelled by the exigencies of domestic politics to perpetuate a bloody stalemate in Vietnam. Bernard Brodie, *War and Politics* (New York, 1973), contains perceptive critiques of both arguments as well as a stimulating overall appraisal of American policy and strategy. George McT. Kahin and John W. Lewis, *The United States in Vietnam* (New York, 1969), an early "dove" study by two specialists in Southeast Asian history, is especially valuable for its analysis of the Vietnamese dimension. Frances FitzGerald, *Fire in the Lake: The Vietnamese and the Americans in Vietnam* (Boston, 1972), romanticizes the Vietnamese Communists but properly emphasizes the cultural gap between Americans and all Vietnamese. David Halberstam, *The Best and the Brightest* (New York, 1972), a massive, rambling, undocumented work, sometimes frustrating, frequently insightful, perhaps better than any other work re-creates the mindset of the policymakers and the intellectual milieu in which U.S. policy was made. James Thomson, "How Could Vietnam Happen? An Autopsy," *Atlantic Monthly*, 221 (April 1968), 47–53, is a stimulating analysis by an insider of the bureaucratic factors leading to intervention. Paul Kattenburg, *The Vietnam Trauma in American Foreign Policy, 1945–1975* (New Brunswick, N.J., 1980), is a scholarly study also informed by the insights of one who was involved in policymaking. Michael Charlton and Anthony Moncrief, *Many Reasons Why* (New York, 1978), contains a number of illuminating interviews with key policymakers.

By the end of the 1970s, the dove interpretation of the war was under fire from conservative "revisionists." Guenter Lewy, *America in Vietnam* (New York, 1978), criticized the military for a faulty and counterproductive strategy but argued that the war should have been fought and could have been won and defends the United States against charges of war crimes. Norman Podhoretz, *Why We Were in Vietnam* (New York, 1982), concludes that the war was unwinnable but argues that the cause was just and the effort worth making.

A useful survey of writing on Vietnam in the early 1980s is Fox Butterfield, "The New Vietnam Scholarship," *New York Times Magazine* (February 13, 1983), 26–32, 45–60. Useful compilations of symposia which reflect recent trends in the literature are Peter Braestrup, ed., *Vietnam as History: Ten Years After the Paris Peace Accords* (Washington, D.C., 1984), which focuses on the instrumental question of why the United States failed, and Harrison Salisbury, ed., *Vietnam Reconsidered* (New York, 1984), more dovish in tone and more concerned with the wisdom, morality, and consequences of U.S. intervention. A recent study which offers some novel interpretations and is particularly good on Vietnamese policy and strategy is Timothy J. Lomperis, *The War Everyone Lost—and Won* (Baton Rouge, La., 1984).

THE FIRST INDOCHINA WAR, 1945–1954

For the origins of the Vietnamese revolution, there is still no better place to begin than Jean Lacouture, *Ho Chi Minh: A Political Biography* (New York, 1968), a highly readable and sympathetic account which stresses Ho's nationalism and charismatic personality. Bernard B. Fall, ed., *Ho Chi Minh on Revolution: Selected Writings, 1920–1966* (New York, 1967), is also useful. John T. McAlister, Jr., *Vietnam: The Origins of Revolution* (New York, 1971), William J. Duiker, *The Rise of Nationalism in Vietnam, 1900–1941* (Ithaca, N.Y., 1976), and David G. Marr, *Vietnamese Anti-Colonialism* (Berkeley, Calif., 1971) and *Vietnamese Tradition on Trial* (Berkeley, Calif., 1982), are fine scholarly analyses that cover only the beginnings but do much to explain why the Vietminh prevailed over other nationalist groups and the French and why North Vietnam ultimately prevailed against South Vietnam and the United States. Robert F. Turner, *Vietnamese Communism: Its Origins and Development* (Stanford, Calif., 1975), dismisses the Vietnamese Communists as usurpers. Douglas Pike, *History of Vietnamese Communism* (Stanford, Calif., 1978), is a valuable brief survey that stresses the superiority of the Communists' organizational techniques.

The standard account of the politics and diplomacy of the First Indochina War is Ellen Hammer, *The Struggle for Indochina, 1945–1955* (Stanford, Calif., 1966). A more up-to-date study, particularly valuable for its coverage of French politics, is Ronald E. Irving, *The First Indochina War: French and American Policy, 1945–1954* (London, 1975). Bernard B. Fall, *Street Without Joy* (New York, 1972), dramatically depicts military operations and the frustrations encountered by the French. Useful surveys of military operations include Lucien Bodard, *The Quicksand War: Prelude to Vietnam* (Boston, 1967), and Edgar O'Ballance, *The Indochina*

War, 1945–1954: A Study in Guerrilla Warfare (London, 1964). King C. Chen, *Vietnam and China, 1938–1954* (Princeton, N.J., 1969), a scholarly study based on Chinese and Vietnamese sources, documents China's influence on the ideology of the Vietnamese revolution and its important military contributions in the latter stages of the war with France.

The importance Vietnam eventually assumed for the United States and the declassification of American documents for the period up to 1950 have stimulated much interest among scholars in the origins of U.S. involvement. Because his trusteeship scheme seemed in retrospect to have offered an alternative to thirty years of war, Franklin Roosevelt's policies have provoked extensive study. Although they differ in emphasis, Gary R. Hess, "Franklin D. Roosevelt and Indochina," *Journal of American History*, LIX (September 1972), 353–368, Walter LaFeber, "Roosevelt, Churchill and Indochina, 1942–1945," *American Historical Review*, 80 (December 1975), 1277–1295, Christopher Thorne, "Indochina and Anglo-American Relations, 1942–1945," *Pacific Historical Review*, XLV (February 1976), 73–96, Christopher Thorne, *Allies of a Kind: The United States, Britain, and the War against Japan, 1941–1945* (New York, 1978), and William Roger Louis, *Imperialism at Bay: The United States and the Decolonization of the British Empire* (New York, 1978), all make clear that Roosevelt's scheme was more an expression of personal prejudice and intent than a carefully thought-out policy. George C. Herring, "The Truman Administration and the Restoration of French Sovereignty in Indochina," *Diplomatic History*, I (Spring 1977), 97–117, stresses the importance of the Soviet threat in Europe in the reorientation of Indochina policy in 1945. Gary R. Hess, "United States Policy and the Origins of the French-Vietminh War, 1945–1946," *Peace and Change*, III (Summer–Fall 1975), 21–33, also emphasizes European factors in shaping the American response to the outbreak of war in Indochina. The early Office of Strategic Services missions to Indochina are recounted by a scholar in Ronald H. Spector, *Advice and Support: The Early Years* (Washington, D.C., 1983), and by a participant in Archimedes L. Patti, *Why Vietnam? Prelude to America's Albatross* (Berkeley, Calif., 1981).

The reorientation of American Far Eastern policy in 1949–1950, of which the commitment to France in Indochina was only one part, has recently received extensive scholarly treatment. The most comprehensive study is Robert M. Blum, *Drawing the Line: The Origin of the American Containment Policy in East Asia* (New York, 1982). Dorothy Borg and Waldo Heinrichs, *Uncertain Years: Chinese-American Relations, 1947–1950* (New York, 1980), although it does not deal specifically with Indochina, sheds much light on the broader policy problem. Michael Schaller, "Securing the Great Crescent: Occupied Japan and the Origins of Containment in Southeast Asia," *Journal of American History*, 69 (September 1982), 392–414, Andrew Rotter, "The Triangular Route to Vietnam: The United States, Great Britain, and Southeast Asia, 1945–1950," *International History Review*, VI (August 1984), 404–423, and William Borden, *The Pacific Alliance: United States Foreign Economic Policy and Japanese Trade Recovery, 1947–1955* (Madison, Wis., 1984), place the decision in the broader framework of American and European political and economic interests in East and Southeast Asia.

The Franco-American partnership in Indochina during the Truman years has not been studied by scholars. Insights into the dilemmas facing U.S. policymakers can be gained from Dean Acheson, *Present at the Creation* (New York, 1969), Gaddis Smith, *Dean Acheson* (New York, 1970), David McLellan, *Dean Acheson: The State Department Years* (New York, 1976), Stephen Jurika, Jr., ed., *From Pearl Harbor to Vietnam: The Memoirs of Admiral Arthur W. Radford* (Stanford, Calif., 1980), John Melby, "Vietnam–1950," *Diplomatic History*, 6 (Winter 1982), 97–109, and particularly from Robert Shaplen, *The Lost Revolution: The U.S. in Vietnam, 1946–1966* (New York, 1966). The mood of these years is best captured in Graham Greene's classic novel *The Quiet American* (London, 1955).

The most up-to-date analysis of American diplomacy during the Dienbienphu crisis is George C. Herring and Richard H. Immerman, "Eisenhower, Dulles and Dienbienphu: The 'Day We Didn't Go to War' Revisited," *Journal of American History*, 72 (September 1985), 343–363. The older work by Melvin Gurtov, *The First Vietnam Crisis: Chinese Communist Strategy and United States Involvement, 1953–1954* (New York, 1967), is still valuable. The French reaction to the crisis can be traced in Paul Ely, *Memoires: l'Indochine dans la Tourmente* (Paris, 1964), and Henri Navarre, *Agonie de l'Indochine, 1953–1954* (Paris, 1956). Bernard B. Fall, *Hell in a Very Small Place* (Philadelphia, 1966), and Jules Roy, *The*

Battle of Dienbienphu (New York, 1965), are excellent accounts of an epic battle, and Stewart Menaul, "Dien Bien Phu," in Noble Frankland and Christopher Dowling, eds., *Decisive Battles of the Twentieth Century* (London, 1976), pp. 305–318, is a good brief study. The Vietnamese perspective can be found in Vo Nguyen Giap, *Dien Bien Phu* (Hanoi, 1962). Robert F. Randle, *Geneva 1954: The Settlement of the Indochinese War* (Princeton, N.J., 1969), is the standard work on the conference that ended one war and laid the basis for another, although it should be supplemented with Francois Joyaux, *La Chine et le règlement du premier conflict d'Indochine (Geneve 1954)* (Paris, 1979), an important study which adds new and important findings from the French archives, and by David Carlton, *Anthony Eden* (London, 1981), an up-to-date biography of a key figure.

THE DIEM ERA, 1954–1963

Ralph B. Smith, *Revolution Versus Containment* (New York, 1983), seeks to place the Second Indochina War in an international perspective. The best overall study of South Vietnam during the Diem years remains Robert Scigliano, *South Vietnam: Nation Under Stress* (Boston, 1964), a comprehensive analysis, ending in 1962, by a political scientist who worked with the Michigan State University advisory group. Scigliano and Guy Fox, *Technical Assistance in Vietnam: The Michigan State Experience* (New York, 1965), is a valuable study of a major aspect of the economic aid program. Official histories based on research in military archives are invaluable for coverage of the military assistance program. Spector, *Advice and Support,* authoritatively covers the army's role, while Robert H. Whitlow, *U.S. Marines in Vietnam: The Advisory and Combat Assistance Era, 1954–1964* (Washington, D.C., 1976), and Edwin Hooper et al., *The United States Navy and the Vietnam Conflict: The Setting of the Stage to 1959* (Washington, D.C., 1976), deal with the other services. Jean Lacouture, *Vietnam Between Two Truces* (New York, 1966), is still useful, as are two biographies of Diem: Denis Warner, *The Last Confucian* (New York, 1963), and Anthony Bouscaren, *The Last of the Mandarins: Diem of Vietnam* (Pittsburgh, 1965). Edward G. Lansdale, *In the Midst of Wars* (New York, 1972), recounts his important role in the birth of South Vietnam and J. Lawton Collins his in *Lightning Joe: An Autobiography* (Baton Rouge, La., 1979). William Colby, *Honorable Men* (New York, 1978), notes some of the activities of the CIA in the nation-building years.

The origins and evolution of the insurgency in South Vietnam provide the subject for a sizable literature filled with controversy. FitzGerald, *Fire in the Lake*, and Douglas Pike, *Viet Cong: National Liberation Front of South Vietnam* (rev. ed.; Cambridge, Mass., 1972), offer conflicting interpretations regarding the success of the front. Jeffrey Race, *War Comes to Long An: Revolutionary Conflict in a Vietnamese Province* (Berkeley, Calif., 1972), James Trullinger, *Village at War: An Account of Revolution in Vietnam* (New York, 1980), and William Andrews, *The Village War: Vietnamese Communist Revolutionary Activity in Dinh Truong Province, 1960–1964* (Columbia, Mo., 1973), are all excellent "micro" studies, exploring the origins and evolution of the war at the village and province levels. King C. Chen, "Hanoi's Three Decisions and the Escalation of the Vietnam War," *Political Science Quarterly*, 90 (Summer 1975), 239–259, is an important, scholarly contribution based on North Vietnamese sources. Edwin E. Moise, *Land Reform in China and North Vietnam: Consolidating the Revolution at the Village Level* (Chapel Hill, N.C., 1983), provides important information and insights about North Vietnam immediately after Geneva.

Memoirs and biographies provide one of the best ways to approach the study of U.S. policy in Vietnam during the Kennedy years. Herbert Parmet, *JFK: The Presidency of John F. Kennedy* (New York, 1983), is the most up-to-date and balanced of the many Kennedy biographies and contains important information on Vietnam policy. Among the numerous memoirs, Roger Hilsman, *To Move a Nation* (New York, 1967), is the most valuable for Vietnam because of the author's role in counterinsurgency policy and in the overthrow of Diem. Maxwell D. Taylor, *Swords and Ploughshares* (New York, 1972), is also thorough and detailed. John Kenneth Galbraith, *Ambassador's Journal: A Personal Account of the Kennedy Years* (Boston, 1969), Henry Cabot Lodge, *The Storm Has Many Eyes* (New York, 1973), and Walt W. Rostow, *The Diffusion of Power: An Essay in Recent History* (New York, 1972), are all useful. Arthur M. Schlesinger, Jr.'s two classics, *A Thousand Days* (Boston, 1965) and *Robert Kennedy and His Times* (Boston, 1978), offer the most spirited defense of the Kennedy policies. John Mecklin, *Mission in Torment: An Intimate Account of the U.S. Role in Vietnam* (Garden City, N.Y., 1965), vividly portrays the turmoil and confusion in the U.S. Embassy in Saigon during this period, while David Halberstam, *The Making of a Quagmire* (New York, 1964), reveals the anger and disillusionment of the dissident journalists. Richard Tregaskis, *Vietnam Diary* (New York, 1963), is a little-known account by a veteran war correspondent which reveals much about the attitudes of the early U.S. advisers in Vietnam. Stephen Pelz, "John F. Kennedy's 1961 Vietnam War Decisions," *Journal of Strategic Studies,* 4 (December 1981), 356–385, is a valuable scholarly article. Geoffrey Warner's articles, "The United States and the Fall of Diem," Part I: "The Coup That Never Was," *Australian Outlook,* 28 (December 1974), 245–258, and Part II: "The Death of Diem," *Australian Outlook,* 29 (March 1975), 3–17, although based primarily on the *Pentagon Papers,* still provide the best study of that subject.

THE SECOND INDOCHINA WAR, 1964–1968

An introduction to the literature of the Johnson era is George C. Herring, "The War in Vietnam," in Robert A. Divine, ed., *Exploring the Johnson Years* (Austin, Tex., 1981), pp. 27–62. Gelb and Betts, *Irony of Vietnam,* is the best analysis of the mindset of the policymakers, although it overstates Johnson's willingness to accept a stalemate. Halberstam, *Best and the Brightest,* is also useful. Johnson's memoirs, *The Vantage Point* (New York, 1971), are dull and defensive, but they do contain material from some of the President's personal files not yet available to scholars. Vaughan Bornet, *The Presidency of Lyndon B. Johnson* (Lawrence, Kans., 1983), the most up-to-date evaluation of the administration, contains several chapters on Vietnam. There is no scholarly biography of Johnson. Doris Kearns, *Lyndon Johnson and the American Dream* (New York, 1976), is less than successful as psychobiography, but it contains valuable insights into Johnson's personality, leadership style, and Vietnam policies. Henry Graff, *The Tuesday Cabinet* (Englewood Cliffs, N.J., 1970), a collection of interviews with Johnson and his top advisers spanning the period from 1965 to 1968, graphically reveals the shift from cautious optimism to great frustration. Warren Cohen, *Dean Rusk* (Totawa, N.J., 1980) is an excellent study of LBJ's Secretary of State. There is no comparable volume on Robert S. McNamara, but Alain C. Enthoven and K. Wayne Smith, *How Much Is Enough?* (New York, 1971), Henry Trewhitt, *McNamara* (New York, 1971), Lawrence Korb, *The Joint Chiefs of Staff: The First Twenty-Five Years* (Bloomington, Ind., 1976), and the highly critical Gregory Palmer, *The McNamara Strategy and the Vietnam War* (Westport, Conn., 1978), help explain the Pentagon's response to Vietnam. Larry Berman, *Planning a Tragedy* (New York, 1982), covers in depth the crucial decisions of July 1965.

The Gulf of Tonkin incident produced a spate of books. All were of the exposé variety and were based on the Congressional hearings of 1968, but their principal findings have held up very well. These include Anthony Austin, *The President's War* (Philadelphia, 1971), John Galloway, *The Gulf of Tonkin Resolution* (Rutherford, N.J., 1970), Joseph C. Goulden, *Truth Is the First Casualty: The Gulf of Tonkin Affair—Illusion and Reality* (New York, 1969), and Eugene C. Windchy, *Tonkin Gulf* (Garden City, N.Y., 1971).

The literature on American military operations has mushroomed in recent years, and the subject has remained highly controversial. For an introduction to the controversy, see George C. Herring, "American Strategy in Vietnam: The Postwar Debate," *Military Affairs*, 46 (April 1982), 57–63. Dave Richard Palmer, *Summons of the Trumpet* (San Rafael, Calif., 1978), a readable survey by a senior Army officer, criticizes the attrition strategy as no strategy at all but accepts Westmoreland's argument that the conditions he faced left him no choice. Westmoreland also blames the civilians for losing a war that could have been won in his bland and defensive memoirs, *A Soldier Reports* (Garden City, N.Y., 1976), a view advanced more emotionally in U.S. Grant Sharp, *Strategy for Defeat* (San Rafael, Calif., 1978). Robert L. Gallucci, *Neither Peace Nor Honor: The Politics of American Military Policy in Vietnam* (Baltimore, Md., 1975), analyzes the decision-making process and finds military professionalism and a closed bureaucratic system primarily responsible for a strategy flawed in its premises and methods. Lewy, *America in Vietnam*, is also highly critical of the military for its strategic failure and suggests that a strategy based on counterinsurgency doctrine might have worked. Harry G. Summers, Jr., *On Strategy: The Vietnam War in Context* (Carlisle Barracks, Pa., 1981), and Bruce Palmer, Jr., *The 25-Year War:*

America's Military Role in Vietnam (Lexington, Ky., 1984), criticize civilian and military leaders for failing to think strategically and argue that a conventional-war strategy isolating North from South Vietnam might have succeeded. Douglas Kinnard, *The War Managers* (Hanover, N.H., 1977), surveys the postwar opinions of senior U.S. Army officers as to what went wrong and finds remarkable diversity. Wallace J. Thies, *When Governments Collide: Coercion and Diplomacy in the Vietnam Conflict, 1964–1968* (Berkeley, Calif., 1980), analyzes the Johnson administration's strategy and diplomacy in terms of coercion theory and offers some persuasive explanations for its failure. Richard A. Hunt and Richard H. Shultz, Jr., *Lessons from an Unconventional War* (Elmsford, N.Y., 1981), contains a series of scholarly essays dealing with numerous topics related to strategy.

Various specific aspects of the war have received extensive treatment. Raphael Littauer and Normal Uphoff, eds., *The Air War in Indochina* (Boston, 1972), remains the best study of that subject, although the more recent Drew Middleton, *Air War—Vietnam* (New York, 1978), and James Clay Thompson, *Rolling Thunder: Understanding Policy and Program Failure* (Chapel Hill, N.C., 1980), are also useful. Marine Corps operations are well covered in Allan R. Millett, *Semper Fidelis: The History of the United States Marine Corps* (New York, 1980), and in the official histories. The Army's official histories dealing with combat operations are yet to be published. In the meantime, its monograph series is useful. Of these volumes, Bernard W. Rogers, *Cedar Falls–Junction City: A Turning Point* (Washington, D.C., 1974), and Joseph A. McChristian, *The Role of Military Intelligence, 1965–1967* (Washington, D.C., 1974) are worthwhile. The important battle of the Ia Drang is analyzed in Harry G. Summers, Jr., "The Bitter Triumph of Ia Drang," *American Heritage*, 35 (February–March 1984), 50–58.

The war produced a huge volume of personal accounts of combat by GIs and a distinguished fiction literature. Among the best are Philip Caputo, *A Rumor of War* (New York, 1977), Robert Mason, *Chickenhawk* (New York, 1983), Michael Herr, *Dispatches* (New York, 1977), James Webb, *Fields of Fire* (New York, 1978), Tim O'Brien, *Going After Cacciato* (New York, 1978), and John DelVecchio, *The Thirteenth Valley* (New York, 1982). Al Santoli, *Everything We Had* (New York, 1981), Mark Baker, *Nam* (New York, 1982), and Wallace Terry, *Bloods: An Oral History of the*

War by Black Veterans (New York, 1984), are valuable collections of oral histories. Dale Reich, "One Year in Vietnam: A Young Soldier Remembers," *Wisconsin Magazine of History*, 64 (Spring 1981), 163–180, is excellent. The legal, moral, and ethical issues raised by combat in Vietnam are explored in Lewy, *America in Vietnam*, and in Richard A. Falk, ed., *The Vietnam War and International Law* (4 vols.; Princeton, N.J., 1967–1976).

The best study of the various pacification programs is Douglas S. Blaufarb, *The Counterinsurgency Era: U.S. Doctrines and Performance* (New York, 1977), a broad evaluation of the American experience with counterinsurgency after World War II. Lawrence E. Grinter, "South Vietnam: Pacification Denied," *Southeast Asia Spectrum*, 3 (July 1975), 49–78, is well researched and balanced in its appraisal. J. K. McCallum, "CORDS Pacification Organization in Vietnam: A Civilian-Military Effort," *Armed Forces and Society*, 10 (Fall 1983), 105–122, studies the organizational aspect of the pacification program. Important studies of specific pacification programs include William D. Parker, *U.S. Marine Corps Civil Affairs in I Corps, Republic of South Vietnam* (Washington, D.C., 1970), an official history, and Francis J. West, *The Village* (New York, 1972), a firsthand account of pacification in the village of Binh Nghia.

For politics in South Vietnam, the most valuable studies remain the older works by Kahin and Lewis and FitzGerald cited above. Also useful is Robert Shaplen, *The Road from War: Vietnam, 1965–1970* (New York, 1970), a collection of perceptive reports by one of America's most knowledgeable journalists. Nguyen Cao Ky, *Twenty Years and Twenty Days* (New York, 1976), and Tran Van Don, *Our Endless War: Inside South Vietnam* (San Rafael, Calif., 1978), two memoirs by top South Vietnamese officials, offer insights into the problems that vexed the Saigon government throughout the war. Allan E. Goodman, *Politics in War: The Bases of Political Community in South Vietnam* (Cambridge, Mass., 1973), is a scholarly analysis of the political structure of South Vietnam after the 1967 elections. Samuel L. Popkin, *The Rational Peasant* (Berkeley, Calif., 1979), studies the political economy of rural Vietnam and reaches some surprising conclusions. Lawrence E. Grinter, "Bargaining Between Saigon and Washington: Dilemmas of Linkage Politics During War," *Orbis*, 18 (Fall 1974), 837–867, argues persuasively that the United States had little leverage over the Saigon government once it made a substantial commitment to South Vietnam.

The best analysis of North Vietnam's response to war remains Jon M. Van Dyke, *North Vietnam's Strategy for Survival* (Palo Alto, Calif., 1972), a sympathetic but scholarly account based primarily on published North Vietnamese sources. Also useful is Patrick J. McGarvey, ed., *Visions of Victory: Selected Vietnamese Communist Military Writings, 1964–1968* (Stanford, Calif., 1969). General Tran Van Tra, *Ending the Thirty Years' War* (Ho Chi Minh City, 1982), focuses primarily on the final campaign of 1975 but also offers important insights into North Vietnamese strategy and tactics in the earlier stages of the war. *Vietnam: The Anti-U.S. Resistance for National Salvation 1954–1975: Military Events* (Hanoi, 1980), is a useful official history. John Mueller, "The Search for the Breaking Point in Vietnam," *Strategic Studies*, 24 (December 1980), 497–519, analyzes on a comparative basis North Vietnam's willingness to absorb enormous losses.

For North Vietnam's relations with its allies, the older study by Donald Zagoria, *Vietnam Triangle: Moscow, Peking, Hanoi* (Indianapolis, 1967), is still useful. W. R. Smyser, *The Independent Vietnamese: Vietnamese Communism Between Russia and China, 1956–1969* (Athens, Ohio, 1980), is more up to date, as is Daniel S. Papp, *Vietnam: The View from Moscow, Peking, Washington* (Salisbury, N.C., 1981). V. C. Funnell, "Vietnam and the Sino-Soviet Conflict," *Studies in Comparative Communism*, 11 (Spring–Summer 1978), 142–199, and J. W. Garver, "Sino-Vietnamese Conflict and Sino-American Rapprochement," *Political Science Quarterly*, 96 (Fall 1981), 445–461, are two excellent articles.

The international aspects of the war have not received the treatment they deserve. On peace negotiations, the older account by David Kraslow and Stuart Loory, *The Secret Search for Peace in Vietnam* (New York, 1968), although remarkably accurate on many points, should be supplemented by the more recent and scholarly Allan E. Goodman, *The Lost Peace: America's Search for a Negotiated Settlement of the Vietnam War* (Stanford, Calif., 1978), a balanced appraisal that makes good use of interviews with U.S. diplomats. Gareth Porter, *A Peace Denied: The United States, Vietnam, and the Paris Agreements* (Bloomington, Ind., 1975), focuses on the 1973 negotiations, but contains several valuable background chapters. Porter is especially good on North Vietnamese motives and strategies, although he is uncritical of Hanoi. Janos Radvanyi, *Delusion and Reality: Gambits, Hoaxes, and Diplomatic One-Upmanship in Vietnam* (South Bend, Ind., 1978), raises serious questions about the sincerity of various East European peace initiatives. Ramesh Thakur, *Peacekeeping in Vietnam: Canada, India, Poland, and the International Commission* (Edmonton, Alberta, 1984), discusses the generally ineffectual role of the peacekeeping commission created at Geneva in 1954.

The best introduction to American public opinion and the war can be found in several general studies of public attitudes by leading analysts: Louis Harris, *The Anguish of Change* (New York, 1973), and Samuel Lubell, *The Hidden Crisis in American Politics* (New York, 1971). Important studies dealing specifically with Vietnam are Sidney Verba et al., "Public Opinion and the War in Vietnam," *American Political Science Review*, 61 (June 1967), 317–333, and Peter W. Sperlich and William L. Lunch, "American Public Opinion and the War in Vietnam," *Western Political Quarterly*, 32 (March 1979), 21–44. John E. Mueller, *War, Presidents and Public Opinion* (New York, 1973), is a valuable, scholarly analysis focusing on Korea and Vietnam.

The antiwar movement has been the subject of extensive analysis. Fred Halstead, *Out Now* (New York, 1978), is an insightful account written by a participant, particularly good on the internal politics of the movement. Thomas Powers, *Vietnam: The War at Home* (New York, 1973), is still good for the period up to 1968. Nancy Zaroulis and Gerald Sullivan, *Who Spoke Up? American Protest Against the War in Vietnam, 1963–1975* (New York, 1984), covers the entire war and contains a wealth of detail but is encyclopedic rather than analytical. The relevant chapters in Charles DeBenedetti, *The Peace Reform in American History* (Bloomington, Ind., 1980), comprise the best introduction to the role and impact of antiwar protest. DeBenedetti, "On the Significance of Citizen Peace Activism: America, 1961–1975," *Peace and Change*, IX (Summer 1983), 6–20, Paul Burstein and William Fredenberg, "Changing Public Policy: The Impact of Public Opinion, Anti-War Demonstrations, and War Costs on Senate Voting on Vietnam War Motions," *American Journal of Sociology*, 84 (1978), 99–122, and Melvin Small, "The Impact of the Antiwar Movement on Lyndon Johnson, 1965–1968," *Peace and Change*, X (Spring 1984), 1–22, attempt to weigh the impact of antiwar protest on policy. Todd Gitlin, *The Whole World Is Watching* (Berkeley, Calif., 1980), explores the influence of the media in the rise and fall of the New Left. Little has been done to date on the erosion of Congressional support for the war. Mark A. Stoler, "What Did He *Really* Say? The 'Aiken Formula' for Vietnam Revisited," *Vermont History*, 46 (Spring 1978), 100–108, and David Turner, "Mike Mansfield and the Vietnam War" (doctoral dissertation, University of Kentucky, 1984), make clear the limitations of the critique of the war by Senate doves. Congressional Research Service, *The U.S. Government and the Vietnam War—Executive and Legislative Roles and Relationships*, Part I (Washington, 1984), and Part II (Washington, 1984), is a superbly researched project that now carries the story to 1964 and will eventually fill a major void in the literature.

The domestic impact of Vietnam can best be studied in Lawrence A. Baskir and William A. Strauss, *Chance and Circumstance* (New York, 1978), a detailed analysis of the effects of the draft on the lives of the "Vietnam generation," and in Gloria Emerson, *Winners and Losers: Battles, Retreats, Gains, Losses and Ruins from a Long War* (New York, 1976), and Myra McPherson, *Long Time Passing: Vietnam and the Haunted Generation* (New York, 1984). Robert M. Stevens, *Vain Hopes, Grim Realities: The Economic Consequences of the Vietnam War* (New York, 1976), and J. F. Walter and H. G. Valter, Jr., "Princess and the Pea; or the Alleged Vietnam War Origins of the Current Inflation," *Journal of Economic Issues*, 16 (June 1982), 597–608, analyze the economic impact of the war.

Not surprisingly, the Tet Offensive of 1968 and the policy debate that followed have attracted a great deal of attention. The best brief appraisal is Bernard Brodie, "The Tet Offensive," in Noble Frankland and Christopher Dowling, eds., *Decisive Battles of the Twentieth Century* (London, 1976), pp. 321–334, an incisive account by a noted student of strategy. Don Oberdorfer, *Tet!* (Garden City, N.Y., 1971), is a highly readable narrative by a distinguished journalist. Clark M. Clifford, "A Viet Nam Reappraisal," *Foreign Affairs*, 47 (July 1969), 601–622, and Townsend Hoopes, *The Limits of Intervention* (New York, 1970), recount the efforts of two top Defense Department officials to turn the war around, although they probably exaggerate the extent to which they actually succeeded. Herbert Y. Schandler, *The Unmaking of a President: Lyndon Johnson and Vietnam* (Princeton, N.J., 1977), a meticulously detailed scholarly study based on extensive interviews with top administration officials, supersedes all previous work on the policy debates after Tet. Robert Pisor, *The End of the Line: The Siege of Khe Sanh* (New York, 1982), is a highly readable account of that famous battle.

The role of media coverage of the war, particularly at Tet, has been one of the most controversial issues to emerge from a war filled with controversy. The charge that the media and especially television lost the war is issued in Robert Elegant, "How to Lose a War," *Encounter*, LVII (August 1981), 73–90. A more persuasive critique of journalists' performance at Tet is the massively detailed study by Peter Braestrup, *Big Story!* (2 vols.; Boulder, Colo., 1977), which argues that the reporting, especially in the early stages, was impressionistic and misleading. Major scholarly analyses of the role of the media include Lawrence W. Lichty, "The War We Watched on Television," *American Film Institute Report*, 4 (Winter 1973), 30–37, George Bailey, "Television War: Trends in Network Coverage of Vietnam 1965–1970," *Journal of Broadcasting*, 20 (Spring 1976), 147–158, Michael Mandelbaum, "Vietnam: The Television War," *Daedalus*, 111 (Fall 1982), 157–168, and Daniel C. Hallin, "The Media, the War in Vietnam, and Political Support: A Critique of the Thesis of an Oppositional Media," *Journal of Politics*, 46 (1984), 2–24. Michael Arlen, *The Living Room War* (New York, 1969), persuasively challenges the widely accepted notion that nightly exposure to violence soured Americans on Vietnam. Clarence R. Wyatt, "'Truth from the Snares of Crisis': The American Press in Vietnam" (M.A. thesis, University of Kentucky, 1984), assesses the performance of the press in covering three major battles.

Seymour Hersh, *My Lai 4* (New York, 1970), is the standard journalistic account of that infamous incident. The best introduction to the My Lai controversy is Joseph Goldstein, Burke Marshall, and Jack Schwartz, *The My Lai Massacre and Its Cover-Up: Beyond the Reach of Law?* (New York, 1976), which includes the Army's investigation of the incident as well as commentary by several noted lawyers.

THE END OF THE WAR AND THE AFTERMATH

Nixon and Kissinger's views of the crisis they inherited can be found in Richard M. Nixon, "Asia After Vietnam," *Foreign Affairs*, 46 (October 1967), 111–125, and Henry A. Kissinger, "The Vietnam

Negotiations," *Foreign Affairs*, 47 (January 1969), 211–234. Richard M. Nixon, *RN: The Memoirs of Richard Nixon* (New York, 1978), is defensive and apologetic but quite valuable for the excerpts from the author's diaries and private papers. Henry Kissinger, *White House Years* (Boston, 1979), and *Years of Upheaval* (Boston, 1983), despite the sometimes querulous tone, will probably stand as one of America's classic political memoirs and are especially full on Vietnam-related issues. Among the numerous other memoirs by Nixon aides, the most useful are William Safire, *Before the Fall* (New York, 1975), and U. Alexis Johnson, *The Right Hand of Power* (Englewood Cliffs, N.J., 1984).

Kissingerology became a veritable rage in the mid-1970s, resulting in a number of useful studies. Marvin and Bernard Kalb, *Kissinger* (Boston, 1974), is a sympathetic and semi-authorized account by two journalists. John Stoessinger, *Kissinger: The Anguish of Power* (New York, 1976), and Roger Morris, *An Uncertain Greatness: Henry Kissinger and American Foreign Policy* (New York, 1977), are early critical appraisals. Seymour M. Hersh, *The Price of Power: Kissinger in the Nixon White House* (New York, 1983), is an often vicious indictment of the man and his policies based on extensive interviews.

Among the handful of specialized studies, a few stand out. William Shawcross, *Sideshow: Kissinger, Nixon and the Destruction of Cambodia* (New York, 1979), as the title implies, accuses the administration of destroying a nation for reasons peripheral to Cambodia itself. Martin F. Herz, *The Prestige Press and the Christmas Bombing* (Washington, D.C., 1980) is highly critical of the major newspapers' response to Nixon's policies. C. Stuart Callison, *The Land-to-the-Tiller Program and Rural Resource Mobilization in the Mekong Delta of South Vietnam* (Athens, Ohio, 1974), is a good brief analysis of land reform in the last stages of direct U.S. involvement.

The Nixon-Kissinger foreign policy produced a number of valuable contemporary studies. Among the best are Henry Brandon, *The Retreat of American Power* (New York, 1974), and Robert E. Osgood, *Retreat from Empire? The First Nixon Administration* (Baltimore, 1973). Jonathan Schell, *The Time of Illusion* (New York, 1975), is a frequently brilliant critique of Nixon's image-making in domestic and foreign policy, and Tad Szulc, *The Illusion of Peace: Foreign Policy in the Nixon Kissinger Years* (New York, 1978), is also highly critical.

The best analysis of the postwar war is Arnold R. Isaacs, *Without Honor: Defeat in Vietnam and Cambodia* (Baltimore, 1983), a thoroughly researched and highly critical study by a journalist who was in Indochina at the time. William E. LeGro, *Vietnam from Cease-Fire to Capitulation* (Washington, D.C., 1981), a volume in the Center of Military History's monograph series, is also useful. Tra, *Ending the Thirty Years' War,* provides insights into North Vietnamese planning, as does Van Tien Dung, *Our Great Spring Victory* (New York, 1977), a frankly exuberant memoir by the architect of the North Vietnamese triumph. Stuart A. Herrington, *Peace with Honor? An American Reports on Vietnam* (San Rafael, Calif., 1983), is a valuable analysis that is part memoir, part history. P. Edward Haley, *Congress and the Fall of South Vietnam and Cambodia* (Rutherford, N.J., 1982), is highly critical of the Congressional role. Stephen T. Hosmer et al., *The Fall of South Vietnam* (New York, 1980), is based on interviews with South Vietnamese leaders and provides valuable insights into South Vietnamese thinking and policies.

The fall of South Vietnam is treated with great drama in a number of accounts by journalists: John Pilzer, *The Last Day* (New York, 1976), Alan Dawson, *55 Days: The Fall of South Vietnam* (Englewood Cliffs, N.J., 1977), Tiziano Terzani, *Giai Phong! The Fall and Liberation of South Vietnam* (New York, 1976), and David Butler, *The Fall of Saigon* (New York, 1985). Frank Snepp, *Decent Interval: An Insider's Account of Saigon's Indecent End* (New York, 1977), a memoir by an official who served in the U.S. Embassy, indicts Ambassador Martin and the Washington policymakers for failure to anticipate and prepare for the fall of Saigon.

The legacy of the war must be studied from the perspective of individual topics. There is no comprehensive analysis of postwar Vietnam, but yearly developments can be followed in the issues of *Asian Survey.* William Shawcross, *The Quality of Mercy: Cambodia, Holocaust, and Modern Conscience* (New York, 1984), indicts, among others, the various charitable agencies for Cambodia's plight. For the problems of American veterans, Robert J. Lifton, *Home from the War* (New York, 1973), is still valuable, and Peter Goldman, *Charlie Company: What Vietnam Did to Us* (New York, 1983), and John Wheeler, *Touched with Fire: The Future of the Vietnam Generation* (New York, 1984), are good.

The debate on lessons of Vietnam began before the war ended and continues unabated. For an introduction to the topic, see the

Herring article in *Military Affairs* cited above. Earl C. Ravenal, *Never Again: Learning from America's Foreign Policy Failures* (Philadelphia, 1978), is an early and perceptive critique of the lessons and the lesson-makers. Ole R. Holsti and James N. Rosenau, *American Leadership in World Affairs: Vietnam and the Breakdown of Consensus* (Winchester, Mass., 1984), is a searching analysis of elite views toward Vietnam and general foreign policy issues based on extensive polling data. Walter H. Capps, *The Unfinished War: Vietnam and the American Conscience* (New York, 1982), is a less-than-successful effort to combat Vietnam "revisionism."

INDEX

Abrams, Creighton W.: replaces
Westmoreland, 208; changes
strategy, 212; and Vietnamization, 212–213, 233; endorses
bombing halt, 216; protests troop
withdrawals, 233, 240; proposes
invasion of Cambodia, 235; urges
bombing of North Vietnam, 247
Accelerated Pacification Campaign,
212, 231
Acheson, Dean G.: on Ho Chi Minh,
14; and Bao Dai solution, 15; on
France in Indochina, 18–19; op-
poses U.S. ground troops in Indo-
china, 21–22, 25; and French
"blackmail," 23, 29; and French
secretiveness, 23–24; and French
war-weariness, 24–25; and Diem,
49; urges deescalation, 206; on
U.S. war-weariness, 243
Adair, Ross, 122
Afghanistan, 270, 276
Agent Orange, 151
Agroville Program, 68–69, 89
Aiken, George, 248, 255, 261
Ali, Muhammad, 171, 172
American Friends of Vietnam, 43, 57
An Loc, battle of (1972), 246
Annam, 6, 7, 48
Antiwar movement, 171–173, 182,
215–216, 227, 229, 238, 240–
242
Ap Bac, battle of (1963), 88
Apocalypse Now, 275
Army of the Republic of Vietnam
(ARVN): U.S. aid for buildup of,
57–59, 86–87; takes offensive
(1962), 87; loses initiative, 88,
118; and Buddhist protests, 96;
desertion in, 118, 136, 180, 213,
231, 233, 264; defeats suffered
by, 69, 128; role of (1965–1967),

130–131, 136, 155; U.S. attitudes
toward, 92, 94, 131, 136, 155,
163, 164, 232–233, 265; and Revolutionary Development,
158–159; and Tet Offensive,
190–191; improvements in, 204,
213, 231, 232; and Vietnamization, 196, 198, 208–209, 212,
229, 231–233, 241; and pacification, 212; invades Laos, 241; invades Cambodia, 234; and 1972
campaigns, 246–247, 249; after
cease-fire, 258–259, 262; impact
of U.S. aid cuts on, 262–264; collapse of, 264–265, 267
Australia, 13, 31, 45n

Baez, Joan, 172
Ball, George W., 125, 138, 142, 143,
145, 176, 206n
Ban Me Thuot, battle of (1975), 264,
265
Bao Dai: heads Vietnam government,
15, 16; role of, 17; U.S. and, 19;
and Vietnamese nationalists, 28;
and Geneva Conference, 39;
post-Geneva government of, 46;
Dulles and, 51; and Diem, 48,
49, 54; and 1955 elections, 55
Bay of Pigs, 77, 106
Bay Vien, 52
Ben Tre, 192
Berlin, 76, 80, 82, 83, 115, 193
Bidault, Georges, 36, 37
Bien Hoa, attack on (1964), 124
Binh Xuyen, 52–55
Boat People, 270. *See also* Refugees
Body count, 153–154, 155–156, 183
Bombing of North Vietnam: U.S. con-
siders, 117, 119, 124–126; as re-
prisal after Gulf of Tonkin, 121;
FLAMING DART, 128; ROLL-

ABOUT THE AUTHOR

George C. Herring is professor of history at the University of Kentucky and is the editor of *Diplomatic History*, the quarterly journal. He received his M.A. and Ph.D. degrees from the University of Virginia. His publications include *Aid to Russia, 1941–1946: Strategy, Diplomacy, the Origins of the Cold War* (Columbia University Press, 1973); *The Secret Diplomacy of the Vietnam War* (University of Texas Press, 1983); and, with Kenneth Coleman, *The Central American Crisis* (Scholarly Resources, Inc., 1985).